Exploring the World With Blockchain Through Cryptotravel

Riktesh Srivastava
City University, Ajman, UAE

Varinder Singh Rana
City University, Ajman, UAE

Mohd Abu Faiz
City University, Ajman, UAE

IGI Global
Scientific Publishing
Publishing Tomorrow's Research Today

Vice President of Editorial — Melissa Wagner
Managing Editor of Acquisitions — Mikaela Felty
Managing Editor of Book Development — Jocelynn Hessler
Production Manager — Mike Brehm
Cover Design — Phillip Shickler

Published in the United States of America by
IGI Global Scientific Publishing
701 East Chocolate Avenue
Hershey, PA, 17033, USA
Tel: 717-533-8845
Fax: 717-533-8661
E-mail: cust@igi-global.com
Website: https://www.igi-global.com

Library of Congress Cataloging-in-Publication Data

Names: Srivastava, Riktesh, 1974- editor. | Rana, Varinder Singh, editor. | Faiz, Mohammad, 1973- editor.
Title: Exploring the world with blockchain through cryptotravel / edited by Riktesh Srivastava, Varinder Rana, Mohammad Faiz.
Description: Hershey, PA : IGI Global Scientific Publishing, [2025] | Includes bibliographical references and index.
Identifiers: LCCN 2024049408 (print) | LCCN 2024049409 (ebook) | ISBN 9798369365625 (hardcover) | ISBN 9798369365632 (paperback) | ISBN 9798369365649 (ebook)
Subjects: LCSH: Tourism--Information technology. | Tourism--Data processing. | Blockchains (Databases) | Cryptocurrencies.
Classification: LCC G156.5.I5 E96 2025 (print) | LCC G156.5.I5 (ebook) | DDC 910.285/57588--dc23/eng/20241220
LC record available at https://lccn.loc.gov/2024049408
LC ebook record available at https://lccn.loc.gov/2024049409

British Cataloguing in Publication Data
A Cataloguing in Publication record for this book is available from the British Library.

Table of Contents

Detailed Table of Contents

Cryptotravel represents a transformative convergence of cryptocurrency technology and the travel industry, heralding a new era of innovation and disruption. This research explores the anticipated innovations, including seamless digital currency payments, decentralized booking systems, and blockchain-based loyalty programs, which promise to enhance security, reduce transaction fees, and improve transparency in travel transactions. Despite these promising advancements, the sector faces significant challenges, including regulatory uncertainties, technological adoption barriers, and cryptocurrency volatility. This paper examines the potential impacts of cryptotravel on travelers, industry stakeholders, and global travel dynamics, highlighting both the opportunities for creating a more inclusive and efficient travel ecosystem and the risks associated with this technological shift. By navigating these challenges, the travel industry can leverage the benefits of cryptotravel to redefine traditional business models and pave the way for a more connected and secure future in global travel.

The purpose of this critical reflection is to investigate blockchain technology and its ability to unleash the Internet of Value (IoV) throughout the hospitality and travel sectors through the five realms of the emerging financial technologies and economies, which are cryptocurrencies, decentralized finance, metaverse, non-fungible token, central bank digital currency. Thus, in evolving electronic markets across the hospitality and tourism industry the blockchain technology could unleash the IoV. Nevertheless, certain challenges of blockchain technology such as its applications, privacy, legal frameworks, and environmental impact have to be discussed as all of these facets are critically important in order to optimize the benefits of cutting-edge technology. With the rising opportunities across the IoV, the hospitality and tourism businesses can improve and advance the hospitality and tourism operations by utilizing blockchain technology.

This chapter examines the evolution of travel booking, highlighting key developments from traditional methods to blockchain solutions. Initially reliant on brick-and-mortar travel agencies and phone reservations, the industry was transformed by the internet and Online Travel Agencies (OTAs), which offered increased convenience and real-time updates through mobile technology. Social media and metasearch engines further influenced booking behaviour, while AI and machine learning enabled personalized recommendations and predictive analytics. The rise of the sharing economy introduced peer-to-peer platforms like Airbnb and Uber. Recently, blockchain technology has promised enhanced transparency and security. Despite these advancements, challenges such as security concerns and user adoption persist. Future trends, including augmented reality (AR), voice-activated bookings, and sustainable travel solutions, are poised to shape the industry's future.

Digital technology has transformed various sectors with aviation not being exceptional. Digiyatra a government-promoted app enhances the traveller's experience by streamlining the operation. A blockchain-based identity management system Digiyatra uses a digital identity system which stores travelers' information on a distributed ledger. The airports and the airlines adopt the system to enhance the security of travellers, reduce the waiting queues in airports, and provide seamless travel and great experience. The chapter explores the revolutionary role of Digiyatra in air travel in India. The study uses online reviews of travellers about their experience using the app. The findings of the study state that security, experience, efficiency, and digitization are key factors for adopting digiyatra. The study's results will assist the government in understanding adopting digital technologies which can redefine the Indian aviation industry and make it future-ready

Cryptocurrency, based on block-chain technology is defined as a decentralized digital peer-to-peer currency. The emergence of cryptocurrency is a boon for future economy; it has been tagged along with innumerable practical and legal issues including risks associated with consumer's protection such as theft, misinformation, and unpredictability; complexity surrounding the legal characterization of cryptocurrencies, illegal activities driven through cryptocurrencies and lack of uniform comprehensive global legislation to address the issues and challenges associated with it. Though valiant efforts have been made by few countries like Canada, United Kingdom, Switzerland, El Salvador etc. to formulate broad range of rules and regulations for digital currency but other developed and developing economies has largely remained silent on the debate surrounding the regulation of cryptocurrencies. This chapter seeks to explore into risk posed by digital currency

where local communities will be real gatekeepers of their lands in the contemporary globalization environment.

Blockchain technology is a disruptive innovation in travel business processes because of its decentralized, secure nature. However, assessing its success is challenging. This paper recommends utilizing MG1 queuing models to analyze and develop blockchain systems in the travel business. By evaluating critical indicators like queue length and wait time, businesses may uncover bottlenecks and scalability problems. The integration of MG1 models enhances operational efficiency, allowing businesses to maximize blockchain's involvement in travel operations, assuring scalability and minimizing expenses.

In the context of dynamic changes in the hospitality industry, the issue of customer loyalty remains one of the primary cornerstones of business continuity. In light of the emergence of the industry's 4.0 concepts, this study aims to identify new tendencies in the paradigm of customer retention and how AI technologies contribute to those changes. Industry 4.0 can be described as the fourth interrelated transformation and is characterized by the integration of digital technologies, AI, and advanced automation impacting operational models across industries including hospitality. Machine Learning, one of the branches of AI, has the capability of handling large amounts of customer data for Analysis, Modelling, and Personalization reducing time, cost, and efforts in improving customer engagement and loyalty. Further, using AI in the form of virtual products such as chatbots and virtual assistants, they continue to provide consistent and efficient services to the customers hence supporting the causes of customer retention.

offers valuable insights into the comprehensive cybersecurity strategies that include risk assessment, employee training, and the adoption of established frameworks. Cybersecurity awareness can strengthen the defence, safeguard sensitive data, and guarantee long term sustainability of the hospitality industry with leveraging cutting edge technologies.

The advent of the realm of cryptocurrency has undoubtedly emancipated a single turn in the domain of outweighing sectors and its stride had shed its limelight over travel as well. The chapter delves into examining the domineering scope of travel accelerated by blockchain technology and digital currencies. Addition to the discussion regarding its potentiality superseding innovation, the chapter denounces the foregrounds that hamper the adoption of wide spread crypto travel these include regulatory uncertainty, scalability problem and concerns regarding volatility and legal compliance all of which must be taken in to account to drastically render upon block chain technology in the travel sector. Ranging from the expansion of tokenized Loyalty program to the disclosure of decentralized travel market places and the incorporation of virtual reality experiences, the possibilities of innovations are thoroughly breath taking.

Preface

INTRODUCTION

In an era marked by rapid technological advancements, blockchain stands out as a transformative force reshaping industries across the globe. Among the most intriguing and promising applications of this groundbreaking technology is its impact on the travel sector. As editors of *Exploring the World With Blockchain Through Cryptotravel*, we are delighted to present a comprehensive examination of how blockchain is revolutionizing travel, making it more secure, efficient, and exhilarating.

This book is the culmination of extensive research and insights from a diverse group of experts, including ourselves from City University Ajman, along with esteemed contributors who bring a wealth of knowledge and experience to this discourse. Our objective is clear: to illustrate the multifaceted ways in which blockchain is redefining the travel experience, from booking processes to data security, and from cryptocurrency payments to smart contracts.

Blockchain technology, with its decentralized nature and robust security features, offers innovative solutions to many of the challenges faced by the travel industry. Traditional booking methods, often marred by inefficiencies and vulnerabilities, are being transformed by blockchain's transparency and reliability. This book explores how blockchain enhances guest experiences, safeguards personal information, and streamlines transactions through smart contracts. It also delves into the evolving role of digital currencies in travel, providing a glimpse into a future where financial transactions are seamlessly integrated into the travel experience.

We begin with an exploration of the intersection between blockchain and travel, setting the stage for understanding its potential impact. The book progresses through discussions on various aspects of blockchain's application in the travel sector, including decentralized identity verification, loyalty programs, and the ethical considerations of blockchain-powered tourism. We also address the challenges and barriers to adoption, providing a balanced perspective on the current landscape and future developments.

As travel industry professionals, blockchain enthusiasts, academicians, researchers, and avid travelers, we have crafted this book to serve as a valuable resource for anyone interested in the convergence of blockchain technology and travel. Our goal is to offer a thorough analysis that not only informs but also inspires, illustrating how blockchain can enhance safety, convenience, and enjoyment in travel.

The future of travel is upon us, and blockchain technology is poised to play a pivotal role in shaping it. We invite you to embark on this journey with us, exploring the revolutionary potential of blockchain in the realm of travel and uncovering the myriad ways it is making the world a more interconnected and accessible place.

Chapter 1: Crypto Travel and Its Future Implications

The first chapter sets the stage for exploring the transformative potential of blockchain and digital currencies in the travel sector. It offers an in-depth analysis of how blockchain technology is accelerating the evolution of travel, highlighting innovations such as tokenized loyalty programs and decentralized travel marketplaces. The discussion extends to virtual reality experiences, showcasing how these advancements could revolutionize travel. However, the chapter does not shy away from addressing the significant barriers to widespread adoption, including regulatory uncertainty, scalability issues, and concerns over volatility and legal compliance. By examining these aspects, the chapter provides a comprehensive overview of both the promising possibilities and the challenges that lie ahead in the realm of crypto travel.

Chapter 2: Concept, Applications, Challenges and Security Threats of Blockchain Technology in the Tourism Industry

This chapter delves into the transformative impact of blockchain technology on the tourism industry, exploring its core principles of decentralization, transparency, and immutability. The chapter outlines how these principles can address key challenges in tourism, such as enhanced security and trustless transactions. Despite the promising benefits, the chapter also highlights critical issues such as scalability, high implementation costs, regulatory uncertainty, and significant security threats like cyberattacks and vulnerabilities in smart contracts. The chapter underscores the necessity for the industry to navigate these challenges through strategic investments in infrastructure, security, and compliance to fully leverage blockchain's potential.

Chapter 3: The Emergence of Crypto Travel - Revolutionizing Global Tourism with Blockchain and Digital Currencies

Chapter 3 explores the burgeoning concept of "crypto travel," where digital currencies like Bitcoin and Ethereum are becoming increasingly integral to travel services. It examines how blockchain enhances transparency, reduces transaction fees, and secures financial data. The chapter highlights platforms such as Travala and various major travel companies experimenting with crypto payments, demonstrating how these innovations could reshape the tourism landscape. Nevertheless, it also addresses the challenges of market volatility, limited merchant adoption, and regulatory uncertainties. By doing so, it provides a balanced perspective on the evolving role of digital currencies in global tourism.

Chapter 4: Exploring the Evolution of Cryptotravel - Anticipated Innovations, Challenges, and Impacts

This chapter investigates the transformative potential of cryptotravel, focusing on anticipated innovations such as seamless digital currency payments and decentralized booking systems. It examines how these innovations promise to enhance security, reduce transaction fees, and increase transparency in travel transactions. Despite these advancements, the chapter identifies significant challenges, including regulatory uncertainties and technological adoption barriers. It explores the potential impacts of cryptotravel on travelers, industry stakeholders, and global travel dynamics, highlighting both opportunities and risks associated with this technological shift.

Chapter 5: The Evolution of Travel Booking - From Traditional Methods to Blockchain Solutions

Chapter 5 provides a historical perspective on the evolution of travel booking methods, tracing developments from traditional brick-and-mortar agencies to modern blockchain solutions. It covers the transformative impact of the internet, Online Travel Agencies (OTAs), social media, and AI on booking behaviors and personalization. The chapter highlights the rise of peer-to-peer platforms and the potential of blockchain to further enhance transparency and security in travel bookings. It also addresses ongoing challenges such as security concerns and user adoption while discussing future trends like augmented reality (AR) and voice-activated bookings.

Chapter 6: Navigating Cryptocurrency Regulation - Trailblazing Legal Strategies for a Borderless Future

This chapter explores the legal complexities surrounding cryptocurrency and the need for comprehensive regulatory frameworks. It examines practical and legal issues including consumer protection, the legal characterization of cryptocurrencies, and the lack of uniform global legislation. Despite efforts by some countries to establish regulatory guidelines, many economies remain silent on the matter. The chapter advocates for the development of robust legal structures to address these issues and ensure the safe and effective use of digital currencies.

Chapter 7: Revolutionizing Air Travel in India - The Impact of Digiyatra

Chapter 7 examines the impact of Digiyatra, a blockchain-based identity management system introduced in India to enhance air travel. It discusses how Digiyatra improves traveler security, reduces airport wait times, and streamlines the travel experience. By analyzing online reviews and user experiences, the chapter highlights the system's contributions to security, efficiency, and digitization in the Indian aviation industry. It provides insights into how digital technologies like Digiyatra can redefine air travel and make it future-ready.

Chapter 8: Exploring the Growing Threat of Cyber Risks and Vulnerabilities in the Hospitality Industry

This chapter addresses the critical issue of cybersecurity in the hospitality sector, where digital systems make hotels prime targets for cyberattacks. It details major cyber threats such as malware, phishing, and Distributed Denial of Service (DDoS) attacks, and their impact on customer confidence and financial stability. Through case studies of notable breaches, the chapter emphasizes the importance of comprehensive cybersecurity strategies, including risk assessment, employee training, and adherence to established frameworks, to safeguard sensitive data and ensure long-term industry sustainability.

Chapter 9: Enhancing Guest Experience and Data Security in Hospitality - The Role of Blockchain Technology

Chapter 9 explores how blockchain technology can significantly enhance data security and guest experience in the hospitality industry. It explains how blockchain's decentralized and transparent nature offers robust solutions for managing guest interactions and protecting personal data. The chapter highlights the use of smart contracts to automate processes and improve operational efficiency. By presenting case studies and real-world examples, it demonstrates the practical benefits of blockchain in hospitality, while also addressing challenges such as technical scalability and regulatory issues.

Chapter 10: Analyzing Blockchain Systems Using MG1 Queue Models for Travel Business Processes

This chapter proposes the use of MG1 queue models to evaluate and develop blockchain systems in the travel industry. It focuses on assessing key performance indicators like queue length and wait time to identify bottlenecks and scalability issues. By integrating MG1 models, the chapter aims to enhance operational efficiency and optimize blockchain's role in travel operations, ultimately helping businesses maximize the benefits of this technology while minimizing costs.

Chapter 11: Customer Retention in the Hospitality Sector - A Glimpse into Industry 4.0 through AI Lens

Chapter 11 explores how Industry 4.0 concepts, particularly AI technologies, are reshaping customer retention in the hospitality sector. It highlights the role of machine learning and AI in analyzing customer data, personalizing interactions, and improving engagement. The chapter discusses how virtual products like chatbots and virtual assistants enhance customer service and support loyalty. It provides insights into how AI-driven advancements are transforming customer relationship management and operational models in the hospitality industry.

Chapter 12: Decentralized Fundraising - A Web3 Crowdfunding Platform with Blockchain Integration

Chapter 12 introduces a Web3 crowdfunding platform that leverages blockchain technology to facilitate decentralized fundraising campaigns. It covers the platform's integration with MetaMask for wallet management and Solidity for smart contracts, emphasizing the transparency, security, and decentralization offered by blockchain. The chapter explains how this platform transforms traditional fundraising by enabling users to manage funds and transactions securely, thereby providing a user-friendly and efficient crowdfunding experience.

Chapter 13: Examine the Adoption of Blockchain Technology Among Tourists - An Emerging Economy Perspective

This chapter investigates the adoption of blockchain technology among tourists in emerging economies, with a focus on India. It examines factors influencing the ease of use and effectiveness of blockchain systems, including effort expectancy, security, and social influence. Through a study conducted in Raipur, the chapter highlights key facilitators of blockchain adoption and offers valuable insights into how emerging markets are embracing this technology to enhance tourism experiences.

Chapter 14: Beyond Traditional CRM - Enhancing Customer Guest Experience and Operational Efficiency with Deep Learning and Blockchain in the Hotel Industry

Chapter 14 explores how deep learning and blockchain technologies can enhance customer experience and operational efficiency in the hotel industry. It discusses the integration of AI-driven CRM systems, which use customer data to improve engagement and loyalty. The chapter highlights how blockchain technology can complement these advancements by providing secure and transparent management of customer interactions. It provides a comprehensive look at how these technologies together are reshaping the hospitality sector.

Chapter 15: Empowering Local Communities through Blockchain Tourism Initiatives

This chapter highlights the potential of blockchain technology to empower local communities within the tourism sector. It explores how blockchain can facilitate direct peer-to-peer transactions, smart contracts, and sustainable tourism practices. By reducing intermediaries and enabling local service providers to access international markets, blockchain offers new opportunities for crowdfunding and resource management. The chapter calls for further research into digital accessibility, regulatory policies, and cross-platform integration to maximize blockchain's benefits for local economies.

Chapter 16: Decentralized Identity Verification - Revolutionizing Travel Documentation

Chapter 16 proposes a decentralized identity management system using blockchain technology to enhance travel documentation. It introduces the Self-Sovereign-Identity (SSI) model and the InterPlanetary File System (IPFS) for secure and transparent document management. The chapter discusses the practical challenges and future prospects of implementing this system, aiming to provide a safe and efficient solution for verifying identity and authenticity in the travel industry.

Chapter 17: Blockchain Technology and Internet of Value in the Hospitality and Tourism Industry

This chapter critically examines how blockchain technology can unlock the Internet of Value (IoV) across the hospitality and tourism sectors. It explores the impact of emerging financial technologies such as cryptocurrencies, decentralized finance, and NFTs on the industry. The chapter discusses the opportunities and challenges associated with blockchain, including privacy, legal frameworks, and environmental concerns, and how these technologies can advance operations and enhance value in hospitality and tourism.

Chapter 18: Enhancing Guest Experience in Hospitality through Blockchain Technology

The final chapter explores how blockchain technology can significantly improve guest experiences and operational efficiency in the hospitality industry. It covers various applications of blockchain, including booking systems, payment solutions, identity verification, and loyalty programs. By leveraging blockchain's transparency and security features, hospitality businesses can streamline operations, reduce costs, and offer more personalized services. The chapter also addresses the challenges of adoption and integration, emphasizing the need for collaboration among industry stakeholders to fully realize blockchain's transformative potential.

CONCLUSION

As we draw our exploration of blockchain's impact on the travel and hospitality sectors to a close, it is clear that we stand on the cusp of a transformative era. "Exploring the World With Blockchain Through Cryptotravel" has been crafted with the vision of shedding light on how this innovative technology is not only disrupting but enhancing the travel experience. From secure and transparent booking processes to the revolutionary potential of cryptocurrency payments and decentralized identity verification, blockchain's promise is as profound as it is expansive.

Our journey through this book has taken us from the foundational concepts of blockchain to its practical applications and challenges in the travel industry. We have seen how blockchain can streamline operations, protect personal data, and even empower local communities through decentralized initiatives. The chapters have provided a detailed examination of how blockchain's principles are being woven into the fabric of travel and hospitality, driving forward advancements while navigating the hurdles of adoption and regulation.

The contributions from our esteemed authors, including insights from City University Ajman and other leading experts, offer a comprehensive perspective on both the potential and the pitfalls of blockchain technology in this dynamic field. From analyzing security threats and regulatory challenges to exploring the integration of artificial intelligence and deep learning, this book has aimed to provide a holistic view of how blockchain is reshaping the travel experience.

As we look towards the future, it is evident that the journey of blockchain in travel is far from complete. The technology is evolving rapidly, and so too are its applications and implications. For industry professionals, technologists, researchers, and travelers alike, this book serves as a guide and a source of inspiration. It underscores the importance of embracing innovation while addressing the real-world challenges that come with it.

We hope that this book has not only informed but also inspired you to explore the exciting possibilities that blockchain offers in the realm of travel and hospitality. The future is here, and blockchain technology is poised to play a pivotal role in making the world more interconnected, secure, and accessible. As you delve into the chapters, we encourage you to envision the ways in which blockchain can further enhance your travel experiences and contribute to the ongoing evolution of this vibrant industry.

Thank you for embarking on this journey with us. The exploration of blockchain's impact on travel is just beginning, and we look forward to witnessing the continued innovations and advancements that will shape the future of this remarkable field.

Riktesh Srivastava
City University Ajman UAE

Varinder Rana
City University Ajman. UAE

Mohammad Faiz
City University Ajman. UAE

Chapter 1
Exploring the Evolution of Cryptotravel:
Anticipated Innovations, Challenges, and Impacts

Vikas Sharma
https://orcid.org/0009-0009-3174-5965
Bhikaji Cama Subharti College of Hotel Management, Swami Vivekanand Subharti University, Meerut, India

Shiv Mohan Verma
Bhikaji Cama Subharti College of Hotel Management, Swami Vivekanand Subharti University, Meerut, India

Ankit Srivastava
Bhikaji Cama Subharti College of Hotel Management, Swami Vivekanand Subharti University, Meerut, India

ABSTRACT

Cryptotravel represents a transformative convergence of cryptocurrency technology and the travel industry, heralding a new era of innovation and disruption. This research explores the anticipated innovations, including seamless digital currency payments, decentralized booking systems, and blockchain-based loyalty programs, which promise to enhance security, reduce transaction fees, and improve transparency in travel transactions. Despite these promising advancements, the sector faces significant challenges, including regulatory uncertainties, technological adoption barriers, and cryptocurrency volatility. This paper examines the potential impacts of cryptotravel on travelers, industry stakeholders, and global travel dynamics, highlighting both the opportunities for creating a more inclusive and efficient travel ecosystem and the risks associated with this technological shift. By navigating these

DOI: 10.4018/979-8-3693-6562-5.ch001

challenges, the travel industry can leverage the benefits of cryptotravel to redefine traditional business models and pave the way for a more connected and secure future in global travel.

1. INTRODUCTION

The travel industry, an ever-evolving landscape, continuously adapts to technological advancements and changing consumer preferences. Among the latest transformative trends is the emergence of "cryptotravel," which integrates cryptocurrency and blockchain technology into the travel sector. This development promises to reshape how travelers interact with various services, from booking flights and hotels to managing loyalty programs and making on-the-go purchases.

Cryptocurrencies, like Bitcoin and Ethereum, have gained widespread attention and acceptance since their inception. Initially conceived as decentralized digital currencies, they offer a secure, transparent, and efficient means of transaction, free from the constraints of traditional financial systems (Nakamoto, 2008). Their underlying technology, blockchain, ensures immutability and transparency of transactions, which is particularly advantageous in an industry like travel, where trust and security are paramount (Tapscott & Tapscott, 2016).

The integration of cryptocurrency into the travel industry presents several anticipated innovations. One of the most significant is the facilitation of seamless payments. Unlike conventional payment systems, cryptocurrencies enable instant, borderless transactions with minimal fees. This is particularly beneficial in the travel industry, where currency exchange rates and international transaction fees can be cumbersome and costly (Holub & Johnson, 2018). Companies like TravelbyBit and CheapAir have already begun accepting cryptocurrencies for flight and hotel bookings, signaling a shift towards broader acceptance (Shah & Krishnan, 2019).

Decentralized booking platforms represent another innovative application of blockchain technology in travel. These platforms eliminate intermediaries, reducing costs and increasing efficiency for both travelers and service providers. By using smart contracts, travelers can book accommodations, flights, and other services directly from providers, ensuring transparency and security throughout the transaction process (Werbach, 2018). Moreover, blockchain can enhance loyalty programs by creating interoperable, tokenized reward systems. This allows travelers to accumulate and redeem rewards across various providers seamlessly, thereby enhancing customer satisfaction and engagement (Kshetri, 2017). Despite these promising innovations, the adoption of cryptotravel faces several challenges. Regulatory uncertainty is a significant hurdle, as governments worldwide grapple with how to classify and regulate cryptocurrencies (Zohar, 2015). The lack of a unified regulatory framework can lead to confusion and hesitancy among both consumers and businesses. Furthermore, the technological barriers to adoption cannot be overlooked. Implementing blockchain solutions requires significant investment in infrastructure and expertise, which may be prohibitive for smaller companies (Catalini & Gans, 2016).

Another critical challenge is the volatility of cryptocurrencies. The value of digital currencies can fluctuate dramatically, posing a risk to both travelers and service providers who accept them as payment (Cheah & Fry, 2015). This volatility can undermine the stability and predictability needed for everyday transactions in the travel industry.

The impact of cryptotravel on the industry and its stakeholders is multifaceted. For travelers, the benefits include greater financial inclusivity, as cryptocurrencies can be accessed and used by anyone with an internet connection, regardless of their location or access to traditional banking services (Narayanan et al., 2016). This democratization of financial services aligns well with the global nature of travel. For industry stakeholders, the adoption of cryptocurrency and blockchain technology offers opportunities to streamline operations, reduce costs, and enhance customer experiences. However, realizing these benefits requires navigating the associated risks and challenges effectively. Cryptotravel stands at the intersection of technological innovation and travel, poised to redefine traditional paradigms. By embracing cryptocurrency and blockchain technology, the travel industry can unlock new efficiencies, enhance security, and provide a more inclusive and seamless experience for travelers worldwide. However, addressing the regulatory, technological, and economic challenges will be crucial to fully realizing the potential of cryptotravel. As the industry evolves, continued research and collaboration among stakeholders will be essential to navigating this transformative landscape successfully.

2. LITERATURE REVIEW

The integration of cryptocurrency and blockchain technology into the travel industry, termed "cryptotravel," has garnered significant academic and industry interest. This literature review delves into the evolution of cryptocurrency, its application in the travel sector, the potential benefits and challenges of cryptotravel, and its broader implications.

2.1. Evolution of Cryptocurrency

Cryptocurrency, first conceptualized by Satoshi Nakamoto with the introduction of Bitcoin in 2008, marked the beginning of a new era in digital finance. Nakamoto (2008) proposed Bitcoin as a peer-to-peer electronic cash system, emphasizing decentralization, security, and transparency. The underlying technology, blockchain, serves as a distributed ledger that records transactions immutably and transparently (Narayanan et al., 2016). Over the years, numerous cryptocurrencies have emerged, each offering unique features and applications (Holub & Johnson, 2018).

2.2. Application of Cryptocurrency in the Travel Sector

The travel industry, characterized by its global reach and diverse customer base, presents an ideal landscape for cryptocurrency integration. Cryptocurrencies offer several advantages over traditional payment methods, including lower transaction fees, faster cross-border transactions, and enhanced security (Catalini & Gans, 2016). Companies such as TravelbyBit and CheapAir have begun accepting Bitcoin and other cryptocurrencies for flight and hotel bookings, demonstrating the practicality of cryptotravel (Shah & Krishnan, 2019).

2.3. Innovations in Cryptotravel

2.3.1. Seamless Payments

One of the most significant innovations in cryptotravel is the facilitation of seamless payments. Traditional payment systems often involve intermediaries, leading to high transaction fees and delays, especially for international transactions. Cryptocurrencies eliminate the need for intermediaries, enabling instant, borderless payments with minimal fees (Holub & Johnson, 2018). This efficiency is particularly beneficial for travelers who frequently engage in international transactions.

2.3.2. Decentralized Booking Platforms

Blockchain technology enables the creation of decentralized booking platforms, which eliminate intermediaries and reduce costs for both travelers and service providers. These platforms use smart contracts to automate and secure transactions, ensuring transparency and trust. For example, Winding Tree, a decentralized travel marketplace, allows direct interaction between travelers and service providers, reducing costs and enhancing efficiency (Werbach, 2018).

2.3.3. Blockchain-Based Loyalty Programs

Traditional loyalty programs often suffer from fragmentation and inefficiency, limiting their effectiveness. Blockchain technology can revolutionize these programs by creating interoperable, tokenized reward systems. These systems allow travelers to accumulate and redeem rewards across various providers seamlessly, enhancing customer satisfaction and engagement (Kshetri, 2017). For instance, companies like Loyyal are leveraging blockchain to create universal loyalty programs that transcend traditional boundaries.

2.4. Challenges of Cryptotravel

2.4.1. Regulatory Uncertainty

Regulatory uncertainty poses a significant challenge to the adoption of cryptotravel. Governments worldwide are grappling with how to classify and regulate cryptocurrencies, leading to a fragmented regulatory landscape (Zohar, 2015). This uncertainty can hinder the adoption of cryptocurrencies in the travel industry, as businesses and consumers may be wary of potential legal repercussions.

2.4.2. Technological Barriers

The implementation of blockchain solutions requires substantial investment in infrastructure and expertise, which may be prohibitive for smaller companies. Additionally, the integration of cryptocurrency payment systems necessitates technical knowledge and adaptation, posing a barrier to widespread adoption (Catalini & Gans, 2016). Despite these challenges, the potential benefits of blockchain technology in travel are driving continued interest and investment.

2.4.3. Cryptocurrency Volatility

The volatility of cryptocurrencies is a major concern for their use in everyday transactions. The value of digital currencies can fluctuate dramatically, posing risks to both travelers and service providers who accept them as payment (Cheah & Fry, 2015). This volatility can undermine the stability and predictability needed for widespread adoption in the travel industry.

2.5. Broader Implications of Cryptotravel

2.5.1. Financial Inclusivity

Cryptocurrencies have the potential to enhance financial inclusivity by providing access to financial services for individuals who are unbanked or underbanked. With an internet connection, anyone can participate in the global economy, making travel more accessible to a broader population (Narayanan et al., 2016). This democratization of financial services aligns with the global nature of travel, fostering a more inclusive travel ecosystem.

2.5.2. Transformation of Business Models

The integration of cryptocurrency and blockchain technology can transform traditional business models in the travel industry. By reducing transaction costs, increasing transparency, and enhancing security, these technologies can streamline operations and improve customer experiences (Tapscott & Tapscott, 2016). For example, travel agencies and service providers can leverage blockchain to offer more competitive pricing and innovative services.

2.6. Case Studies and Industry Examples

2.6.1. TravelbyBit

TravelbyBit, an Australian startup, exemplifies the practical application of cryptocurrency in the travel industry. The company allows travelers to book flights and accommodations using Bitcoin and other cryptocurrencies, highlighting the feasibility and benefits of cryptotravel (Shah & Krishnan, 2019). TravelbyBit's success demonstrates the growing acceptance of cryptocurrency payments in the travel sector.

2.6.2. Winding Tree

Winding Tree, a decentralized travel marketplace, showcases the potential of blockchain technology to revolutionize travel booking platforms. By eliminating intermediaries, Winding Tree reduces costs and increases efficiency for both travelers and service providers (Werbach, 2018). The platform's use of smart contracts ensures transparency and security, addressing common concerns in traditional booking systems.

2.7. Future Prospects and Research Directions

The future of cryptotravel is promising, with ongoing research and development aimed at addressing current challenges and unlocking new opportunities. Future research could explore the impact of regulatory developments on the adoption of cryptotravel, the potential for integrating advanced technologies such as artificial intelligence with blockchain, and the long-term implications of cryptocurrency volatility on the travel industry. Collaborative efforts among industry stakeholders, regulators, and researchers will be crucial in navigating the evolving landscape of cryptotravel. The integration of cryptocurrency and blockchain technology into the travel industry holds significant potential to enhance efficiency, security, and inclusivity. While there are notable challenges, including regulatory uncertainty, technological barriers, and cryptocurrency volatility, the potential benefits make cryptotravel a compelling area of exploration and development. As the industry continues to evolve, ongoing research and collaboration will be essential in realizing the full potential of cryptotravel, paving the way for a more connected and secure future in global travel.

3. OBJECTIVES

To examine the Integration of Cryptocurrency in the Travel Industry.
To evaluate the Benefits and Challenges of Cryptotravel.
To assess the Impact of Cryptotravel on Travelers and Industry Stakeholders.

4. HYPOTHESES

H1. The adoption of cryptocurrency in the travel industry is significantly influenced by the perceived benefits of cost savings and transaction efficiency.
H2. Regulatory uncertainty and cryptocurrency volatility are major deterrents to the widespread adoption of cryptocurrency payments in the travel sector.
H3. Early adopters of cryptocurrency payments in the travel industry will experience a competitive advantage in terms of customer satisfaction and market share.

5. MATERIAL AND METHODOLOGY

The study employed a mixed-methods research design, combining quantitative and qualitative approaches to comprehensively analyze cryptotravel (Johnson & Onwuegbuzie, 2004). This approach ensured a robust understanding of the phenomena by triangulating data from various sources (Creswell & Plano Clark, 2011). Quantitative data collection involved surveys targeting a sample size of 200 travel service providers and 400 travelers who were aware of or had used cryptocurrency (Fink, 2013). Stratified random sampling was used to ensure representation across different regions and types of travel services (Babbie, 2016). Structured questionnaires were distributed online to collect data on cryptocurrency adoption, benefits, and challenges in travel (Dillman, Smyth, & Christian, 2014). Secondary data, including industry reports and financial statements, were analyzed to quantify cryptocurrency adoption trends and its impact on the travel industry (Yin, 2014).

Qualitative data collection methods included interviews with industry experts, executives from cryptocurrency-adopting travel companies, and regulators (Rubin & Rubin, 2012). Semi-structured interview guides were used to explore in-depth perspectives on cryptocurrency and blockchain integration in travel (Seidman, 2013). Additionally, case studies of pioneering cryptotravel companies such as TravelbyBit, CheapAir, and Winding Tree were conducted to understand implementation processes, benefits, challenges, and outcomes (Yin, 2014). Data analysis comprised quantitative techniques like descriptive and inferential statistics, including hypothesis testing, to evaluate relationships between variables (Bryman, 2016). Qualitative analysis methods, such as thematic and content analysis, were used to identify key themes and patterns related to cryptocurrency integration in travel (Guest, MacQueen, & Namey, 2011). Ethical considerations included obtaining informed consent, ensuring confidentiality, and minimizing bias (Guba & Lincoln, 1985). Limitations, such as sample representativeness and rapid technological changes, were acknowledged (Maxwell, 2013). In conclusion, the research methodology provided a comprehensive understanding of cryptocurrency's integration in the travel industry, its benefits, challenges, and impacts on travelers and industry stakeholders.

6. RESULTS AND FINDINGS

The following sections present a detailed analysis of the quantitative and qualitative data collected through surveys, secondary data, interviews, and case studies. This analysis aims to provide a comprehensive understanding of the current state, benefits, challenges, and impacts of cryptotravel.

6.1. Quantitative Data Analysis

Descriptive Statistics

Table 1 presents the descriptive statistics of survey responses from travel service providers and travelers.

Table 1. Descriptive statistics of survey responses

Measure	Mean (Providers)	SD (Providers)	Mean (Travelers)	SD (Travelers)
Awareness of Cryptocurrency	4.2	0.9	4.5	0.7
Adoption of Cryptocurrency	2.8	1.2	3.1	1.1
Perceived Benefits	4.0	0.8	4.2	0.6
Perceived Challenges	3.9	1.0	4.0	0.9

- **Awareness.** Both groups show high awareness of cryptocurrencies, with travelers having slightly higher awareness than providers.
- **Adoption.** The adoption rate is moderate, indicating that while interest is high, actual implementation is still in progress.
- **Perceived Benefits.** Both groups recognize significant benefits, with travelers slightly more positive.
- **Perceived Challenges.** Both groups perceive considerable challenges, indicating barriers to wider adoption.

Inferential Statistics

Hypothesis Testing.

H1. The adoption of cryptocurrency in the travel industry is significantly influenced by the perceived benefits of cost savings and transaction efficiency.

- **Regression Analysis.**
    - o Dependent Variable. Adoption of Cryptocurrency
    - o Independent Variables. Perceived Cost Savings, Transaction Efficiency

Table 2. Regression analysis results

Variable	Coefficient (β)	Standard Error	t-Value	p-Value
Perceived Cost Savings	0.35	0.08	4.375	<0.01
Transaction Efficiency	0.30	0.07	4.286	<0.01
R^2	**0.48**			

• Both perceived cost savings and transaction efficiency significantly influence the adoption of cryptocurrency ($p < 0.01$), with a combined R^2 of 0.48, indicating that these factors explain 48% of the variance in adoption rates.

H2. Regulatory uncertainty and cryptocurrency volatility are major deterrents to the widespread adoption of cryptocurrency payments in the travel sector.

- **Chi-Square Test.**
  - o Variables. Adoption of Cryptocurrency (Yes/No) and Perceived Regulatory Uncertainty/Volatility

Table 3. Chi-Square test results

Variable	χ^2	Degrees of Freedom	p-Value
Regulatory Uncertainty	22.47	1	<0.01
Cryptocurrency Volatility	18.34	1	<0.01

• Both regulatory uncertainty and cryptocurrency volatility are significant deterrents to the adoption of cryptocurrency in the travel sector ($p < 0.01$).

H3. Early adopters of cryptocurrency payments in the travel industry will experience a competitive advantage in terms of customer satisfaction and market share.

- **T-Test.**
  - o Variables. Customer Satisfaction, Market Share (Early Adopters vs. Non-Adopters)

Table 4. T-Test results

Variable	Mean (Early Adopters)	Mean (Non-Adopters)	t-Value	p-Value
Customer Satisfaction	4.4	3.8	3.45	<0.01
Market Share Growth	3.6	3.0	2.98	<0.01

• Early adopters report significantly higher customer satisfaction and market share growth compared to non-adopters ($p < 0.01$), indicating a competitive advantage.

6.2. Qualitative Data Analysis

1. Thematic Analysis

Interviews with 20 industry experts and case studies were analyzed to identify key themes.

Key Themes Identified.

- **Innovation and Efficiency.**

- Cryptocurrency transactions reduce transaction times and fees.
- Case studies like TravelbyBit and CheapAir show increased efficiency and customer convenience.

- **Transparency and Security.**
  - Blockchain's immutable ledger enhances security and transparency.
  - Winding Tree's decentralized platform ensures secure and transparent transactions.
- **Regulatory Hurdles.**
  - Regulatory uncertainty complicates the adoption of cryptocurrency.
  - Different global standards create challenges for international travel service providers.
- **Volatility Concerns.**
  - Price volatility of cryptocurrencies affects their reliability.
  - Both TravelbyBit and CheapAir have strategies to mitigate volatility risks, such as immediate conversion to stable currencies.

2. Content Analysis

Case Study Findings.

TravelbyBit.

- **Implementation.** User-friendly platform accepting multiple cryptocurrencies.
- **Benefits.** Enhanced customer convenience, increased international bookings.

CheapAir.

- **Implementation.** Accepts Bitcoin and other cryptocurrencies for flight and hotel bookings.
- **Benefits.** Reported increased international bookings, highlighting the demand for alternative payment methods.

Winding Tree.

- **Implementation.** Decentralized travel marketplace using blockchain.
- **Benefits.** Reduced costs, increased efficiency, and enhanced transparency by eliminating intermediaries.

Summary of Findings

Quantitative Insights.

- High awareness of cryptocurrencies among travel service providers and travelers.

- Moderate adoption rates, influenced positively by perceived cost savings and transaction efficiency.
- Significant regulatory and volatility challenges.
- Competitive advantages for early adopters in terms of customer satisfaction and market share.

Qualitative Insights.

- Cryptocurrencies offer innovation and efficiency benefits, reducing transaction times and fees.
- Enhanced security and transparency through blockchain technology.
- Significant regulatory hurdles and volatility concerns.
- Case studies demonstrate practical benefits and challenges.

7. RECOMMENDATIONS

Based on the detailed analysis of quantitative and qualitative data, several recommendations are proposed to address the challenges and leverage the opportunities associated with integrating cryptocurrency and blockchain technology in the travel industry.

For Travel Service Providers. Travel service providers should consider adopting cryptocurrency payment options to cater to the growing segment of tech-savvy travelers. This can be facilitated through partnerships with established cryptocurrency payment processors to ensure smooth transactions and immediate conversion to stable currencies if necessary. Providers should also invest in blockchain technology to enhance transparency, security, and efficiency in their operations, such as using blockchain for booking systems, loyalty programs, and identity verification processes. Additionally, implementing risk management strategies to mitigate the impact of cryptocurrency volatility is crucial. This includes automatic conversion to stablecoins or fiat currencies upon receipt of payment to maintain financial stability while offering innovative payment options.

For Industry Stakeholders and Regulators. Industry stakeholders and regulators should collaborate to develop a clear and unified regulatory framework for using cryptocurrencies in the travel industry. This framework should address key concerns such as consumer protection, anti-money laundering (AML), and combating the financing of terrorism (CFT). Promoting education and awareness about the benefits and risks associated with cryptocurrencies is also essential. This can be achieved through organizing workshops, seminars, and creating informational resources to raise awareness and promote informed decision-making. Additionally, supporting innovation and research in blockchain and cryptocurrency technologies is vital.

Governments and industry bodies should provide grants, subsidies, and partner with academic institutions to explore new applications and improve existing systems.

For Travelers. Travelers interested in using cryptocurrencies should stay informed about the latest developments, including which travel providers accept cryptocurrencies, the benefits, and potential risks. This knowledge will help them make informed choices and maximize the advantages of cryptotravel. Using secure and reputable cryptocurrency wallets and platforms for transactions is crucial to ensure the security of their digital assets and enjoy a hassle-free travel experience. Moreover, travelers should look for travel providers offering blockchain-based loyalty programs, which are often more flexible and rewarding than traditional ones, allowing them to earn and redeem points across various service providers seamlessly.

For Early Adopters. Early adopters should continuously monitor market trends and regulatory developments to stay ahead of the curve. Keeping abreast of changes will help them adapt quickly and maintain their competitive advantage. Leveraging data and analytics to understand customer preferences and behavior better is also recommended. This insight can help tailor services and marketing strategies to attract more customers and enhance satisfaction. Furthermore, fostering collaboration with other industry players, technology providers, and regulatory bodies can help early adopters navigate challenges and create a more robust ecosystem for cryptotravel. Building strategic partnerships can lead to shared resources, expertise, and innovation.

8. CONCLUSION

The detailed analysis confirms the potential of cryptocurrency and blockchain technology to transform the travel industry by enhancing efficiency, security, and inclusivity. However, significant challenges such as regulatory uncertainty and cryptocurrency volatility must be addressed to achieve widespread adoption. Early adopters have already demonstrated competitive advantages, suggesting that continued investment and innovation in cryptotravel could reshape the travel landscape.

Future research should focus on monitoring regulatory developments, exploring advanced technological integrations, and devising strategies to mitigate volatility to harness the full potential of cryptotravel.

REFERENCES

Catalini, C., & Gans, J. S. (2016). Some Simple Economics of the Blockchain. *National Bureau of Economic Research*. https.//DOI: 10.3386/w22952

Catalini, C., & Gans, J. S. (2016). Some Simple Economics of the Blockchain. *National Bureau of Economic Research*. https.//DOI: 10.3386/w22952

Cheah, E.-T., & Fry, J. (2015). Speculative bubbles in Bitcoin markets? An empirical investigation into the fundamental value of Bitcoin. *Economics Letters, 130*, 32-36. https.//DOI: 10.1016/j.econlet.2015.02.029

Holub, M., & Johnson, J. (2018). Bitcoin research across disciplines. *The Information Society, 34*(2), 114-126. https.//DOI: <ALIGNMENT.qj></ALIGNMENT>10.1080/01972243.2018.1413556

Holub, M., & Johnson, J. (2018). Bitcoin research across disciplines. *The Information Society, 34*(2), 114-126. https.//DOI: <ALIGNMENT.qj></ALIGNMENT>10.1080/01972243.2018.1413556

Kshetri, N. (2017). Will blockchain emerge as a tool to break the poverty chain in the Global South? *Third World Quarterly, 38*(8), 1710-1732. https.//DOI: <ALIGNMENT.qj></ALIGNMENT>10.1080/01436597.2017.1282992

Nakamoto, S. (2008). Bitcoin. A Peer-to-Peer Electronic Cash System.

Nakamoto, S. (2008). Bitcoin. A Peer-to-Peer Electronic Cash System.

Narayanan, A., Bonneau, J., Felten, E., Miller, A., & Goldfeder, S. (2016). *Bitcoin and Cryptocurrency Technologies*. Princeton University Press.

Narayanan, A., Bonneau, J., Felten, E., Miller, A., & Goldfeder, S. (2016). *Bitcoin and Cryptocurrency Technologies*. Princeton University Press.

Shah, A., & Krishnan, R. (2019). Decentralized travel booking platforms using blockchain technology. An empirical study. *Journal of Travel Research, 58*(7), 1234-1245. https.//DOI: <ALIGNMENT.qj></ALIGNMENT>10.1177/0047287518807639

Tapscott, D., & Tapscott, A. (2016). *Blockchain Revolution. How the Technology Behind Bitcoin Is Changing Money, Business, and the World*. Penguin.

Werbach, K. (2018). *The Blockchain and the New Architecture of Trust*. MIT Press. DOI: 10.7551/mitpress/11449.001.0001

Werbach, K. (2018). *The Blockchain and the New Architecture of Trust*. MIT Press. DOI: 10.7551/mitpress/11449.001.0001

Zohar, A. (2015). Bitcoin. under the hood. *Communications of the ACM, 58*(9), 104-113. https.//DOI: 10.1145/2699415

Chapter 2
Examine the Adoption of Blockchain Technology Among Tourists:
An Emerging Economy Perspective

Pramendra Sahu
https://orcid.org/0009-0004-8458-2999
MATS University, Raipur, India

Shailja Bakshi
https://orcid.org/0009-0007-3531-7234
MSBS, MATS University, Raipur, India

Pravin Chandra Singh
https://orcid.org/0000-0002-6002-0703
MATS University, Raipur, India

Kumari Neelam
Mahatma Gandhi Kashi Vidyapith, Varanasi, India

Divya Kr
CT University, India

Pankaj Kumar
United University, Prayagraj, India

Sujay Vikram Singh
https://orcid.org/0000-0002-7113-2698
Banaras Hindu University, India

Utkarsh Keshari
Institute of Management Studies, Varanasi, India

Vishal Kumar Singh
https://orcid.org/0000-0002-5381-3027
School of Management Sciences, Varanasi, India

ABSTRACT

Blockchain technology has become a hot topic of interest and has gained considerable attention in a range of research fields, including the tourism industry. It has completely transformed the way tourists experience things, but there is still ongoing

DOI: 10.4018/979-8-3693-6562-5.ch002

research on its impact in the field of tourism. This study aims to identify the facilitators that help in the adoption of blockchain technology in an emerging economy like India. The study examines various factors that contribute to the ease of use and effectiveness of a system, including expectations of effort, security, availability of resources, social influence, and expectations of performance. Conducted in Raipur, the capital city of Chhattisgarh, with a sample size of 380 using convenience sampling. Findings indicate that all facilitators significantly impact blockchain adoption among tourists. Effort Expectancy was found to be the most influential factor, while Social Influence had the least impact. This study offers valuable insights into the adoption of blockchain technology among tourists, specifically in central India.

1. INTRODUCTION

Technological advancements have the ability to revolutionize whole fields in cycles. In terms of the tourist sector, the advent of digitalization has been of great significance over the last few decades. It has paved the way for commercial contacts between private persons on a wide scale and established patterns that have reshaped the market by developing new trends. Around the course of the last several years, academics all around the world have shown an increasing interest in blockchain technology (BT) in a broad variety of study fields. The exponential growth of investments in blockchain-based solutions for the tourism sector indicates that the advancement of blockchain systems will significantly influence the industry's trajectory in the coming years. Through its disruptive innovation, BT is well positioned to redefine the way in which the tourist sector will evolve in the future by offering passengers with experiences that are integrated and seamless (Khan et al., 2017). Despite the rising interest in BT, the literature on its use in the tourist industry is still in its early phases. This is particularly true when compared to other technologies associated to the internet (Erol et al., 2022). There is a lack of a complete overview that explains and predicts the problems that are associated with the installation and adoption of BT within the tourist sector, even though there is understanding of the potential advantages that BT may give to the business (Irannezhad & Mahadevan, 2021). In this respect, scholars accept the necessity for a more in-depth examination of the factors that drive and discourage the adoption of BT, as well as the ramifications of its incorporation into the tourist setting from a theoretical and managerial standpoint (Valeri & Baggio, 2021). Previous studies have come under fire for failing to consider the point of view of end users, with much of their attention being directed on the technical architecture of BT (Önder & Gunter, 2022). In particular, the fact that visitors' views and their behavioural intentions toward the adoption of BT are not well understood is the root cause of the gap in the existing body of studies

(Balasubramanian et al., 2022; Nur Muharam et al., 2024; Zavolokina et al., 2023). Thus, in this study factors which acts as a facilitator in the adoption of block chain technology will be explored and their respective influence on tourist's intention towards block chain will be studied.

2. THEORETICAL BACKGROUND

2.1. Unified Theory of Acceptance and Use of Technology

UTAUT, or the Unified Theory of Acceptance and Use of Technology, is a conceptual framework that attempts to provide an explanation for and forecast the acceptance and utilization of technology by individuals. The Technology Acceptance Model (TAM), the Theory of Reasoned Action (TRA), and the Theory of Planned Behaviour (TPB) are among the established theories and models that UTAUT incorporates, as proposed by (Venkatesh et al., 2003). According to UTAUT2, desire to use increased by 18% and technology acceptability increased by 12%. These numbers show how technology benefits customers (Tamilmani et al., 2021). The present study seeks to understand the elements that impact Indians' block chain technology adoption.

3. LITERATURE REVIEW AND HYPOTHESIS DEVELOPMENT

3.1. Behavioural Intention

The concept of behavioural intention is inextricably linked to the level of trust that individuals place in technology and their propensity to continue using it in subsequent instances (Waris et al., 2020). It is crucial to consider how individuals perceive their preparedness to utilize technology when evaluating intentions. Individuals will derive their intentions from their own perceptions of the ease of use and utility, and these intentions can predict the future level of technology acceptance (Szajna, 1996).

3.2. Effort Expectancy

The ease and simplicity with which a technology is used is referred to as Effort expectancy (Venkatesh et al., 2003). Therefore, any novel technological advancement should incorporate a user-friendly interface (Falwadiya & Dhingra, 2022). It is observed that argue that users would experience overall satisfaction when employing

BT due to its minimal complexity and effort requirements (Chang et al., 2022a; P. Jain et al., 2023). Thus, following hypothesis has formulated:

H1: Effort expectancy has a positive influence on tourists' behavioural intention to use blockchain technology.

3.3. Security

For a tourist's protection of their personal data is a serious concern (Wut et al., 2021) It is observed that blockchain based technology help the tourist to increase their security and ownership over data they disclose to tourism service provider (Tyan et al., 2020). Tourists experience a heightened sense of safety when they have faith in the technological security measures in place, as this instills confidence in them regarding the potential compromise of their confidential or financial information during transactions (Ruangkanjanases et al., 2023). Hence security positively influence tourists' intention to use blockchain technology. Thus, following hypothesis has formulated:

H2: Security has a positive influence on tourists' behavioural intention to use blockchain technology.

3.4. Facilitating Conditions:

According to (Venkatesh, 2022), FCs concern an individual's conviction regarding the existence of a technical and organizational framework that facilitates the application of a particular technology. Contrary to the initial model proposed by (Venkatesh et al., 2003), which posits that FC does not exert a substantial impact on BI, the Theory of Planned Behaviour (Azjen, 1988) demonstrates that FCs are represented as a direct precursor to utilization. Recent studies have established that FCs play a significant role in fostering increased consciousness and have a strong correlation with intentions (Huang & Chueh, 2022); consequently, they are regarded as predictors when analysing intentions to utilize technology. Thus, following hypothesis has formulated:

H3: Facilitating conditions has a positive influence on tourists' behavioural intention to use blockchain technology.

3.5. Social Influence

In addition to the technology itself, the social environment in which it is used is a significant factor in determining whether or not a person intends to employ BT-based services (Batwa & Norrman, 2021). As a result, it is essential to consider social influence, which may be described as the extent to which people sense that significant references (such as family and friends) believe that they need to make use of a certain technology (Venkatesh et al., 2003). Customers select a particular technology based not only on their own motivations and personal preferences, but also on the advice and views of others. Individual behaviour is thus impacted by the intentions of others regarding its utilization, which they perceive because of technology adoption (Radic et al., 2022). Thus, following hypothesis has formulated:

H4: Social Influence has a positive influence on tourists' behavioural intention to use blockchain technology.

3.6. Performance Expectancy

Performance expectancy is defined as the extent to which the anticipated benefits of performing tasks can be obtained by individuals through the implementation of a novel technology (Chowdhury et al., 2023). Numerous studies have corroborated its impact on technology adoption in diverse technological contexts over the years (Wong et al., 2020). Presently, it is regarded as a reliable predictor of the intention to implement a particular technology. Thus, following hypothesis has formulated:

H5: Performance Expectancy has a positive influence on tourists' behavioural intention to use blockchain technology.

Figure 1. Conceptual framework

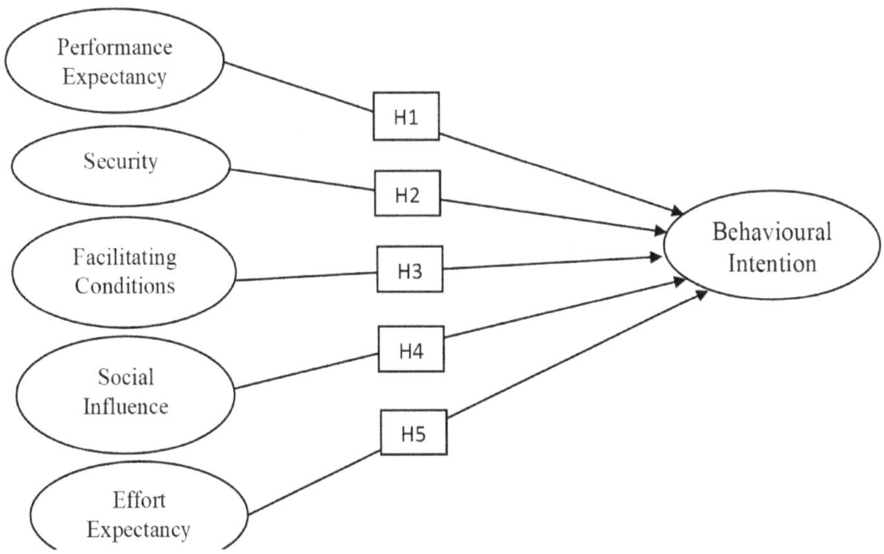

4. RESEARCH METHODOLOGY

4.1. Data Collection

The data was gathered via the use of an unstructured questionnaire that was created with the assistance of Google Form and sent to respondents in the English language through various social media platform. For the sake of this investigation, a Likert scale that allows for five potential responses—strongly agree, agree, neutral, disagree, and strongly disagree—is used. The sample size was 380 and convenience sampling is being employed to gather data.

4.2. Construct Measurement

The items considered for this research were taken from different sources available in the literature and were adapted to fit in the context of present study (**Table-1**).

Table 1. Measurement instruments

Constructs	No of Items	Source
Performance Expectancy	3	(Pham & Thi Nguyet, 2023)
Security	3	(Khalilzadeh et al., 2017)
Facilitating Conditions	3	(Chang et al., 2022)
Social Influence	3	(Venkatesh & Davis, 2000)
Effort Expectancy	3	(Chang et al., 2022; G. Jain et al., 2022)
Behavioral Intention	4	(Khalilzadeh et al., 2017)

4.3. Respondents Profile

The people that took part in this research were residents of Raipur (Central India), which is located in Chhattisgarh. The following is a characterization of the participants' demographic characteristics: Male participants made up 52% of the total, while female participants made up 48% of the total. Most of the participants in the research were male. The participants in the research ranged in age from 18 to 60 years old, with a significant proportion falling within the age range of 25 to 35 years old.

5. DATA ANALYSIS

To conduct the analysis of the data, a two-step technique known as EFA and CFA was used. For data analysis and association testing, SPSS and AMOS were utilized. According to (Field, 2009), the KMO value is 0.848, which is higher than the required limit of 0.6. Additionally, the $\chi 2$ value is 5551.550, the DF value is 171, and the p-value is less than 0.001 (Table-2). These findings indicate that there is a suitable correlation between the statements for doing principal component analysis. All the variables that were observed had a factor loading that is more than 0.50, which is higher than the value that was recommended (Table-3). For all constructs, the composite average Cronbach values are higher than the specified levels of $\geq$0.70 (Cronbach, 1951), which indicates that the constructs have a high degree of internal consistency (Table-4).

Table 2. KMO and Bartlett's test

Kaiser-Meyer-Olkin Measure of Sampling Adequacy.		**0.848**
Bartlett's Test of Sphericity	Approx. Chi-Square	5551.550
	Df	171
	Sig.	.000

Source: Analysis Output

Table 3. Factor loading and Cronbach alfa

Construct	Items	Factor Loading
Performance Expectancy		
	BT allows me to improve/enhance the purchasing experience	0.809
	BT helps me access tourist information more accurately	0.807
	BT helps me timesaving in researching information, avoiding misinformation	0.786
Security		
	BT allows data to be saved securely	0.860
	BT ensures secure transactions and less exposure to fraud	0.826
	Facilities transactions by securely transmitting sensitive information	0.862
Facilitating Conditions		
	I think I have the resources (technological devices) to use BT	0.883
	I think I have the required expertise to use BT	0.869
	I believe it is easy to purchase tourism products/services through BT	0.877
Social Influence		

continued on following page

Table 3. Continued

Construct	Items	Factor Loading
	People whose opinions I appreciate would prefer that I use BT, rather than other innovative technologies	0.929
	People who can influence my decision motivate me to use BT	0.947
	If many people in my community or my friends use BT, I will also use this technology Facilitating conditions (FC) FC1 I think I have the resource	0.911
Effort Expectancy		
	BT is easy to use	0.878
	The use of BT is reliable and saves time in the purchasing process	0.896
	BT simplifies the decision-making process	0.884
Behavioural Intention		
	I intend to adopt BT within 3 years	0.816
	I expect to use the BT	0.817
	I will recommend the use of BT to friends and acquaintances	0.823
	I will pioneer the use of BT in tourism	0.756

Source: Analysis Output

Table 4.

Cronbach's Alpha	No of Items
0.898	19

Source: Analysis Output

Figure 2. Measurement model

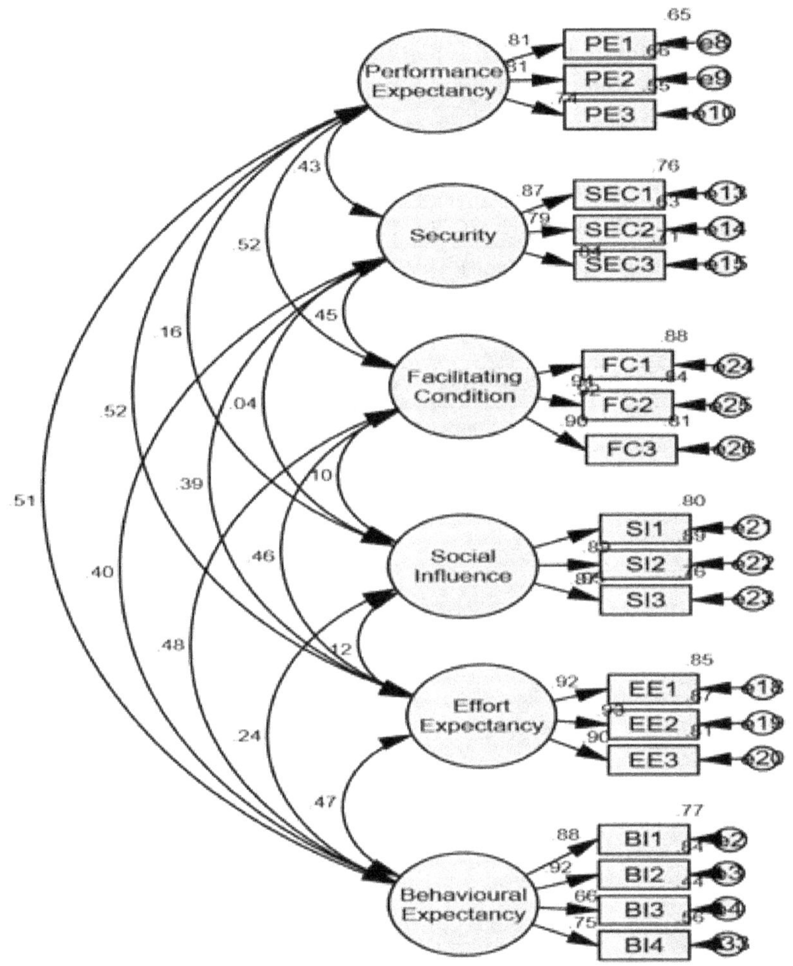

Source: Analysis Output

5.1. SEM Analysis

To evaluate the structural model of the conceptual research model that was hypothesized, SEM was implemented. It indicates that all values arriving after the SEM analysis are within the prescribed range i.e. the average variance extracted is greater than the maximum shared variance and average shared variance, as stated by (AVE>MSV>ASV) (Hair et al., 2010). The values of model fit indices are as follows: chi-square/df: 2.352; CFI: 0.966; GFI: 0.917; RMSEA: 0.060 (Fornell &

Larcker, 1981; MacCallum et al., 1996; Mulaik, 1987). The structural model's estimations, critical ratio, and equations based on the SEM are represented as Table 5.

Based on the indices, the SEM remains within acceptable limits and is deemed a viable model. The values validated all hypotheses from H1 to H5.

Table 5. Direct relationship

Direct Relationship	Estimate	S.E.	C.R.	P-values	Significance	Hypotheses
BI<--- PE	0.446	.095	4.701	***	Significant	H_1 accepted
BI<---SEC	0.355	.085	4.183	***	Significant	H_2 accepted
BI<--- FC	0.338	.075	4.521	***	Significant	H_3 accepted
BI<---SI	0.170	.048	3.542	***	significant	H_4 accepted
BI<---EE	0.574	.058	4.441	***	Significant	H_5 accepted

Source: Analysis Output

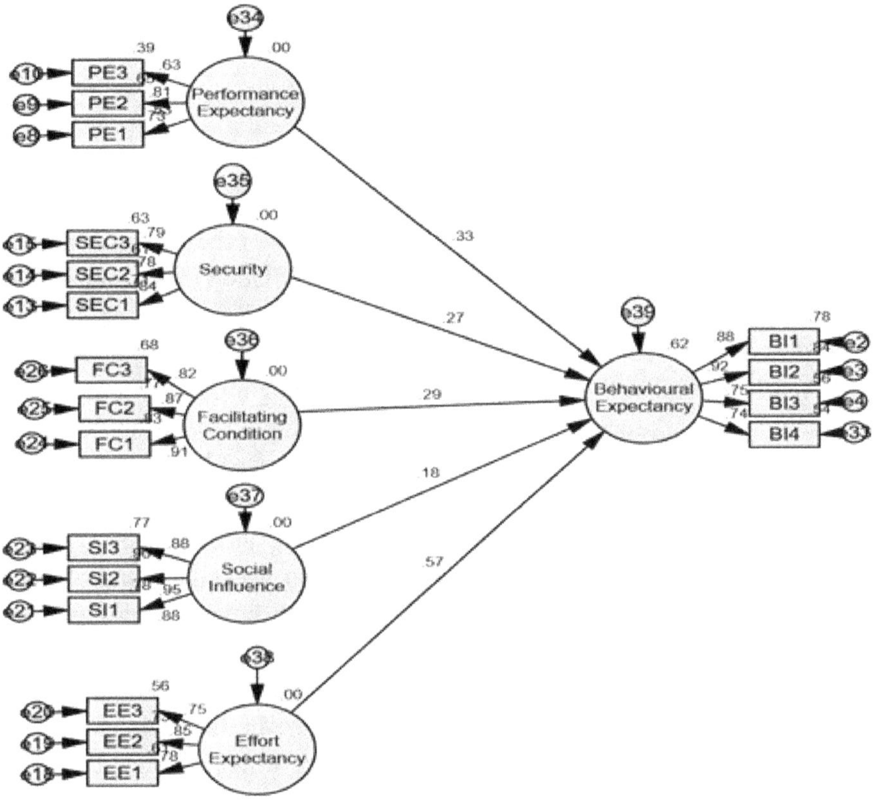

Source: Analysis Output

The route diagram for the structural equation model is depicted in Figure 3. The study conducted has revealed that the consumer's behavioural intention regarding the adoption of blockchain technology is significantly influenced by several factors, including performance expectancy, security, facilitating conditions, social influence, and effort expectancy.

6. CONCLUSION

6.1. Findings

This study looks at the factors that lead to consumers in the travel industry accepting BT. The results demonstrate that travellers' readiness to embrace BT is dependent on a complex procedure. Study reveals that all the factors are significantly influencing the tourist's intention to adopt blockchain technology and this is in line with the previous studies. Out of the five factors effort expectancy has come out as the most significant predicators of tourist's intentions to adopt blockchain technology while social influence is the weakest predicator.

6.2. Theoretical and Managerial Implications

This study is an effort to enhance our understanding of the fundamental factors that influence the behavioural intentions of visitors in relation to the adoption of BT within the tourism sector from a theoretical perspective. This research illuminates the complex interplay between motivations and objections by examining the antecedents that influence these intentions, thereby contributing to a more comprehensive understanding of the process by which technology adoption decisions are made in the tourism sector. Regarding the managerial ramifications, blockchain service providers have to use their resources to guarantee that the intended clientele establishes a favourable association between belief variables (Performance Expectancy, Security, Facilitating Conditions, Social Influence and Effort Expectancy) and blockchain technology. It is suggested that while incorporating blockchain technology marketers should makes it user friendly and when tourists are facing minimum complexity while using blockchain it will enhance their level of satisfaction. While using BT tourist's should have a sense of safety and ownership over their personal data, that is why marketers should incorporate latest software which protects the tourist's data from unauthorised use. It is also evident from this study that marketers should facilitate the tourist's with training with respect to BT use will be beneficial to the BT service providers. This study further reveals that family, friends, peers etc have a significant impact on tourist's intention to use BT technology; It helps in developing a rational and emotional viewpoint with respect to use of BT technology. Finally, this study reveals that markets should convenience the targeted audience regarding the performance and benefits of the novel technology (BT) and it will lead to a positive intention towards that technology.

6.3. Limitations and Scope for Future Research

First, since BT adoption is still in its early phases, it may be difficult to extrapolate survey findings due to respondents' ignorance of the technology's workings. Surveys based on a deeper comprehension of the respondents' BT knowledge and awareness levels may be conducted in future study, together with the introduction of an experimental design research methodology. The methodology was not compromised by the sample size, although it does restrict how broadly the findings can be applied. Therefore, it is advised that large-scale research be done in the future.

REFERENCES

Azjen, I. (1988). *Attitudes, personality and behavior*. Open University Press.

Balasubramanian, S., Sethi, J. S., Ajayan, Ş., & Paris, C. M. (2022). An enabling Framework for Blockchain in Tourism. *Information Technology & Tourism*, 24(2), 165–179. Advance online publication. DOI: 10.1007/s40558-022-00229-6

Batwa, A., & Norrman, A. (2021). Blockchain Technology and Trust in Supply Chain Management: A Literature Review and Research Agenda. *OPERATIONS AND SUPPLY CHAIN MANAGEMENT*, 14(2), 203–220. DOI: 10.31387/oscm0450297

Chang, M., Walimuni, A. C. S. M., Kim, M., & Lim, H. (2022a). Acceptance of tourism blockchain based on UTAUT and connectivism theory. *Technology in Society*, 71, 102027. Advance online publication. DOI: 10.1016/j.techsoc.2022.102027

Chang, M., Walimuni, A. C. S. M., Kim, M., & Lim, H. (2022b). Acceptance of tourism blockchain based on UTAUT and connectivism theory. *Technology in Society*, 71, 102027. Advance online publication. DOI: 10.1016/j.techsoc.2022.102027

Chang, M., Walimuni, A. C. S. M., Kim, M., & Lim, H. (2022c). Acceptance of tourism blockchain based on UTAUT and connectivism theory. *Technology in Society*, 71, 102027. Advance online publication. DOI: 10.1016/j.techsoc.2022.102027

Chowdhury, S., Rodriguez-Espindola, O., Dey, P., & Budhwar, P. (2023). Blockchain technology adoption for managing risks in operations and supply chain management: Evidence from the UK. *Annals of Operations Research*, 327(1), 539–574. DOI: 10.1007/s10479-021-04487-1 PMID: 34629606

Cronbach, L. J. (1951). Coefficient alpha and the internal structure of tests. *Psychometrika*, 16(3), 297–334. DOI: 10.1007/BF02310555

Erol, I., & Neuhofer, I. O., Dogru (Dr. True), T., Oztel, A., Searcy, C., & Yorulmaz, A. C. (. (2022). Improving sustainability in the tourism industry through blockchain technology: Challenges and opportunities. *Tourism Management*, 93. Advance online publication. DOI: 10.1016/j.tourman.2022.104628

Falwadiya, H., & Dhingra, S. (2022). Blockchain technology adoption in government organizations: A systematic literature review. *J. Global Oper. Strat. Sourcing*, 15(3), 473–501. DOI: 10.1108/JGOSS-09-2021-0079

Field, A. (2009). *Discovering statistics using spss*. sage.

Fornell, C., & Larcker, D. F. (1981). Evaluating structural equation models with unobservable variables and measurement error. *JMR, Journal of Marketing Research*, XVIII(February), 39–50. DOI: 10.1177/002224378101800104

Hair, F. J., Black, C. W., Babin, J. B., & Amderson, E. R. (2010). Multivariate Data Analysis (7th ed.). pearson prentice Hall.

Huang, D. H., & Chueh, H. E. (2022). Behavioral intention to continuously use learning apps: A comparative study from Taiwan universities. *Technological Forecasting and Social Change*, 177(1), 121531. DOI: 10.1016/j.techfore.2022.121531

Irannezhad, E., & Mahadevan, R. (2021). Is blockchain tourism's new hope? In *Journal of Hospitality and Tourism Technology* (Vol. 12, Issue 1, pp. 85–96). Emerald Group Holdings Ltd. DOI: 10.1108/JHTT-02-2019-0039

Jain, G., Kamble, S. S., Ndubisi, N. O., Shrivastava, A., Belhadi, A., & Venkatesh, M. (2022). Antecedents of Blockchain-Enabled E-commerce Platforms (BEEP) adoption by customers – A study of second-hand small and medium apparel retailers. *Journal of Business Research*, 149(1), 576–588. DOI: 10.1016/j.jbusres.2022.05.041

Jain, P., Singh, R. K., Mishra, R., & Rana, N. (2023). Emerging dimensions of blockchain application in tourism and hospitality sector: A systematic literature review. *Journal of Hospitality Marketing & Management*, 32(3), 1–23. DOI: 10.1080/19368623.2023.2184440

Khalilzadeh, J., Ozturk, A. B., & Bilgihan, A. (2017). Security-related factors in extended UTAUT model for NFC based mobile payment in the restaurant industry. *Computers in Human Behavior*, 70, 460–474. DOI: 10.1016/j.chb.2017.01.001

Khan, M. S., Woo, M., Nam, K., & Chathoth, P. K. (2017). Smart city and smart tourism: A case of Dubai. *Sustainability (Basel)*, 9(12), 2279. Advance online publication. DOI: 10.3390/su9122279

MacCallum, R. C., Browne, M. W., & Sugawara, H. M. (1996). Power analysis and determination of sample size for covariance structure modeling. *Psychological Methods*, 1(2), 130–149. DOI: 10.1037/1082-989X.1.2.130

Mulaik, S. A. (1987). A Brief History of the Philosophical Foundations of Exploratory Factor Analysis. *Multivariate Behavioral Research*, 22(3), 267–305. DOI: 10.1207/s15327906mbr2203_3 PMID: 26776378

Nur Muharam, I., Tussyadiah, I. P., & Kimbu, A. N. (2024). A theoretical model of user acceptance of blockchain-based peer-to-peer accommodation. *Current Issues in Tourism*, 27(7), 1008–1025. DOI: 10.1080/13683500.2022.2164485

Önder, I., & Gunter, U. (2022). Blockchain: Is it the future for the tourism and hospitality industry? *Tourism Economics*, 28(2), 291–299. DOI: 10.1177/1354816620961707

Pham, C. T., & Thi Nguyet, T. T. (2023). Determinants of blockchain adoption in news media platforms: A perspective from the Vietnamese press industry. *Heliyon*, 9(1), e12747. Advance online publication. DOI: 10.1016/j.heliyon.2022.e12747 PMID: 36685429

Radic, A., Quan, W., Antonio, A. M., Lee, J. S., & Han, H. (2022). You can't hold the tide with a broom: Cryptocurrency payments and tourism in South Korea and China. *Tourism Management Perspectives*, 43(1), 101000. DOI: 10.1016/j.tmp.2022.101000

Ruangkanjanases, A., Qhal, E. M. A., Alfawaz, K. M., & Hariguna, T. (2023). Examining the Antecedents of Blockchain Usage Intention: An Integrated Research Framework. *Sustainability (Basel)*, 15(4), 3500. Advance online publication. DOI: 10.3390/su15043500

Szajna, B. (1996). Empirical Evaluation of the Revised Technology Acceptance Model. *Management Science*, 42(1), 85–92. DOI: 10.1287/mnsc.42.1.85

Tamilmani, K., Rana, N. P., Wamba, S. F., & Dwivedi, R. (2021). The extended Unified Theory of Acceptance and Use of Technology (UTAUT2): A systematic literature review and theory evaluation. *International Journal of Information Management*, 57(1), 102269. DOI: 10.1016/j.ijinfomgt.2020.102269

Tyan, I., Yagüe, M. I., & Guevara-Plaza, A. (2020). Blockchain technology for smart tourism destinations. *Sustainability (Basel)*, 12(22), 1–11. DOI: 10.3390/su12229715

Valeri, M., & Baggio, R. (2021). A critical reflection on the adoption of blockchain in tourism. *Information Technology & Tourism*, 23(2), 121–132. DOI: 10.1007/s40558-020-00183-1

Venkatesh, V. (2022). Adoption and use of AI tools: A research agenda grounded in UTAUT. *Annals of Operations Research*, 308(1–2), 641–652. DOI: 10.1007/s10479-020-03918-9

Venkatesh, V., & Davis, F. D. (2000). Theoretical extension of the Technology Acceptance Model: Four longitudinal field studies. *Management Science*, 46(2), 186–204. DOI: 10.1287/mnsc.46.2.186.11926

Venkatesh, V., Smith, R. H., Morris, M. G., Davis, G. B., Davis, F. D., & Walton, S. M. (2003). User acceptance of information technology: Toward a unified view. *Management Information Systems Quarterly*, 27(3), 425–478. DOI: 10.2307/30036540

Waris, A., Malang, P. N., Rachmawati, I. K., Bukhori, M., Majidah, Y., & Hidayatullah, S. (2020). Analysis Of Use Of Mobile Banking With Acceptance And Use Of Technology (UTAUT) Article in. *International Journal of Scientific & Technology Research*. www.ijstr.org

Wong, L. W., Tan, G. W. H., Lee, V. H., Ooi, K. B., & Sohal, A. (2020). Unearthing the determinants of Blockchain adoption in supply chain management. *International Journal of Production Research*, 58(7), 2100–2123. DOI: 10.1080/00207543.2020.1730463

Wut, T. M., & Xu, J. (Bill), & Wong, S. mun. (2021). Crisis management research (1985–2020) in the hospitality and tourism industry: A review and research agenda. In *Tourism Management* (Vol. 85). Elsevier Ltd. DOI: 10.1016/j.tourman.2021.104307

Zavolokina, L., Zani, N., & Schwabe, G. (2023). Designing for Trust in Blockchain Platforms. *IEEE Transactions on Engineering Management*, 70(3), 849–863. DOI: 10.1109/TEM.2020.3015359

Chapter 3
The Emergence of Crypto Travel:
Revolutionizing Global Tourism With Blockchain and Digital Currencies

Ashish Raina
https://orcid.org/0000-0001-5812-5920
CT University, India

ABSTRACT

The rapid advancement and growth in adoption of crypto-currencies are revolutionizing the global travel industry. This chapter explores the emergence of "crypto travel," where digital currencies such as Bitcoin and Ethereum are increasingly used for travel services. The chapter examines how blockchain enhances transparency, reduces transaction fees, and ensures the privacy and security of financial data. Platforms like Travala, alongside major travel companies experimenting with crypto payments, are leading this shift. However, the chapter also discusses challenges, including market volatility, limited merchant adoption, and regulatory uncertainties. As crypto travel evolves, it offers the potential to reshape the tourism landscape, providing tech-savvy travelers with innovative payment options while driving efficiency. The integration of digital currencies and blockchain technology marks a significant milestone in the future of global tourism.

DOI: 10.4018/979-8-3693-6562-5.ch003

INTRODUCTION

Crypto travel refers to the integration of crypto-currencies and blockchain technology within the travel industry, enhancing payment methods and operational efficiencies. This emerging trend is characterized by the use of digital currencies for transactions related to travel services, such as booking accommodations and transportation. Blockchain technology facilitates secure payment systems, contract management, and identity verification, which can streamline travel processes (Vinod, 2020). The adoption of crypto-currencies allows for flexible payment options, enabling travelers to choose between fiat and digital currencies at the point of sale (Wnuk, 2017). Crypto-currencies offer advantages like lower transaction fees and increased security; however, they also present risks such as volatility and cyber threats (Vijaikanth & Boyle, 2023 ; Silva & Filho, 2024). Factors influencing the adoption of crypto-currencies in travel include perceived usefulness, ease of use, and security concerns (Silva & Filho, 2024). While crypto travel presents innovative opportunities, it also faces significant challenges that must be addressed to ensure widespread acceptance and security in transactions.

Crypto travel enables travelers to use digital currencies for booking flights, hotels, and other travel services. As blockchain technology and crypto-currencies gain mainstream acceptance, the travel industry has started exploring its potential to streamline transactions, reduce costs, and increase global access. One major advantage of crypto travel is the reduction of transaction fees. Traditional payment methods, especially international transfers, often involve high fees and lengthy processing times. Crypto-currencies, by contrast, offer near-instantaneous transactions with minimal costs. This is particularly beneficial for travelers dealing with currency exchange and cross-border payments. Crypto travel also appeals to privacy-conscious consumers. Many travelers prefer decentralized systems that allow them to bypass traditional banking infrastructure and avoid sharing sensitive financial information.

However, crypto travel faces challenges, such as market volatility and limited merchant adoption. While some travel platforms, like Expedia (through third-party services) and Travala, accept crypto-currencies, the wider adoption by hotels, airlines, and tourism services is still developing. As regulatory clarity and technological advancements continue, crypto travel is poised to grow, offering innovative solutions for modern, tech-savvy travelers.

CRYPTO TRAVEL AND LOCAL COMMUNITIES

The intersection of crypto-currency and local communities presents innovative opportunities for economic engagement and social cohesion. Various blockchain applications are emerging that leverage local currencies to enhance community participation and support local businesses. Crypto travel, the use of crypto-currencies like Bitcoin for travel-related transactions, is gaining traction, offering new opportunities for local communities. By enabling peer-to-peer transactions, crypto travel reduces reliance on traditional financial intermediaries, allowing more direct interaction between travelers and local service providers. This decentralization can empower small businesses, particularly in developing regions where banking infrastructure is limited. For instance, local hotels, guides, and artisans can accept crypto-currencies, bypassing high transaction fees associated with credit cards or international transfers. This financial inclusivity fosters local economic development by allowing community members to capture more value from tourism.

Moreover, blockchain technology enhances transparency and trust within the tourism sector. Smart contracts can ensure secure, automated transactions, reducing fraud risks for both travelers and local vendors. Communities that embrace crypto payments can also market themselves as innovative, attracting tech-savvy tourists seeking unique travel experiences. El Salvador's adoption of Bitcoin as legal tender, for example, has attracted a wave of crypto tourists, spurring local economies. However, the volatility of crypto-currencies poses risks for small businesses, which may face income fluctuations. Additionally, low digital literacy and lack of infrastructure in rural or marginalized communities could limit the benefits of crypto travel. Despite these challenges, with education and infrastructure investments, crypto travel holds promise for promoting economic empowerment and financial inclusion, ultimately creating more equitable opportunities for local communities within the global tourism landscape.

Currencies, Community Engagement and Crypto Travel

Local currencies, facilitated by blockchain technology, enable secure transactions within specific geographical areas, promoting local commerce and consumer loyalty (Shaw, 2018). Projects like Encointer propose community crypto-currencies that provide universal basic income, fostering economic stability and participation among residents (Brenzikofer, 2019). The token economy framework allows for diverse mechanisms that incentivize community involvement, with various projects exploring different governance models and token distribution strategies (Domenicale et al., 2024). Digital-community currencies can address socio-economic disparities and enhance community resilience, although challenges remain regarding sustainability and participant motivation (Nishibe, 2020).

Local currencies, community engagement, and crypto-currency are interconnected themes that are significantly shaping the modern economic and social landscapes, especially in the realm of travel. Local currencies, often issued by towns, cities, or regions, serve as an important tool to encourage residents and visitors to spend money within the local economy. These alternative currencies, such as the Bristol Pound in the UK or the BerkShares in Massachusetts, promote regional economic sustainability by reducing financial outflows to large corporations and instead directing funds to local businesses. This practice helps strengthen local economies, creates a sense of community ownership, and enhances social ties by fostering direct relationships between consumers and local entrepreneurs. Community engagement plays a crucial role in the success of such currency systems, as they depend on active participation, trust, and shared values within the local population. Without widespread community involvement, the impact of these currencies is often limited.

On the other hand, the rise of crypto-currency, such as Bitcoin, Ethereum, and other decentralized digital assets, presents a globalized alternative to traditional financial systems. In the context of travel, "crypto travel" refers to the growing trend of tourists using crypto-currencies to pay for goods and services, such as accommodations, flights, and local experiences. This trend has gained momentum in regions that aim to attract tech-savvy travelers, particularly those interested in the benefits of decentralized finance (DeFi) and blockchain technology. Crypto-currency offers advantages such as lower transaction fees, faster cross-border payments, and increased transparency through blockchain's secure, immutable ledgers. Moreover, blockchain technology ensures transparency and security, enhancing trust in peer-to-peer transactions, a critical factor for travelers concerned with fraud or fluctuating currency exchange rates. While crypto-currency challenges traditional local currencies, it also opens new pathways for engaging communities in the global economy. Integrating decentralized financial systems into local ecosystems may offer unique opportunities for fostering both local economic growth and global connectivity. Ultimately, the combination of local currencies, community engagement, and crypto-currency in the travel sector represents a shift toward more diversified, resilient, and inclusive economic models that balance local benefits with global access.

Future of Crypto Travel

The future of crypto travel is set to evolve significantly as blockchain technology and crypto-currencies become more integrated into global economies. With the rising popularity of decentralized finance (DeFi) and digital currencies like Bitcoin, Ethereum, and stablecoins, the travel industry is exploring new ways to cater to tech-savvy consumers seeking efficient, transparent, and secure travel solutions. As blockchain technology advances, the potential for smart contracts in the travel industry is another area of interest. Smart contracts can automate and streamline various aspects of travel bookings, insurance claims, and loyalty programs. For example, travelers could book flights and hotels using a smart contract that automatically refunds the amount if the service is canceled or delayed, reducing the need for third-party intermediaries. The future of crypto travel will likely involve greater integration with decentralized finance (DeFi) systems. DeFi platforms enable peer-to-peer financial services like lending and insurance, which could be applied to travel services. Imagine a scenario where travelers can take out crypto-based travel insurance or use decentralized platforms to pool resources for discounted group travel rates.

Currently, several travel platforms are beginning to accept crypto-currencies as a form of payment. Notable examples include Travala, a blockchain-based travel booking platform, and companies like Expedia and Booking.com, which have explored crypto payments through partnerships with third-party providers like BitPay. This trend is expected to grow as the demand for crypto payments increases, especially among younger travelers, many of whom are comfortable with digital currencies. As more people hold crypto-currencies as part of their portfolios, the incentive to spend them directly on travel services will rise. Major airlines and hotel chains are also showing interest in accepting crypto payments. For instance, AirBaltic and LOT Polish Airlines have already introduced Bitcoin as a payment method. As more airlines and hotels recognize the efficiency and global nature of crypto-currencies, adoption is likely to expand.

One of the key drivers of the future of crypto travel is the benefit it offers both consumers and businesses. Crypto-currencies provide fast, borderless transactions with low fees, making them an attractive alternative to traditional payment methods, particularly for international travel. Traditional cross-border payments often involve high fees and delays due to intermediaries like banks and payment processors. In contrast, crypto-currencies can be transferred almost instantaneously at a fraction of the cost. For travelers, this means avoiding the hassle and expense of exchanging currencies in foreign countries. It also allows them to bypass some of the complications related to credit card usage abroad, such as international transaction fees or blocked cards due to fraud alerts. Crypto wallets are accessible globally, allowing travelers from countries with limited financial infrastructure to book and pay for services easily. Moreover, the privacy and security features of blockchain technology can help address concerns over data breaches and identity theft, which are prevalent in the travel industry. Since crypto-currency payments do not require travelers to share sensitive personal information, they may be less vulnerable to hacking and fraud.

The future of crypto travel looks promising as the world moves towards digitalization. With increasing adoption, technological innovation, and the growing appeal of decentralized systems, the travel industry is poised to transform. However, overcoming challenges like regulatory uncertainty and market volatility will be key to realizing its full potential. As these barriers diminish, crypto travel may become a staple of the global tourism industry, offering greater convenience, security, and financial inclusivity. The future of crypto travel is poised for significant transformation as crypto-currencies gain traction in the tourism sector. This evolution is driven by technological advancements, changing consumer preferences, and the potential for enhanced security and convenience in transactions.

Crypto-currencies are increasingly being accepted by hotels, travel agencies, and entertainment services, reflecting a growing trend towards digital currencies in tourism (Açiksözlü et al., 2022). A systematic review identified key factors influencing tourists' adoption of crypto-currencies, including perceived usefulness, ease of use, and security concerns (Silva & Filho, 2024). Blockchain technology, integral to crypto-currencies, is seen as a facilitator for sustainable tourism by democratizing economic participation and enhancing trust among stakeholders (Tham & Sigala, 2020). The potential for crypto-currencies to support sustainable tourism goals is being explored, emphasizing their role in creating inclusive economic systems(Tham & Sigala, 2020).

Challenges and Opportunities

Despite the promising outlook, challenges such as regulatory compliance and security concerns remain significant barriers to widespread adoption ("Crypto-currency as a method of payment in the tourism sector", 2023). The demand for secure and user-friendly crypto-currency payment methods is critical for the tourism industry's future ("Crypto-currency as a method of payment in the tourism sector", 2023). While the integration of crypto-currencies in travel presents exciting opportunities, it also necessitates addressing regulatory and security challenges to ensure a smooth transition into this new financial landscape. Despite its promising potential, crypto travel faces several significant challenges that hinder its widespread adoption in the tourism industry.

One of the most prominent issues is the volatility of crypto-currencies. Digital currencies like Bitcoin and Ethereum are known for dramatic price fluctuations, which create uncertainty for both travelers and service providers. A traveler who books a hotel using Bitcoin may find that the currency's value has dropped substantially by the time of payment, creating financial unpredictability for both parties. Conversely, sudden price surges could lead to dissatisfaction if services were purchased at a higher rate.

Another critical challenge is limited merchant adoption. While a few platforms, such as Travala and AirBaltic, have embraced crypto payments, the majority of hotels, airlines, and tourism-related services still rely on traditional payment systems. Without broader adoption by major players in the travel industry, crypto travel remains a niche option rather than a mainstream solution.

Furthermore, regulatory uncertainty around crypto-currencies presents a formidable barrier. Many countries have yet to establish clear legal frameworks for digital currencies, leading to inconsistent rules on their use for transactions, taxation, and compliance. This creates complications for businesses operating across multiple jurisdictions, as they must navigate diverse regulatory landscapes.

Cybersecurity concerns also pose significant risks. While blockchain technology is generally secure, crypto wallets and exchanges are frequent targets for hackers, putting travelers at risk of theft or fraud.

Additionally, the lack of user familiarity and digital literacy among consumers and service providers alike slows the adoption of crypto travel. Many people are hesitant to use digital currencies due to a lack of understanding, while businesses may find it technically challenging to integrate crypto payments into their systems. Together, these challenges underscore the complexities that must be addressed for crypto travel to gain broader traction in the global tourism market.

Crypto travel faces significant challenges that impede its broader adoption. The volatility of digital currencies creates financial unpredictability for both travelers and service providers. Limited merchant acceptance and regulatory uncertainty further complicate integration into mainstream travel services. Cybersecurity risks and a lack of digital literacy among users and businesses also pose substantial barriers. Addressing these issues is crucial for unlocking the full potential of crypto travel in the global tourism industry.

CONCLUSION

Scope of Research in Crypto Travel

Future research in crypto travel offers a wealth of possibilities to explore and address the emerging complexities of this evolving sector. One key area of investigation could be the development of more stable digital currencies, such as stablecoins, which aim to minimize volatility and provide a more reliable medium of exchange for travel transactions. Researchers could also examine innovative blockchain applications, such as smart contracts, which could automate and secure various aspects of travel bookings, insurance claims, and loyalty programs. Additionally, exploring regulatory frameworks and their impact on global crypto travel adoption would provide valuable insights into creating a more harmonized legal environment. The study of consumer behavior and digital literacy could reveal strategies for increasing user adoption and trust in crypto travel solutions. Finally, research into cybersecurity measures tailored to crypto travel platforms could help mitigate risks and enhance user protection. By delving into these areas, future research could significantly contribute to the advancement and mainstream acceptance of crypto travel in the global tourism industry.

REFERENCES

Aaron, T. (2020, January 13). Marianna, Sigala. (2020). 2. Road block(chain): Bit(coin)s for tourism sustainable development goals? *Journal of Hospitality and Tourism Technology*, 11(2), 203–222. Advance online publication. DOI: 10.1108/JHTT-05-2019-0069

Alain, B. (2019). 3. encointer — Local Community Crypto-currencies with Universal Basic Income. arXiv: Cryptography and Security

Ben, V. (2020). 1. Blockchain in travel. *Journal of Revenue and Pricing Management*, 19(1), 2–6. Advance online publication. DOI: 10.1057/s41272-019-00213-6

Bingjie, Liu., William, C., Norman. (2016). 4. Developing a conceptual framework to understand local residents' contribution in online travel communities

Gislainy, Laise, da, Silva., Luiz, Mendes, Filho. (2024). 5. Proposição de Fatores que influenciam o uso de Criptomoedas para Pagamento de Serviços Turísticos: Uma Revisão Sistemática da Literatura e Bibliometria. DOI: 10.18226/21789061.v16i1p140

Gislainy, Laise, da, Silva., Luiz, Mendes, Filho. (2024). 3. Proposição de Fatores que influenciam o uso de Criptomoedas para Pagamento de Serviços Turísticos: Uma Revisão Sistemática da Literatura e Bibliometria. DOI: 10.18226/21789061.v16i1p140

Horst, T. Daniel, T., Leung., Andrei, O., J., Kwok., Aaron, Tham. (2021). 3. Crypto-currency adoption in travel and tourism – an exploratory study of Asia Pacific travellers. *Current Issues in Tourism*. Advance online publication. DOI: 10.1080/13683500.2020.1863928

Horst, T. Daniel, T., Leung., Andrei, O., J., Kwok., Aaron, Tham. (2021). 5. Crypto-currency adoption in travel and tourism – an exploratory study of Asia Pacific travellers. *Current Issues in Tourism*. Advance online publication. DOI: 10.1080/13683500.2020.1863928

Irene, Domenicale., Cristina, Viano., Claudio, Schifanella. (2024). 1. Blockchain for local communities: an exploratory review of token economy aspects. Frontiers in blockchain, DOI: 10.3389/fbloc.2024.1426802

John, Matthew, Wnuk. (2017). 2. Flexible payment services for travel and credit cards

Makoto, N. (2020). *5. The present and future of digital-community currencies: RAMICS 2019 in Hida–Takayama keynote speech.* Evolutionary and Institutional Economics Review., DOI: 10.1007/s40844-020-00177-y

Norman, Shaw. (2018). 2. Helping the Local Community with Crypto-Currency: A Case Study.. DOI: 10.1007/978-3-319-91716-0_52

Övgü, Açiksözlü., Ilbey, Varol., Nur, Neşe, Şahin. (2022). 1. Touristic coins: evaluation of the use of crypto coins in tourism businesses by tourism students. Social science development journal, DOI: 10.31567/ssd.759

Vijendran, Vijaikanth., A, Boyle. (2023). 4. The Use of Crypto-currencies as a Tool for the Development of Marketing in Tourism. Smart Innovation, Systems and Technologies, DOI: 10.1007/978-981-19-9099-1_1

Chapter 4

Concept, Applications, Challenges, and Security Threats of Blockchain Technology in the Tourism Industry

Ashish Raina
https://orcid.org/0000-0001-5812-5920
CT University, India

Sarita Rani
APS Miran Sahib, India

Gaurav Bathla
https://orcid.org/0000-0002-6992-811X
CT University, India

ABSTRACT

Blockchain technology, a decentralized, transparent, and immutable system, has emerged as a transformative force across various sectors, including tourism and hospitality. Originally developed for cryptocurrencies, blockchain's core principles—such as enhanced security, decentralized data management, and trustless transactions—are now being applied to address key challenges in the tourism industry. Despite its numerous advantages, blockchain presents several challenges and security threats to the hospitality industry. Issues such as scalability, high implementation costs, regulatory uncertainty, and data privacy concerns complicate its adoption. Furthermore, the risk of cyberattacks, including 51% attacks and vulnerabilities

DOI: 10.4018/979-8-3693-6562-5.ch004

in smart contracts, poses significant security threats. The chapter concludes by acknowledging blockchain's potential while emphasizing the need for the industry to navigate these challenges carefully, particularly through strategic investment in infrastructure, security, and compliance.

1.0 INTRODUCTION TO BLOCKCHAIN

Block-chain technology is a combination of various digital mechanisms like cryptography, data management, and networking which supports capturing, validation, and execution of transactions between the communicating users. Block chains are basically tamper evident and tamper resistant distributed digital ledgers implemented with a decentralized repository and has no central authority. It is a distributed and public database of all transactions executed and shared among participating parties. Basically, they enable a group of users to record transactions in a shared ledger and do not allow transactions to be changed once published (Chhabra et. al., 2017). The block chain contains a verifiable record of every transaction ever made which is verified by consensus of the participants in the system. Block chain can be technically defined as

Block chain is a peer-to-peer, distributed ledger that is crypto graphically secure, append only, immutable (extremely hard to change), and updateable only via consensus or agreement among peers (Bashir et. al., 2018).

In block chains the crypto graphically signed transactions are grouped in to blocks. Each block is crypto graphically linked to the previous block making the chain tam-per evident. New blocks are added after validation using the consensus mechanism and replicated across the ledger of the network.

Blockchain technology, introduced in 2008 with the advent of Bitcoin by an anonymous entity known as Satoshi Nakamoto, has evolved into one of the most transformative technological advancements of the 21st century. It is a decentralized, distributed ledger system that facilitates the recording of transactions across multiple computers in such a way that ensures the security, transparency, and immutability of data. At its core, blockchain is designed to enable trustless, peer-to-peer networks where parties can transact without the need for intermediaries like banks or governments, making it highly disruptive in industries reliant on third-party validation and verification.

2.0 ORIGIN OF BLOCKCHAIN TECHNOLOGY

The blockchain generally comprises several fields like software engineering, distributed computing, cryptography, and game theory. Real-world blockchain applications are usually defined discussed under the umbrella of what is known as crypto economics. Crypto economics (Sultan et. al., 2018) is defined as, "a discipline concerned with the production, consumption and transfer of wealth using computer networks, cryptography,and game theory to enhance prosperity of groups in current and future digital market economies."

Block chain is a basis of Bitcoin. Satoshi Nakamo to is considered as the inventor of blockchain. He published a research article to a cryptography forum outlining technique to counter the double-spend scenario. Early crypto currencies suffered from the problem of double spending. He described his technique by using a series of hashed timestamps, without explicitly defining blockchain. "Each timestamp includes the previous timestamp in its hash, forming a chain, with each additional timestamp reinforcing the ones behind it" (Nakamoto, 2019). The original method was modified to adapt the needs of Bitcoin, and was defined as—cryptographically linked chain of blocks, where each block uses hash digest of previous block for security.

3.0 KEY FEATURES OF BLOCKCHAIN

One of the defining features of blockchain is its decentralized nature. Traditional systems, such as banking or cloud computing, rely on centralized servers that store all the data and act as the authoritative source of truth. In contrast, blockchain relies on a distributed network where every participant, known as a node, has a copy of the entire ledger. This eliminates single points of failure and makes it more resilient to hacking and system failures.

The concept of immutability is another cornerstone of blockchain technology. Once a transaction is recorded on a blockchain, it is nearly impossible to alter. This is achieved through cryptographic hashing, which transforms transaction data into a fixed-size string of characters that is uniquely tied to the data in a block. Each block in the chain contains a hash of the previous block, forming a secure and verifiable chain of transactions. To alter any transaction would require changing all subsequent blocks, which becomes computationally prohibitive as the chain grows longer, making the blockchain tamper-proof.

Transparency is also a significant advantage. In a public blockchain, such as the one underpinning Bitcoin, all transaction data is visible to every participant in the network. This fosters a level of accountability not possible in traditional financial systems, where access to transaction records is typically restricted. Even in private or permissioned blockchains, where access to data may be limited, the architecture ensures that every participant is aware of the validity and integrity of transactions they are authorized to see.

4.0 APPLICATIONS AND IMPLICATIONS

Blockchain's initial application in cryptocurrencies demonstrated its potential in decentralizing financial systems, but its utility extends far beyond digital currencies. Industries as diverse as supply chain management, healthcare, real estate, and government are exploring blockchain to improve transparency, efficiency, and security. For example, in supply chain management, blockchain can provide an immutable record of product origins and movements, enabling greater traceability and reducing the risk of fraud. In healthcare, it offers a secure platform for managing patient records, ensuring data integrity while protecting privacy.

Furthermore, blockchain's potential to disrupt financial markets is enormous. Through decentralized finance (DeFi), blockchain enables services like lending, borrowing, and trading to occur directly between users without intermediaries, potentially reducing costs and increasing accessibility to financial services, especially in underbanked regions.

5.0 BLOCK CHAIN AND TOURISM INDUSTRY

Blockchain technology, initially developed for cryptocurrencies like Bitcoin, is increasingly being adopted across various industries, including the tourism sector. The core principles of blockchain—decentralization, transparency, security, and immutability—are transforming how travel companies, airlines, hotels, and tourists engage in transactions and manage data. Blockchain's decentralized structure provides opportunities to address some of the tourism industry's long-standing challenges, such as fraud, inefficiencies in bookings and payments, loyalty programs, and the management of personal data.

5.1 Enhanced Payment Systems

One of the most significant ways blockchain is revolutionizing tourism is through improved payment systems. Traditionally, international travel involves currency conversions and high transaction fees when paying for services in foreign countries. Blockchain can eliminate the need for intermediaries like banks or payment processors by facilitating direct, peer-to-peer transactions using crypto-currencies. This reduces costs and speeds up transaction times. Moreover, using blockchain-based payment systems can improve security, as the encrypted nature of blockchain transactions makes it difficult for hackers to tamper with financial records.

For instance, tourists can book flights, hotels, and other services using cryptocurrencies like Bitcoin or Ethereum, bypassing traditional payment gateways and their associated fees. This is particularly beneficial for travelers from regions with limited access to conventional banking services or in areas where currency fluctuations are unpredictable. By offering more streamlined, transparent, and cost-effective payment options, blockchain enhances the overall travel experience.

5.2 Streamlined Booking and Reservation Processes

Blockchain technology can also improve booking and reservation processes in the tourism sector. Currently, many travel bookings are managed by intermediaries such as online travel agencies (OTAs), which charge high commission fees to airlines, hotels, and customers. By using blockchain, travel companies can directly connect with customers, cutting out these intermediaries and reducing costs. This allows for a more transparent and efficient booking system, where both service providers and travelers can see real-time availability and prices.

For example, blockchain-based platforms can automate and manage bookings with smart contracts—self-executing contracts with predefined conditions coded into them. Once a customer books a hotel or flight, the smart contract ensures that the payment is only processed when the service is delivered, reducing the risk of fraud or miscommunication. This makes the booking process more secure and trustworthy.

5.3 Improved Customer Loyalty Programs

Blockchain can also transform loyalty programs in the tourism industry. Traditionally, loyalty programs offered by airlines, hotels, and travel agencies are often fragmented, with points earned from one company not transferrable to others. This creates inefficiencies and reduces the value of the points earned. Blockchain can consolidate these programs into a unified, decentralized platform where customers can earn and redeem points across various service providers.

With blockchain, loyalty points can be tokenized, enabling travelers to accumulate and spend them more easily across different platforms. This allows for a more flexible and user-friendly rewards system, where points from different programs can be used interchangeably, thereby improving customer satisfaction.

5.4 Enhanced Security and Privacy

In an era where data privacy is a growing concern, blockchain offers enhanced security for managing personal information. When booking travel services, tourists often provide sensitive data, including passports and credit card details, which are vulnerable to hacking and misuse. Blockchain's decentralized and encrypted nature provides a safer way to store and share personal data. Instead of relying on centralized databases that can be breached, blockchain stores data across a distributed network, making it difficult for unauthorized users to access.

Blockchain can also simplify the verification process for travel documents such as visas and passports, reducing waiting times at airports and borders. Digital identities stored on a blockchain are immutable and easily verifiable, allowing travelers to securely share only the necessary information with service providers.

Blockchain technology is poised to revolutionize the tourism industry by improving payment systems, enhancing the booking process, consolidating loyalty programs, and providing greater security for personal data. While still in the early stages of adoption, blockchain has the potential to address some of the key challenges in tourism, creating a more efficient, secure, and transparent ecosystem for travelers and service providers alike.

6.0 BLOCKCHAIN POSSIBILITIES IN HOSPITALITY INDUSTRY

Blockchain technology, known for its decentralized, secure, and transparent nature, is gradually transforming various sectors, including the hospitality industry. This technology, which originated with cryptocurrencies like Bitcoin, has applications far beyond finance. In the hospitality industry, it offers the potential to enhance operations, improve customer experiences, reduce fraud, streamline payments, and create more efficient loyalty programs. As hotels, restaurants, and other service providers increasingly adopt blockchain, they can leverage its unique capabilities to create a more efficient and seamless guest experience.

6.1 Streamlining Payments and Reducing Transaction Costs

One of the most immediate benefits blockchain offers to the hospitality industry is the ability to streamline payments. Traditionally, international travelers must deal with currency conversions, high transaction fees, and delays when using traditional banking systems. Blockchain, through the use of cryptocurrencies, enables direct peer-to-peer transactions that bypass these intermediaries, reducing costs for both service providers and customers.

By using blockchain-based payment systems, hotels and restaurants can accept cryptocurrencies like Bitcoin or Ethereum, offering a faster and more cost-effective alternative to traditional payment methods. The decentralized nature of blockchain ensures that payments are processed almost instantaneously, eliminating the need for third-party payment processors, which can slow down transactions and charge high fees. This is particularly beneficial for international tourists who often face steep currency exchange fees and transaction delays when paying for services abroad.

Moreover, blockchain's encryption ensures the security of financial transactions, reducing the risk of fraud. The immutability of the blockchain ledger makes it extremely difficult for hackers to alter payment records, thereby offering greater trust and security to both businesses and consumers.

6.2 Enhancing Guest Identification and Data Security

In the hospitality industry, securing personal data is of paramount importance. Hotels, for example, collect sensitive information such as passport details, credit card numbers, and home addresses, making them prime targets for cyber-attacks. Blockchain technology can significantly enhance the security of this data through its decentralized and encrypted ledger system.

Rather than storing guest information on a centralized server, which is vulnerable to hacking, blockchain allows data to be distributed across a secure network, making it more difficult for malicious actors to breach. This decentralized approach also gives guests more control over their personal data, as blockchain can enable them to share only the necessary information with hotels or service providers.

Blockchain can also streamline the check-in process by simplifying guest identification. By using blockchain-based digital identities, guests can securely verify their identity without needing to share sensitive personal information repeatedly. For example, a guest could present a digital identity stored on the blockchain at check-in, where the hotel can instantly verify their booking and identity, making the process quicker and more secure.

6.3 Improving Booking and Reservation Systems

Blockchain can also revolutionize booking and reservation systems by eliminating intermediaries, such as online travel agencies (OTAs), which often charge high commissions and complicate the reservation process. The current system often involves multiple intermediaries, including booking platforms and payment gateways, which can lead to higher costs and inefficiencies.

By using blockchain-based platforms, hotels can directly connect with customers, allowing for a more transparent and efficient booking system. Smart contracts—self-executing contracts with the terms of the agreement written into code—can automate and secure bookings, ensuring that reservations are confirmed once the payment is made. These contracts execute automatically when predefined conditions are met, reducing the risk of double bookings, cancellations, or fraud.

For instance, once a guest books a room and makes a payment, the smart contract can instantly verify the transaction and lock in the reservation. This can eliminate disputes and reduce the risk of overbooking. Additionally, blockchain's transparent nature means that both customers and hotels can verify reservations and payments in real-time, making the booking process more reliable and secure.

6.4 Reinventing Loyalty Programs

Loyalty programs are a crucial part of the hospitality industry, but they are often fragmented and complex, with points difficult to transfer or redeem across different service providers. Blockchain can simplify and unify these programs, allowing for more flexible, transparent, and efficient systems.

Blockchain enables the tokenization of loyalty points, meaning that points can be stored, transferred, and redeemed on a decentralized platform. This allows guests to accumulate points from various hotels, restaurants, or airlines and use them across multiple businesses, making loyalty programs more appealing and user-friendly. Moreover, the transparency of blockchain ensures that guests can track their points in real-time, reducing confusion and improving customer satisfaction.

By removing the need for intermediaries in managing loyalty programs, blockchain also lowers costs for hospitality providers and enables more seamless integration with other businesses in the ecosystem, such as airlines or tour operators.

7.0 CHALLENGES, AND SECURITY THREATS BLOCKCHAIN CAN CREATE IN THE HOSPITALITY INDUSTRY

Blockchain technology, known for its decentralized, transparent, and immutable nature, has the potential to transform various sectors, including hospitality. While the technology offers numerous advantages, such as increased efficiency, transparency, and security, it also brings with it unique challenges and security threats that can impact the hospitality industry. These challenges primarily stem from the complexity of implementing blockchain, the evolving nature of the technology, and the risks associated with cybersecurity.

7.1 Complexity and Scalability Issues

One of the primary challenges blockchain introduces to the hospitality industry is its complexity and scalability. Blockchain's decentralized nature means that data is shared across a network of nodes, with each transaction verified by consensus mechanisms. For the hospitality industry, which handles vast amounts of transactional data—such as reservations, customer records, payments, and loyalty points—this poses a significant challenge. Public blockchains, which are commonly used for cryptocurrencies, struggle with scalability, particularly as transaction volumes increase.

For instance, Bitcoin and Ethereum blockchains can handle only a limited number of transactions per second (7 and 15, respectively). For a global industry like hospitality, where real-time transactions are essential, this lack of scalability can result in slow processing times, reducing the efficiency that blockchain is supposed to bring. Implementing private or permissioned blockchains can alleviate some of these concerns, but this often comes at the cost of reduced decentralization and transparency, which are core features of blockchain technology.

7.2 Cost of Implementation and Integration

Another significant challenge is the high cost associated with implementing and integrating blockchain technology into existing systems. The hospitality industry operates on various legacy systems, and migrating to blockchain involves significant investment in both infrastructure and expertise. Blockchain requires highly skilled professionals to develop, maintain, and troubleshoot the system, driving up costs for companies, especially smaller or mid-sized firms that may not have the financial resources to adopt such advanced technology.

Moreover, integrating blockchain with other technologies that hotels and resorts rely on, such as property management systems (PMS) and customer relationship management (CRM) systems, can be cumbersome and time-consuming. Compatibility issues can arise, leading to costly delays and interruptions in daily operations. This creates a barrier for the widespread adoption of blockchain in hospitality, limiting its benefits to only those companies willing and able to absorb these costs.

7.3 Data Privacy and Compliance Concerns

While blockchain is often praised for its security features, its transparency can also pose risks, particularly concerning data privacy. In the hospitality industry, guest information—such as identification details, payment records, and personal preferences—must be handled with great care to comply with regulations like the General Data Protection Regulation (GDPR) in Europe and the California Consumer Privacy Act (CCPA) in the U.S.

Blockchain's immutability means that once data is entered into the ledger, it cannot be deleted or altered. This presents a challenge in complying with regulations that grant individuals the "right to be forgotten" or the right to request deletion of their data. While some solutions, such as off-chain data storage or encryption, have been proposed, they complicate the blockchain infrastructure, potentially reintroducing centralization and defeating the purpose of using blockchain in the first place.

7.4 Cyber Security Threats and Vulnerabilities

Despite blockchain's inherent security features—such as cryptographic hashing and decentralized control—it is not immune to cyberattacks. In the hospitality industry, blockchain-based systems could still be vulnerable to various security threats, including 51% attacks, where a single entity gains majority control over the blockchain network, allowing them to alter the transaction history or double-spend tokens. Although this risk is more prominent in smaller blockchain networks with fewer nodes, it remains a potential threat as blockchain technology becomes more prevalent in the hospitality industry.

Smart contracts, self-executing contracts embedded with predefined rules, are often touted as a way to streamline transactions in hospitality, such as booking reservations or processing payments. However, smart contracts are not foolproof and can contain vulnerabilities or coding errors that hackers can exploit. For example, in 2016, a major smart contract platform known as "The DAO" was hacked, resulting in the loss of millions of dollars' worth of cryptocurrency. In the hospitality sector, a flawed smart contract could lead to erroneous charges, invalid reservations, or unauthorized access to guest data.

7.5 Regulatory Uncertainty

Blockchain technology exists in a complex and often unclear regulatory environment. Governments around the world have been slow to adopt comprehensive regulations concerning the use of blockchain, particularly in industries like hospitality, where its applications are still emerging. Regulatory uncertainty creates risks for companies that wish to adopt blockchain, as they may face unforeseen legal challenges or compliance issues.

For example, blockchain-based payments in cryptocurrencies may be subject to different financial regulations than traditional payment systems. Taxation, anti-money laundering (AML) laws, and know-your-customer (KYC) regulations may all be affected by how blockchain is used in hospitality transactions, and companies could face penalties if they fail to comply with new or evolving standards.

While blockchain technology offers significant potential for transforming the hospitality industry by improving transparency, efficiency, and security, it also brings several challenges and security threats. Scalability issues, high costs of implementation, privacy concerns, and cybersecurity vulnerabilities pose substantial risks. Additionally, the lack of clear regulatory frameworks adds another layer of uncertainty for businesses adopting blockchain. To fully realize the benefits of blockchain, the hospitality industry will need to navigate these challenges carefully, investing in robust security measures, infrastructure, and compliance to mitigate risks associated with this emerging technology.

8.0 CONCLUSION

Blockchain technology has emerged as a disruptive force across multiple industries, and its potential within the tourism sector is vast and transformative. As explored throughout this chapter, blockchain offers a range of applications that can reshape how transactions are conducted, data is managed, and trust is established between consumers and service providers in tourism. At its core, blockchain's decentralized, immutable, and transparent nature provides an innovative framework for addressing many of the inefficiencies and challenges that currently plague the tourism industry.

8.1. Enhancing Transparency and Efficiency

One of blockchain's most significant contributions to the tourism industry is its ability to enhance transparency and efficiency in various operations. By eliminating the need for intermediaries in transactions, blockchain reduces costs and streamlines processes such as bookings, payments, and loyalty programs. The use of smart contracts automates and secures transactions, ensuring that they are executed based on predefined conditions, thereby reducing the risk of fraud, miscommunication, and disputes between service providers and travelers. As a result, blockchain can create a more trustworthy and seamless experience for consumers, while enabling service providers to operate more efficiently.

In payment systems, blockchain enables peer-to-peer transactions, bypassing traditional banks and financial institutions that often charge high fees for international transactions. This has particular relevance for international tourists, who can benefit from the speed, security, and reduced costs associated with blockchain-based payments. Moreover, the adoption of crypto-currencies further simplifies the process for travelers from underbanked regions or areas with fluctuating currency values.

8.2. Strengthening Security and Data Privacy

Data security and privacy are critical issues in the tourism sector, particularly as more personal information is shared online during booking and payment processes. Blockchain's decentralized and encrypted nature provides enhanced protection for sensitive data, reducing the likelihood of cyberattacks and breaches. By storing guest information across a distributed ledger, blockchain offers an added layer of security, minimizing the vulnerability of centralized databases that are frequently targeted by hackers.

Moreover, blockchain's potential to streamline identity verification processes, such as passports and visas, can significantly improve security while enhancing the efficiency of airport and border operations. Digital identities stored on a blockchain are easily verifiable and secure, allowing travelers to share only the necessary information with service providers, protecting their privacy while speeding up verification processes.

8.3 Revolutionizing Loyalty Programs and Customer Engagement

Blockchain also presents a unique opportunity to revolutionize loyalty programs in the tourism industry. Current loyalty programs are often fragmented, making it difficult for travelers to redeem rewards across different service providers. Blockchain can consolidate these programs into a single, unified system where travelers can earn and redeem points across a wide range of companies. Tokenizing loyalty points on a blockchain platform allows for seamless transfers and redemptions, increasing customer engagement and satisfaction.

The flexibility that blockchain offers in managing rewards systems can help companies create more personalized and user-friendly experiences, which is becoming increasingly important in a competitive tourism market. By simplifying loyalty programs and enhancing customer engagement, blockchain can drive long-term customer loyalty and business growth in the tourism industry.

8.4. Challenges and Security Threats

Despite the clear advantages, blockchain technology also faces numerous challenges and security threats that need to be addressed for widespread adoption in tourism. Scalability remains a major concern, as public blockchains, such as Bitcoin and Ethereum, struggle to handle high volumes of transactions. For a global industry like tourism, which processes millions of transactions daily, the limitations of current blockchain infrastructures must be resolved to achieve the desired level of efficiency and speed.

Additionally, the cost of implementing blockchain technology is a significant barrier, particularly for small and mid-sized companies. Integrating blockchain into legacy systems is not only expensive but also requires specialized knowledge and expertise. This raises questions about whether the benefits of blockchain can be fully realized across the entire tourism industry or if it will remain limited to larger, more resourceful companies.

From a regulatory perspective, blockchain also operates in a largely ambiguous legal environment. Regulatory bodies worldwide have yet to establish comprehensive frameworks governing the use of blockchain in industries such as tourism. This regulatory uncertainty adds to the complexity of adopting blockchain and creates potential risks for businesses that may face unforeseen legal challenges or compliance issues.

Finally, cybersecurity threats persist despite blockchain's built-in security features. While blockchain is inherently secure due to its decentralized and cryptographically secured nature, vulnerabilities such as 51% attacks and smart contract flaws remain potential risks. As blockchain technology continues to evolve, businesses must be proactive in developing robust security measures to mitigate these risks and ensure the safety of both financial and personal data.

8.5. The Future of Blockchain in Tourism

Looking ahead, blockchain technology holds the potential to transform the tourism industry into a more secure, transparent, and efficient ecosystem. Its applications in improving payment systems, streamlining booking and reservation processes, enhancing data privacy, and creating unified loyalty programs can address many of the industry's existing challenges. However, the successful adoption of blockchain requires overcoming its inherent challenges, including scalability, regulatory uncertainty, and high implementation costs.

As blockchain technology matures and becomes more scalable, its integration with other emerging technologies—such as artificial intelligence (AI), the Internet of Things (IoT), and big data—could further enhance its impact on the tourism sector. By enabling real-time data sharing, predictive analytics, and personalized experiences, these synergies could propel tourism into a new era of digital innovation.

In conclusion, while blockchain is not a panacea for all the issues facing the tourism industry, its promise to enhance efficiency, security, and transparency makes it a critical technology to watch. Industry stakeholders, including travel companies, hotels, airlines, and governments, must collaborate to address the challenges of blockchain implementation while fostering innovation that can ultimately redefine the travel experience. As adoption grows, blockchain technology is poised to play an increasingly central role in the evolution of the global tourism landscape.

REFERENCES

Bashir, I. (2018). *Mastering Blockchain:Distributed Ledger Technology,Decentralization,and Smart Contracts Explained.* Packt Publishing Ltd.

Chhabra, A. S., Choudhury, T., Srivastava, A. V., & Aggarwal, A. (2017, December). Prediction for big data and IoT in 2017. In *2017 International Conference on Infocom Technologies and Unmanned Systems (Trends and Future Directions) (ICTUS)* (pp. 181-187). IEEE.

Garg, G., Sharma, S., Choudhury, T., & Kumar, P. (2017, August). Crop productivity based on IoT. In *2017 International Conference On Smart Technologies For Smart Nation (SmartTechCon)* (pp. 223-226). IEEE.

Nakamoto, S. (2019). *Bitcoin: A Peer-to-peer Electronic Cash System. Technical report*. Manubot.

Sultan, K., Ruhi, U., & Lakhani, R. (2018). Conceptualizing blockchains: Characteristics & applications. *arXiv preprint arXiv:1806.03693.*

Chapter 5
Beyond Traditional CRM: Enhancing Customer Guest Experience and Operational Efficiency With Deep Learning and Blockchain in the Hotel Industry

Harish Uppilappatta Chennelleri
City University, Ajman, UAE

Dhanya Neelamana Mani
De MontFort University, Dubai, UAE

ABSTRACT

Travellers of the current era are more technology savvy and they prefer all the services and information to be available online. Technology is used effectively by tourism industry participants to enhance the customer experience by meeting the needs of the new age travellers and this is one of the significant trends seen worldwide. Technology is used in various ways in online booking, self-service check-ins, contactless payments, mobile boarding, and resolving customer grievances. The industry is one of the most customer centric industry relying heavily on positive customer interactions and Customer Relationship Management (CRM) plays a critical part. With the exponential growth in the amount of customer related data available today as well as the advancements in data analytical methodologies, the importance of CRM has further strengthened.

DOI: 10.4018/979-8-3693-6562-5.ch005

INTRODUCTION

Travel and tourism industry is seen as one of the most important sectors for economic growth. Travel and tourism sector contributed to 9.1% to the global GDP in 2023 and created 27 million new jobs in 2023 according to a report by World Travel & Tourism Council. With the growth in the industry reaching closer to the pre-pandemic levels, members of the hospitality sector is looking to embrace newer evolving technologies to enhance customer experience.

Travellers of the current era are more technology savvy and they prefer all the services and information to be available online. Technology is used effectively by tourism industry participants to enhance the customer experience by meeting the needs of the new age travellers and this is one of the significant trends seen world-wide. Technology is used in various ways in online booking, self-service check-ins, contactless payments, mobile boarding, and resolving customer grievances.

The industry is one of the most customer centric industry relying heavily on positive customer interactions and Customer Relationship Management (CRM) plays a critical part. With the exponential growth in the amount of customer related data available today as well as the advancements in data analytical methodologies, the importance of CRM has further strengthened. The hospitality industry, especially the traditional participants of the industry seem to be slow to embrace the latest data analytical methods and employ them as part of CRM (Aluri et.al., 2019). With the help of AI enabled data analysis tools like machine learning, deep learning and natural language processing, new insights about customer trends and customer preferences can be generated that helps in enhancing customer experiences and improving the operational efficiency of the hotel. Today it is also possible to access real time data and the analysis can be used effectively to improve personalization and customization of offerings and services by improving the capabilities in customer interaction and customer responsiveness (Sota et.al., 2020).

The deep learning models can help the decision makers to predict the types of customers, their length of stay, food preferences, their activities of interests, seasonal trends etc. These models can be then used by the hotel managers to optimise their pricing, raise customer satisfaction levels, and increase overall operational efficiency. Apart from prediction, artificial intelligence-based technologies like image recognition, voice recognition and sensory data analysis can be employed in real time operations to enhance security and improve operational efficiency.

This industry is being restructured with new types of service providers entering the sector using latest technologies and traditional participants are also trying to remodel themselves by integrating technology. One of the disruptive technology is blockchain technology which provides a secure and transparent alternative to collect and store data and information. Blockchain technology can be efficiently utilized to improve information sharing, prevent pilferage, remove inefficient transactions and fraud (Sharma et.al., 2021). As discussed in the previous paragraphs, though there is a great potential to use artificial intelligence technologies to improve personalized guest experience, the concern is of ethical issues surrounding data privacy. (Said, S. 2023). This necessitates the requirement of improving security and transparency which capabilities of blockchain technology can provide. Blockchain technology will also help the companies to improve customer verification process and can ensure that the customer information in its CRM is accurate, reliable and is available in real time. Studies have shown that strengthening CRM with AI and blockchain can improve customer satisfaction, customer loyalty, business efficiency and revenue (Idian, et.al., 2023).

The chapter proposes a deep learning model using guest data to predict customer preferences, customer satisfaction, and trends. The study uses deep learning frameworks like ANN, and RNN for processing customer data that comprises numerical as well as textual data. The dataset of a typical CRM contains booking details, location, room types and amenities, length of stay, customer reviews etc. before applying deep learning tools, data will be cleaned and pre-processed for managing missing values, outlier removing, encoding categorical data, and data scaling. After preprocessing, suitable model for the dataset like MLP, LSTM, will be selected, then the data training is carried out. Then the trained model is applied on data to predict relevant attributes.

LITERATURE REVIEW

Customer Relationship Management (CRM) is a multifaceted concept that has evolved significantly over time. CRM's origins lie in relationship marketing, which emphasizes long-term engagement with customers rather than transactional interactions. Berry (1983) defined relationship marketing as attracting, maintaining, and enhancing customer relationships. This foundational concept underscored the importance of sustained customer interactions, setting the stage for more structured CRM definitions.

As technology advanced, CRM began to be defined in terms of its technological components and processes. Swift (2001) described CRM as an enterprise approach to understanding and influencing customer behavior through meaningful communication to improve customer acquisition, retention, and profitability and emphasized CRM systems' role in automating and managing customer-related data and interactions.

Payne and Frow (2005) defined CRM as a strategic approach that integrates internal processes and functions, and external networks, to create and deliver value to targeted customers at a profit. This broader perspective highlighted CRM's role in aligning business processes with customer needs to enhance overall performance.

CRM plays an important role in fostering meaningful customer experiences and engagements, supported by insights from data analytics and social media interactions. Buttle and Maklan (2015) defined CRM as the core business strategy that integrates internal processes and functions, and external networks, to create and deliver value to targeted customers at a profit.

Recent definitions of CRM reflect the integration of advanced technologies such as AI and machine learning. Kumar and Reinartz (2018) described CRM as a strategic process that uses information technologies to manage customer interactions and data throughout the customer lifecycle. This contemporary view incorporates predictive analytics and automation to enhance customer relationships and business intelligence.

Scholars like Berry (1983) and Grönroos (1994) emphasized the importance of building long-term relationships with customers rather than focusing solely on transactional marketing. These foundational theories laid the groundwork for the development of CRM systems that aimed to enhance customer loyalty and satisfaction.

In the late 20th century, CRM began to evolve with technological advancements. Davenport et al. (2001) documented the transition from simple contact management systems to more sophisticated databases that integrated various customer-related functions. This era saw the rise of Sales Force Automation (SFA) systems, which automated sales processes and improved data management.

Rigby et al. (2002) emphasized the strategic importance of CRM in achieving competitive advantage. These systems allowed for a more holistic approach to managing customer relationships, moving beyond siloed functions. Chen and Popovich (2003) provide a comprehensive examination of CRM as a multifaceted business strategy. The authors emphasize that successful CRM implementation requires a balanced integration of people, processes, and technology.

The advent of cloud computing brought significant changes to CRM, as documented by scholars like Fjermestad and Romano (2003). Cloud-based CRM systems, notably Salesforce, democratized access to CRM tools, making them scalable and more affordable for small and medium-sized enterprises (SMEs). Payne and Frow (2005) provides a comprehensive and strategic perspective on Customer Relationship Management (CRM). The authors propose a detailed framework for understanding and implementing CRM, emphasizing its role as a strategic business process.

The integration of social media into CRM systems marked the rise of Social CRM. Greenberg (2010) provided comprehensive insights into how businesses leveraged social media to enhance customer engagement and gather valuable customer insights.

Recent literature has focused on the integration of artificial intelligence (AI) and machine learning (ML) into CRM systems. Authors like Kumar and Reinartz (2018) have explored how AI-driven analytics can provide predictive insights, automate tasks, and enhance personalization. This era represents the cutting edge of CRM technology, promising greater efficiency and deeper customer understanding.

The research article by Idian, Hassan, and Terzungwe (2023) explores the integration of artificial intelligence (AI), blockchain, and machine learning (ML) into customer relationship management (CRM). It examines how these technologies enhance CRM by improving data security, personalization, and predictive analytics. AI and ML algorithms provide deeper insights into customer behaviors, allowing for tailored marketing strategies, while blockchain ensures secure and transparent data transactions. The study underscores the synergistic potential of these technologies in revolutionizing CRM practices, leading to more efficient, personalized, and secure customer interactions. The authors highlight the transformative impact on various industries, with a focus on practical applications and future research directions.

Gupta & Kumar (2022) states that usage of technologies like Artificial Intelligence (AI), and the Internet of Things (IoT) with CRM systems has enabled organizations to be in continuous touch with customers, track their movements, collect data to analyze their buying patterns, product usage patterns. The companies are using AI tools like machine learning and deep learning to analyze why customers shift loyalty.

METHODOLOGY

This study uses a customer dataset of airbnb properties inorder to apply artificial intelligence models that can help in improving the understanding of customer preferences. The methods that are used for analysis are explained below. The objective of the methodology applied is to build a model that classifies a property as highly rated and low rating based on the features of the property. The model helps the Airbnb hosts to make changes to the property they are listing in order to boost the customer satisfaction and attract potential bookings. This can be used as the baseline of the factors that contribute to the popularity and the rating of the property.

Logistic Regression

Logistic regression is a statistical method used for binary classification tasks in machine learning. It models the probability that a given input belongs to a particular class. Unlike linear regression, which predicts a continuous output, logistic regression predicts a binary outcome (0 or 1) by applying a logistic function (also known as the sigmoid function) to a linear combination of input features. This results in an S-shaped curve that outputs values between 0 and 1, which can be interpreted as probabilities.

Decision Tree Classifier

A decision tree classifier is a versatile machine learning algorithm used for both classification and regression tasks. It works by recursively splitting the data into subsets based on the value of input features, creating a tree-like model of decisions.

Random Forest

A Random Forest classifier is an ensemble learning method that builds multiple decision trees and merges them to get a more accurate and stable prediction. It is an extension of decision tree classifiers that aims to reduce the risk of overfitting and improve generalization.

Naive Bayes Classifier

Naive Bayes classifiers rely on Bayes' Theorem, a fundamental concept in probability, to make predictions. The "naive" aspect comes from the assumption that features (attributes) used for classification are independent of each other given the class label. While this assumption may not always hold true in reality, Naive Bayes often performs well in practice.

Support Vector Machines (SVM)

Support Vector Machines (SVMs) are another powerful machine learning algorithm family used for classification and regression tasks. They are known for their ability to handle high-dimensional data and perform well even with limited training data.SVMs aim to find an optimal hyperplane that separates data points belonging to different classes with the maximum possible margin. The margin refers to the distance between the hyperplane and the closest data points of each class, called support vectors.

Multi-Layer Perceptrons

Multi-Layer Perceptrons (MLPs) are a type of artificial neural network architecture widely used for classification tasks. They are powerful because they are considered universal function approximators. This means that, given enough hidden layers and neurons, an MLP can theoretically learn and represent any complex relationship between the input data and the desired output (class labels) for a classification problem.

Convolutional Neural Networks (CNN)

Convolutional Neural Networks (CNNs) are traditionally used for image and spatial data due to their ability to capture local patterns through convolutional layers. However, CNNs can also be adapted for numeric data, especially when the data can be structured in a way that allows the network to learn local dependencies and hierarchies.Numeric data must be reshaped into a format that suits CNNs, often as a 1D or 2D array depending on the context.

Dataset Explanation

The primary dataset for predicting the listing price and host property rating is sourced from Kaggle. This dataset includes features that describe the properties of a listing, such as the number of bathrooms and bedrooms, number of reviews, review score, neighborhood, GPS coordinates, and description of the listing.

The dataset comprises a mix of continuous, categorical, nominal, ordinal, and Boolean features. Continuous variables include log_price, number of reviews, and review score rating. Categorical variables encompass Property_type, Room_type, Amenities, Description, Bed_type, Name of the rental, and Neighborhood. Nominal variables include Accommodates, Bathrooms, and Bedrooms. The ID is classified as an ordinal variable. Boolean variables include Cleaning fee, Host_has_profile_pic, Host_identity_verified, and Instant bookable. The remaining features are either temporal variables (such as first review, host since) or geographical variables (latitude and longitude).

Airbnb datasets are popular resources for data science and machine learning projects related to the short-term rental market. They typically contain information about Airbnb listings, hosts, and reviews. Here's a breakdown of the common data points you might find:

Listing Information

- Listing ID: A unique identifier for each Airbnb listing.
- Listing Name: The title or name of the listing.
- Neighbourhood/Location: The neighborhood or area where the listing is situated.
- Room Type: The type of accommodation offered (entire home/apartment, private room, shared room).

- Property Type: The type of property (apartment, house, bungalow, etc.).
- Accommodates: The number of guests the listing can accommodate.
- Price: The nightly price of the listing.
- Amenities: A list of amenities offered by the listing (e.g., Wi-Fi, kitchen, laundry, etc.).
- Description: A textual description of the listing provided by the host.
- Minimum Stay: The minimum number of nights required for a reservation.
- Availability: Information about the dates the listing is available for booking.
- Host ID: A unique identifier for the host who listed the property.
- Number of Reviews: The total number of reviews the listing has received.
- Review Scores: Scores on various aspects of the listing (e.g., cleanliness, location, communication).
- Latitude/Longitude: Geographical coordinates of the listing.

Host Information

- Host Name: The name of the host who listed the property.
- Number of Listings: The total number of listings hosted by this user.
- Response Rate: The percentage of inquiries the host responds to within a certain timeframe.
- Is Superhost: A flag indicating if the host is a designated Superhost by Airbnb.

Review Information

- Review ID: A unique identifier for each review.
- Reviewer ID: A unique identifier for the guest who wrote the review.
- Review Text: The textual content of the review.
- Review Date: The date the review was written.
- Overall Rating: A numerical rating given to the listing by the reviewer.

Pre-Processing the Data

We possess the attractions.csv file, which offers the latitude and longitude of the top 3 attractions in each of the 6 states, and we utilize this data to determine the distance from the listing to each of those locations. A few columns had missing data and it is filled appropriately according to the data type. Fields such as host_has_profile_pic, host_identity_verified the values were present in the form of string “t” and “f” and it is converted into boolean variables for applying the models.

Latent Dirichlet Allocation (LDA) is a topic modeling technique in natural language processing and machine learning that discovers hidden topics within a collection of documents by assuming that each document is a mixture of topics and each topic is a mixture of words. LDA topic modeling is applied to an Airbnb dataset to identify hidden themes within property descriptions. By analyzing the text data, LDA assumes each document (e.g., review or listing) is a mixture of various topics, and each topic is characterized by a distribution of words, allowing for the discovery of patterns and prevalent themes in the Airbnb dataset. After LDA new features are created such as Sentiment_intensity LDA_attractions LDA_transport LDA_amenities LDA_property_desc. This is added to the existing features to enhance the rating prediction.

The amenities column were present as a list in the original dataset, which was converted into a series of columns such as 24-hour check-in', 'Accessible Room', 'Air purifier',etc . This will allow add extra features of boolean columns to the dataset which plays important role in predicting the rating.

Further pre-processing is done to make the rating into a series of bins to prepare the data for classification problem. We created equal probability bins and converted into three classes. The distribution of these classes are represented in the figure 1 below.

Figure 1. Rating bins for analysis

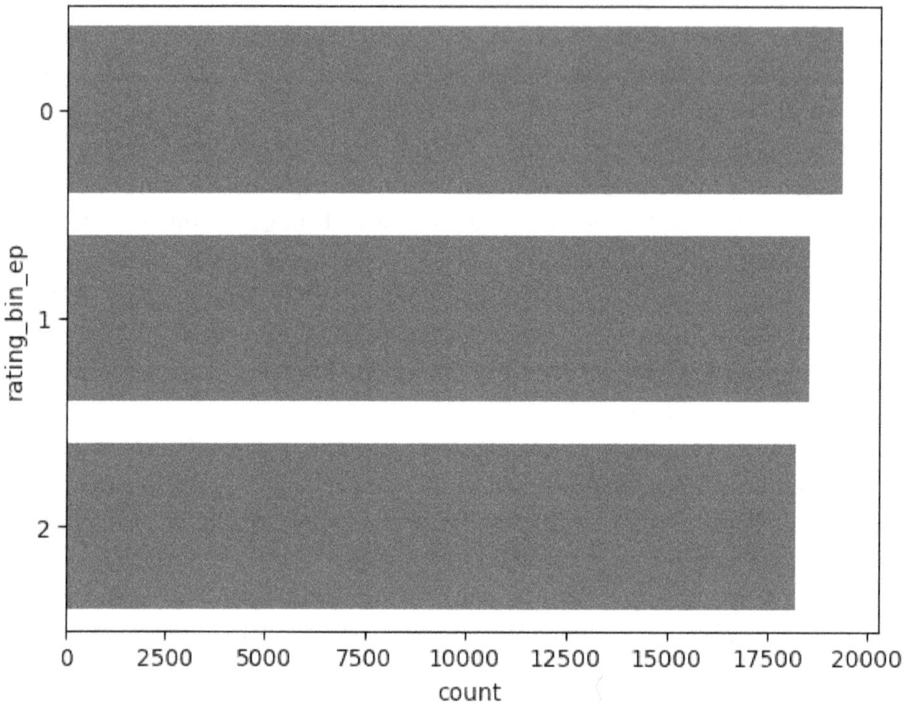

The data after all these changes and pre-processing are split for training and testing and the models are applied to this data.

RESULTS AND DISCUSSIONS

Figure 2. Property type

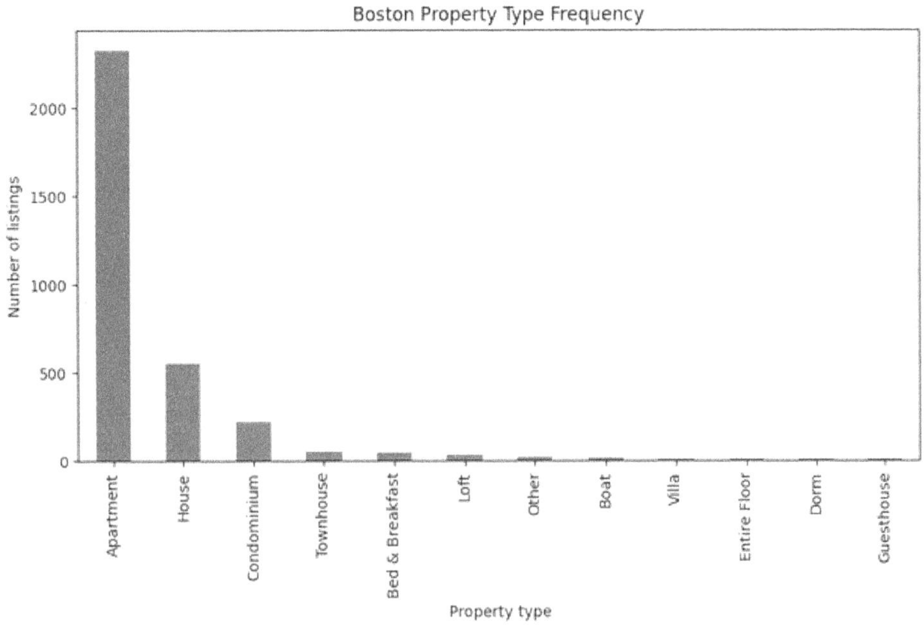

It is seen that customers prefer apartment type among the various types of properties as seen in Figure 2.

Analysis of Review Comments

The paper has analyzed the reviews provided by the customers and samples of reviews are given below.

Sample of Negative Review

"We didn t meet Izzy at all After we arrived nobody was there except some spanish speaking people Our room was disgusting It smelted like mold and was very dirty The Bathroom wasn t cleaned either and my friend and i wanted to leave right after we came The Dryer or washer was not usable because the assistant from Izzy washed all the time The Neighborhood is not safe at all and

every other morning u could hear people fight Don t stay there It s nothing like u would expect it And it s definitely to expensive for this nasty place
We were very disappointed On the pictures the apartment looked very nice but it was dirty especially in the bathroom and the blankets There was an aggravating smell in the flat and especially in the staircase The wardrobes were broken and also the skirting boards But Jordan was friendly and accessible at any time"

Sample for a Positive Review

"My stay at islam's place was really cool! Good location, 5min away from subway, then 10min from downtown. The room was nice, all place was clean. Islam managed pretty well our arrival, even if it was last minute ;) i do recommand this place to any airbnb user:)"
The room was clean and very comfortable. Having a key for this room also made it very safe. Getting to downtown is also very easy and fast. The whole is also very nice from the inside offering everything needed. I would definitely come back!"

Text polarity refers to the sentiment of a piece of text, whether it's positive, negative, or neutral. It's a fundamental aspect of sentiment analysis, which is a type of natural language processing (NLP) used to understand the feeling or opinion expressed in text.

Here's a breakdown of text polarity:

- *Positive polarity* indicates a favorable sentiment, like enjoyment, satisfaction, or approval.
- *Negative polarity* reflects an unfavorable sentiment, such as dislike, disappointment, or anger.
- *Neutral polarity* means the text expresses no particular sentiment or opinion.

Text polarity is often measured on a scale, with positive values representing positive sentiment and negative values representing negative sentiment. In some cases, the scale may range from 0 to 1, with 0 being neutral and 1 being extremely positive or negative. Other systems might use a scale from -1 to 1, where -1 is entirely negative and 1 is entirely positive.

Text subjectivity refers to the degree to which a piece of text expresses personal opinions, beliefs, or feelings, as opposed to factual information. It's another aspect analyzed in sentiment analysis tasks alongside polarity.

Here's a breakdown of text subjectivity:

- *High subjectivity*: Text that expresses personal opinions, judgments, or evaluations. Examples include reviews, blog posts, or social media comments.
- *Low subjectivity*: Text that presents facts and information in an objective manner. Examples include news articles, scientific papers, or technical manuals.

Similar to polarity, text subjectivity can be measured on a scale, typically ranging from 0 to 1.

Here's a general interpretation:

- **0:** Completely objective, presenting only facts.
- **1:** Highly subjective, expressing personal opinions and emotions.

Figure 3. Polarity and subjectivity analysis

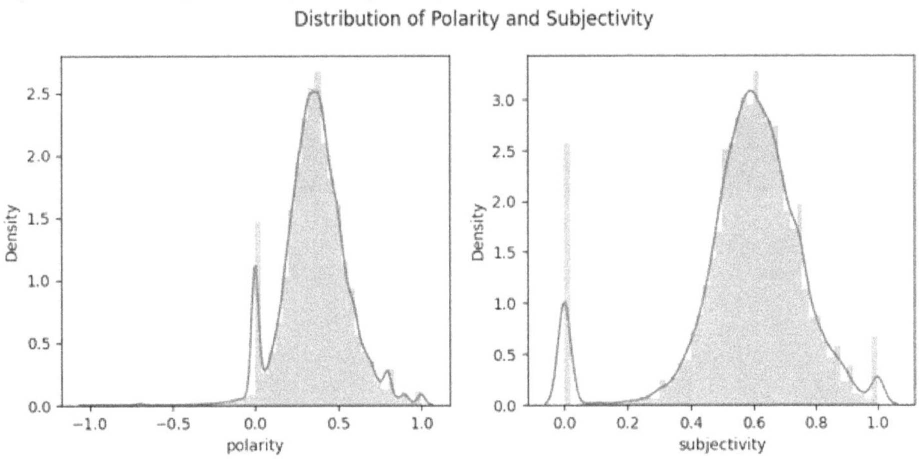

Figure 3 shows that positive reviews are more showing that generally the customers are satisfied with the properties. Subjectivity shows that most of the reviews are based on emotions and opinions. We can also see that there is a peak at zero, showing there are reviews that are completely objective. This analysis shows that the reviews are an important element to be considered in the operations of a property and in managing customer relations.

Figure 4 and figure 5 shows word cloud for positive and negative reviews.

Figure 4. Negative reviews word cloud

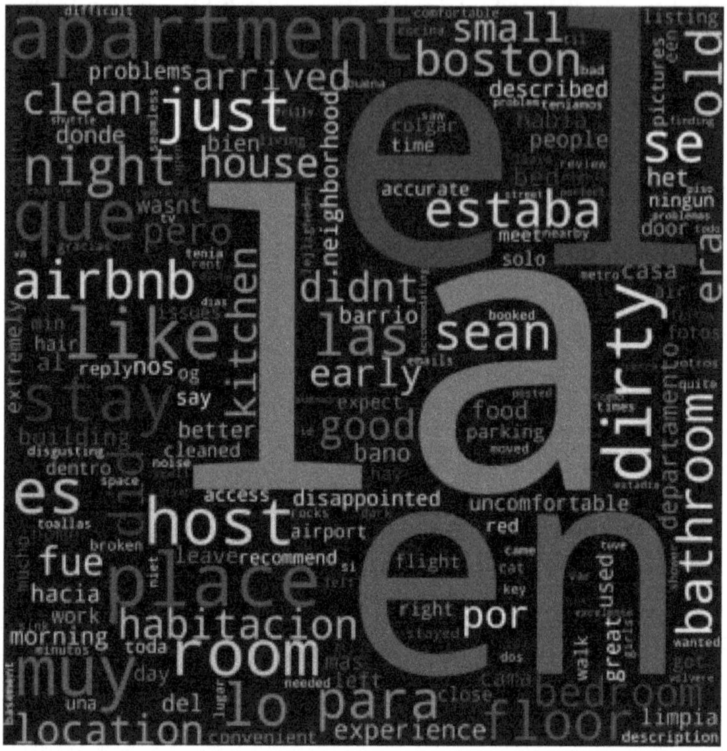

Figure 5. Positive reviews word cloud

Table 1. Comparative analysis of prediction models

Model	Accuracy	Precision	Recall	F1 Score
Logistic Regression	0.462	0.47	0.49	0.48
Decision Tree classifier	0.44	0.46	0.44	0.45
Random Forest	0.56	0.58	0.56	0.57
Naive bayes classifier	0.61	0.64	0.61	0.62
SVM	0.36	0.36	0.40	0.42
MLP	0.72	0.67	0.71	0.74
CNN	0.82	0.79	0.84	0.83

The metrics we considered for this classification task and the results obtained is given in the table. The accuracy score is comparatively low in basic methods like logistic regression and it is getting better in deep learning-based approach. Deep learning models like convolutional neural networks (CNNs) can capture complex, non-linear relationships through their hidden layers. This allows them to learn more intricate patterns in the data.Deep learning models can automatically learn features directly from the data. These features made the model to predict the review classes more accurately than rest of the models. The performance of SVM is very low. The performance of SVMs can be sensitive to hyperparameters like the C parameter (regularization) and gamma (kernel coefficient). Hyperparameter tuning may help in improving the accuracy.

Figure 6. Predicted features

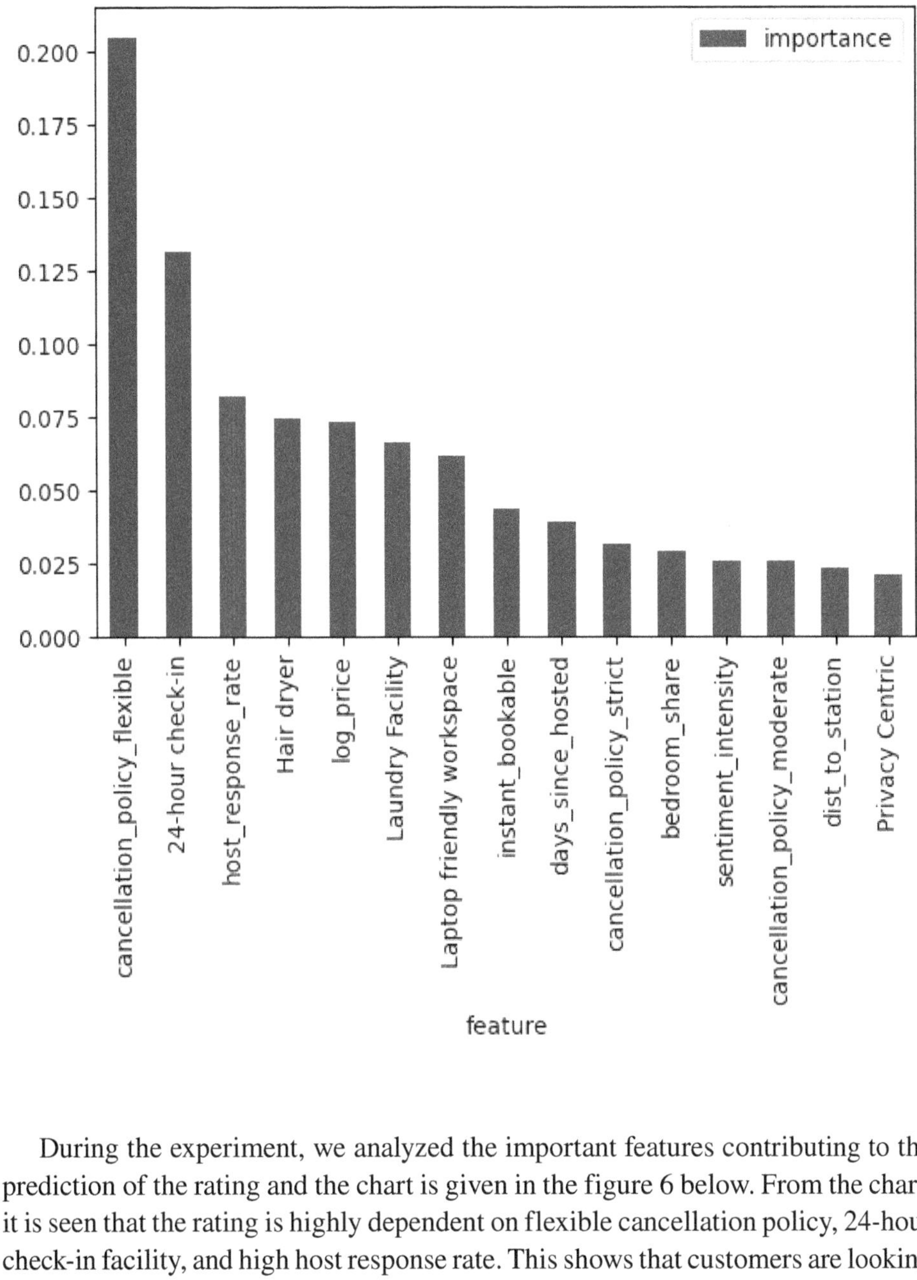

During the experiment, we analyzed the important features contributing to the prediction of the rating and the chart is given in the figure 6 below. From the chart, it is seen that the rating is highly dependent on flexible cancellation policy, 24-hour check-in facility, and high host response rate. This shows that customers are looking for flexibility and responsiveness as an important feature. Other critical features are laundry facility, laptop friendly workplace, and instant booking facility. Analysing these features can improve the overall rating of the Airbnb.

REFERENCES

https://wttc.org/research/economic-impact

https://www.unwto.org/news/tourism-s-importance-for-growth-highlighted-in-world-economic-outlook-report

Aluri, A., Price, B. S., & McIntyre, N. H. (2019). Using Machine Learning To Cocreate Value Through Dynamic Customer Engagement In A Brand Loyalty Program. *Journal of Hospitality & Tourism Research (Washington, D.C.)*, 43(1), 78–100. DOI: 10.1177/1096348017753521

Berry, L. L. (1983). Relationship marketing. In Berry, L. L., Shostack, G. L., & Upah, G. D. (Eds.), *Emerging Perspectives on Services Marketing*.

Buttle, F., & Maklan, S. (2015). *Customer Relationship Management: Concepts and Technologies*. Routledge. DOI: 10.4324/9781315764597

Chen, I. J., & Popovich, K. (2003). Understanding customer relationship management (CRM): People, process and technology. *Business Process Management Journal*, 9(5), 672–688. DOI: 10.1108/14637150310496758

Davenport, T. H., Harris, J. G., & Kohli, A. K. (2001). How do they know their customers so well? *MIT Sloan Management Review*.

Fjermestad, J., & Romano, N. C.Jr. (2003). Electronic customer relationship management: Revisiting the general principles of usability and resistance – an integrative implementation framework. *Business Process Management Journal*, 9(5), 572–591. DOI: 10.1108/14637150310496695

Greenberg, P. (2010). The impact of CRM 2.0 on customer insight. *Journal of Business and Industrial Marketing*, 25(6), 410–419. DOI: 10.1108/08858621011066008

Gupta, C. P., & Kumar, V. R. (2022, June). Artificial Intelligence and Internet of Things: Revolutionizing the implementation of Customer Relationship Management. In *2022 ASU International Conference in Emerging Technologies for Sustainability and Intelligent Systems (ICETSIS)* (pp. 60-66). IEEE. DOI: 10.1109/ICETSIS55481.2022.9888821

Idian, M. J. I., Hassan, M. K., & Terzungwe, A. S. (2023). Artificial Intelligence, Blockchain, Machine Learning, and Customer Relationship Management. Bincang Sains dan Teknologi, 2(01), 16-20.

Kumar, V., & Reinartz, W. (2018). *Customer Relationship Management: Concept, Strategy, and Tools*. Springer. DOI: 10.1007/978-3-662-55381-7

Kumar, V., & Reinartz, W. (2018). *Customer Relationship Management: Concept, Strategy, and Tools*. Springer. DOI: 10.1007/978-3-662-55381-7

Payne, A., & Frow, P. (2005). A strategic framework for customer relationship management. *Journal of Marketing*, 69(4), 167–176. DOI: 10.1509/jmkg.2005.69.4.167

Payne, A., & Frow, P. (2005). A strategic framework for customer relationship management. *Journal of Marketing*, 69(4), 167–176. DOI: 10.1509/jmkg.2005.69.4.167

Rigby, D. K., Reichheld, F. F., & Schefter, P. (2002). Avoid the four perils of CRM. *Harvard Business Review*. PMID: 11894676

Said, S. (2023). The Role of Artificial Intelligence (AI) and Data Analytics in Enhancing Guest Personalization in Hospitality. *Journal of Modern Hospitality*, 2(1), 1–13. DOI: 10.47941/jmh.1556

Sharma, M., Sehrawat, R., Daim, T., & Shaygan, A. (2021). Technology assessment: Enabling Blockchain in hospitality and tourism sectors. *Technological Forecasting and Social Change*, 169, 120810. DOI: 10.1016/j.techfore.2021.120810

Sota, S., Chaudhry, H., & Srivastava, M. K. (2020). Customer relationship management research in hospitality industry: A review and classification. *Journal of Hospitality Marketing & Management*, 29(1), 39–64. DOI: 10.1080/19368623.2019.1595255

Storbacka, K., Strandvik, T., & Grönroos, C. (1994). Managing customer relationships for profit: The dynamics of relationship quality. *International Journal of Service Industry Management*, 5(5), 21–38. DOI: 10.1108/09564239410074358

Swift, R. S. (2001). *Accelerating Customer Relationships: Using CRM and Relationship Technologies*. Prentice Hall.

Chapter 6
Blockchain Technology and Internet of Value in the Hospitality and Tourism Industry

Aleksandar Radic
https://orcid.org/0000-0001-7760-5495
Independent Researcher, Croatia

ABSTRACT

The purpose of this critical reflection is to investigate blockchain technology and its ability to unleash the Internet of Value (IoV) throughout the hospitality and travel sectors through the five realms of the emerging financial technologies and economies, which are cryptocurrencies, decentralized finance, metaverse, non-fungible token, central bank digital currency. Thus, in evolving electronic markets across the hospitality and tourism industry the blockchain technology could unleash the IoV. Nevertheless, certain challenges of blockchain technology such as its applications, privacy, legal frameworks, and environmental impact have to be discussed as all of these facets are critically important in order to optimize the benefits of cutting-edge technology. With the rising opportunities across the IoV, the hospitality and tourism businesses can improve and advance the hospitality and tourism operations by utilizing blockchain technology.

DOI: 10.4018/979-8-3693-6562-5.ch006

INTRODUCTION

A technological breakthrough is a delicate time where a single design is applied to multiple use cases (Lee et al., 2021). In the digital age, we are witnessing the developments of blockchain and distributed ledger technology, as the hospitality and tourism companies explore various use cases in order to apply blockchain technology. The main reason behind the embracement of blockchain technology in touristry is its ability to provide outstanding money transfers, which are effortless and direct (Irannezhad & Mahadevan, 2021). Thus, blockchain technology serves as a the stage that facilitates innovation of the Internet of Information (IoI) towards the Internet of Value (IoV) in today's asset driven hospitality and tourism businesses.

The IoV in the service and leisure sectors can be potrayed as an economic system of countless assets, which owns the commercial value for people. Hence, idea behind the IoV is to transfigurate fabrics of quantitative values into a simplified structure that persist on blockchain (Treiblmaier, 2022a). More precisely, IoV is a digital nexus that permits a value transfer in the absence of governance (Treiblmaier, 2022a). Money is easily transferred within the IoV, which is similar to today's information movement, since blockchain technology removes intermediaries, which include financial institutions, bureaucracy, and various administrations, and it lowers payment fees, provides wide inclusion, and offers fidelity, privacy, and robust security (Lacity, 2020). In the hospitality and tourism sectors, the demands for payments are reciprocal to the increasing revenue, so the hospitality and tourism companies require seamless, interoperable, inclusive, certain, cost effective, and real time payments (Demirciftci et al., 2020).

The blockchain technology holds specific features that can unlock the IoV across the hospitality and tourism sectors, because various hospitality and tourism companies, supporting businesses, worldwide destinations, and many other stakeholders can set up their own ecosystem that is tokenized, interoperable, which is within and outside the particular business silos, and trustworthy for all the participants (Rashideh, 2020). Thus, the hospitality and tourism businesses are increasing their blockchain technology adoption in order to allure the emerging venture capitalists and streamline their networks (Su et al., 2022). Furthermore, blockchain technology enables business to lower their energy consumption and carbon footprints within the hospitality and tourism sector, capture the benefits of the central bank digital currencies (CBDC), extend the hospitality products and travel destinations into the metaverses, accelerate crypto transactions, offer valuable loyalty programs, and tap into the decentralized finance (DeFi) and tokenize physical assets, such as festivals, amusement parks, heritage sites, hotels, and resorts spaces in the form of non-fungible tokens (NFTs).

In 2017, the cryptocurrency market experienced exponential growth in value, which was followed by a rapid decline and consolidation up until the 2020/2021 bull run when the market cap for cryptocurrencies reached 2.8 trillion $USD (Hajric, 2022). Scholars around the world are exploring the direction of digital currencies, which is a result of the shared trust concerning the use cases of cryptocurrency based on blockchain technology and their impact on financial technology and the evolving economic ecosystem. Hence, Mofokeng and Fatima (2018) outlined that the tourism industry will experience a wide adoption of cryptocurrencies as payment systems in the years to come, because the benefits of these types of payment systems are appealing to the hospitality and tourism businesses. Moreover, Mantas et al. (2022) suggested that memorable touristic experiences could be tokenized on a platform that provides a personalized digital memento in a form of an NFT. This way various hospitality and tourism businesses can collaborate on a blockchain powered platform, because all the participants can co-create memorable touristic experiences using mobile technologies (Mantas et al., 2022). However, there are some skepticisms related to DeFi and its promises. Aramonte et al. (2021) argued in particular that DeFi inherently poses certain centralization. They stated that absolute decentralization is an illusion, because a certain level of centralization is inevitable within the constitutional details of a system where this type of structure allows a small group of participants to form a concentration of power. Furthermore, this type of concentration of power within the elite participants could undermine the financial stability, because of higher debts than equity cause a mismatch between the market liquidity of assets and the funding liquidity of liabilities as well as the lack of shock absorbers (Aramonte et al., 2021). Finally, Valeri and Baggio (2020) outlined a gap in the tourism management literature with the recent critical reflection about the adoption of blockchain technology in the tourism industry. Furthermore, the previously authors have incited the need for further research in regard to the better understanding of blockchain technology applicability in the hospitality and tourism sector with special attention to the integrated systems for value creation, the improvements in financial technology and the potential economics, and the operational and social impacts (Valeri & Baggio, 2020).

As a result, the purpose of this paper is to investigate blockchain technology and its ability to unlock the IoV across the hospitality and tourism sectors via the five realms that are described in the following sections. Moreover, we hope that our conceptual framework will be useful for the decision makers in regard to the benefits of implementing new technology in the holiday industry, and we hope that our paper will serve as a forum for further discussions that generate subsequent research avenues.

BLOCKCHAIN AND WEB 3.0 IMPLICATIONS IN HOSPITALITY AND TOURISM INDUSTRY

The hospitality and tourism industry is divided into various sectors, such as flights, car rentals, resorts/hotels, tours, and various hospitality services. Each of these facets is prone to the heavy burden of operational expenses, long intermediation chains, overselling, and any human errors that lead to service delivery failures. As a result, blockchain is regarded a valuable technology to use in order to improve and advance the hospitality and travel experiences. Due to the decentralized nature of blockchain technology, the hospitality and tourism service providers and the end users are able to seamlessly interact, because the intermediaries are reduced.

The blockchain fundamental data composition is comprised of 1-megabyte files that are called *blocks*, which are tied into the *chain* through a complex mathematical proof. The inception of blockchain lies with the intelligent incorporation of the existing technologies for novel causes where cryptographic authorization, distributed computing, immutability, and validation play key roles (Duan et al., 2020; Kollmann et al., 2020). All system rules for blockchain are known and enforced by all the participants through the validation process, because the validation removes the system administrative functions, enables the public state and public rules, and empowers the participants to enforce the rules (Xiong et al., 2020). Accordingly, blockchain offers the mediators a compelling advanced instrument, since it empowers the people and organizations with respect to mutual trust as well as to conduct peer-to-peer businesses. Furthermore, blockchain technology permits the establishment of a CBDC that is grounded on Distributed Ledger Technology (DLT) and the conventional central bank architecture, which is where tourism and hospitality businesses can access liquidity, rapidness, inexpensive, and more coherent payments with business to business (B2B), person-to-person (P2P), and cross-border transactions (Radic et al., 2022a).

In 2008, Satoshi Nakamoto, which is the name that is being used by the supposed unidentified person or persons, created Bitcoin as a response to the 2008 financial crisis. Bitcoin was meant to serve as an improved version of the monetary system. Blockchain is seen analogously as the internet successfully distributes knowledge, which is due to disruptive technology that could decentralize financial transactions. Thus, Bitcoin was the first technology to arrive at this stage, so we are seeing today the diversification of blockchain for divergent use cases. Bitcoin is more precisely similar to Web 1.0, because they both mark the first stage of the fundamental beginning (Ragnedda & Destefanis, 2020). However, Web 1.0 is a set of static websites, whereas Bitcoin through its Proof of Work (PoW) algorithm failed as world currency, which is due to its high fees, high carbon footprint, and inability to handle contracts or trust agreements (Voshmgir, 2020). Nevertheless, Bitcoin has proven itself to be a robust store of value that is equivalent to digital gold. The second stage is similar to Web 2.0 as well as Ethereum and smart contracts. Web 2.0 introduced inventiveness, cooperation, and social distribution, whereas Ethereum through its Proof of Stake (PoS) algorithm manages digital assets without enforcing the platform ownership. Also, it offers agreements between parties on blockchain through its smart contracts (Ragnedda & Destefanis, 2020). However, the Ethereum network has proven to be congested, and it carries high fees for the confirmation of executed transactions. The third stage is described with a rise of Web 3.0 and the proliferation of blockchain technologies, such as XRP Ledger (Treiblmaier, 2022a). Web 3.0 essentially empowers its users to engage in the control and performance of the protocols (Voshmgir, 2020). Thus, people can become contributors and shareholders as opposed to just pure consumers of products (Ragnedda & Destefanis, 2020). The XRP Ledger algorithm relies on Consensus Protocol in order to validate account balances and perform transactions (Treiblmaier, 2022a). The XRP Ledger Consensus Protocol has proven to be superior because it offers a real time settlement system that is secure and scalable. Furthermore, blockchain technology enables the creation of a CBDC that is based on Distributed Ledger Technology (DLT) and he conventional central bank architecture, which is where tourism and hospitality businesses can access cash flow, velocity, affordable, and comprehensible payments with business to business (B2B), person-to-person (P2P), and cross-border transactions (Takeda & Ito, 2021).

Web 3.0 is set of protocols that can involve artificial intelligence with the genuine purpose of decentralizing control over the internet (Ragnedda & Destefanis, 2020). Thus, one can argue that the purpose of Web 3.0 is the liberation of the end users from the control of today's technological monsters that control the internet (Treiblmaier, 2022a). The decentralization of the internet is proliferating within the metamorphosis of Web 3.0, and the hospitality and tourism participants are offered peculiar and decentralized platform applications, which can be used anywhere without handing over a person's sensitive or personal data. For instance, using smart contracts for internet-based hospitality and tourism services completely avoid human intermediaries, so people can freely engage with each other without any approvals from the companies or governments. Moreover, people who work for or manage hospitality and tourism businesses and who are not able to access the standard financial services for various reasons are now able to receive these types of services without permissions from banks or other financial service companies with DeFi. Web 3.0 is often accordingly seen as the structural synonym for the metaverse, because their essence is about constructing interactions and networks that use various digital and blockchain assets (Voshmgir, 2020). Thus, the end users' digital identity is entirely under their control, which allows them to choose what pieces of data they want to share or even sell for crypto, within the hospitality and tourism metaverse. Furthermore, Web 3.0 offers a cooperative governance structure in the hospitality and tourism sectors for the end users, because they can tokenize their tourist or travel experiences, dining or pub memes, private photos or videos, social media outputs, destination or hospitality services reviews, museums, festivals or concerts experiences, heritage sites tours, hotel and resorts experiences, conference participations, and many other hospitality and tourism products. However, in order to achieve the democratization of the access and ownership of wealth in the service and travel field, the holiday businesses and their end users cannot purely rely on technology, which is what is required for a change of the societal mindset that is accompanied by regulatory, monetary, and fiscal policies.

Figure 1 is the graphical presentation of the blockchain ability to unlock the IoV in the hospitality and tourism industry.

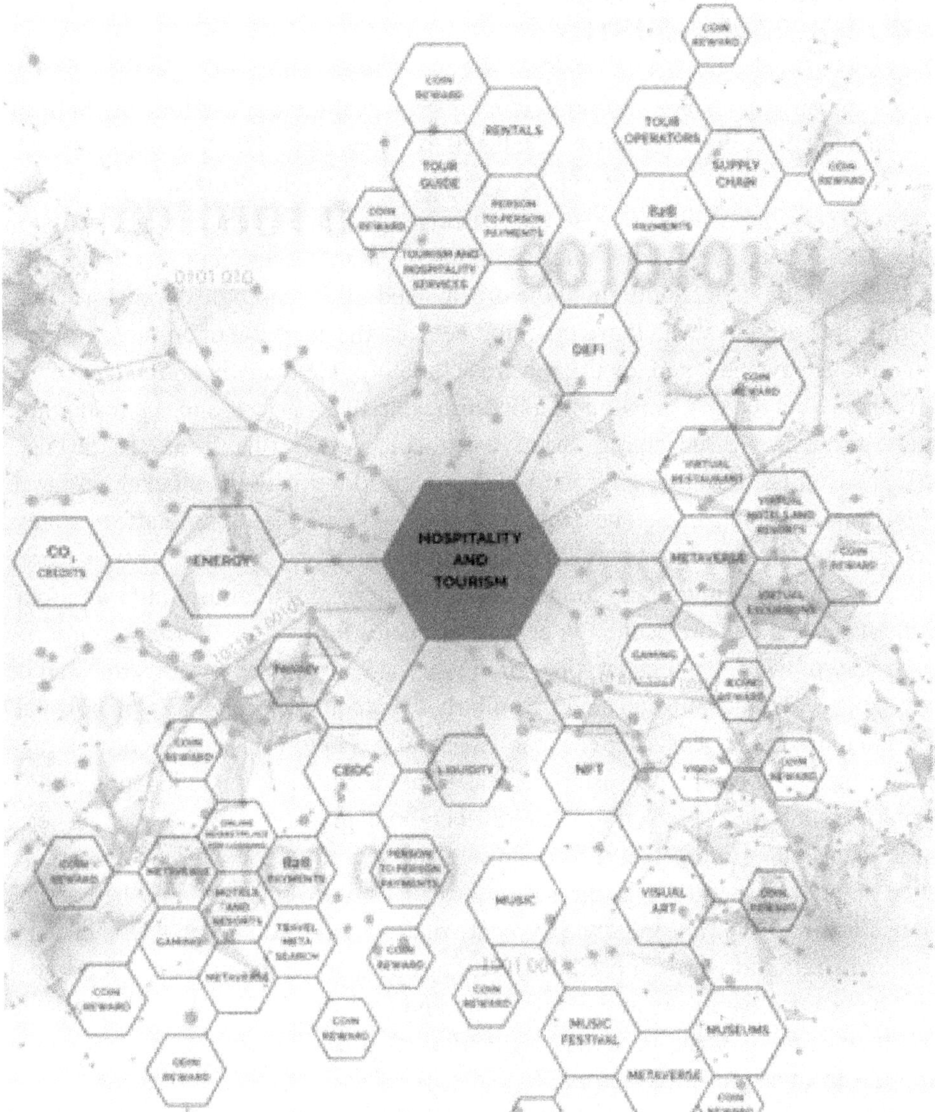
HOSPITALITY AND TOURISM
DEFI
TOUR OPERATORS
SUPPLY CHAIN
B2B PAYMENTS
RENTALS
TOUR GUIDE
PERSON TO PERSON PAYMENTS
TOURISM AND HOSPITALITY SERVICES
COIN REWARD
METAVERSE
VIRTUAL RESTAURANT
VIRTUAL EXCURSIONS
GAMING
ENERGY
CO_2 CREDITS
CBDC
LIQUIDITY
NFT
VIDEO
B2B PAYMENTS
MOTELS AND RESORTS
TRAVEL META SEARCH
GAMING
MUSIC
VISUAL ART
MUSIC FESTIVAL
MUSEUMS
METAVERSE

CRYPTOCURRENCIES IN THE HOSPITALITY AND TOURISM INDUSTRY

Cryptocurrencies are decentralized, encrypted, digital assets that are built on blockchain technology (Tham & Sigala, 2020; Thies et al., 2022; Bachmann et al., 2022, Treiblmaier, 2022b). Cryptocurrencies can be interchanged globally, and they can serve as an alternative to the fiat currencies. In a recent critical discussion about blockchain technology and its implications to service and travel industry, Kizildag et al. (2020) highlighted the urgent need for technological transformation within the hospitality and tourism sector, because the adoption of cryptocurrencies for various payments and loyalty rewards could provide many benefits. Hence, we are witnessing today a growing number of hospitality services, such as restaurants and cafés, which are accepting various cryptocurrencies for payments (Radic et al., 2022b). Similarly, there is the robust mainstream adoption of the blockchain-based travel booking platforms. These blockchain-based travel booking platforms are a competitive alternative to the traditional booking methods as they offer transparent booking process without any hidden costs. Furthermore, the hospitality and tourism businesses that are accepting cryptocurrencies for payments are also engaged in loyalty programs, which are providing real-value tokenized rewards that can be saved or spent for leisure and travel. Similarly, cryptocurrency payments in hospitality and tourism services offer cashback that can be kept for passive income, which makes the cryptocurrency user/holder a shareholder that is eligible for future travel benefits. Thus, the blockchain-based travel booking platforms can offer a long-term investment opportunity that also addresses the shared user experience concerns, such as multiple redirects and registrations that a user experiences when she/he books a single trip. Essentially, payments that are based on cryptocurrencies are fast and straightforward. Subsequently, it appears that the mainstream adoption of cryptocurrency payments in the hospitality and tourism industry are a direct result of the previous bull run in the crypto market, as such favorable conditions attract support from new investors.

Non-Fungible Tokens (NFTs) and Their Role in the Hospitality and Tourism Industry

NFTs are the tokens that are the most commonly used as digital proof-of-ownership of underlying assets. In the service and leisure industry, the NFTs fits as representations of various forms of digital art, or they can also be used for the tokenization of various hospitality and tourism assets from the hotels, resorts, restaurants, cafés memberships and cultural and heritage products (Treiblmaier, 2021). Thus, this ecosystem makes them digitally tradable as every issued token represents a unique non-fungible asset. Moreover, small hospitality and tourism businesses can create context specific platforms that run on open access blockchain where the users can issue NFT's, which are used as collateral for loans. The utility of the NFTs can also be seen in gaming as various hotels/resorts, amusement parks, museums, and even cultural heritage sites can build games that combine the playing aspect with the economics and sustainability. These types of games are called Play-to-Earn (P2E), and in such games the users compete using NFTs, and their earnings are dedicated to the upkeep of various cultural heritage sites or to the development of the local societies where the hospitality and tourism services are based. Furthermore, the restaurants and cafés can sell their memberships in the form of NFTs, as the NFT owners can use tokens in order to gain access to culinary, cultural, and social experiences. Museums can also share their contents through various projects that can be minted and offered for auction in the form of an NFT. Thus, the museum NFT owners can enjoy special privileges such as limited access the peculiar museums cultural and social experiences. The art and music festivals can also sell their tickets in the form of NFT for their showcases, exhibits, and live performances. Finally, all the aspects of hospitality and tourism management, which include purchases, leases, timesharing, prepaid leasing, and the licensing of property-based experiences can be placed on blockchain-powered platforms and tokenized using NFTs as a digital certification and reward solutions.

The Metaverse as Extended Reality in the Hospitality and Tourism Industry

The metaverse is the concept of a three-dimensional (3D) universe that involves multiple different virtual spaces where the users persistently interact with each other in an online environment. The metaverse is seen as the future of the internet. However, the metaverse does not fully exist yet, and the video games are the closest to providing a metaverse experience (Han et al., 2022). In the hospitality and tourism industry, the metaverse is a virtual space that allows the users to work, meet, entertain, learn, create, play games, and socialize with each other. The hotels/resorts, amusement parks, museums, and cultural heritage sites can create a virtual reality platform powered by blockchain technology, on which end users can co-create and monetize their touristic experience using various hospitality contents and tourism applications. Furthermore, users can also purchase plots of various destinations, parts of hotels, resorts, and amusement parks. The metaverse also allows its users to create their own museums, music festivals, and even recreate cultural heritage sites that they can navigate, build upon, and monetize. Amusement parks, hotels, resorts, and national parks can build a simulated reality, which include places where the visitors can enjoy via their mobile phones in order to initiate and extend individualized 3D impression onto the close physical surroundings. The metaverse in the aforementioned cases permits incredibly immersive and realistic 3D virtual user experiences beyond the need for the users to use augmented reality viewing devices. In the hospitality and tourism metaverse, time-sharing real estate can use NFTs in order to make the touristic properties scarce as well as valuable. In this type of hospitality metaverse, the users can own part of the real estate that will increase in value as the demand for the space increases, which they can sell at that point. As nanotechnology gets more sophisticated and makes revolutionary progress with real life use cases, people will be able to implant some type of brain–machine interfaces that would allow them to access the various metaverse platforms at a glance.

Decentralized Finance (DeFi) and its Potential in Hospitality and Tourism

DeFi is an open decentralized financial system powered by blockchain technology that provides transparency, to a great extent control and the authority to its users. In hospitality and tourism sectors, DeFi takes out the intermediary, eliminates fees, charges, and any penalties (Kizildag et al., 2020). The hospitality and tourism services, small tour operators, freelancer tour guides, privately owned rentals and participants in supply chain can engage in various DeFi projects that rely on smart contracts. By doing so aforementioned entities can have direct access to the commercial use such as loan and cash flow beyond the need of a middlemen. Within DeFi financial system everyone in hospitality and tourism services can access liquidity and earn fees on blockchain based stablecoin exchange as issued tokens maximize rewards for its liquidity providers. Moreover, as property rentals, tour guides and tour operators deposit tokens into the DeFi agreement, the tokens are consequently combined and loaned to borrowing rate participants. Subsequently, the accumulated interest is then divided proportionally to all consignors, who can earn quite attractive annual percentage yield. Furthermore, DeFi is an expanding community of genuine, operating set of rules, which are transmitting value to many hospitality and tourism service providers. Hence, if tour operators or property rentals are in need of a loan, they can access DeFi platform as secured loans are depending on the assets that aforementioned hospitality business can boost their loan-to-deposit ratio and enhance business liquidity. Such loans might not be the greatest return on capital employed; however, it permits loans to be free from restrictions and spontaneous. Looking at P2P and B2B payments in hospitality and tourism sectors, DeFi protocols offer fiat-pegged tokens to strength price firmness of the international payments. Finally, DeFi protocols combine the price firmness and broad application of fiat currencies that enable affordable payments and fast cross border settlements.

Central Bank Digital Currency (CBDC) and Financial Stability Implications in Hospitality and Tourism

A CBDC is a new form of digital money that is contrasting orthodox cash that is in circulation, deposits, and settlement accounts. Nevertheless, CBDC is fully backed to fiat currencies, and it is distributed and govern by trustworthy financial entities. The main purpose of a CBDC in the hospitality and tourism sectors is to regulate monetary and fiscal policies and accelerate the financial inclusion through blockchain technology (Kim et al., 2022). Furthermore, the efficiency and reliability of a CBDC that is DTL and the central bank infrastructure offers various hospitality and tourism businesses fast and secure B2B, P2P, and financial transactions with precise detectability, accountability, and uniformity within the complicated, fallible, and slow payment systems in the service and travel sector. During a global crisis, such as the current COVID-19 pandemic, Liu et al. (2021) outlined the outmost importance of government financial stimulus packages for the heavily affected hospitality industry and households. Thus, CBDC based on a DTL can boost liquidity and offer payments that are cheap, fast, scalable, and reliable (Radic et al., 2020). The demand for fast, 24/7, high fidelity, and real-time global payments in the travel and leisure industry are rising (Cheng et al., 2021), accordingly, central banks with a CBDC can offer these types of services, as the ultimate goal is to move money smoothly and continuously like information on the internet. Furthermore, more and more restaurants, hotels, resorts, and other service and leisure businesses are extending into the crypto market, so it becomes clearer that the travel and leisure industry can gain from a CBDC. Thus, CBDC with their centralized system, are able to aid service and leisure businesses in the integration with traditional finance. Lastly, CBDCs are needed, as they can assist leisure businesses to bring the money into the crypto market (including gaming and the metaverse) from mainstream finance as well as providing them with an exit route in fast and reliable manner.

Energy Consumption and Carbon Credits in the Hospitality and Tourism Industry

Lowering energy consumption and carbon footprints as well as managing carbon credits are important aspects of the climate action goals that were set by the United Nations Sustainable Development. Hospitality and tourism businesses are engaging in various environmental initiatives in order to provide a green experience for their users with hopes that these types of practices can create robust and enduring partnerships (Wu et al., 2018). Cash payments are a common method of settlement in the travel and leisure industry. In regard to the modern fiat money system, which include all bank deposits and cash that are used for payments, there is a great opportunity to lower the carbon footprint, because maintaining the modern fiat money system leaves a heavy carbon footprint. Hence, the hospitality and tourism businesses that use carbon neutral blockchains, such as XRP Ledger for their payments and cross border settlements are in position to create carbon credits, which would allow them to compensate for their other greenhouse gas emissions. Furthermore, blockchain technology can also offer a climate-based solution program, which could manage the reforestation operation and verify each planted tree. Blockchain technology possesses a robust and significant positive effect on energy consumption as well as carbon credits in the travel and tourism operations, accordingly, Sharma et al. (2020) outlined eco-innovative practices that should be appropriately measured and included in the conceptual frameworks.

DISCUSSION AND IMPLICATIONS

The emergence of blockchain technology has generated a groundbreaking nexus that is revolutionizing the operations across a wide range of industries. This paper expands the body of knowledge by critically reviewing the function of blockchain technology and its capacity to unleash the IoV across the travel and leisure. This study reviews the implications of Web 3.0 in order to facilitate blockchain technology applications, and it delineates the potentials of the five domains, which include cryptocurrency, NFT's, the metaverse, DeFi, and CBDC. Also, this paper discusses the prospects of the blockchain in the service and leisure industry, and it brings to the light the significance of novel technology in regard to environmental sustainability.

Blockchain technology holds promising potential in regard to transforming the hospitality and tourism business models. We are experiencing fundamental changes in the global economy where blockchain technology is reshaping the financial sector and e-commerce with the inception of the IoV as digital technologies advance (Önder & Gunter, 2022). Hence, the IoI is evolving under the influence of blockchain technology because various intermediaries are being removed from accumulation, transfers, and management of the value. The winds of changes are blowing towards the travel and tourism sectors with the novel technology potential to revolutionize the global economy. The IoV is gaining momentum in the service and leisure industry as the novel technology has the prospect to crumble silos so that value can circulate as effortlessly as information does (Willie, 2019).

Due to the powerful changes that are driven by the blockchain technology, it is particularly important to understand the IoV implications in regard to service and travel industry. Despite the fact that blockchain technology is an emerging technology and the IoV is not yet fully understood when it comes to the applications to the vacation industry, it is important to identify and address all the limitations at early stages so that the adoption of the IoV can be quickly embraced. Certain limitations in regard to the widespread of the IoV in the service and leisure industry are mostly related to the understanding of technical difficulties, like modularity, biodata, and technological parity. There are certain technical challenges, which are related to the security, that need to be addressed when considering application of the blockchain technology in service and travel industry. However, these security breaches are mostly affiliated to the user error as opposed to the fundamental technology. Therefore, delving into the consumer behaviors, sustainable growth, and regulatory frameworks are deemed necessary for the accomplishment of triumphant implementation of blockchain technology in the vacation industry.

Blockchain technology is creating a powerful and meaningful effect on hospitality and tourism businesses and societies because the IoV offers secured and direct exchanges of value, experiences, intellectual properties, and various other assets without the involvement of traditional intermediaries. With opportunities across the IoV, hotels/resorts, tour operators, restaurants, and any other hospitality and tourism businesses can solve their operational problems in P2P/B2B payments, cross border settlements, the metaverse interoperability, liquidity/finances, smart contracts, sales, carbon footprint and supply chain operations by utilizing blockchain technology. Thus, to obtain increased understanding of the novel technology and the IoV with its full implications across the hospitality and tourism sectors, more empirical studies in different domains of hospitality and tourism are needed.

In addition to the lack of assets and the derivatives liquidity in the traditional markets there are great opportunities for DeFi provided the devastating impact of the COVID-19 pandemic on the global hospitality and tourism industry. Web 3.0 and the metaverse are expected to rise, so DeFi is gradually progressing in the hospitality and tourism sectors, where NFT marketplaces will witness an influx of users and growth. NFT has captured the hospitality and tourism businesses, as we are seeing a rise of P2E gaming, which is becoming a growing economic force. The NFT concept will subsequently evolve across the hospitality and tourism sectors in new ways as users and businesses are starting to see more value with having open interoperability between platforms. This change will be the cornerstone of more sustainable concepts, as staking and rewarding with cryptocurrencies will have an impactful role.

Finally, the central governments are rapidly exploring avenues for the implementation of a CBDC, because more and more businesses are adopting cryptocurrencies for payments. A CBDC can offer many benefits to the hospitality and tourism sectors, but it is important that the values of our society as well as user privacy and control are not abused by monetary policy manipulation. Thus, upcoming studies should address the impacts of a CBDC on social, political, philosophical, and legal aspects in the leisure and service sectors.

Despite the promising outlook of blockchain technology, insights into the role of blockchain technology and how it contributes to the IoV for the hospitality and tourism industry is largely under-explored in the literature (Sharma et al., 2021), thus, an abundance of research agenda needs to be opened up. An inadequate understanding of issues that pertain to acceptance of blockchain technology inhibits the business uptake of the technology as well as operational innovation, which will inevitably result in a disadvantaged market position (Filimonau & Naumova, 2020). In order to transform blockchain technology into smart hospitality and tourism, the blockchains should be effectively incorporated into business models and managed in a way that the industry can reap the benefits of the IoV. In light of the promising opportunities for utilization of blockchain technology in the leisure operations, an understanding of how the various stakeholders' take on blockchain technology and its impact commercial activity and customer experience will provide evidence to the potential applications of blockchain, which will in turn heighten the IoV. As a result, we urge the hospitality and tourism technology scholars to conduct research that analyzes the viability of blockchain technologies that include cryptocurrency, non-fungible token, the metaverse, decentralized finance, and central bank digital currency, in the hospitality and tourism operations. Investigating the motivators and inhibitors of blockchain technology adoption within the hospitality and tourism sectors will be a promising research opportunity.

CONCLUSION

Suggestions for Future Research

The information is essential for the promotion of IoV across the service and travel industry. However, the IoV across the leisure industry depends on the blockchain technology diffusion. Moreover, shedding light on the consequence of novel technology on the chain of distribution within the context of smart hospitality and tourism will be a fruitful research path. The knowledge should include specific, useful recommendations about how blockchain technology can improve efficiency with the hospitality and tourism operations. Advancing protocols using comprehensive analysis of blockchain technology situation are deemed necessary at some time in future in view to promoting the process of adoption. The points of view of the industry professionals, practitioners, decision makers, policy makers, and above all, consumers should be holistically pursued. Thus, opening the possibilities for the blockchain technology and the IoV to become everyday reality that could reshape the future of the leisure industry.

Blockchain holds the key to unleashing the IoV across the service and leisure sectors. However, in order to fully grasp the aforementioned potential of the IoV and its implications, robust frameworks, which are solidly grounded in theoretical logics, are needed. Thus, we call upon the scholars and practitioners to engage in this cutting-edge and promising research topic, because various studies about the IoV in the service and and travel industry can provide new conceptual perspectives as well as enhance business practices.

REFERENCES

Aramonte, S., Huang, W., & Schrimpf, A. (2021). *DeFi risks and the decentralisation illusion*. BIS Quarterly Review.

Bachmann, N. M., Drasch, B., Fridgen, G., Miksch, M., Regner, F., Schweizer, A., & Urbach, N. (2022). Tarzan and chain: Exploring the ICO jungle and evaluating design archetypes. *Electronic Markets*, 32(3), 1707–1723. DOI: 10.1007/s12525-021-00463-6

Cheng, N. T. Y., Fong, L. H. N., & Law, R. (2021). Mobile payment technology in hospitality and tourism: A critical review through the lens of demand, supply and policy. *International Journal of Contemporary Hospitality Management*, 33(10), 3636–3660. DOI: 10.1108/IJCHM-02-2021-0261

Demirciftci, T., Chen, C., & Erdem, M. (2020). A tabulation of information technology and consumer behavior in hospitality revenue management research. *Journal of Hospitality and Tourism Technology*, 11(3), 575–587. DOI: 10.1108/JHTT-02-2019-0018

Duan, J., Kang, L., Chen, Z., Peng, T., & Wang, Y. (2020). A photo-sharing social network based on blockchain technology. *International Journal of Technology Management*, 84(1/2), 70–85. DOI: 10.1504/IJTM.2020.112078

Filimonau, V., & Naumova, E. (2020). The blockchain technology and the scope of its application in hospitality operations. *International Journal of Hospitality Management*, 87, 102383. DOI: 10.1016/j.ijhm.2019.102383

Hajric, V. (2022). Crypto Crash Erases More Than $1 Trillion in Market Value". *Bloomberg*, 22 January 2022. Available at: https://www.bloomberg.com/news/articles/2022-01-21/crypto-meltdown-erases-more-than-1-trillion-in-market-value (accessed 10 December 2022).

Han, D.-I. D., Bergs, Y., & Moorhouse, N. (2022). Virtual reality consumer experience escapes: Preparing for the metaverse. *Virtual Reality (Waltham Cross)*, 26(4), 1443–1458. Advance online publication. DOI: 10.1007/s10055-022-00641-7

Irannezhad, E., & Mahadevan, R. (2021). Is blockchain tourism's new hope? *Journal of Hospitality and Tourism Technology*, 12(1), 85–96. DOI: 10.1108/JHTT-02-2019-0039

Kim, J. J., Radic, A., Chua, B. L., Koo, B., & Han, H. (2022). Digital currency and payment innovation in the hospitality and tourism industry. *International Journal of Hospitality Management*, 107, 103314. DOI: 10.1016/j.ijhm.2022.103314

Kizildag, M., Dogru, T., Zhang, T., Mody, M. A., Altin, M., Ozturk, A. B., & Ozdemir, O. (2020). Blockchain: A paradigm shift in business practices. *International Journal of Contemporary Hospitality Management*, 32(3), 953–975. DOI: 10.1108/IJCHM-12-2018-0958

Kollmann, T., Hensellek, S., de Cruppe, K., & Sirges, A. (2020). Toward a renaissance of cooperatives fostered by Blockchain on electronic marketplaces: A theory-driven case study approach. *Electronic Markets*, 30(2), 273–284. DOI: 10.1007/s12525-019-00369-4

Lacity, M. C. (2020). *Blockchain Foundations: For the Internet of Value*. University of Arkansas Press.

Lee, M., Ahn, J., Shin, M., Kwon, W., & Back, K.-J. (2021). Integrating technology to service innovation: Key issues and future research directions in hospitality and tourism. *Journal of Hospitality and Tourism Technology*, 12(1), 19–38. DOI: 10.1108/JHTT-01-2019-0013

Liu, M. T., Wang, S., McCartney, G., & Wong, I. A. (2021). Taking a break is for accomplishing a longer journey: Hospitality industry in Macao under the COVID-19 pandemic. *International Journal of Contemporary Hospitality Management*, 33(4), 1249–1275. DOI: 10.1108/IJCHM-07-2020-0678

Mantas, P., Ioannou, Z.-M., Viennas, E., Pavlidis, G., & Sakkopoulos, E. (2022). Digital gifts and tourism mementos: A sustainable approach. *Sustainability (Basel)*, 14(1), 98. DOI: 10.3390/su14010098

Mofokeng, N., & Fatima, T. (2018). Future tourism trends: Utilizing non-fungible tokens to aid wildlife conservation. *African Journal of Hospitality, Tourism and Leisure*, 7(4), 1–20.

Önder, I., & Gunter, U. (2022). Blockchain: Is it the future for the tourism and hospitality industry? *Tourism Economics*, 28(2), 291–299. DOI: 10.1177/1354816620961707

Radic, A., Law, R., Lück, M., Kang, H., Ariza-Montes, A., Arjona-Fuentes, J. M., & Han, H. (2020). Apocalypse now or overreaction to coronavirus: The global cruise tourism industry crisis. *Sustainability (Basel)*, 12(17), 6968. DOI: 10.3390/su12176968

Radic, A., Quan, W., Ariza-Montes, A., Lee, J. S., & Han, H. (2022b). You can't hold the tide with a broom: Cryptocurrency payments and tourism in South Korea and China. *Tourism Management Perspectives*, 43, 101000. DOI: 10.1016/j.tmp.2022.101000

Radic, A., Quan, W., Koo, B., Chua, B. L., Kim, J. J., & Han, H. (2022a). Central bank digital currency as a payment method for tourists: Application of the theory of planned behavior to digital Yuan/Won/Dollar choice. *Journal of Travel & Tourism Marketing*, 39(2), 152–172. DOI: 10.1080/10548408.2022.2061677

Ragnedda, M., & Destefanis, G. (2020). Blockchain: A disruptive technology. Ragnedda, M. & Destefanis, G. (Eds.). *Blockchain and Web 3.0: Social, Economic, and Technological Challenges*. Routledge, New York, NY.

Rashideh, W. (2020). Blockchain technology framework: Current and future perspectives for the tourism industry. *Tourism Management*, 80, 104125. DOI: 10.1016/j.tourman.2020.104125

Sharma, M., Sehrawat, R., Daim, T., & Shaygan, A. (2021). Technology assessment: Enabling blockchain in hospitality and tourism sectors. *Technological Forecasting and Social Change*, 169, 120810. DOI: 10.1016/j.techfore.2021.120810

Sharma, T., Chen, J., & Liu, W. Y. (2020). Eco-innovation in hospitality research (1998-2018): A systematic review. *International Journal of Contemporary Hospitality Management*, 32(2), 913–933. DOI: 10.1108/IJCHM-01-2019-0002

Su, K.-W., Chiu, P.-C., & Lin, T.-H. (2022). Establishing a blockchain online travel agency with a human–computer interaction perspective. *Journal of Hospitality and Tourism Technology*, ahead-of-print .DOI: 10.1108/JHTT-01-2021-0038

Takeda, A., & Ito, Y. (2021). A review of FinTech research. *International Journal of Technology Management*, 86(1), 67–88. DOI: 10.1504/IJTM.2021.115761

Tham, A., & Sigala, M. (2020). Road block(chain): Bit(coin)s for tourism sustainable development goals? *Journal of Hospitality and Tourism Technology*, 11(2), 203–222. DOI: 10.1108/JHTT-05-2019-0069

Thies, F., Wallbach, S., Wessel, M., Besler, M., & Benlian, A. (2022). Initial coin offerings and the cryptocurrency hype - the moderating role of exogenous and endogenous signals. *Electronic Markets*, 32(3), 1691–1705. DOI: 10.1007/s12525-021-00460-9

Treiblmaier, H. (2021). The token economy as a key driver for tourism: Entering the next phase of blockchain research. *Annals of Tourism Research*, 91, 103177. DOI: 10.1016/j.annals.2021.103177

Treiblmaier, H. (2022a). Defining the Internet of Value. Vadgama, N., Xu, J. & Tasca, P. (Eds.). *Enabling the Internet of Value: How Blockchain Connects Global Business*. Springer Nature, Switzerland, 3-13. DOI: 10.1007/978-3-030-78184-2_1

Treiblmaier, H. (2022b). Do cryptocurrencies really have (no) intrinsic value? *Electronic Markets*, 32(3), 1749–1758. DOI: 10.1007/s12525-021-00491-2

Valeri, M., & Baggio, R. (2020). A critical reflection on the adoption of blockchain in tourism. *Information Technology & Tourism*, 23(2), 121–132. DOI: 10.1007/s40558-020-00183-1

Voshmgir, S. (2020). *Token Economy: How the Web3 reinvents the Internet* (2nd ed.). BlockchainHub Berlin.

Willie, P. (2019). Can all sectors of the hospitality and tourism industry be influenced by the innovation of Blockchain technology? *Worldwide Hospitality and Tourism Themes*, 11(2), 112–120. DOI: 10.1108/WHATT-11-2018-0077

Wu, H.-C., Cheng, C.-C., Chen, Y.-C., & Hong, W. (2018). Towards green experiential loyalty: Driving from experiential quality, green relationship quality, environmental friendliness, green support and green desire. *International Journal of Contemporary Hospitality Management*, 30(3), 1374–1397. DOI: 10.1108/IJCHM-10-2016-0596

Xiong, Y., Xia, S., & Wang, X. (2020). Artificial intelligence and business applications, an introduction. *International Journal of Technology Management*, 84(1/2), 1–7. DOI: 10.1504/IJTM.2020.112615

Chapter 7
The Evolution of Travel Booking:
From Traditional Methods to Blockchain Solutions

G. Sowmya
https://orcid.org/0000-0002-9275-7726
MLR Institute of Technology, India

R Sridevi
Jawaharlal Nehru Technological University, India

K. S. Sadasivarao
Sri Indu College of Engineering and Technology, India

ABSTRACT

This chapter examines the evolution of travel booking, highlighting key developments from traditional methods to blockchain solutions. Initially reliant on brick-and-mortar travel agencies and phone reservations, the industry was transformed by the internet and Online Travel Agencies (OTAs), which offered increased convenience and real-time updates through mobile technology. Social media and metasearch engines further influenced booking behaviour, while AI and machine learning enabled personalized recommendations and predictive analytics. The rise of the sharing economy introduced peer-to-peer platforms like Airbnb and Uber. Recently, blockchain technology has promised enhanced transparency and security. Despite these advancements, challenges such as security concerns and user adoption persist. Future trends, including augmented reality (AR), voice-activated bookings, and sustainable travel solutions, are poised to shape the industry's future.

DOI: 10.4018/979-8-3693-6562-5.ch007

1. INTRODUCTION

Travel booking has undergone a remarkable transformation from its early days of manual reservations and in-person consultations to the sophisticated, digital-driven processes we see today. Initially, travellers relied heavily on traditional methods such as visiting brick-and-mortar travel agencies, making phone reservations, and using printed travel guides. The introduction of the internet marked a pivotal change, leading to the rise of Online Travel Agencies (OTAs) and mobile applications, which provided unprecedented convenience and access to a plethora of travel options. Social media platforms, metasearch engines, and the sharing economy further revolutionized the industry, making travel booking more personalized and accessible. Recently, blockchain technology has emerged as a promising solution for enhancing transparency, security, and efficiency in travel bookings. (Thees, Erschbamer, & Pechlaner, 2020)Technological advancements have been crucial in shaping the modern travel booking landscape. The internet's arrival made it possible to book flights, accommodations, and other travel services online, democratizing access to travel information and deals. Mobile technology and travel apps have enabled travellers to book and manage their trips on the go, offering real-time updates and seamless experiences. Artificial Intelligence (AI) and Machine Learning (ML) have introduced personalized recommendations, predictive analytics, and virtual assistants, improving user experience and operational efficiency. The sharing economy, powered by peer-to-peer platforms like Airbnb and Uber, has expanded travel options and fostered a more connected global community. Blockchain technology, with its potential to enhance security and transparency, represents the latest frontier in travel booking innovations. These technological advancements not only streamline the booking process but also provide travellers with more choices, greater convenience, and improved security, ultimately transforming how we explore the world. (Balasubramanian, Sethi, Ajayan, & Paris, 2022)

2. TRADITIONAL TRAVEL BOOKING METHODS

2.1 Historical Perspective on Travel

Travel, as we know it today, has deep historical roots. Initially, travel was primarily for trade, exploration, and pilgrimage. Over time, it evolved into a leisure activity. The early 20th century saw the rise of organized travel, with railways and steamships making distant destinations more accessible. Travel during this period was often a luxury reserved for the affluent, facilitated through personal connections and bespoke arrangements. (Elhaj, 2012)

2.2 Travel Agencies: Brick-and-Mortar Beginnings

The concept of travel agencies emerged in the mid-19th century. Thomas Cook, often credited as the pioneer of organized travel, founded one of the first travel agencies in 1841. These agencies offered a range of services, from booking transportation and accommodations to organizing entire tours. Clients would visit the agency in person to consult with travel agents, who provided expert advice and handled all arrangements. The physical presence of travel agencies played a crucial role in building trust and offering personalized service.

2.3 Phone Reservations and Direct Hotel Bookings

As telephone technology became widespread, it revolutionized the travel booking process. Travelers could now make reservations directly by calling hotels, airlines, and other service providers. This method offered greater convenience compared to visiting a travel agency. Hotels and airlines set up dedicated call centers to handle reservations, providing a more direct and often quicker way to secure travel arrangements. Despite the convenience, this method still relied heavily on manual processes and human intermediaries. Figure 1 shows the evolution of different travel booking platforms.

Figure 1. Evolution of travel booking methods

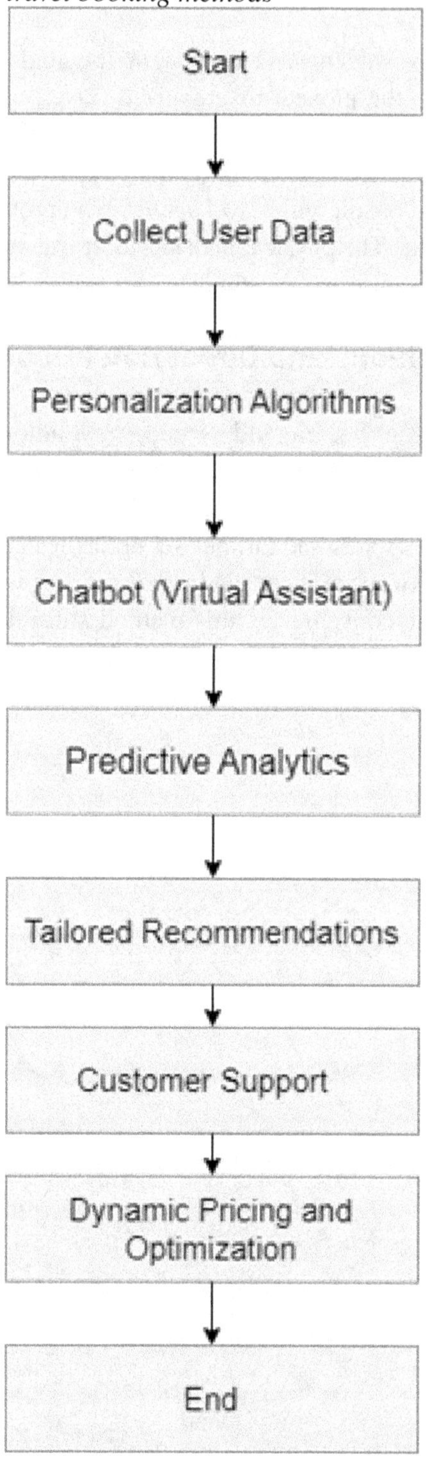

2.4 Printed Travel Guides and Brochures

Before the digital age, printed travel guides and brochures were essential resources for travellers. Guidebooks from publishers like Baedeker and Michelin provided detailed information on destinations, including maps, cultural insights, and recommended accommodations and restaurants. Travel brochures, distributed by agencies and service providers, offered curated packages and promotional deals. These printed materials were highly valued for their comprehensive and reliable content, helping travellers plan their trips with confidence and a sense of adventure. (Liao, 2020)

Traditional travel booking methods laid the groundwork for the modern travel industry. While they relied heavily on personal interaction and manual processes, these methods were instrumental in shaping the travel experiences of millions and establishing trust in the travel industry.

3. THE ADVENT OF THE INTERNET AND ONLINE TRAVEL AGENCIES (OTAS)

3.1 Emergence of the Internet in the Travel Industry

The internet's arrival in the mid-1990s marked a revolutionary shift in the travel industry. Initially, travel information and booking processes were digitized, making it easier for travellers to access data and make reservations. Websites began to offer details about destinations, accommodations, and transportation, allowing users to gather information from the comfort of their homes. As the internet evolved, it enabled direct connections between travellers and service providers, bypassing traditional intermediaries and reducing the need for physical interactions. (García, Anjos, & Dogan, 2021)

3.2 Rise of Online Travel Agencies (OTAs)

With the internet's proliferation, Online Travel Agencies (OTAs) emerged, fundamentally transforming the travel booking landscape. Companies like Expedia, Priceline, and Travelocity were among the first to capitalize on the new digital marketplace. OTAs provided a one-stop shop for booking flights, hotels, car rentals, and other travel-related services. Their user-friendly platforms allowed travellers to compare prices, read reviews, and make reservations online. This digital shift democratized travel, making it more accessible and convenient for a broader audience

3.3 Advantages of OTAs Over Traditional Methods

OTAs offered several advantages over traditional travel booking methods:

i. **Convenience:** Travelers could book services at any time, from anywhere, without the need to visit a physical agency.
ii. **Price Comparison:** OTAs allowed users to compare prices across multiple providers, ensuring competitive rates and the best deals.
iii. **User Reviews:** Customer reviews and ratings provided valuable insights, helping travelers make informed decisions.
iv. **Comprehensive Options:** OTAs offered a wide range of choices, from budget to luxury options, catering to diverse needs and preferences.
v. **Dynamic Packaging:** Travelers could bundle services (flights, hotels, car rentals) for better deals and streamlined itineraries. (Psefti, Poulaki, Papaioannou, & Katsoni, 2021)

3.4 Popular Online Travel Platforms and Their Impact

Several OTAs have become household names, significantly impacting the travel industry:

i. **Expedia:** One of the largest OTAs, offering extensive travel services and partnerships with numerous airlines, hotels, and car rental companies. (Lee, Denizci Guillet, & Law, 2013)
ii. **Booking.com:** Known for its vast inventory of accommodations, ranging from hotels to vacation rentals, with a strong focus on user experience and customer service. (Martin-Fuentes & Mellinas, 2018)
iii. **Airbnb:** Revolutionized the accommodation sector by introducing a peer-to-peer model, allowing individuals to rent out their homes or rooms. (Ding, Niu, & Choo, 2023)
iv. **Priceline:** Introduced innovative pricing models like "Name Your Own Price," enabling travellers to bid on hotel rooms and rental cars.
v. **TripAdvisor:** Initially a review site, it expanded to include booking capabilities, leveraging its vast database of user-generated reviews to guide travellers' choices. (Gretzel & Yoo, 2008)These platforms have not only made travel booking more accessible and efficient but have also introduced greater transparency and competition in the market. They have empowered travellers with more control over their travel planning and have driven the travel industry towards continuous innovation and improvement.

4. THE IMPACT OF MOBILE TECHNOLOGY

4.1 Smartphone Revolution and Travel Apps

The widespread adoption of smartphones has revolutionized the travel industry. With powerful computing capabilities and constant internet connectivity, smartphones have become indispensable tools for travellers. The development of travel apps has further enhanced this revolution, offering a wide array of functionalities that cater to every aspect of travel planning and management. Apps from airlines, hotels, OTAs, and independent developers provide services such as booking flights and accommodations, checking in, accessing itineraries, and receiving real-time notifications. (Dias & Afonso, 2021)

4.2 On-the-Go Booking and Real-Time Updates

Mobile technology allows travellers to make bookings on-the-go, providing unparalleled convenience and flexibility. Whether it's a last-minute hotel reservation, a sudden change in flight plans, or booking activities and excursions, mobile apps enable travellers to manage their plans seamlessly from anywhere. Additionally, real-time updates and notifications keep travellers informed about their schedules, such as flight delays, gate changes, or weather conditions, ensuring they can adjust their plans accordingly and reduce stress during their journeys.

4.3 Integration of Maps and Navigation in Travel Apps

One of the most significant advancements in travel apps is the integration of maps and navigation services. Apps like Google Maps and Apple Maps offer comprehensive navigation features, helping travellers find directions, explore points of interest, and discover local amenities. These apps provide real-time traffic updates, public transportation options, and estimated travel times, making it easier for travellers to navigate unfamiliar locations. Many travel apps also integrate with these map services to offer additional functionalities, such as locating nearby hotels, restaurants, and tourist attractions, enhancing the overall travel experience. (Muñoz, del Vas, & Yi, 2019) Mobile technology has fundamentally changed how travellers plan, book, and manage their trips. The convenience of on-the-go booking, real-time updates, and advanced navigation capabilities has made travel more accessible, efficient, and enjoyable, solidifying smartphones as essential travel companions.

5. THE ROLE OF SOCIAL MEDIA IN TRAVEL BOOKING

5.1 Influence of Social Media on Travel Decisions

Social media has profoundly influenced how travellers make decisions about their trips. Platforms like Facebook, Instagram, Twitter, and Pinterest provide a wealth of visual and narrative content that inspires and informs potential travellers. Photos, videos, and stories shared by friends, family, influencers, and brands offer authentic glimpses into destinations, accommodations, and activities. These social cues play a significant role in shaping travellers' preferences, encouraging them to explore new places and experiences they might not have considered otherwise.

5.2 User-Generated Content and Reviews

User-generated content (UGC) and reviews on platforms such as TripAdvisor, Yelp, and Google Reviews have become crucial resources for travellers. Authentic reviews and ratings from fellow travellers provide valuable insights into the quality and reliability of hotels, restaurants, tours, and attractions. This peer feedback helps travelers make more informed choices, reducing the risk of disappointing experiences. The transparency and trust associated with UGC have made it a vital component of modern travel planning.

5.3 Social Media Platforms as Marketing Tools for Travel Companies

Travel companies leverage social media platforms as powerful marketing tools to reach and engage potential customers. By creating visually appealing content and interactive campaigns, companies can showcase their offerings and attract a wider audience. Influencer partnerships are particularly effective, as influencers share their travel experiences with large, engaged followings, often leading to increased brand visibility and credibility. Social media advertising, targeted through sophisticated algorithms, allows travel companies to reach specific demographics and interests, maximizing their marketing impact. (Xiang & Gretzel, 2010)Social media has transformed travel booking by influencing decisions, providing trustworthy user-generated content, and serving as a dynamic marketing platform for travel companies. This integration of social media into the travel ecosystem has made the process of discovering, planning, and booking travel more interactive, personalized, and engaging.

6. METASEARCH ENGINES AND AGGREGATORS

6.1 Definition and Functionality of Metasearch Engines

Metasearch engines are specialized search engines that aggregate data from multiple sources to provide a comprehensive overview of available travel options. Unlike traditional OTAs, which sell travel products directly, metasearch engines compare prices and availability from various OTAs, airlines, hotels, and other travel providers. When a user searches for a flight, hotel, or rental car, the metasearch engine compiles results from different websites, displaying them in a unified format. Users are then redirected to the provider's site to complete their bookings. This functionality enables travellers to efficiently compare options and find the best deals without visiting multiple websites. (Meng, 2009)

6.2 Comparison of OTAs and Metasearch Engines

i. **Business Model:** OTAs act as intermediaries that handle the booking process and payments, earning commissions on each sale. Metasearch engines, on the other hand, generate revenue primarily through referral fees and advertising, as they redirect users to the providers' websites to complete bookings.
ii. **User Experience:** OTAs offer a seamless booking experience within their platforms, managing the entire transaction. Metasearch engines provide a broader view of options, facilitating price and feature comparisons across multiple providers, but users must navigate to external sites to finalize bookings.
iii. **Scope and Focus:** While OTAs typically focus on providing a wide range of services within their ecosystem, metasearch engines aim to cover the entire market, including smaller and less-known providers, to offer the most comprehensive comparison. (Dudás, Boros, & Vida, 2017)

6.3 Major Players in the Metasearch Market

i. **Kayak:** One of the leading metasearch engines, Kayak offers comprehensive search capabilities for flights, hotels, car rentals, and vacation packages. It provides filters and tools to help users find the best deals and track price changes.
ii. **Skyscanner:** Known for its user-friendly interface and extensive global coverage, Skyscanner compares flight, hotel, and car rental options. It is popular for its flexible search options, such as searching for the cheapest month to travel.

iii. **Google Flights:** Leveraging Google's powerful search algorithms, Google Flights offers fast and flexible flight searches, including fare predictions and alternative route suggestions. It integrates seamlessly with other Google services.
iv. **TripAdvisor:** Originally a review site, TripAdvisor has expanded its metasearch capabilities, allowing users to compare prices for hotels, flights, and restaurants. It integrates user reviews and ratings into the search results, enhancing decision-making. (Domínguez Vila, Araújo, Brea, & Alén, 2017)
v. **Trivago:** Specializing in hotel comparisons, Trivago aggregates data from numerous booking sites, providing a detailed overview of hotel options. Its interface allows users to filter results by price, location, and amenities.

Metasearch engines and aggregators have become indispensable tools for modern travelers, offering comprehensive and efficient ways to compare travel options and find the best deals. Their ability to aggregate data from multiple sources and present it in an accessible format has significantly enhanced the travel booking process, empowering users to make more informed and cost-effective choices.

7. AI AND MACHINE LEARNING IN TRAVEL BOOKING

7.1 Personalization and Recommendation Algorithms

Artificial Intelligence (AI) and Machine Learning (ML) have significantly enhanced personalization in travel booking. By analyzing vast amounts of user data, including past bookings, search history, and preferences, AI algorithms can deliver tailored recommendations for flights, hotels, activities, and destinations. These personalized suggestions improve user experience by presenting relevant options, thereby increasing the likelihood of booking. For instance, an AI-powered travel app might suggest hotels based on a user's previous stays or recommend destinations aligned with their interests and travel history. (Bulchand-Gidumal, 2020)

7.2 Chatbots and Virtual Travel Assistants

Chatbots and virtual travel assistants, powered by AI, have revolutionized customer service in the travel industry. These tools provide 24/7 support, handling a wide range of inquiries from booking modifications to travel advice. Chatbots can process natural language queries, offer instant responses, and guide users through the booking process. For example, a chatbot on a travel website can help users find flights, book hotels, and answer questions about travel policies. Virtual assistants like Siri, Google Assistant, and Amazon Alexa also integrate with travel services, allowing users to book trips and receive travel updates through voice commands (Khan, Irfan, & Muley, 2023). Figure 2 shows how AI and ML useful in Travel booking.

Figure 2. AI and ML in travel booking

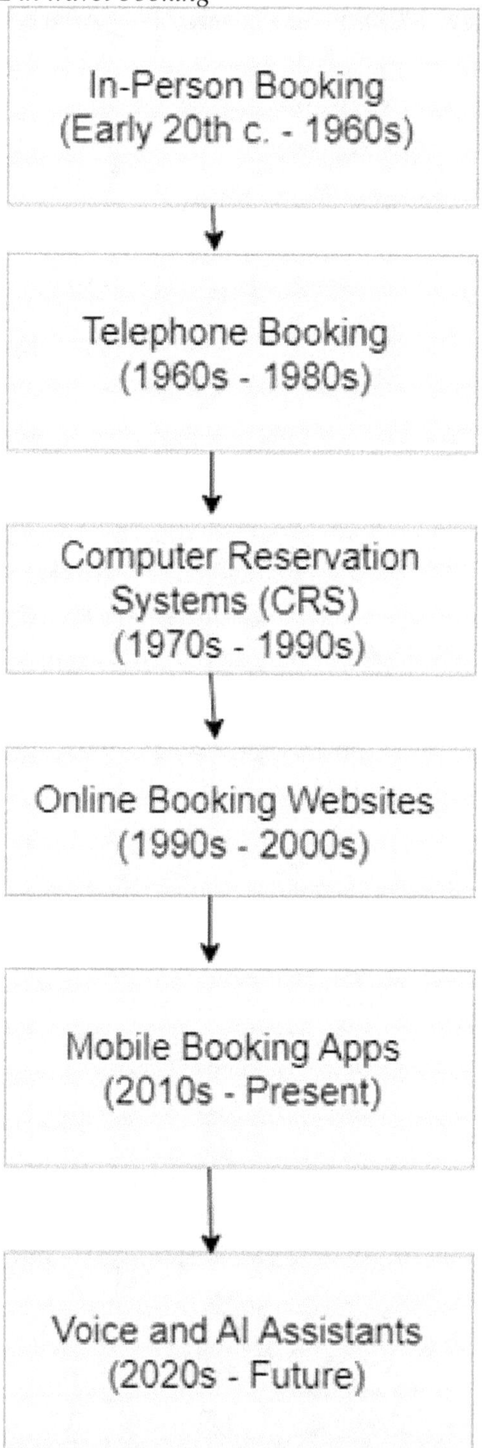

7.3 Predictive Analytics for Dynamic Pricing and Demand Forecasting

Predictive analytics, driven by AI and ML, enables dynamic pricing and demand forecasting in the travel industry. By analyzing historical data, current trends, and various external factors (such as weather, holidays, and economic conditions), predictive models can forecast demand and adjust prices in real time. Airlines, hotels, and car rental companies use these insights to optimize pricing strategies, ensuring they maximize revenue while remaining competitive. For instance, an airline might increase prices for flights during peak travel periods based on predicted high demand or offer discounts during off-peak times to fill seats.

AI and ML are transforming the travel booking landscape by providing personalized recommendations, improving customer service with chatbots and virtual assistants, and optimizing pricing through predictive analytics. These technologies enhance user experience, increase operational efficiency, and drive revenue growth, making them essential components of modern travel booking systems. (Guizzardi, Pons, Angelini, & Ranieri, 2020)

8. THE SHARING ECONOMY AND PEER-TO-PEER BOOKING PLATFORMS

8.1 Rise of the Sharing Economy in Travel

The sharing economy has dramatically reshaped the travel industry, emphasizing access over ownership and community-driven experiences. This economic model leverages technology to enable individuals to share resources, such as accommodations, transportation, and services, directly with others. The rise of the sharing economy in travel has been driven by factors such as the increased connectivity provided by the internet, a growing preference for unique and personalized travel experiences, and the desire for more cost-effective options. This shift has led to the emergence of numerous peer-to-peer platforms that facilitate the sharing of resources. (Hong, 2018)

8.2 Peer-to-Peer Accommodation and Transport Services

Peer-to-peer accommodation and transport services are at the forefront of the sharing economy in travel. These services allow individuals to rent out their homes, apartments, or even spare rooms to travelers, as well as share their vehicles or offer rides.

i. **Accommodation:** Platforms like Airbnb, Vrbo, and HomeAway enable property owners to list their spaces for short-term rentals. Travelers can choose from a wide range of accommodations, from single rooms to entire homes, often at lower prices than traditional hotels. These platforms also provide a more personalized and local experience, as hosts often share insider tips and recommendations with their guests.
ii. **Transport:** Ride-sharing services such as Uber, Lyft, and BlaBlaCar connect drivers with passengers looking for convenient and affordable transportation. These platforms offer various options, from private rides to carpooling, catering to different needs and budgets. They also provide greater flexibility and availability compared to traditional taxi services. (Pesonen & Tussyadiah, 2017)

8.3 Impact of Platforms like Airbnb and Uber

Platforms like Airbnb and Uber have had a profound impact on the travel industry, influencing both consumers and traditional service providers.

a. Consumer Impact:
    i. **Cost Savings:** Peer-to-peer services often offer more affordable options compared to traditional hotels and taxis, making travel more accessible.
    ii. **Diverse Choices:** Travelers have access to a broader range of accommodation and transport options, from budget-friendly to luxury, and can choose unique stays that align with their preferences.
    iii. **Local Experiences:** Staying in local homes and using local drivers provide travelers with a more authentic and immersive experience, fostering cultural exchange and understanding. (Hall et al., 2022)
b. Industry Impact:
    i. **Competition:** Traditional hotels and taxi services face increased competition, pushing them to innovate and improve their offerings to retain customers.
    ii. **Regulatory Challenges:** The rapid growth of peer-to-peer platforms has led to regulatory challenges, as cities and countries struggle to update laws and regulations to address issues such as safety, taxation, and fair competition.
    iii. **Economic Effects:** The sharing economy has created new income opportunities for individuals, allowing property owners and drivers to monetize their assets. This has contributed to economic growth and provided financial benefits to local communities.

The sharing economy and peer-to-peer booking platforms have revolutionized the travel industry by providing cost-effective, diverse, and personalized options for travelers. Platforms like Airbnb and Uber have not only enhanced the travel experience but also challenged traditional service providers to adapt and innovate in response to changing consumer preferences and market dynamics.

9. BLOCKCHAIN TECHNOLOGY IN TRAVEL BOOKING

9.1 Introduction to Blockchain and Its Basic Principles

Blockchain technology, a decentralized digital ledger system, allows the secure recording and verification of transactions across multiple computers. Its core principles include decentralization, immutability, transparency, and security. Each block in a blockchain contains a list of transactions, and once a block is added to the chain, it cannot be altered. This ensures that the data remains consistent and tamper-proof. Blockchain relies on consensus mechanisms, such as proof of work or proof of stake, to validate transactions and maintain the integrity of the network. (Namasudra & Akkaya, 2023)

9.2 Potential Applications of Blockchain in Travel

Blockchain technology offers several potential applications in the travel industry, aiming to enhance various aspects of travel booking and management:

i. **Identity Verification:** Blockchain can streamline and secure the identity verification process, making it easier for travelers to move through airports and other checkpoints without repeated checks.
ii. **Payment Systems:** Cryptocurrencies and blockchain-based payment systems can reduce transaction fees and increase the speed and security of payments between travellers and service providers.
iii. **Loyalty Programs:** Blockchain can unify disparate loyalty programs across airlines, hotels, and other services, allowing travelers to easily manage and redeem their rewards. (Takale, Damke, Mehra, Burkule, & Tadge, 2024)
iv. **Smart Contracts:** These self-executing contracts with terms directly written into code can automate various travel-related transactions, such as hotel bookings, car rentals, and insurance claims, reducing the need for intermediaries.
v. **Baggage Tracking:** Blockchain can provide an immutable record of baggage handling, improving transparency and reducing the chances of lost or mishandled luggage.

9.3 Benefits of Blockchain: Transparency, Security, and Efficiency

i. **Transparency:** Blockchain's public ledger system ensures that all transactions are visible and traceable, fostering trust among users. This transparency can reduce fraud and increase accountability in travel bookings and transactions.
ii. **Security:** The decentralized and encrypted nature of blockchain makes it highly secure against hacking and unauthorized access. This enhances the protection of sensitive traveller information and financial transactions.
iii. **Efficiency:** By eliminating intermediaries and automating processes through smart contracts, blockchain can significantly reduce administrative costs and processing times. This leads to more efficient operations and faster service delivery for travellers.

9.4 Case Studies of Blockchain Solutions in Travel

i. **Winding Tree:** This blockchain-based travel distribution platform aims to create a decentralized marketplace for travel services. By using blockchain, Winding Tree reduces the need for intermediaries, lowering costs for both service providers and travellers. Lufthansa and Air New Zealand are among the airlines that have partnered with Winding Tree to explore blockchain applications.
ii. **Webjet:** An Australian online travel agency, Webjet has developed a blockchain solution for hotel bookings to address issues of overbooking and double bookings. By creating a transparent and secure ledger of hotel inventory and transactions, Webjet ensures accurate availability and reduces booking errors.
iii. **LockTrip:** This blockchain-based travel platform offers hotel and vacation rental bookings with zero commissions. By utilizing blockchain, LockTrip provides transparent pricing and reduces costs for both travellers and property owners. It also integrates cryptocurrency payments, enhancing security and efficiency.
iv. **TUI Group:** One of the world's largest travel companies, TUI has implemented a blockchain-based inventory management system. This system allows TUI to manage and distribute hotel room availability more efficiently, reducing reliance on intermediaries and improving operational transparency.

Blockchain technology has the potential to revolutionize the travel booking industry by enhancing transparency, security, and efficiency. Through innovative applications and successful case studies, blockchain demonstrates its ability to address longstanding challenges in the travel sector, paving the way for more streamlined and trustworthy travel experiences.

10. CHALLENGES AND LIMITATIONS OF MODERN TRAVEL BOOKING TECHNOLOGIES

10.1 Security and Privacy Concerns

As travel booking technologies have advanced, security and privacy concerns have become more prominent. The vast amount of personal and financial data processed by OTAs, travel apps, and blockchain systems makes them prime targets for cyberattacks. Issues such as data breaches, identity theft, and fraudulent transactions pose significant risks to both travelers and service providers. Ensuring robust security measures, such as encryption, secure payment gateways, and compliance with data protection regulations (like GDPR), is crucial to mitigating these risks. Additionally, maintaining user privacy by implementing transparent data usage policies and giving users control over their personal information is essential for building trust.

10.2 Market Fragmentation and Competition

The travel booking industry is highly fragmented, with numerous OTAs, metasearch engines, peer-to-peer platforms, and traditional travel agencies vying for market share. This intense competition can lead to inconsistent pricing, with different platforms offering varying rates for the same services. Travelers may find it challenging to navigate through the plethora of options, leading to decision fatigue. Moreover, smaller or newer platforms may struggle to compete with established giants, limiting their ability to innovate and offer unique services. This fragmentation also complicates the integration of new technologies, such as blockchain, which require widespread adoption to realize their full potential. (Tandafatu, Ermilinda, & Darkel, 2024)

10.3 User Trust and Adoption Barriers

Adopting new travel booking technologies can be hindered by user trust and familiarity issues. Many travelers are hesitant to switch from traditional methods to new platforms due to concerns about reliability, security, and usability. For instance, while blockchain technology promises enhanced transparency and security, its complexity and association with cryptocurrencies can deter mainstream users. Similarly, the use of AI and machine learning for personalized recommendations may raise concerns about data privacy and algorithmic bias. Building user trust requires clear communication about the benefits and safety measures of new technologies, as well as providing seamless, user-friendly experiences that demonstrate tangible improvements over traditional methods.

While modern travel booking technologies offer numerous advantages, they also face significant challenges and limitations. Addressing security and privacy concerns, managing market fragmentation and competition, and overcoming user trust and adoption barriers are critical to the continued evolution and success of these technologies in the travel industry.

11. FUTURE TRENDS IN TRAVEL BOOKING

Integration of Augmented Reality (AR) and Virtual Reality (VR) will revolutionize the way travelers plan and experience trips by offering immersive previews of destinations, accommodations, and activities, allowing users to explore places virtually before booking. The rise of voice-activated bookings, facilitated by smart assistants like Alexa, Siri, and Google Assistant, will make the process more convenient and hands-free, enabling travelers to make reservations and access information through simple voice commands. Additionally, there will be a growing emphasis on sustainable and eco-friendly travel booking solutions, with platforms offering options that prioritize environmental responsibility, such as eco-friendly accommodations, carbon offset programs, and sustainable transportation choices. These trends will collectively enhance user experience, accessibility, and environmental consciousness in the travel industry. - The Role of Big Data and Analytics in Shaping Future Trends

12. CONCLUSION

The trajectory of travel booking has evolved from traditional methods to a digital landscape infused with advanced technologies. As we move forward, the integration of emerging technologies such as Augmented Reality (AR) and Virtual Reality (VR) will redefine the booking experience, offering immersive previews of destinations. Additionally, the rise of voice-activated bookings and a growing emphasis on sustainability promise to enhance convenience and environmental consciousness in the travel industry, shaping a more seamless, responsible, and personalized journey for travellers worldwide.

REFERENCES

Balasubramanian, S., Sethi, J. S., Ajayan, S., & Paris, C. M. (2022). An enabling Framework for Blockchain in Tourism. *Information Technology & Tourism*, 24(2), 165–179. DOI: 10.1007/s40558-022-00229-6

Bulchand-Gidumal, J. (2020). *Impact of Artificial Intelligence in Travel*. Tourism, and Hospitality., DOI: 10.1007/978-3-030-05324-6_110-1

Dias, S., & Afonso, V. (2021). Impact of Mobile Applications in Changing the Tourist Experience. European Journal of Tourism. *Hospitality and Recreation.*, 11(1), 113–120. DOI: 10.2478/ejthr-2021-0011

Ding, K., Niu, Y., & Choo, W. C. (2023, June 8). The evolution of Airbnb research: A systematic literature review using structural topic modeling. *Heliyon*, 9(6), e17090. DOI: 10.1016/j.heliyon.2023.e17090 PMID: 37484274

Dudás, G., Boros, L., & Vida, G. (2017). Comparing the temporal changes of air-fares on online travel agency websites and metasearch engines. *Tourism (Zagreb)*, 65, 187–203.

Elhaj, M. (2012). Preferences for Online vs. Traditional Travel Reservation. *Asean Journal of Hospitality and Tourist.*, 10(2), 100–109. DOI: 10.5614/ajht.2011.10.2.03

García, G., Dos Anjos, S., & Doğan, S.GARCİA. (2021). Online Travel Agencies and Their Role in the Tourism Industry. [AHTR]. *Advances in Hospitality and Tourism Research*, 10(3), 361–386. Advance online publication. DOI: 10.30519/ahtr.865546

Gretzel, U., & Yoo, K.-H. (2008). Use and Impact of Online Travel Reviews. *Information and Communication Technologies in Tourism*, 2008, 35–46. DOI: 10.1007/978-3-211-77280-5_4

Guizzardi, A., Pons, F., Angelini, G., & Ranieri, E. (2020). Big data from dynamic pricing: A smart approach to tourism demand forecasting. *International Journal of Forecasting*, 37(3), 1049–1060. Advance online publication. DOI: 10.1016/j.ijforecast.2020.11.006

Hall, C. M., Prayag, G., Safonov, A., Coles, T., Gössling, S., & Naderi Koupaei, S. (2022). Airbnb and the sharing economy. *Current Issues in Tourism*, 25(19), 3057–3067. DOI: 10.1080/13683500.2022.2122418

Hong, J. (2018). Rise of the Sharing Economy and the Future of Travel and Tourism Industry. *Journal of Business and Hotel Management.*, 07(2). Advance online publication. DOI: 10.4172/2169-0286.1000180

Khan, Ms & Irfan, Zainab & Muley, Kirti. (2023). CHATBOT ADOPTION IN TRAVEL AND TOURISM SERVICES. 2.

Lee, H., & Guillet, D. (2013). An Examination of the Relationship between Online Travel Agents and Hotels: A Case Study of Choice Hotels International and Expedia. com. *Cornell Hospitality Quarterly*, 54(1), 95–107. DOI: 10.1177/1938965512454218

Liao, Rouya. (2020). The value of traditional travel agency in the digital age.

Martin-Fuentes, E., & Mellinas, J. (2018). Hotels that most rely on Booking.com – online travel agencies (OTAs) and hotel distribution channels. *Tourism Review*, 73(4), 465–479. DOI: 10.1108/TR-12-2017-0201

Meng, Weiyi. (2009). Metasearch Engines. .DOI: 10.1007/978-0-387-39940-9_217

Muñoz, Andrés & del Vas, Ginesa & Yi, Yee. (2019). An integral mobile application for pre-travel, on-site and post-travel stages. 4. 7-17.

Namasudra, Suyel & Akkaya, Kemal. (2023). Introduction to Blockchain Technology. .DOI: 10.1007/978-981-19-8730-4_1

Pesonen, Juho & Tussyadiah, Iis. (2017). Peer-to-peer accommodation: drivers and user profiles. .DOI: 10.1007/978-3-319-51799-5

Psefti, Dimitra & Poulaki, Ioulia & Alkistis, Papaioannou & Katsoni, Vicky. (2021). The Evolution of Online Travel Agencies in the Last Decade: E-Travel SA as an Exceptional Paradigm. .DOI: 10.1007/978-3-030-72469-6_40

Takale, Dattatray & Damke, Sahil & Mehra, Sujal & Burkule, Sanskruti & Tadge, Nidhi. (2024). Applications of Blockchain in Tourism Industry.

Tandafatu, N., Ermilinda, L., Darkel, M., & Brekmans, Y. (2024). Digital Transformation in Tourism: Exploring the Impact of Technology on Travel Experiences. *International Journal of Multidisciplinary Approach Sciences and Technologies.*, 1(1), 55–64. DOI: 10.62207/w3vsg352

Thees, H., Erschbamer, G., & Pechlaner, H. (2020). The Application of Blockchain in Tourism: Use Cases in the Tourism Value System. *European Journal of Tourism Research*, 26, 2602. Advance online publication. DOI: 10.54055/ejtr.v26i.1933

Domínguez Vila, Trinidad & Araújo, Noelia & Brea, José Antonio & Alén, Elisa. (2017). Tourism Search and Metasearch Engines for Online Booking:. .DOI: 10.4018/978-1-5225-1054-3.ch003

Xiang, Z., & Gretzel, U. (2010). Role of Social Media in Online Travel Information Search. *Tourism Management*, 31(2), 179–188. DOI: 10.1016/j.tourman.2009.02.016

Chapter 8
Revolutionizing Air Travel in India:
The Impact of Digiyatra

Partho Pratim Seal
https://orcid.org/0000-0001-6867-8713
Welcomgroup Graduate School of Hotel Admininstration, India & Manipal Academy of Higher Education, India

Nagendra Yadav
https://orcid.org/0009-0008-9743-9250
Welcomgroup Graduate School of Hotel Administration, India & Manipal Academy of Higher Education, India

Rupam Konar
https://orcid.org/0000-0002-3235-3842
Centre for Research and Innovation in Tourism, Taylor's University, Malaysia

ABSTRACT

Digital technology has transformed various sectors with aviation not being exceptional. Digiyatra a government-promoted app enhances the traveller's experience by streamlining the operation. A blockchain-based identity management system Digiyatra uses a digital identity system which stores travelers' information on a distributed ledger. The airports and the airlines adopt the system to enhance the security of travellers, reduce the waiting queues in airports, and provide seamless travel and great experience. The chapter explores the revolutionary role of Digiyatra in air travel in India. The study uses online reviews of travellers about their experience using the app. The findings of the study state that security, experience, efficiency, and digitization are key factors for adopting digiyatra. The study's results will assist the government in understanding adopting digital technologies which can redefine

DOI: 10.4018/979-8-3693-6562-5.ch008

the Indian aviation industry and make it future-ready

INTRODUCTION

The aviation sector in the last decade has witnessed a rapid transformation which is influenced by external factors and innovative digital technologies (Pereira et al., 2021).Air travel has become a main mode of travel in Asian countries including India (Chaouk et al., 2019). Domestic travel in India has received tremendous growth in the last few years. India currently is one of the largest (domestic) civil aviation markets of the world with more than seventy per cent of travellers being domestic. The increase in aviation demand is mainly because of the rising working population especially the rising middle class and the business and leisure travel. It is advised that travellers arrive at the airport at least two hours before a domestic flight and at least three hours before an international flight for security check as it takes about 1.5 to 3 hrs for visa process checking of documents and passports which sometimes have long queues (Sorenson, 2018).

With the increase and the massive volume of air travellers streamlining them along with securing the airport is of prime importance. Considering streamlining of security in airports across the world requires the adoption of innovative technology for enhancing the travellers' journeys. It is believed that there will be a paradigm shift from paper to paperless with the usage of biometrics at airports. The efficiency in the airports is reimagined by offering an incredibly seamless and hassle-free experience (Sorenson, 2018). Passengers at the airport go through a cumbersome process of planning and scheduling, check-in steps, baggage management and security clearance which many times do reduce the overall satisfaction of air travellers. The emerging technologies use blockchain to enhance the digital identity and data privacy (Back, 2017) of travelers at the airport with the usage of facial recognition systems.

The facial recognition system is a technology-driven application which can identify and verify individual images and match them with digital images which is already inscribed. The recognition systems are computer-based security systems which detect and identify the human face. The main function of a facial recognition system is the neural mechanism system for face perception like the distance between the eyes, the shape of cheekbones along with other distinguishable features. The measures are tallied with the entire database of pictures to obtain the perfect match (Guleria et al., 2024). The face identification research and match it against a database to identify the face of an individual. As it is difficult to remember the name and face of an individual who may have been on the wanted list, facial recognition will automatically identify a person entering the airport as it will track the image of an individual and compare it with a database of photographs. The facial recognition tracks by capturing images of individuals and then using an algorithm to compare them with the database of photographs and alerts the security if there is a match. Any filter does not influence the system like age, gender, race, or country of origin (Khan & Efthymiou, 2021). The facial recognition in airports could also restrict employees to only those areas where they are authorized to enter and can alert security if any unauthorized entry happens. Facial recognition technology is used autonomously to process passengers at checkpoints from entry at the airport to aeroplane boarding.

Knowing about the traveller's composition and passenger evaluation of airline services helps in planning aviation infrastructure to meet the future demands of aviation in Indian cities. The traveller identification procedure in India has consistently been manual verification with paperwork, creating bottlenecks. The usage of hard copies of paper-based identification like identity proofs, flight tickets and boarding passes at each touch point does influence both the security personnel and also the traveller's experience. The multiple-identity verification with travel documents at the airport causes inconvenience to the passenger and is not suitable considering the passenger growth in larger airports in India. In developing countries like India although there is a concern about applying digital technologies the application of it in real-time is not as in some developed nations. For this, facilities like self-check-in are necessary for travellers to make their lives more convenient (La & Heiets, 2021). With the growing number of travellers at the airport and the security concern, the government of India conceptualized a national biometric digital identification system for air travel in 2016. Digitalization is the adaptation of using different digital technologies to change various aspects of people's surroundings (Gray & Rumpe, 2015). Researchers (Lenka et al., 2017) believe that digitalization helps industry and firms to change their strategy and performance. The core of digitalization is not restricted to data as it needs to be modelled by analyzing and summarizing the characteristics along with the obtained modes of digitization which is required for resolving requirements in various fields. After policy debate and technological planning, the Digi Yatra program was approved for country-wide implementation. The DigiYatra enables paperless travel and rejects repeated identity checks. The main motto was to provide a seamless travel experience by eliminating multiple time presenting of identity cards and other travel documents. The Digi Yatra provides a seamless air travel experience by removing the need for presenting identity information and travel documents for security checks. The travellers instead have to enroll once in Digi Yatra and they can upload their biometric authentication at the airport security check areas. The study considers examining Digi Yatra to check regarding improving the travellers experience and also security as the entire digitized process is encrypted for end-to-end air journeys. The research aims to find if Digi Yatra could enhance the travellers' experience along with the necessary security required for air travel. The study will also state the travelers challenges and perceptions which are linked to the digital ID system. The findings will help Digi Yatra to be more robust and contribute to a broader global discourse by creating appropriate infrastructure for air travel in India.

REVIEW OF LITERATURE

Digi Yatra is a central biometrics–linked database which recognizes boarding passes and flight details. The traveller at a respective location has to pass through a facial recognition scan which is tallied with the database for verification at all entry points, security checkpoints, and also at boarding gates. The program was launched in August 2022 in the country and is currently operational in 13 airports and 14 more airports are to be added soon. The advent of Digi Yatra is a major change towards modernization and digital air travel in the country. Although it is a technological transformation still there are concerns regarding privacy, exclusion and optimum implementation of the project. DigiYatra uses facial recognition technology, which makes terminal entry and security seamless, without any hassles and a paperless process. The DigiYatra application is a decentralized mobile-based identification storage platform which can store identification documents and travel documents. The platform introduced by a combination of the Ministry of Civil Aviation (MOCA) and DigiYatra Foundation is for creating a digital society. DigiYatra is the future for air travel which enables the automatic digital processing of flyers reducing the travelers' waiting time and making the boarding process faster and seamless as in Figure 1. The concept of DigiYatra is on four pillars connecting travellers, connected flying, connected airports, and connected systems which ensures easy entry at all checkpoints. The data in DigiYatra is saved in an encrypted format with blockchain technology being used. All the data is stored in the passenger's phones and the data shared with the airport is removed 24 hours after the traveler completes the journey. DigiYatra ensures enhanced security at the airport as the passenger data is validated along with the airline's departure control system which allows only designated passengers to enter the terminal.

Figure 1. Flow chart

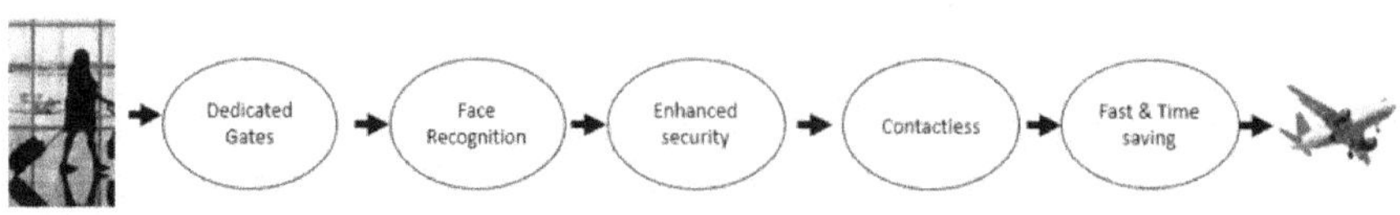

The DigiYatra foundation is engaged in DigiYatra central ecosystem which aims to provide a seamless and memorable digital experience and considers a real-time selfie-based facial biometric validation for its authentication purpose. The main mission of the DigiYatra assures a seamless journey with a firm sense of ease for passengers from embarkation to arrival. DigiYatra prioritizes sustainability with a transition to a complete paperless automated authentication and verification process slashing the carbon emissions and moving towards a more ecologically responsible future. To preserve data security and privacy DigiYatra adopts a technology of decentralized identity, self-sovereign identity and verified credentials enabling authentication and verification which does not store or accumulate data on the server. The blockchain technology used by DigiYatra works in the background enabling it to maintain privacy. The blockchain runs on computers which are in multiple locations so the data is not stored in a single database to avoid the risk associated with one central database. The transparency of blockchain provides increased confidence as transactions are observable and irretrievable and also the clearance of recorded transactions (Tapscott & Tapscott, 2017). With utilizing DigiYatra application the user undergoes authentication followed by retrieving data from either DigiLocker or Aadhaar. After the retrieval of data, the same is matched with the Aadhaar. On confirmation, the authenticated selfie along with user information including name, gender, date of birth, and masked Aadhaar form a verified credential stored in Digi Yatra Wallet. The data obtained from the Aadhar is deleted as nothing is stored on any server. The entities which are integrated into the DigiYatra platform like airports readily acknowledge and validate verified credentials which allow entry to the airport. The exchange of information along with validation is initiated by the user for accessing the services and the important data is shared by the traveller when a boarding pass is necessary mostly 24-48 hrs before the journey. After the departure of the flight the airport automatically deletes the travelers' data. Audits regularly ensure compliance along with checks at airports that verify timely data. For security reasons a mandatory policy is made by which no minors can create a verifiable credential without the consent of the guardian. At first, the guardian or the parent has to create their verified credential before the same is created for the minors. The DigiYatra an ambitious biometric facial recognition program aims to transform the end-to-end air transit experience with touchless, paperless processing by digital identity authentication. Biometrics is used for authentication and identification as it is challenging to match the data with what was taken previously. The authentication is used for verifying and a final decision is made on the degree of similarity. The biometric system tallies the scanned data with those already captured for comparison. The biometric technologies consist of both hardware and software, the identification device is the hardware that helps to collect, read and compare the biometric data. The biometric data are obtained from an individual unique to that person. The software fixed in the biometric technology processes the biometric data. The software and the hardware ensure that the data is captured and extracted match. The user adoption pattern is used to understand the acceptance of the facial recognition digital ID and the apprehensions that impact voluntary enrollment. The pace of adoption depends on how the travellers switch over to biometrics-based air travel.

The usage of biometric identification is widely accepted in the development of modern airports. A lot of research has happened to examine the application, opportunities and challenges which are associated with incorporating biometric systems at the airports. Initial studies (Souto et al., 2013) analyzed facial recognition systems and later used for travellers at the Miami and Washington Dallas airports to have a fair improvement in processing times at airports. A study on the initial implementation of biometrics in UK airports discussed the privacy concerns of travellers. Trials with facial biometrics to expedite the security check at the airport in Australia are also considered (Bromberg et al., 2020). The biometric facial recognition software does identify people by crosschecking different facial features and allowing the face to be used for access at the airport. Along with other countries opting for biometric and facial recognition systems India pioneered an Aadhar-based biometric ID system which integrates travellers' data with the Aadhar data for aviation security. There has been a risk to data privacy and surveillance of Aadhar as some of the data was leaked and automatic facial recognition increases the risk of data stealing. The pace by which the transformation to digitalization depends critically on how the travellers embrace the biometrics air travel model. The research study provides a framework to find whether a digital innovation like DigiYatra achieves its goal when implemented on a large scale across all airports.

This study is conducted to understand the implementation of DigiYatra and how it will provide a seamless, futuristic air transit for the citizens of India. The study focuses mainly on passenger experience, security, and adoption aspects of Digi Yatra and how it will enhance future travellers' convenience by reducing the time spent. The study adopted a qualitative approach with semi-structured interviews to assess the traveller's perception of a hassle-free air travel facility with biometrics and facial recognition. It will also probe the impact of DigiYatra on airport security as data privacy and surveillance risks are common for any centralized biometric database. It also considers how digitized passenger verification will be for convenience reducing the time spent on travel. The study findings will help to obtain the key learnings about DigiYatra and how India can make biometric travel more efficient, trusted, and inclusive for travellers. It will also display globally how facial recognition could be used for digital identity by the aviation sector. As India moves on with its digital transformation of air transit it can lead to other countries considering similar initiatives. The research aims to provide evidence-based insights which support balancing innovation aspiration with ground realities for maximum benefit of the public. We can summarize that the study will help to understand how the biometric digital ID system delivers a smoother, safer and more modern air transit for one of the world's fastest-growing aviation market and a road for the country's digital journey.

METHODOLOGY

The study adopted a qualitative approach by using semi-structured interviews. The qualitative method allows us to obtain answers to questions which are difficult for the quantitative methods to conclude with (Savin-Baden & Major, 2013). The qualitative study helps to identify variables which can be later analyzed quantitatively, or quantitative measures may not describe them appropriately (Marshall & Rossman, 2014). The face-to-face interviews were conducted for the study with extreme care taken to follow up while collecting and analyzing the data. The study targeted frequent air travellers using the airports which had DigiYatra facilities. The travellers who had used DigiYatra were the only respondents in the study and had used it at least once in three months. The data was collected in two cities Delhi and Bengaluru as they were the major airports in North and South India where DigiYatra facility is available. The semi-structured questions asked in the interview were refined with consultation of academicians and industry practitioners. The questions were open-ended to obtain maximum input and the best insights (Marshall & Rossman, 2014). To minimise the bias during the interview and for data analysis precautionary steps were taken in which initially the questions were generic followed by specific questions. A purposive sampling was used in the study and appropriate care was taken during the interview so the interviewee would not be influenced. During the interview process few steps were followed the conversation was followed with the interviewee with proper referencing stating the objective, considering travelers' experience with the DigiYatra platform and also interviewing the respondent with a semi-structured question. The responses were collected from travellers during March, April, and May 2024 with each interview lasting 25 to 30 min.

The data obtained from the travellers were analyzed by thematic analysis where the data was narrowed for coding the interviews and then they were categorized further into themes and sub-themes as necessary. To ensure the reliability and consistency of data adequate interviews were conducted considering that similar responses will be obtained for saturation. The process was conducted till the responses obtained reached a saturation point. All the respondent's points were considered and the outcome was reported. Care and consistency were undertaken for collecting and recording data to confirm the intended meaning of the respondent which was reviewed.

RESULTS AND FINDINGS

The study findings state that travellers have adopted Digiyatra at airports which provide their services. The themes developed from the study fall under four main categories security, experience digitization, and efficiency. Figure 2 presents the framework that categorizes each of the themes of travellers using DigiYatra. The preference for adopting Digiyatra is for security as there is no reason for travellers to carry their boarding passes and identity proofs. The experience of the travellers opting for Digiyatra is quite satisfactory with some having a great experience. The digitization of the entire process is also a reason why travellers have adopted for it. Digiyatra has changed how travellers' time is spent at the airport entry and in the security check area as the efficiency of the process has a positive impact on travellers.

Figure 2. Chart

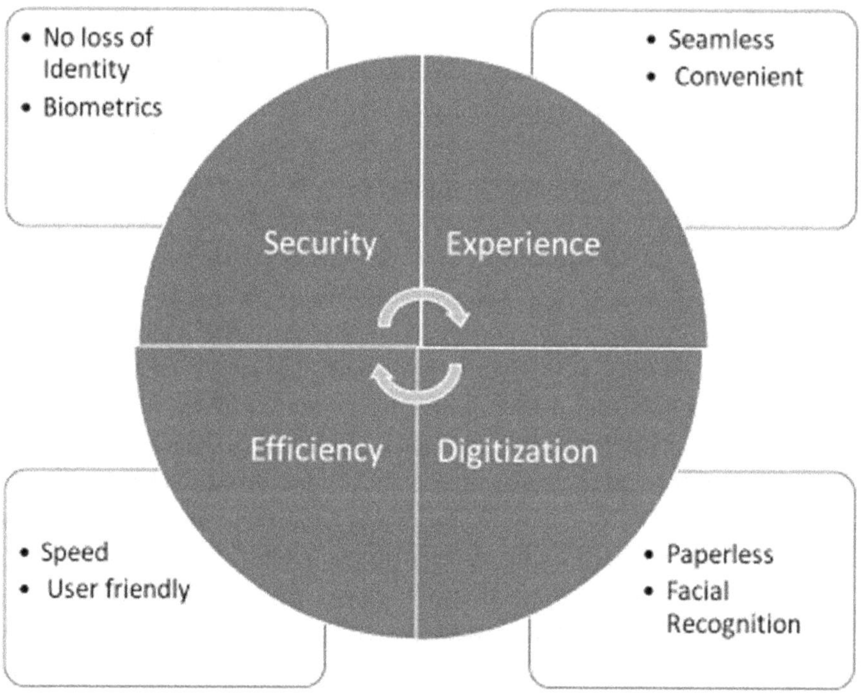

Security

Facial recognition and biometrics are used to authenticate the traveller's identity at an airport to meet the needs of the customs department and protect the country's borders.

"There is a risk of the use of sensitive biometric data for boarding which is essentially shared or will this over-surveillance extend in time to every single movement an individual does? As an individual who is the owner of the data, do I have any confidence that there are adequate controls in place for the entire lifecycle of the data, including deletion?

The biometric data is held on the device in a secure wallet. The transmission is encrypted from end to end and the server purges data 24 hours after flight departure. The document says they at least confirm to NIST CSF, ISO 27001 and the Data Privacy Act.

The security feature of Digi Yatra does not open the gates if the flight departure time is beyond a certain period of about 6 hrs. Digiyatra will be more secure while non-Digiyatra will ask for more scrutiny."

Most travellers believe that biometric authentication has enhanced airport security and reduced the risk associated with forged identities and documents. The Digiyatra also strengthened the security protocol with other identity databases which are necessary for law enforcement.

Experience

The travel experience is arbitrated also by speed, the coherence of a service and also on its reliability (Mahmoudi & Duman, 2015).

"Used DigiYatra 20 + times during the last few quarters, and surprisingly has been a seamless experience, saving time especially Delhi airport. Also with so much of personally identifiable data openly available and shared, it makes little difference in opting out of a single/ app service like DigiYatra.

Yes it has made our lives simpler. The airports are anyways high- security zones with scores of cameras recording our moves. We assume that this data will be with the government but do we know or care with which entity? All-in-all, it is a fair deal to use the app if it saves time as our data is anyway public.

I had to take an early flight out of Hyderabad. I reached the airport at 4.45 Am after completing check -in online with just a cabin bag in hand. By 4.52 Am I was at the gate having been able to skip the lines thanks to Digiyatra. Considering that the seven-minute timeframe included the time it took for me to walk from the car to the departure ramp to the airport entrance. Overall experience is great."

The findings do state that Digiyatra has improved the convenience of the travellers by reducing time spent in the airport queues. The verification process of the travellers has also been quick, leading to faster movement of the travellers to the boarding gates.

Digitization

The digital transformation in airports applies to the self-service check kiosks at airport entry points and on self-check boarding gates. Air travel digitisation has been the focus with biometric boarding, digital bag drop, and electronic passports with automated passenger processing and luggage handling being implemented at various airports in the country.

> *"Big fan of Digiyatra as I use it frequently at Mumbai, Delhi, and Bengaluru airports. I had put my bag & laptop through screening and just walked through the security check-in 30 seconds. With Digiyatra you don't need to carry your boarding pass & driving license you can just flash your face & smile. Recently though Digiyatra in Delhi, I reached the boarding gate from the airport entrance in just 15 minutes.*
>
> *The credentials are validated after the photograph of the self is validated against the Aadhar as this and the uploaded boarding pass help a smooth entry to the airport."*

Digitization in India is by Aadhaar biometrical identification which is a digital database comprising data of almost all Indian citizens and creates a seamless, paperless travel experience. Aadhaar from the beginning was a surveillance project disguised as a development intervention (Abraham, 2019). It is stated to be the first step for the digitalisation of India.

Efficiency

> *"Digiyatra since its launch has been a breeze at the airports. I mostly travel for business trips which makes it easier with DigiYatra which has separate entry gates"*
>
> *Digiyatra is a great time saver and gives you a VIP feel as you bypass the queue and enter the airport without waiting. No boarding passes, ID proofs, as you just stand and wait for the gate to be opened as soon as your scan is done. My last few travels were without hard copies of the boarding pass at the entrance. Truly Digital India.*
>
> *Digiyatra is still faster. From a technical standpoint, the system has to authenticate your face with only those who are expected to enter the airport in the next few hours as it is faster than the overworked CISF staff"*

The DigiYatra has reduced the average passenger processing time by 10-12 minutes. The queues in large airports especially in the morning were too long and travellers had to be in the airport quite ahead of schedule. With DigiYatra the traveller's time in entry and the security check has been considerably reduced.

DISCUSSION AND CONCLUSION

The study findings suggest that the DigiYatra program expedites air travel by reducing time and improving the convenience of airport officials by enhancing speed and efficiency. The data from the interview also states that enrollment in DigiYatra is less because of low awareness, registration complexities and the fear of data misuse. Some travellers are also apprehensive about surveillance of their facial data misuse although biometrics is essential for security. It is also observed that Digiyatra improved security by reducing the forgery of paper documents. The centralized database assists in real-time verification however the effectiveness is based on how the data is kept secure from leaks. Although digitization has shown early chances of achieving goals there are challenges to the adoption and travellers perception which are to be addressed. For the Digi Yatra to be operational to its full potential it necessitates upgraded infrastructure, creating awareness amongst the travellers and building trust. A combined interpretation of the sentiments of all stakeholders could help guide India towards a more responsible, sustainable, and digitized journey.

The study investigates the role of DigiYatra in air travel in India. The study has few limitations as the data was collected from only two big airports in India and the opinion of travellers and their experience in other airports could not be generalized. Though the respondents were briefed before about the purpose of the study the questions were answered by the travellers as per their own experience and understanding. Most of the travellers were in a hurry as they were leaving the airport and the response was brief and not detailed. The travellers in the study were mostly business travellers so the experience of the leisure travellers could not be ascertained. Future studies should be undertaken to understand the leisure travellers' perspectives on Digiyatra and compare and contrast the same with business travellers.

In the future, research may also look into other unexplored dimensions like air-ground transport integration and other airline perspective, comparing studies across nations, and evaluating cybersecurity concerns in depth which will assist in air travel digitization. The study findings will help us understand the travellers' different views about the various aspects of Digiyatra. To this, the present study provides the Digiyatra operators and managers with options to formulate strategies to utilize both facial recognition and biometrics for the digitization of airports in the country.

The findings of the current study also state how the combination of biometric authentication with facial recognition and the centralized database helps to heighten the security of travellers at the airport. However, it also acknowledges the challenges requiring refinement so that Digiyatra can be efficient and safe and implemented in airports nationwide.

REFERENCES

Back, A. (2017). Using Blockchain for Digital Identity & Crypto Assets. Retrieved from medium.com/blockchain-review/self-sovereign-identity-and-the-digitization -of-realworld-assets-738e87dc530c

Bromberg, D. E., Charbonneau, É., & Smith, A. (2020). Public support for facial recognition via police body-worn cameras: Findings from a list experiment. *Government Information Quarterly*, 37(1), 101415. Advance online publication. DOI: 10.1016/j.giq.2019.101415

Chaouk, M., Pagliari, R., & Miyoshi, C. (2019). A critical review of airport privatisation in the Kingdom of Saudi Arabia: Case study of Medina Airport. *Case Studies on Transport Policy*, 7(2), 433–442. DOI: 10.1016/j.cstp.2019.02.001

Gray, J., & Rumpe, B. (2015). Models for Digitalization. *Software & Systems Modeling*, 4(4), 1319–1320. DOI: 10.1007/s10270-015-0494-9

Guleria, A., Krishan, K., Sharma, V., & Kanchan, T. (2024). *Global adoption of facial recognition technology with special reference to India—Present status and future recommendations*. Medicine, Science and the Law/Medicine, Science and the Law., DOI: 10.1177/00258024241227717

Khan, N., & Efthymiou, M. (2021). The use of biometric technology at airports: The case of customs and border protection (CBP). *International Journal of Information Management Data Insights,* 1 (2) 2021.100049, ISSN 2667-0968

La, J., & Heiets, I. (2021). The Impact Of Digitalization And Intelligentization On Air Transportation System. *Aviation*, 25(3), 159–170. DOI: 10.3846/aviation.2021.15336

Lenka, S., Parida, V., & Wincent, J. (2016). Digitalization capabilities as enablers of Value Co-Creation in servitizing firms. *Psychology and Marketing*, 34(1), 92–100. DOI: 10.1002/mar.20975

Mahmoudi, N., & Duman, E. (2015). Detecting credit card fraud by modified Fisher discriminant analysis. *Expert Systems with Applications*, 42(5), 2510–2516. DOI: 10.1016/j.eswa.2014.10.037

Marshall, C., & Rossman, G. B. (2014). *Designing Qualitative Research.* Sage publications.

Pereira, B. A., Lohmann, G., & Houghton, L. (2021). Innovation and value creation in the context of aviation: A Systematic Literature Review. *Journal of Air Transport Management*, 94, 102076. DOI: 10.1016/j.jairtraman.2021.102076

Savin-Baden, M., & Major, C. H. (2013). *Qualitative Research: The Essential Guide to Theory and Practice*. Routledge.

Sorenson, A. (2018). A Paradigm Shift in How We Travel. Retrieved from https://www.linkedin.com/pulse/paradigm-shift-how-we-travel-arne-sorenson1/?trackingId=a4BJrFrz9F1wMNEGQ6Yyxg%3D%3D&lipi=urn%3Ali%3Apage%3 Ad_flagship3_search_srp_content%3BnWePi4GxTuq7E3Fm%2FwAfdQ%3D%3D&licu=urn%3Ali%3Acontrol%3Ad_flagship3_search_srp_co

Souto, T., Baptista, A., Tavares, D., Queirós, C., & António, M. (2013). Facial emotional recognition in schizophrenia: Preliminary results of the virtual reality program for facial emotional recognition. *Archives of Clinical Psychiatry*, 40(4), 129–134. DOI: 10.1590/S0101-60832013000400001

Tapscott, D., & Tapscott, A. (2017). How blockchain will change organizations. *MIT Sloan Management Review*, 58(2), 10–13.

Chapter 9 Navigating Cryptocurrency Regulation: Trailblazing Legal Strategies for a Borderless Future

Bhupinder Singh
https://orcid.org/0009-0006-4779-2553
Sharda University, India

Christian Kaunert
https://orcid.org/0000-0002-4493-2235
Dublin City University, Ireland & University of South Wales, UK

ABSTRACT

Cryptocurrency, based on block-chain technology is defined as a decentralized digital peer-to-peer currency. The emergence of cryptocurrency is a boon for future economy; it has been tagged along with innumerable practical and legal issues including risks associated with consumer's protection such as theft, misinformation, and unpredictability; complexity surrounding the legal characterization of cryptocurrencies, illegal activities driven through cryptocurrencies and lack of uniform comprehensive global legislation to address the issues and challenges associated with it. Though valiant efforts have been made by few countries like Canada, United Kingdom, Switzerland, El Salvador etc. to formulate broad range of rules and regulations for digital currency but other developed and developing economies has largely remained silent on the debate surrounding the regulation of cryptocurrencies. This chapter seeks to explore into risk posed by digital currency and provide a need for formulation of legal structure appropriate for regulating

DOI: 10.4018/979-8-3693-6562-5.ch009

the cryptocurrencies.

1. INTRODUCTION

Cryptocurrency, a form of Fiat money is a digital/electronic currency without any physical existence but represents value (Thapaliya & Sharma, 2023). Whereas, blockchain technology is an electronic database that is distributed among the nodes of a peer-to-peer network, it assists in collection and storage of information when a cryptocurrency is bought, sold, or exchanged (Djenna et al., 2023) (Awajan, 2023). The current state of cryptocurrency is opaque and its swift evolution in the last decade has led to increased regulatory scrutiny by the international organisations and government of various jurisdictions worldwide to formulate a comprehensive legislation or regulation to address the risk and opportunities offers (Attaran & Deb, 2018) (Brotcke, 2022). Cryptocurrencies are digital "coins" or "tokens" secured through cryptography (Abebe et al., 2020) (Elluri et al., 2023). These assets exist entirely in digital form and utilize blockchain or other decentralized ledger technologies (DLTs) to operate on a decentralized network (Hagendorff, 2019) (Singh & Kaunert, 2024). This setup allows users to transact directly without the need for a central authority (Thapaliya & Sharma, 2023) (Dash et al., 2022).

Cryptocurrencies can be instantly transferred at a peer-to-peer (P2P) level without intermediaries like banks or central banks (Barocas et al., 2023) (Narayana & Sreedevi, 2023). In principle and barring additional cryptographic measures or security breaches, cryptocurrency transactions are fully traceable and immutable with users remaining pseudonymous unless their assets are linked to a validated know your customer (KYC) file through an exchange (Mhlanga, 2021) (Pocher et al., 2023). Regulators worldwide should develop frameworks to responsibly monitor and guide cryptocurrency activities within their jurisdictions (Chen et al., 2018) (Tyagi et al., 2020). These frameworks should ensure fair market conduct, competition, the application and enforcement of tax rules, and consumer protection, while also fostering the growth of a lucrative cryptocurrency-based economy (Cao et al., 2021). Given that cryptocurrencies are cross-jurisdictional, regulatory challenges extend beyond national borders (Alazab et al., 2023). Regulators should strive for cross-jurisdictional standards to create regulatory clarity, close loopholes and mitigate regulatory arbitrage, while ensuring inclusivity for all users (Zhang et al., 2022). Well-designed cryptocurrency regulations in various jurisdictions have already encouraged crypto-based innovations and efficiencies in finance and commerce, especially for cross-border transactions (Singh, 2023). Regulators should examine these examples to enhance their understanding of the essential parameters and variables in designing regulatory frameworks (Lee & Shin, 2020).

Figure 1. Displays the dimensions of the introduction split sections

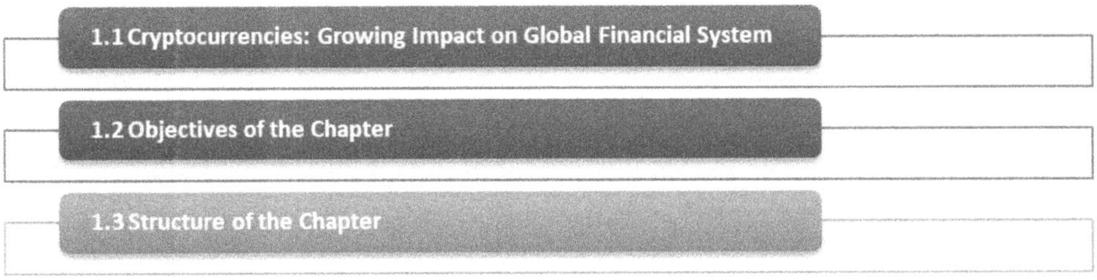

(Source- Original)

1.1 Cryptocurrencies: Growing Impact on Global Financial System

Macroeconomically speaking, careful examination is necessary to understand how the usage of cryptocurrencies and the function of commercial banks in the world's financial services industry interact (AJ & Kaythry, 2023). Financial regulators believe that the present cryptocurrency systems are deficient in crucial aspects that sovereign monetary regimes need in order to oversee and regulate a nation's financial stability (Li et al., 2020). Cryptocurrencies are unable to respond to threats to price stability and the economy by modifying supply in response to shocks to demand since they often lack flexible monetary policies (Cheng et al., 2021). Like supply shocks in traditional financial markets, monetary authorities cannot dampen the impact of supply shocks on cryptocurrency prices by influencing demand (Bhuvaneshwari & Kaythry, 2023). The lack of central banks acting as the lender of last resort (LOLR) for cryptocurrencies may make runs more likely in the event that this central banking function is removed (Muhlhoff, 2021). A further worry for central banks is that if cryptocurrencies become widely used, a nation's monetary sovereignty may be compromised if fewer people use the local unit of account (Saltz et al., 2019). Central bankers are concerned that, even if there aren't any examples of this happening just yet, it would increase domestic price volatility since the central bank would be less successful in implementing monetary policy (Hoijtink & Planque-van Hardeveld, 2022).

1.2 Objectives of the Chapter

This chapter has the following objectives to:

Examine Current Regulatory Frameworks

- Analyse regulatory frameworks that are currently in place for cryptocurrencies in different jurisdictions.

Propose Novel Legal Techniques

- Put forth novel legal techniques that can efficiently control cryptocurrencies in a globalized and quickly changing digital landscape.

Discuss Future Directions

- Recognize and prepare for potential obstacles to cryptocurrency regulation, such as those pertaining to international trade, consumer safety, sound financial practices, and emerging technologies.

Figure 2. Illuminates the objectives of the chapter

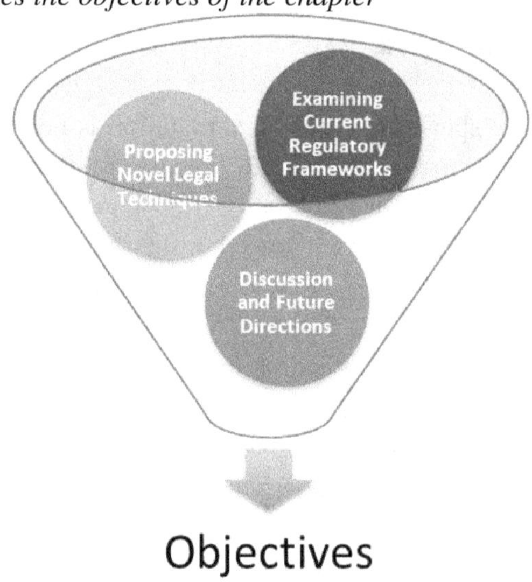

(Source- Original)

1.3 Structure of the Chapter

This chapter deeply dives into the multifarious dimensions of Navigating Cryptocurrency Regulation: Trailblazing Legal Strategies for a Borderless Future. Section 2 elaborates the Current Regulatory Landscape: Regulatory Approaches. Section 3 highlights the Challenges in Cryptocurrency Regulation. Section 4 discusses the Legal Implications of Emerging Technologies. Section 5 explores the Trailblazing Legal Strategies. Finally, Section 6 Conclude the Chapter with Future Scope.

Figure 3. Expresses the flow of this chapter

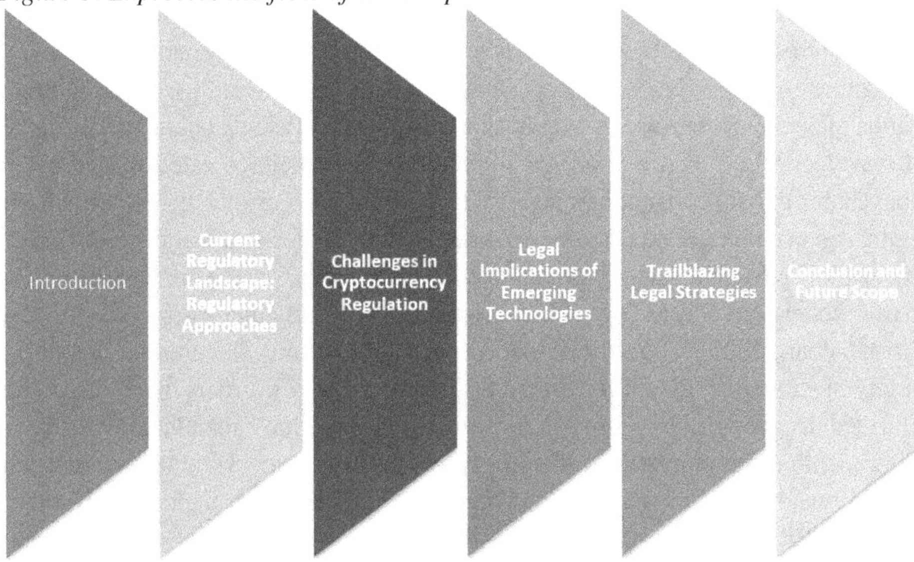

(Source- Original)

2. CURRENT REGULATORY LANDSCAPE: REGULATORY APPROACHES

Cryptocurrency is a digital asset not issued by any government, based on cryptographic algorithms, whose existence and transfer are confirmed and recorded on a ledger distributed across a network of independent computers known as "validators" (Utami et al., 2022) (Zhang et al., 2022) (Baker & Robinson, 2020). Before a cryptocurrency's existence or transfer can be recorded, the network's validators must reach consensus according to the network's protocol (Aziz & Andriansyah, 2023). This decentralized validator network architecture is designed to establish trust without a central authority, such as a government (Bao et al., 2022). Multiple entities operate independently under a shared governance framework, eliminating a single point of failure or control (McKendrick, 2019). This setup reduces the risk of double-spending while maintaining pseudonymity in transactions (Rai & Sahu, 2020). Validators use cryptographic tools extensively (but not exclusively) to ensure security (Sharma et al., 2023) (Varma et al., 2022).

Cryptocurrency is utilized as a utility on the network to incentivize node operators to validate transactions and guard against spam, distributed denial of service (DDoS), and other attacks (Tippins et al., 2021) (Lui & Lamb, 2018). Cryptocurrencies function as their own unit of account, though their acquisition price is often quoted in government-issued fiat currency (Mijwil et al., 2023) (Schmitt, 2020). Most cryptocurrency projects allow account addresses to be issued and currency to be transferred between sender and recipient without a central party and without requiring personal identification (Siwakoti et al., 2023) (Zhang et al., 2020). There are two types of cryptocurrencies: traditional cryptocurrencies, created by standalone blockchains like BTC (Bitcoin) and ETH (Ethereum), and cryptocurrencies that are digital representations of other assets, such as fiat-backed stablecoins like USDC issued by Circle 9Nassar & Kamal, 2021) (Alruwaili, 2023). This focuses solely on traditional cryptocurrencies, which are considered mathematics-driven protocols (Grimm et al., 2021). The nations that do provide consumer safeguards are using a variety of strategies (Dhoni & Kumar, 2023). To assist consumers in making more informed decisions, countries such as France and India have mandated that advertising mention the dangers involved in investing in cryptocurrencies (Kordzadeh & Ghasemaghaei, 2022) (Mijwil & Aljanabi, 2023). To lower the danger of theft, cryptocurrency asset service providers in South Korea, including exchanges and wallets, are required to receive an information security certificate from the Korea Internet and Security Agency (Sambasivan et al., 2021) (Singh, 2023). The laws against deceitful behavior and fraud have been put in place in nations like Australia and Japan (Singh, 2023). Even if these instances show the efforts being made by certain nations, legislators must work more to enact consumer protection laws in order to guarantee the security of cryptocurrency marketplaces (Zhang et al., 2023) (Singh, 2023) (Katyal, 2019).

3. CHALLENGES IN CRYPTOCURRENCY REGULATION

There are dozens of cryptocurrency networks and projects out there right now and each one has its own features, structures, and designs (Irfan et al., 2023) (Selbst & Barocas, 2018) (Chohan et al., 2023). The majority of these projects use distributed ledger systems, but there are two basic kinds of permissions for access: (1) permissionless, in which networks are open and any entity can send transactions, read the transaction history (ledger) or take part in transaction verification; and (2) permissioned, in which a governance framework restricts participation in these activities and the former, permissionless crypto currencies (Singh et al., 2023) (Sowmya et al., 2023) (Daugherty & Wilson, 2018) Also, there are differences in the ways such networks reach agreement among participating validators; some employ additional processes in addition to proof of stake (like ADA) and proof of labor (like BTC) (Swiatkowska, 2020) (Berk et al., 2021).

The use of cryptocurrency and digital assets by businesses, investors, and even certain central banks is generating increased interest and acceptance at the institutional and retail levels which is driving up regulatory activity in this area (Abbas, et al., 2024) (Sudhakar & Kumar, 2023) (Kochhar et al., 2023). The United States' regulatory environment is changing in tandem with market development, as lawmakers and state and federal authorities consider ways to bring clarity to the regulatory framework (Kaushik, 2024) (Liu et al., 2024). Protections for investors and customers, dangers associated with fraud and financial crimes, licensing, and chartering are some of the major topics being addressed (Rajkumar et al., 2023) (Nisha & Muthurajkumar, 2023). Regulators have several difficulties, one of which is correctly classifying the current crop of cryptocurrencies (Shukla et al., 2024). The recent developments in digital technology have led directly to the emergence of crypto assets, which provide new opportunities for financial transactions, investment, and trading (Paddalwar et al., 2023) (Itani et al., 2023). Cryptocurrencies are inherently complicated and disruptive, which makes classification challenging (Odeh & Abu Taleb, 2023) (Ortiz-Ruiz et al., 2024). The fast rate of innovation and market developments provide a challenge to regulators, perhaps resulting in oversight gaps (Ali et al., 2024).

It is difficult to obtain a thorough categorization in the market (Hamad, 2023). A method that's frequently employed is contrasting cryptocurrency assets with fiat money (Latif et al., 2024) (Anis et al., 2023) (Abdalrdha et al., 2023). The European Parliament's extensive investigation indicates that cryptocurrency assets are still not widely used as regular payment methods (AL-Dosari et al., 2024). A lot of researchers contend that tokens that behave like securities constitute a whole new class of assets, which includes cryptocurrencies (Ambika, 2024) (Aljuhani et al., 2023). Cryptocurrency assets are often regarded as investments because of their inherent worth and related advantages (Lone et al., 2023) (Messai & Seba, 2023). Customers who trade in cryptocurrency run a serious risk (Manimaran et al., 2023) (Nehinbe et al., 2023). Theft is becoming more prevalent, and one of the key features of cryptocurrency markets is their volatility, which is frequently caused by speculators (Ali & Farooq, 2023) (Escorcia-Gutierrez et al., 2023). Also, misleading advertising and misinformation make informed investment difficult (Kongsorot et al., 2023). It discovered that, in spite of these dangers, only one-third of the nations under investigation had put laws in place to safeguard consumers (Costa & Sofikitis, 2024) (Ali et al., 2024) (Tok & Chattopadhyay, 2023). There could be legal safeguards for participants in cryptocurrency marketplaces in other nations, but they are sometimes unproven or ambiguous laws (Wu et al., 2023) (Segovia-Vargas, 2024) (Lipsa & Dash, 2023).

Figure 4. Showcase the challenges in cryptocurrency regulation

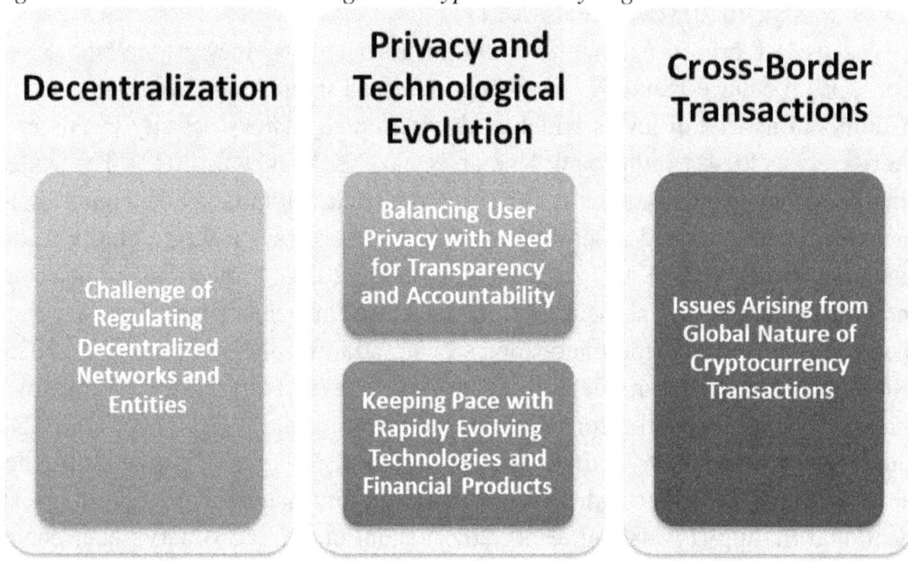

(Source- Original)

4. LEGAL IMPLICATIONS OF EMERGING TECHNOLOGIES

Since the launch of Bitcoin in 2009, cryptocurrencies have become a cutting-edge asset class that provide a substitute for conventional fiat money (Virmani et al., 2023) (Messai & Seba, 2023) (Venkatasubramanian et al., 2023). The improved transactional transparency, quicker processing, and easier access to financial services especially in areas with little banking are some of its advantages (Vatambeti & Mamidisetti, 2023) (Singh et al., 2024) (Das et al., 2023). With a market value of $1.6 trillion, the cryptocurrency industry has expanded rapidly over time to become a major player in the global financial ecosystem. This expansion is a result of cryptocurrencies' growing economic integration (Kumar et al., 2023) (Alabdulkreem et al., 2023) (Nandan & Dey, 2023). Cryptocurrencies do carry some danger, though, despite their growing appeal and the innovation they provide to the financial services industry as well as other industries (Priyadarshini et al., 2023) (Moustafa et al., 2023) (Afrifa et al., 2023).

The best approaches to address the distinct and occasionally unforeseen problems posed by cryptocurrencies are a constant source of assessment for regulators and politicians throughout the globe (Soliman et al., 2023) (Cao et al., 2024) (Abbas et al., 2024). In a short amount of time, cryptocurrencies have gone from being symbols of alternative systems and ideologies to becoming well-known assets that draw attention from investors, businesses, and even whole nations (Saha, 2024) (Al-Quayed et al., 2024) (Kumar et al., 2024). This asset class is becoming more popular, and with it, so is the regulatory environment around cryptocurrencies (Vasan et al., 2024) (Rathee et val., 2024). Cryptocurrencies and the underlying blockchains, building on earlier advances in distributed computing and encryption, present a new paradigm for the safe transmission, storing, and access of data and values (Sharma & Annaboina, 2024) (Gangula et al., 2024). This progression can be compared to how the internet developed (Niu et al., 2024) (Shaikh et al., 2024).

Figure 5. Displays the legal implications of emerging technologies

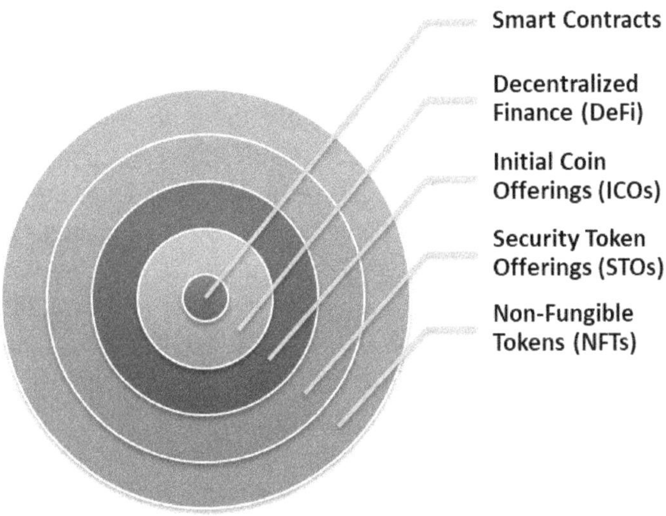

(Source- Original)

The regulatory environment that now governs cryptocurrencies and digital assets is dispersed and changing quickly (Plageras et al., 2024) (Demir & Serkan, 2024). A transaction may be subject to the authority of many federal and state agencies, depending on the particular circumstances and asset structure (Rakha et al., 2024) (Nikoro et al., 2024). With licensed banking institutions creating crypto infrastructure such as custody services and crypto technology companies integrating with regular financial systems, regulatory loopholes and overlaps are appearing in the sector as it grows (Alrubayyi et al., 2024). Legislative reforms may be required in order to properly define an adequate regulatory system, which would include licensing and chartering agencies, and this might also affect key markets (Samsudeen & Thomas, 2024) (Sakthibalan et al., 2024). It should think about passing new legislation, according to an interagency assessment, to guarantee that stablecoins and stablecoin arrangements are governed by a uniform and extensive federal prudential framework (din et al., 2024) (Hemamalini et al., 2024). Further steps would restrict issuers to insured depository institutions, subject companies handling stablecoin operations (such digital wallets) to federal regulation, and limit issuer-commercial entity relationships (Tejasvi et al., 2024). If stablecoins are categorized as securities, commodities, or derivatives, the SEC and CFTC have both shown a desire to have more control over them (Devan et al., 2024) (Reddy et al., 2024). Stablecoin arrangements and other cryptocurrency assets are being subjected to the application of current rules and principles by international standard setters including the FSB, BCBS, and FATF (Pritee et al., 2024) (Zhang et al., 2024).

5. TRAILBLAZING LEGAL STRATEGIES

There are prominent economic entities, like the European Union (EU), have cautioned about such threats (Li & Dong, 2024) (Nyarko et al., 2024). These worries include the possibility of their use in illegal operations like as financing terrorism and money laundering, in addition to the dangers of tax evasion, market manipulation, and volatility (Ababneh & Aljarrah, 2024) (Montasari, 2024). These dangers draw attention to the intricate system that underpins cryptocurrency operations, weighing the necessity for consumer protection and financial stability against the possibility for innovation (Mishra et al., 2024). For these reasons, it is essential to comprehend how various nations execute cryptocurrency regulatory frameworks (Mittal, 2024). The legislative environment throughout the world is currently fragmented with different governments taking varying positions, ranging from outright prohibitions to acknowledging cryptocurrencies as legal cash (Behiry & Aly, 2024). The rate and magnitude of the continuous rise in the value of cryptocurrency assets are equally noteworthy (Gunavathi & Bharathi, 2024). Authorities think that by taking the right steps, this increasing tendency may be controlled (Saiyed & Al-Anbagi, 2024). The Financial Stability Board (FSB) highlights the necessity of conducting a comprehensive examination of the cryptocurrency market in order to properly manage this expanding trend and create appropriate regulatory frameworks (Dasari & Kaluri, 2024).

The dominance of digital assets is predicted to continue growing for the foreseeable future. Even though they are still relatively young, these virtual assets are developing quickly (Ganji & Afshan, 2024) (Roshanaei, 2024). The increasing value of digital assets, particularly Bitcoin, which has attracted a lot of attention, is noteworthy (Lightbody et al., 2024) (Nguyen et al., 2024). Regulators have difficulties as a result of the cryptocurrency industry's explosive expansion, which is now the most notable trend in financial technology (Bui et al., 2024) (Sahingoz et al., 2024). The development of efficient laws in this area is hampered by a lack of knowledge about the characteristics of the environment and the dangers that are involved (Abdulhussein, 2024). As a result, cooperation is being undertaken by stakeholders from different countries in order to fully comprehend cryptocurrency assets and resolve pertinent issues (Costa & Sofikitis, 2024).

6. CONCLUSION AND FUTURE SCOPE

Cryptocurrencies and their underlying blockchain technology are becoming increasingly influential in the global economy, impacting everything from cross-border retail payments to interbank transfers (AL-Dosari et al., 2024). The widespread adoption and decentralized nature of cryptocurrencies present unique and unprecedented challenges for financial authorities, capital markets regulators, consumer protection and privacy agencies, and tax authorities worldwide (Ziwei et al., 2024). With utilizing the internet, cryptocurrencies provide new digital channels for people and micro, small, and medium-sized businesses (MSMEs) to engage with the global financial system. A new paradigm for the transmission, storage, and access of protected data and value is introduced by cryptocurrencies and blockchain technology (Kumar, 2024). As such, the distinct technological and economic features of cryptocurrencies demand careful regulation that takes into account their special qualities and applications (Singh & Kaunert, 2024). In spite of regulatory and governmental actions, the popularity of cryptocurrencies is growing. Some institutions are challenged by this unrestrained expansion. A climate of uncertainty brought about by regulators' hesitancy reduces the number of investors who are interested in cryptocurrencies (Singh et al., 2024). In order to meet this problem, it is imperative that creative approaches to market regulation be investigated (Singh, 2024). These issues call for a cooperative strategy in which business and government cooperate to create laws that effectively suppress fraud and deal with the spread of phony cryptocurrencies (Singh & Kaunert, 2024). To safeguard investors from fraud, strong security measures must be put in place at the same time. The future trends indicate that cryptocurrency assets will continue to be significant (Singh, 2023). Investors and entrepreneurs drawn to these assets will continue to be active players in the market as long as their value rises. Regulators are essential in this environment (Singh, 2023). It is their duty to maintain security and minimize uncertainty while avoiding interfering with the market system's ability to operate (Singh, 2024).

REFERENCES

ABABNEH, M., & ALJARRAH, A. (2024). CYBERSECURITY: MALWARE MULTI-ATTACK DETECTOR ON ANDROID-BASED DEVICES USING DEEP LEARNING METHODS. *Journal of Theoretical and Applied Information Technology*, 102(1).

Abbas, S., Bouazzi, I., Ojo, S., Al Hejaili, A., Sampedro, G. A., Almadhor, A., & Gregus, M. (2024). Evaluating deep learning variants for cyber-attacks detection and multi-class classification in IoT networks. *PeerJ. Computer Science*, 10, e1793. DOI: 10.7717/peerj-cs.1793 PMID: 38259893

Abbas, S., Bouazzi, I., Ojo, S., Al Hejaili, A., Sampedro, G. A., Almadhor, A., & Gregus, M. (2024). Evaluating deep learning variants for cyber-attacks detection and multi-class classification in IoT networks. *PeerJ. Computer Science*, 10, e1793. DOI: 10.7717/peerj-cs.1793 PMID: 38259893

Abdalrdha, Z. K., Al-Bakry, A. M., & Farhan, A. K. (2023). A Survey on Cybercrime Using Social Media. *Iraqi Journal for Computers and Informatics*, 49(1), 52–65. DOI: 10.25195/ijci.v49i1.404

Abdulhussein, M. (2024). The Impact of Artificial Intelligence and Machine Learning on Organizations Cybersecurity.

Abebe, R., Barocas, S., Kleinberg, J., Levy, K., Raghavan, M., & Robinson, D. G. (2020, January). Roles for computing in social change. In *Proceedings of the 2020 conference on fairness, accountability, and transparency* (pp. 252-260). DOI: 10.1145/3351095.3372871

Afrifa, S., Varadarajan, V., Appiahene, P., & Zhang, T. (2023). Using Machine Learning to Classify Network Abnormalities into Legitimate or Assault in IoT-based Cyber Physical System. *Sensors and Electronic Instrumentation Advances*, 150.

AJ, B., & Kaythry, P. (2023). A Review of Deep Learning Strategies for Enhancing Cybersecurity in Networks.

AL-Dosari, K., Fetais, N., & Kucukvar, M.AL-Dosari. (2024). Artificial intelligence and cyber defense system for banking industry: A qualitative study of AI applications and challenges. *Cybernetics and Systems*, 55(2), 302–330. DOI: 10.1080/01969722.2022.2112539

AL-Dosari, K., Fetais, N., & Kucukvar, M.AL-Dosari. (2024). Artificial intelligence and cyber defense system for banking industry: A qualitative study of AI applications and challenges. *Cybernetics and Systems*, 55(2), 302–330. DOI: 10.1080/01969722.2022.2112539

Al-Quayed, F., Ahmad, Z., & Humayun, M. (2024). A situation based predictive approach for cybersecurity intrusion detection and prevention using machine learning and deep learning algorithms in wireless sensor networks of industry 4.0. *IEEE Access : Practical Innovations, Open Solutions*, 12, 34800–34819. DOI: 10.1109/ACCESS.2024.3372187

Alabdulkreem, E., Alotaibi, S. S., Alamgeer, M., Marzouk, R., Hilal, A. M., Motwakel, A., & Rizwanullah, M. (2023). Intelligent Cybersecurity Classification Using Chaos Game Optimization with Deep Learning Model. *Computer Systems Science and Engineering*, 45(1), 971–983. DOI: 10.32604/csse.2023.030362

Alazab, M., Soman, K. P., Srinivasan, S., Venkatraman, S., & Pham, V. Q. (2023). Deep learning for cyber security applications: A comprehensive survey. *Authorea Preprints*.

Ali, B., & Farooq, A. (2023, May). Ensemble Based AI Detector for Cyber Crimes. In *2023 6th International Conference on Electronics Technology (ICET)* (pp. 619-623). IEEE. DOI: 10.1109/ICET58434.2023.10211904

Ali, H. H., Naif, J. R., & Humood, W. R. (2024, March). Deep learning algorithms for IoT security (survey). In *AIP Conference Proceedings* (Vol. 2885, No. 1). AIP Publishing.

Ali, M., Shahroz, M., Mushtaq, M. F., Alfarhood, S., Safran, M., & Ashraf, I. (2024). Hybrid Machine Learning Model for Efficient Botnet Attack Detection in IoT Environment. *IEEE Access : Practical Innovations, Open Solutions*, 12, 40682–40699. DOI: 10.1109/ACCESS.2024.3376400

Aljuhani, A., Kumar, P., Alanazi, R., Albalawi, T., Taouali, O., Islam, A. N., & Alazab, M. (2023). A deep learning integrated blockchain framework for securing industrial iot. *IEEE Internet of Things Journal*.

Alrubayyi, H., Alshareef, M. S., Nadeem, Z., Abdelmoniem, A. M., & Jaber, M. (2024). Security Threats and Promising Solutions Arising from the Intersection of AI and IoT: A Study of IoMT and IoET Applications. *Future Internet*, 16(3), 85. DOI: 10.3390/fi16030085

Alruwaili, F. F. (2023). Optimal hybrid deep learning enabled attack detection and classification in IoT environment. *Computers, Materials & Continua*, 75(1), 99–115. DOI: 10.32604/cmc.2023.034752

Ambika, N. (2024). Early Detection of Darknet Traffic in Internet of Things Applications. *Automated Secure Computing for Next-Generation Systems*, 139-153.

Anis, G. M., Aboutabl, A. E., & Galal, A. (2023). MACHINE LEARNING FOR DETECTING CYBERCRIME IN THE BANKING SECTOR. *Journal of Southwest Jiaotong University*, 58(5).

Attaran, M., & Deb, P. (2018). Machine learning: The new'big thing'for competitive advantage. *International Journal of Knowledge Engineering and Data Mining*, 5(4), 277–305. DOI: 10.1504/IJKEDM.2018.095523

Awajan, A. (2023). A novel deep learning-based intrusion detection system for IOT networks. *Computers*, 12(2), 34. DOI: 10.3390/computers12020034

Aziz, L. A. R., & Andriansyah, Y. (2023). The Role Artificial Intelligence in Modern Banking: An Exploration of AI-Driven Approaches for Enhanced Fraud Prevention, Risk Management, and Regulatory Compliance. *Reviews of Contemporary Business Analytics*, 6(1), 110–132.

Baker, D. J., & Robinson, P. H. (Eds.). (2020). *Artificial Intelligence and the Law: Cybercrime and Criminal Liability*. Routledge. DOI: 10.4324/9780429344015

Bao, Y., Hilary, G., & Ke, B. (2022). Artificial intelligence and fraud detection. *Innovative Technology at the Interface of Finance and Operations*, I, 223–247. DOI: 10.1007/978-3-030-75729-8_8

Barocas, S., Hardt, M., & Narayanan, A. (2023). *Fairness and machine learning: Limitations and opportunities*. MIT Press.

Behiry, M. H., & Aly, M. (2024). Cyberattack detection in wireless sensor networks using a hybrid feature reduction technique with AI and machine learning methods. *Journal of Big Data*, 11(1), 16. DOI: 10.1186/s40537-023-00870-w

Berk, R., Heidari, H., Jabbari, S., Kearns, M., & Roth, A. (2021). Fairness in criminal justice risk assessments: The state of the art. *Sociological Methods & Research*, 50(1), 3–44. DOI: 10.1177/0049124118782533

Bhuvaneshwari, A. J., & Kaythry, P. (2023). A Review of Deep Learning Strategies for Enhancing Cybersecurity in Networks: DEEP LEARNING STRATEGIES FOR ENHANCING CYBERSECURITY. [JSIR]. *Journal of Scientific and Industrial Research*, 82(12), 1316–1330.

Brotcke, L. (2022). Time to assess bias in machine learning models for credit decisions. *Journal of Risk and Financial Management*, 15(4), 165. DOI: 10.3390/jrfm15040165

Bui, H. T., Aboutorab, H., Mahboubi, A., Gao, Y., Sultan, N. H., Chauhan, A., Parvez, M. Z., Bewong, M., Islam, R., Islam, Z., Camtepe, S. A., Gauravaram, P., Singh, D., Ali Babar, M., & Yan, S. (2024). Agriculture 4.0 and Beyond: Evaluating Cyber Threat Intelligence Sources and Techniques in Smart Farming Ecosystems. *Computers & Security*, 140, 103754. DOI: 10.1016/j.cose.2024.103754

Cao, D. M., Sayed, M. A., Islam, M. T., Mia, M. T., Ayon, E. H., Ghosh, B. P., & Raihan, A. (2024). Advanced Cybercrime Detection: A Comprehensive Study on Supervised and Unsupervised Machine Learning Approaches Using Real-world Datasets. *Journal of Computer Science and Technology Studies*, 6(1), 40–48. DOI: 10.32996/jcsts.2024.6.1.5

Cao, L., Yang, Q., & Yu, P. S. (2021). Data science and AI in FinTech: An overview. *International Journal of Data Science and Analytics*, 12(2), 81–99. DOI: 10.1007/s41060-021-00278-w

Chen, Z., Van Khoa, L. D., Teoh, E. N., Nazir, A., Karuppiah, E. K., & Lam, K. S. (2018). Machine learning techniques for anti-money laundering (AML) solutions in suspicious transaction detection: A review. *Knowledge and Information Systems*, 57(2), 245–285. DOI: 10.1007/s10115-017-1144-z

Cheng, X., Liu, S., Sun, X., Wang, Z., Zhou, H., Shao, Y., & Shen, H. (2021). Combating emerging financial risks in the big data era: A perspective review. *Fundamental Research (Beijing)*, 1(5), 595–606. DOI: 10.1016/j.fmre.2021.08.017

Chohan, M. N., Haider, U., Ayub, M. Y., Shoukat, H., Bhatia, T. K., & Hassan, M. F. U. (2023). Detection of Cyber Attacks using Machine Learning based Intrusion Detection System for IoT Based Smart Cities. *EAI Endorsed Transactions on Smart Cities*, 7(2), e4–e4.

Costa, M. B., & Sofikitis, D. (2024). Applying Deep Learning and Data Analytics to identify Malware Attacks.

Costa, M. B., & Sofikitis, D. (2024). Applying Deep Learning and Data Analytics to identify Malware Attacks.

Das, S., Balmiki, A. K., Mazumdar, K., & Bhowmick, P. (2023). Cyber-Physical Security Issues and Challenges Using Machine Learning and Deep Learning Technologies. In *Artificial Intelligence in Cyber-Physical Systems* (pp. 105–123). CRC Press. DOI: 10.1201/9781003248750-7

Dasari, S., & Kaluri, R. (2024). An Effective Classification of DDoS Attacks in a Distributed Network by Adopting Hierarchical Machine Learning and Hyperparameters Optimization Techniques. *IEEE Access : Practical Innovations, Open Solutions*, 12, 10834–10845. DOI: 10.1109/ACCESS.2024.3352281

Dash, B., Sharma, P., & Ali, A. (2022). Federated learning for privacy-preserving: A review of PII data analysis in Fintech. [IJSEA]. *International Journal of Software Engineering and Its Applications*, 13(4).

Daugherty, P. R., & Wilson, H. J. (2018). *Human+ machine: Reimagining work in the age of AI.* Harvard Business Press.

Demir, B., & Serkan, A. (2024). Cyber Vigilantes: A Deep Dive into the Art and Science of Digital Defense. *Integrated Journal of Science and Technology, 1*(2).

Devan, A. M., Raghul, V., Dhasmana, U., Rath, A., & Jacob, L. (2024). 6 Deep Support Learning Model Decision for Police Investigation. *Artificial Intelligence for Cyber Defense and Smart Policing*, 76.

Dhoni, P., & Kumar, R. (2023). Synergizing generative ai and cybersecurity: Roles of generative ai entities, companies, agencies, and government in enhancing cybersecurity. *Authorea Preprints.*

din, S. M. U., Sharma, R., Rizvi, F., & Sharma, N. (2024). Detection of botnet in IoT network through machine learning based optimized feature importance via ensemble models. *International Journal of Information Technology, 16*(2), 1203-1211.

Djenna, A., Barka, E., Benchikh, A., & Khadir, K. (2023). Unmasking Cybercrime with Artificial-Intelligence-Driven Cybersecurity Analytics. *Sensors (Basel)*, 23(14), 6302. DOI: 10.3390/s23146302 PMID: 37514596

Elluri, L., Mandalapu, V., Vyas, P., & Roy, N. (2023). Recent Advancements in Machine Learning for Cybercrime Prediction. *Journal of Computer Information Systems*, •••, 1–15. DOI: 10.1080/08874417.2023.2270457

Escorcia-Gutierrez, J., Gamarra, M., Leal, E., Madera, N., Soto, C., Mansour, R. F., Alharbi, M., Alkhayyat, A., & Gupta, D. (2023). Sea turtle foraging algorithm with hybrid deep learning-based intrusion detection for the internet of drones environment. *Computers & Electrical Engineering*, 108, 108704. DOI: 10.1016/j.compeleceng.2023.108704

Gangula, R., Vutukuru, M. M., & Kumar, R. (2024). Hybridization of Bottlenose Dolphin Optimization and Artificial Fish Swarm Algorithm with Efficient Classifier for Detecting the Network Intrusion in Internet of Things (IoT). *International Journal of Intelligent Systems and Applications in Engineering*, 12(6s), 220–232.

Ganji, K., & Afshan, N. (2024). A bibliometric review of Internet of Things (IoT) on cybersecurity issues. *Journal of Science and Technology Policy Management.*

Grimm, P. W., Grossman, M. R., & Cormack, G. V. (2021). Artificial intelligence as evidence. *Nw. J. Tech. & Intell. Prop.*, 19, 9.

Gunavathi, R., & Bharathi, K. M. (2024). 2 Cybercrimes in the. *Artificial Intelligence for Cyber Defense and Smart Policing*, 21.

Hagendorff, T. (2019). From privacy to anti-discrimination in times of machine learning. *Ethics and Information Technology*, 21(4), 331–343. DOI: 10.1007/s10676-019-09510-5

Hamad, S. I. (2023). A review of deep learning applied to cyber security. *Texas Journal of Engineering and Technology*, 22, 49–57.

Hemamalini, V., Mishra, A. K., Tyagi, A. K., & Kakulapati, V. (2024). Artificial Intelligence–Blockchain-Enabled–Internet of Things-Based Cloud Applications for Next-Generation Society. *Automated Secure Computing for Next-Generation Systems*, 65-82.

Hoijtink, M., & Planqué-van Hardeveld, A. (2022). Machine learning and the platformization of the military: A study of google's machine learning platform TensorFlow. *International Political Sociology*, 16(2), olab036. DOI: 10.1093/ips/olab036

Irfan, M., Elmogy, M., & El-Sappagh, S. (Eds.). (2023). *The impact of AI innovation on financial sectors in the era of industry 5.0.* IGI Global.

Itani, M., Basheer, H., & Eddine, F. (2023, July). Attack Detection in IoT-Based Healthcare Networks Using Hybrid Federated Learning. In *2023 International Conference on Smart Applications, Communications and Networking (SmartNets)* (pp. 1-7). IEEE. DOI: 10.1109/SmartNets58706.2023.10216144

Katyal, S. K. (2019). Private accountability in the age of artificial intelligence. *UCLA Law Review. University of California, Los Angeles. School of Law*, 66, 54.

Kaushik, K. (2024). Leveraging Deep Learning Techniques for Securing the Internet of Things in the Age of Big Data. *Applying Artificial Intelligence in Cybersecurity Analytics and Cyber Threat Detection*, 309.

Kochhar, S. K., Bhatia, A., & Tomer, N. (2023). Using Deep Learning and Big Data Analytics for Managing Cyber-Attacks. In *New Approaches to Data Analytics and Internet of Things Through Digital Twin* (pp. 146–178). IGI Global.

Kongsorot, Y., Musikawan, P., Aimtongkham, P., You, I., Benslimane, A., & So-In, C. (2023). An Intrusion Detection and Identification System for Internet of Things Networks Using a Hybrid Ensemble Deep Learning Framework. *IEEE Transactions on Sustainable Computing*, 8(4), 596–613. DOI: 10.1109/TSUSC.2023.3303422

Kordzadeh, N., & Ghasemaghaei, M. (2022). Algorithmic bias: Review, synthesis, and future research directions. *European Journal of Information Systems*, 31(3), 388–409. DOI: 10.1080/0960085X.2021.1927212

Kumar, A. (2024). Cybersecurity Threat Detection using Machine Learning and Network Analysis. *Journal of Artificial Intelligence General science (JAIGS) ISSN: 3006-4023, 1*(1), 38-46.

Kumar, A. K., Vadivukkarasi, K., & Dayana, R. (2023, February). A Novel Hybrid Deep Learning Model for Botnet Attacks Detection in a Secure IoMT Environment. In *2023 International Conference on Intelligent Systems for Communication, IoT and Security (ICISCoIS)* (pp. 44-49). IEEE. DOI: 10.1109/ICISCoIS56541.2023.10100396

Kumar, P., Gowda, D. Y., & Prakash, A. M. (2024). Machine Learning in Cybersecurity: A Comprehensive Survey of Data Breach Detection, Cyber-Attack Prevention, and Fraud Detection. *Pioneering Smart Healthcare 5.0 with IoT, Federated Learning, and Cloud Security*, 175-197.

Latif, S., Boulila, W., Koubaa, A., Zou, Z., & Ahmad, J. (2024). DTL-IDS: An optimized Intrusion Detection Framework using Deep Transfer Learning and Genetic Algorithm. *Journal of Network and Computer Applications*, 221, 103784. DOI: 10.1016/j.jnca.2023.103784

Lee, I., & Shin, Y. J. (2020). Machine learning for enterprises: Applications, algorithm selection, and challenges. *Business Horizons*, 63(2), 157–170. DOI: 10.1016/j.bushor.2019.10.005

Li, H., & Dong, S. (2024). Image steganalysis algorithm based on deep learning and attention mechanism for computer communication. *Journal of Electronic Imaging*, 33(1), 013015–013015. DOI: 10.1117/1.JEI.33.1.013015

Li, L., Zhao, T., Xie, Y., & Feng, Y. (2020). Interpretable machine learning based on integration of nlp and psychology in peer-to-peer lending risk evaluation. In *Natural Language Processing and Chinese Computing: 9th CCF International Conference, NLPCC 2020, Zhengzhou, China, October 14–18, 2020* [Springer International Publishing.]. *Proceedings*, 9(Part II), 429–441.

Lightbody, D., Ngo, D. M., Temko, A., Murphy, C. C., & Popovici, E. (2024). Dragon_Pi: IoT Side-Channel Power Data Intrusion Detection Dataset and Unsupervised Convolutional Autoencoder for Intrusion Detection. *Future Internet*, 16(3), 88. DOI: 10.3390/fi16030088

Lipsa, S., & Dash, R. K. (2023). A novel intrusion detection system based on deep learning and random forest for digital twin on IOT platform. *Int. J. Sch. Res. Eng. Technol*, 2, 51–64.

Liu, C., Chen, B., Shao, W., Zhang, C., Wong, K., & Zhang, Y. (2024). Unraveling Attacks in Machine Learning-based IoT Ecosystems: A Survey and the Open Libraries Behind Them. arXiv preprint arXiv:2401.11723.

Lone, A. N., Mustajab, S., & Alam, M. (2023). A comprehensive study on cybersecurity challenges and opportunities in the IoT world. *Security and Privacy*, 6(6), e318. DOI: 10.1002/spy2.318

Lui, A., & Lamb, G. W. (2018). Artificial intelligence and augmented intelligence collaboration: Regaining trust and confidence in the financial sector. *Information & Communications Technology Law*, 27(3), 267–283. DOI: 10.1080/13600834.2018.1488659

Manimaran, M., Dhar, M., Norabuena-Figueroa, R., Mahaveerakannan, R., Saraswathi, S., & Selvakumarasamy, K. (2023). Implementing Machine Learning-based Autonomic Cyber Defense for IoT-enabled Healthcare Devices. *Journal of Artificial Intelligence and Technology*, 3(4), 162–172. DOI: 10.37965/jait.2023.0209

McKendrick, K. (2019). Artificial intelligence prediction and counterterrorism. *London: The Royal Institute of International Affairs-Chatham House, 9.*

Messai, M. L., & Seba, H. (2023, August). IoT Network Attack Detection: Leveraging Graph Learning for Enhanced Security. In *Proceedings of the 18th International Conference on Availability, Reliability and Security* (pp. 1-7). DOI: 10.1145/3600160.3605053

Messai, M. L., & Seba, H. (2023, June). POSTER: Activity Graph Learning for Attack Detection in IoT Networks. In *2023 IEEE 24th International Symposium on a World of Wireless, Mobile and Multimedia Networks (WoWMoM)* (pp. 320-322). IEEE.

Mhlanga, D. (2021). Financial inclusion in emerging economies: The application of machine learning and artificial intelligence in credit risk assessment. *International journal of financial studies, 9*(3), 39.

Mijwil, M., & Aljanabi, M. (2023). Towards artificial intelligence-based cybersecurity: The practices and ChatGPT generated ways to combat cybercrime. *Iraqi Journal For Computer Science and Mathematics*, 4(1), 65–70.

Mijwil, M., Salem, I. E., & Ismaeel, M. M. (2023). The significance of machine learning and deep learning techniques in cybersecurity: A comprehensive review. *Iraqi Journal For Computer Science and Mathematics*, 4(1), 87–101.

Mishra, A. K., Hemamalini, V., & Tyagi, A. K. (2024). Digital Forensics with Emerging Technologies: Vision and Research Potential for Future. *Conversational Artificial Intelligence*, 675-697.

Mittal, H. (2024). Software security: Threats, solutions and challenges. *Computer Software and Media Applications*, 6(1), 3769. DOI: 10.24294/csma.v6i1.3769

Montasari, R. (2024). Machine Learning and Deep Learning Techniques in Countering Cyberterrorism. In *Cyberspace, Cyberterrorism and the International Security in the Fourth Industrial Revolution: Threats, Assessment and Responses* (pp. 135–158). Springer International Publishing. DOI: 10.1007/978-3-031-50454-9_8

Moustafa, N., Koroniotis, N., Keshk, M., Zomaya, A. Y., & Tari, Z. (2023). Explainable intrusion detection for cyber defences in the internet of things: Opportunities and solutions. *IEEE Communications Surveys and Tutorials*, 25(3), 1775–1807. DOI: 10.1109/COMST.2023.3280465

Mühlhoff, R. (2021). Predictive privacy: Towards an applied ethics of data analytics. *Ethics and Information Technology*, 23(4), 675–690. DOI: 10.1007/s10676-021-09606-x

Nandan, M., & Dey, S. (2023). Cybersecurity: Techniques and Applications to Combat Vicious Threats in Modern-Era Indices. In *AI-Aided IoT Technologies and Applications for Smart Business and Production* (pp. 248-270). CRC Press.

Narayana, Y. V., & Sreedevi, M. (2023, October). DDCATF: Deep Learning Approach for Detection of Cybercrime Activities Based on Temporal Features. In *2023 International Conference on Self Sustainable Artificial Intelligence Systems (ICSSAS)* (pp. 462-469). IEEE. DOI: 10.1109/ICSSAS57918.2023.10331644

Nassar, A., & Kamal, M. (2021). Ethical Dilemmas in AI-Powered Decision-Making: A Deep Dive into Big Data-Driven Ethical Considerations. *International Journal of Responsible Artificial Intelligence*, 11(8), 1–11.

Nehinbe, J. O., Benson, J. A., & Chibuzor, L. (2023). The classification of the investigations and punishment for crime syndicates that relate to intrusions against IoT-based healthcare systems. In *Blockchain Technology Solutions for the Security of IoT-Based Healthcare Systems* (pp. 113–131). Academic Press. DOI: 10.1016/B978-0-323-99199-5.00010-0

Nguyen, H., Nawara, D., & Kashef, R. (2024). Connecting the Indispensable Roles of IoT and Artificial Intelligence in Smart Cities: A Survey. *Journal of Information and Intelligence*.

Nisha, S. R., & Muthurajkumar, S. (2023). Semantic Graph Based Convolutional Neural Network for Spam e-mail Classification in Cybercrime Applications. *International Journal of Computers, Communications & Control*, 18(1).

Niu, T., Li, W., & Liu, Y. (2024). DarkGuardNet: A deep learning framework for imbalanced dark web traffic identification and application classification.

Nkoro, E. C., Njoku, J. N., Nwakanma, C. I., Lee, J. M., & Kim, D. S. (2024). Zero-Trust Marine Cyberdefense for IoT-Based Communications: An Explainable Approach. *Electronics (Basel)*, 13(2), 276. DOI: 10.3390/electronics13020276

Nyarko, B. N. E., Bin, W., Zhou, J., Odoom, J., Danso, S. A., & Addai, G. E. S. (2024). Forensic detection of heterogeneous activity in data using deep learning methods. *Intelligent Systems with Applications*, 21, 200303. DOI: 10.1016/j.iswa.2023.200303

Odeh, A., & Abu Taleb, A. (2023). Ensemble-Based Deep Learning Models for Enhancing IoT Intrusion Detection. *Applied Sciences (Basel, Switzerland)*, 13(21), 11985. DOI: 10.3390/app132111985

Ortiz-Ruiz, E., Bermejo, J. R., Sicilia, J. A., & Bermejo, J. (2024). Machine Learning Techniques for Cyberattack Prevention in IoT Systems: A Comparative Perspective of Cybersecurity and Cyberdefense in Colombia. *Electronics (Basel)*, 13(5), 824. DOI: 10.3390/electronics13050824

Paddalwar, S., Ragha, L., & Mane, V. (2023). Cyber threat mitigation using machine learning, deep learning, artificial intelligence, and blockchain. In *Intelligent Approaches to Cyber Security* (pp. 163–179). Chapman and Hall/CRC. DOI: 10.1201/9781003408307-14

Plageras, A., Stergiou, C. L., & Psannis, K. (2024). Secure Edge Communications Over the IoT.

Pocher, N., Zichichi, M., Merizzi, F., Shafiq, M. Z., & Ferretti, S. (2023). Detecting anomalous cryptocurrency transactions: An AML/CFT application of machine learning-based forensics. *Electronic Markets*, 33(1), 37. DOI: 10.1007/s12525-023-00654-3

Pritee, Z. T., Anik, M. H., Alam, S. B., Jim, J. R., Kabir, M. M., & Mridha, M. F. (2024). Machine learning and deep learning for user authentication and authorization in cybersecurity: A state-of-the-art review. *Computers & Security*, 140, 103747. DOI: 10.1016/j.cose.2024.103747

Priyadarshini, I., Mohanty, P., Alkhayyat, A., Sharma, R., & Kumar, S. (2023). SDN and application layer DDoS attacks detection in IoT devices by attention-based Bi-LSTM-CNN. *Transactions on Emerging Telecommunications Technologies*, 34(11), e4758. DOI: 10.1002/ett.4758

Rai, R., & Sahu, C. K. (2020). Driven by data or derived through physics? a review of hybrid physics guided machine learning techniques with cyber-physical system (cps) focus. *IEEE Access : Practical Innovations, Open Solutions*, 8, 71050–71073. DOI: 10.1109/ACCESS.2020.2987324

Rajkumar, S., Sheeba, S. L., Sivakami, R., Prabu, S., & Selvarani, A. (2023). An IoT-Based Deep Learning Approach for Online Fault Detection Against Cyber-Attacks. *SN Computer Science*, 4(4), 393. DOI: 10.1007/s42979-023-01808-y

Rakha, M. A., Khan, I. U., Ouaissa, M., Ouaissa, M., & Ayub, M. Y. (2024). Hybrid Model for IoT-Enabled Intelligent Towns Using the MQTT-IoT-IDS2020 Dataset. In *Cyber Security for Next-Generation Computing Technologies* (pp. 159-176). CRC Press.

Rathee, G., Iqbal, R., Kerrache, C. A., & Song, H. (2024). TrustNextGen: Security Aspects of Trustworthy Next Generation Industrial Internet of Things (IIoT). *IEEE Internet of Things Journal*, 11(15), 25568–25576. DOI: 10.1109/JIOT.2024.3361801

Reddy, B. B., Pasha, S. G., Kameswari, M., Chinkera, R., Fatima, S., Bhargava, R., & Shrivastava, A. (2024). Classification Approach for Face Spoof Detection in Artificial Neural Network Based on IoT Concepts. *International Journal of Intelligent Systems and Applications in Engineering*, 12(13s), 79–91.

Roshanaei, M. (2024). Enhancing Mobile Security through Comprehensive Penetration Testing. *Journal of Information Security*, 15(2), 63–86. DOI: 10.4236/jis.2024.152006

Saha, S. (2024). SECURITY IN IOT USING ARTIFICIAL INTELLIGENCE. *The Fusion of Artificial Intelligence and Soft Computing Techniques for Cybersecurity*.

Sahingoz, O. K., Buber, E., & Kugu, E. (2024). DEPHIDES: Deep Learning Based Phishing Detection System. *IEEE Access : Practical Innovations, Open Solutions*, 12, 8052–8070. DOI: 10.1109/ACCESS.2024.3352629

Saiyed, M. F., & Al-Anbagi, I. (2024). A Genetic Algorithm-and t-Test-Based System for DDoS Attack Detection in IoT Networks. *IEEE Access : Practical Innovations, Open Solutions*, 12, 25623–25641. DOI: 10.1109/ACCESS.2024.3367357

Sakthibalan, P., Saravanan, M., Ansal, V., Rajakannu, A., Vijayalakshmi, K., & Vani, K. D. (2024). A Federated Learning Approach for ResourceConstrained IoT Security Monitoring. In *Handbook on Federated Learning* (pp. 131–154). CRC Press.

Saltz, J., Skirpan, M., Fiesler, C., Gorelick, M., Yeh, T., Heckman, R., & Beard, N. (2019). Integrating ethics within machine learning courses. [TOCE]. *ACM Transactions on Computing Education*, 19(4), 1–26. DOI: 10.1145/3341164

Sambasivan, N., Arnesen, E., Hutchinson, B., Doshi, T., & Prabhakaran, V. (2021, March). Re-imagining algorithmic fairness in india and beyond. In *Proceedings of the 2021 ACM conference on fairness, accountability, and transparency* (pp. 315-328). DOI: 10.1145/3442188.3445896

Samsudeen, S., & Thomas, L. (2024). Cybersecurity Warning System Using Diluted Convolutional Neural Network Framework for IOT Attack Prevention. *International Journal of Intelligent Engineering & Systems*, 17(1).

Schmitt, M. (2020). Artificial intelligence in business analytics, capturing value with machine learning applications in financial services.

Segovia-Vargas, M. J. (2024). Money Laundering in the Age of Cybercrime and Emerging Technologies.

Selbst, A. D., & Barocas, S. (2018). The intuitive appeal of explainable machines. *Fordham Law Review*, 87, 1085.

Shaikh, J., Butt, Y. A., & Naqvi, H. F. (2024). Effective Intrusion Detection System Using Deep Learning for DDoS Attacks. *The Asian Bulletin of Big Data Management*, 4(1). Advance online publication. DOI: 10.62019/abbdm.v4i1.113

Sharma, A., Mansotra, V., & Singh, K. (2023). Detection of Mirai Botnet Attacks on IoT devices Using Deep Learning. *Journal of Scientific Research and Technology*, 174-187.

Sharma, N., & Annaboina, K. (2024). Analytical Study On Prevention And Detection Of Financial Cybercrime And Frauds Using Transaction Pattern Generation Tool. *Journal of Scientific Research and Technology*, 9-31.

Shukla, R. K., & Tiwari, A. K. (2024). Security Analysis of the Cyber Crime. In *The Ethical Frontier of AI and Data Analysis* (pp. 257–271). IGI Global. DOI: 10.4018/979-8-3693-2964-1.ch016

Singh, B. (2023). Federated Learning for Envision Future Trajectory Smart Transport System for Climate Preservation and Smart Green Planet: Insights into Global Governance and SDG-9 (Industry, Innovation and Infrastructure). *National Journal of Environmental Law*, 6(2), 6–17.

Singh, B. (2023). Tele-Health Monitoring Lensing Deep Neural Learning Structure: Ambient Patient Wellness via Wearable Devices for Real-Time Alerts and Interventions. *Indian Journal of Health and Medical Law*, 6(2), 12–16.

Singh, B. (2023). Blockchain Technology in Renovating Healthcare: Legal and Future Perspectives. In *Revolutionizing Healthcare Through Artificial Intelligence and Internet of Things Applications* (pp. 177-186). IGI Global.

Singh, B. (2023). Unleashing Alternative Dispute Resolution (ADR) in Resolving Complex Legal-Technical Issues Arising in Cyberspace Lensing E-Commerce and Intellectual Property: Proliferation of E-Commerce Digital Economy. *Revista Brasileira de Alternative Dispute Resolution-Brazilian Journal of Alternative Dispute Resolution-RBADR*, 5(10), 81–105. DOI: 10.52028/rbadr.v5i10.ART04.Ind

Singh, B. (2023). Blockchain Technology in Renovating Healthcare: Legal and Future Perspectives. In *Revolutionizing Healthcare Through Artificial Intelligence and Internet of Things Applications* (pp. 177-186). IGI Global.

Singh, B. (2023). Unleashing Alternative Dispute Resolution (ADR) in Resolving Complex Legal-Technical Issues Arising in Cyberspace Lensing E-Commerce and Intellectual Property: Proliferation of E-Commerce Digital Economy. *Revista Brasileira de Alternative Dispute Resolution-Brazilian Journal of Alternative Dispute Resolution-RBADR*, 5(10), 81–105. DOI: 10.52028/rbadr.v5i10.ART04.Ind

Singh, B. (2024). Social Cognition of Incarcerated Women and Children: Addressing Exposure to Infectious Diseases and Legal Outcomes. In Reddy, K. (Ed.), *Principles and Clinical Interventions in Social Cognition* (pp. 236–251). IGI Global., DOI: 10.4018/979-8-3693-1265-0.ch014

Singh, B. (2024). Lensing Legal Dynamics for Examining Responsibility and Deliberation of Generative AI-Tethered Technological Privacy Concerns: Infringements and Use of Personal Data by Nefarious Actors. In Ara, A., & Ara, A. (Eds.), *Exploring the Ethical Implications of Generative AI* (pp. 146–167). IGI Global., DOI: 10.4018/979-8-3693-1565-1.ch009

Singh, B., & Kaunert, C. (2024). Integration of Cutting-Edge Technologies such as Internet of Things (IoT) and 5G in Health Monitoring Systems: A Comprehensive Legal Analysis and Futuristic Outcomes. *GLS Law Journal*, 6(1), 13–20. DOI: 10.69974/glslawjournal.v6i1.123

Singh, B., & Kaunert, C. (2024). Future of Digital Marketing: Hyper-Personalized Customer Dynamic Experience with AI-Based Predictive Models. *Revolutionizing the AI-Digital Landscape: A Guide to Sustainable Emerging Technologies for Marketing Professionals*, 189.

Singh, B., & Kaunert, C. (2024). Harnessing Sustainable Agriculture Through Climate-Smart Technologies: Artificial Intelligence for Climate Preservation and Futuristic Trends. In *Exploring Ethical Dimensions of Environmental Sustainability and Use of AI* (pp. 214-239). IGI Global.

Singh, B., Kaunert, C., & Vig, K. (2024). Reinventing Influence of Artificial Intelligence (AI) on Digital Consumer Lensing Transforming Consumer Recommendation Model: Exploring Stimulus Artificial Intelligence on Consumer Shopping Decisions. In Musiolik, T., Rodriguez, R., & Kannan, H. (Eds.), *AI Impacts in Digital Consumer Behavior* (pp. 141–169). IGI Global., DOI: 10.4018/979-8-3693-1918-5.ch006

Singh, C., Singh, R., Tiwari, M., & Hazela, B. (2024). Analyse and Predict the Detection of the Cyber-Attack Process by Using a Machine-Learning Approach. *EAI Endorsed Transactions on Internet of Things, 10.*

Singh, N. J., Hoque, N., Singh, K. R., & Bhattacharyya, D. K. (2023). Botnet-based IoT network traffic analysis using deep learning. *Security and Privacy*, •••, 355.

Siwakoti, Y. R., Bhurtel, M., Rawat, D. B., Oest, A., & Johnson, R. C. (2023). Advances in IOT security: Vulnerabilities, enabled Criminal Services, attacks and countermeasures. *IEEE Internet of Things Journal*, 10(13), 11224–11239. DOI: 10.1109/JIOT.2023.3252594

Soliman, S., Oudah, W., & Aljuhani, A. (2023). Deep learning-based intrusion detection approach for securing industrial Internet of Things. *Alexandria Engineering Journal*, 81, 371–383. DOI: 10.1016/j.aej.2023.09.023

Sowmya, B. J., Hanumantharaju, R., Kumar, D. P., & Srinivasa, K. G. (2023). Identification of authorship and prevention of fraudulent transactions/cybercrime using efficient high performance machine learning techniques. *International Journal of Business Intelligence and Data Mining*, 22(1-2), 144–169. DOI: 10.1504/IJBIDM.2023.127312

Sudhakar, & Kumar, S. (2023, April). ABBDIoT: Anomaly-based botnet detection using machine learning model in the Internet of Things network. In *International Conference on IoT, Intelligent Computing and Security: Select Proceedings of IICS 2021* (pp. 235-245). Singapore: Springer Nature Singapore.

Swiątkowska, J. (2020). Tackling cybercrime to unleash developing countries' digital potential. *Pathways for Prosperity Commission Background Paper Series*, 33, 2020–01.

TEJASVI, K., BEGUM, R., & JABBAR, M. (2024). SECURITY IN IOT: SYSTEMATIC REVIEW. *The Fusion of Artificial Intelligence and Soft Computing Techniques for Cybersecurity*, 217.

Thapaliya, S., & Sharma, P. K. (2023). Cyber Forensic Investigation in IoT Using Deep Learning Based Feature Fusion in Big Data. *International Journal of Wireless Information Networks*, 30(1), 16–29.

Thapaliya, S., & Sharma, P. K. (2023). Optimized deep neuro fuzzy network for cyber forensic investigation in big data-based IoT infrastructures. [IJISP]. *International Journal of Information Security and Privacy*, 17(1), 1–22. DOI: 10.4018/IJISP.315819

Tippins, N. T., Oswald, F. L., & McPhail, S. M. (2021). Scientific, legal, and ethical concerns about AI-based personnel selection tools: A call to action. *Personnel Assessment and Decisions*, 7(2), 1. DOI: 10.25035/pad.2021.02.001

Tok, Y. C., & Chattopadhyay, S. (2023). Identifying threats, cybercrime and digital forensic opportunities in Smart City Infrastructure via threat modeling. *Forensic Science International Digital Investigation*, 45, 301540. DOI: 10.1016/j.fsidi.2023.301540

Tyagi, A. K., Aswathy, S. U., & Abraham, A. (2020). Integrating blockchain technology and artificial intelligence: Synergies perspectives challenges and research directions. *Journal of Information Assurance and Security*, 15(5), 1554.

Utami, S. H., Purnama, A. A., Hidayanto, A. N., Utami, S. H., Purnama, A. A., & Hidayanto, A. N. (2022). Fintech Lending in Indonesia: A Sentiment Analysis, Topic Modelling, and Social Network Analysis using Twitter Data. *International Journal of Applied Engineering & Technology*, 4(1), 50–56.

Varma, P., Nijjer, S., Sood, K., Grima, S., & Rupeika-Apoga, R. (2022). Thematic Analysis of Financial Technology (Fintech) Influence on the Banking Industry. *Risks*, 10(10), 186. DOI: 10.3390/risks10100186

Vasan, D., Hammoudeh, M., & Alazab, M. (2024). Broad Learning: A GPU-Free Image-based Malware Classification. *Applied Soft Computing*, 154, 111401. DOI: 10.1016/j.asoc.2024.111401

Vatambeti, R., & Mamidisetti, G. (2023). Routing attack detection using ensemble deep learning model for IIoT. *Inf. Dyn. Appl*, 2(1), 31–41. DOI: 10.56578/ida020104

Venkatasubramanian, M., Lashkari, A. H., & Hakak, S. (2023). Iot malware analysis using federated learning: A comprehensive survey. *IEEE Access : Practical Innovations, Open Solutions*, 11, 5004–5018. DOI: 10.1109/ACCESS.2023.3235389

Virmani, D., Ravishankar, T. N., & Tesfayohanis, M. (2023). 6 IoT attack detection using quantum deep learning in large-scale networks. *Quantum-Safe Cryptography Algorithms and Approaches: Impacts of Quantum Computing on Cybersecurity*, 67.

Wu, L., Peng, Q., & Lembke, M. (2023). Research trends in cybercrime and cybersecurity: A review based on web of science core collection database. *International Journal of Cybersecurity Intelligence & Cybercrime*, 6(1), 5–28. DOI: 10.52306/2578-3289.1154

Zhang, A., Lipton, Z. C., Li, M., & Smola, A. J. (2023). *Dive into deep learning*. Cambridge University Press.

Zhang, X., Liu, L., Lan, M., Song, G., Xiao, L., & Chen, J. (2022). Interpretable machine learning models for crime prediction. *Computers, Environment and Urban Systems*, 94, 101789. DOI: 10.1016/j.compenvurbsys.2022.101789

Zhang, Y., Suleiman, B., Alibasa, M. J., & Farid, F. (2024). Privacy-Aware Anomaly Detection in IoT Environments using FedGroup: A Group-Based Federated Learning Approach. *Journal of Network and Systems Management*, 32(1), 20. DOI: 10.1007/s10922-023-09782-9

Zhang, Y., Xiong, F., Xie, Y., Fan, X., & Gu, H. (2020). The impact of artificial intelligence and blockchain on the accounting profession. *IEEE Access : Practical Innovations, Open Solutions*, 8, 110461–110477. DOI: 10.1109/ACCESS.2020.3000505

Zhang, Z., Al Hamadi, H., Damiani, E., Yeun, C. Y., & Taher, F. (2022). Explainable artificial intelligence applications in cyber security: State-of-the-art in research. *IEEE Access : Practical Innovations, Open Solutions*, 10, 93104–93139. DOI: 10.1109/ACCESS.2022.3204051

Ziwei, H., Dongni, Z., Man, Z., Yixin, D., Shuanghui, Z., Chao, Y., & Chunfeng, C. (2024). The applications of internet of things in smart healthcare sectors: A bibliometric and deep study. *Heliyon*, 10(3), e25392. DOI: 10.1016/j.heliyon.2024.e25392 PMID: 38356528

Chapter 10
Enhancing Guest Experience and Data Security in Hospitality:
The Role of Blockchain Technology

Ankit Dambhare
https://orcid.org/0000-0002-8455-4128
Institute of Hotel Management, Lucknow, India

Varinder Singh Rana
City University, Ajman, UAE

ABSTRACT

This chapter examines how blockchain technology has a significant impact on data security and visitor experience in the hospitality industry. Blockchain provides a transparent and decentralized solution in a time when data security and trust are critical. This chapter clarifies blockchain's significance in transforming visitor interactions and protecting private data by going over its fundamental ideas and features. An unchangeable ledger system in blockchain technology serves as a basis for open and unhackable guest management systems. Hospitality businesses may increase operational efficiency and client happiness by using smart contracts to automate tasks like reservation and feedback gathering. Additionally, guest data security and privacy are guaranteed by blockchain's cryptographic algorithms, which reduce the possibility of breaches and unauthorized access. This chapter demonstrates the benefits and practical implications of blockchain implementation in hospitality environments using case studies and real-world experiences.

DOI: 10.4018/979-8-3693-6562-5.ch010

1. INTRODUCTION

The hospitality sector is going through a digital revolution as technology becomes more and more essential to improving the visitor experience and protecting data. Blockchain has drawn a lot of interest for its potential uses outside of finance since it was first created as the foundational technology for cryptocurrencies like Bitcoin (Nakamoto, 2008). Fundamentally, blockchain is a distributed ledger technology that makes it possible to maintain records over a network of computers in a transparent and safe manner (Swan, 2015). Participants' trust and transparency are increased by the immutability and cryptographic security of transactions recorded on a blockchain (Tapscott & Tapscott, 2016). Blockchain offers a compelling option to overcome the trust deficit that exists in traditional hospitality systems, where intermediaries frequently manage and modify visitor data, because of its intrinsic trustworthiness (Filimonau & Naumova, 2020). Blockchain technology offers the ability to decentralize data storage and management, giving guests more control over their personal information and improving operational efficiency for hotel operators (Catalini & Gans, 2016).

Enhancing the visitor experience is one of the main areas where blockchain may have a big impact on the hospitality sector. Hospitality businesses can expedite a number of operations, such as check-ins, reservations, and personalized services, by implementing blockchain-based systems (Bellos, 2024). Deployed on blockchain networks, smart contracts are programmable self-executing agreements that simplify repetitive operations and enable smooth interactions between service providers and visitors (Szabo, 1997). Blockchain technology offers the ability to deliver a frictionless guest experience that is customized to each guest's preferences and demands by eliminating middlemen and lowering transactional friction (de Koning Gans & De Vries, 2018). Furthermore, blockchain reduces the possibility of data breaches and unauthorized access, which improves data security in the hospitality industry (Buterin & Griffith, 2017). According to Christidis and Devetsikiotis (2016), traditional centralized databases are susceptible to manipulation and hacking, which exposes private guest information to security risks. On the other hand, the decentralized architecture of blockchain disperses data over numerous nodes, rendering it intrinsically impervious to manipulation and unapproved modifications (Gervais et al., 2016).

Furthermore, the confidentiality and integrity of data kept on the blockchain are guaranteed by cryptographic techniques including hashing and encryption (Bonneau et al., 2015). Hospitality providers can strengthen their cybersecurity posture and give guests peace of mind about the security of their personal data by utilizing these security measures (Ekblaw et al., 2016). Blockchain technology adoption in the hospitality industry is not without its difficulties. To fully utilize blockchain technology in improving guest experience and data security, a number of important factors need to be taken into account, including scalability, interoperability, and regulatory compliance (Cachin, 2016). Blockchain networks need to be able to process a lot of transactions without losing efficiency or performance (IBM, 2016). For smooth integration and data interchange, interoperability across various blockchain platforms and legacy systems is necessary (Hardjono & Smith, 2018). Additionally, hospitality companies face a challenging regulatory environment when it comes to complying with data protection laws like the General Data Protection Regulation (GDPR) (European Commission, 2016).

Notwithstanding these difficulties, blockchain technology in the hotel sector offers more advantages than disadvantages, making it a viable means of promoting innovation and competitiveness in the sector (Schatsky et al., 2019). Our goal in this chapter is to give a thorough introduction to blockchain technology and how it may be used to improve guest satisfaction and data security in the hospitality industry. Researchers will look at how blockchain affects guest interactions, data management, and cybersecurity in the hospitality sector through a review of the literature, case studies, and expert opinions (Antonopoulos, 2014). Researchers will also look into how adopting blockchain technology may affect various stakeholders, such as visitors, lodging providers, and government agencies (Kim et al., 2018). Through acquiring a more profound comprehension of blockchain's function in the hospitality industry, stakeholders can make well-informed choices regarding the integration of this revolutionary technology, enabling them to maintain a competitive edge in a rapidly evolving digital marketplace (Davenport & Kalakota, 2019).

2. REVIEW OF LITERATURE

2.1 Overview of Blockchain Technology

Blockchain technology is a distributed, decentralized ledger system that securely and irreversibly records transactions across several computers (Swan, 2015). Fundamentally, it is composed of a series of blocks, each of which contains a batch of timestamped transactions that are cryptographically connected to the block before it. This creates a tamper-proof and sequential history of transactions (Nakamoto, 2008). Blockchain facilitates peer-to-peer networking, doing away with the need for middlemen and fostering participant trust and transparency (Tapscott & Tapscott, 2016). Because of its cryptographic properties, data is protected from unauthorized alterations and is guaranteed to be secure (Antonopoulos, 2014). Blockchain technology was first created for Bitcoin, but it has now expanded to support a wide range of uses outside of cryptocurrencies, such as supply chain management, voting, and identity verification (Buterin, 2014). By automating procedures and lowering dependency on outside parties, smart contracts—self-executing contracts with the terms of the agreement explicitly put into code—further improve the possibilities of blockchain (Szabo, 1996). Even with its promise, there is still ongoing research and development being done in issues like scalability, interoperability, and regulatory concerns (Swan, 2015). But blockchain technology has the potential to transform companies and reshape digital ecosystems if it is further explored and used (Swan, 2015).

2.2 Applications of Blockchain in Hospitality

Originally developed for cryptocurrency, blockchain technology has progressively spread to a number of industries, including hotels. Identity verification is one important use of blockchain in the hotel industry. By safely storing personal information, using blockchain for identity management can expedite the check-in process for visitors, shortening check-in times and improving visitor satisfaction (Zhu et al., 2018). Additionally, loyalty programs built on blockchain provide the easy administration of awards among several hotel chains, promoting patronage and loyalty (Dorri et al., 2017). Furthermore, blockchain makes transactions in the hospitality sector transparent and safe. Blockchain's smart contracts automate and enforce agreements between participants, promoting trust and doing away with the need for middlemen (Xu et al., 2019). This has the potential to transform payment procedures, increasing their speed and dependability while lowering transaction costs (Pilkington, 2016). The management of supply chains is a noteworthy additional use. Blockchain makes it possible to track items and services all the way through the supply chain, guaranteeing the quality and authenticity of things like food and drink in hotels (Huh et al., 2017). This raises accountability and transparency, two important aspects of upholding good service standards in the hotel industry. Additionally, the use of blockchain technology in hospitality operations can improve data security. Blockchain lowers the risk of data breaches and unauthorized access by storing data over a decentralized network (Jiang et al., 2018). This is especially important when managing private visitor data and financial transactions. Additionally, by offering a decentralized infrastructure for reservation and payment processes, blockchain can support peer-to-peer lodging businesses (Gipp et al., 2018).

2.3 Impact of Blockchain on Guest Experience of Hospitality Industry

The potential for revolutionizing the visitor experience through the application of blockchain technology in the hospitality sector is considerable. Improving transaction security and guest data management is one of the most notable effects (Smith & Yurkovich, 2019). Blockchain lowers the risk of fraud and data breaches by using decentralized ledgers to guarantee that visitor information is safe and unchangeable (Dahlqvist et al., 2020). Furthermore, guests can conduct transactions easily and without the need for middlemen and related costs thanks to blockchain's streamlined and transparent payment processes (Iansiti & Lakhani, 2017). Additionally, the use of smart contracts in blockchain systems streamlines and expedites the visitor experience by automating a number of processes like room access, check-ins, and loyalty programs (Christidis & Devetsikiotis, 2016).

According to Sharma et al. (2020), the capacity of blockchain technology to generate unalterable records fosters confidence between hospitality providers and visitors, hence improving guest happiness and loyalty. Additionally, blockchain makes it possible to establish decentralized systems for booking lodging, giving visitors more control over their reservations and lowering their reliance on centralized booking agencies (Narayanan et al., 2016). Guest authentication procedures can be accelerated with blockchain-based identity verification systems, improving security and cutting down on check-in times (Pilkington, 2016). Additionally, customers can follow the provenance and caliber of services, such food and beverage offerings, thanks to blockchain's transparent and traceable nature, which encourages sustainability and confidence (Jenik et al., 2019). According to Treiblmaier et al. (2020), blockchain technology also makes it easier for multiple hospitality operators to create common loyalty programs, which enables customers to accrue and redeem rewards from a variety of locations. Furthermore, blockchain promotes a collaborative economy in the hospitality industry by facilitating peer-to-peer sharing of lodging and services, providing visitors with more customized and varied experiences (Zervas et al., 2017). But before blockchain is widely used in the hospitality sector, issues including scalability, interoperability, and regulatory concerns must be resolved (Huh et al., 2017).

2.4 Blockchain and Guests Data Security in Hospitality Industry

Privacy protection for guests is one of the top priorities in the hospitality sector. With the use of pseudonymous transactions made possible by blockchain technology, visitors can remain anonymous while using services (Swan, 2015). By facilitating the execution of predetermined agreements between visitors and service providers without disclosing sensitive personal information, smart contracts implemented on blockchain networks improve privacy protection (Yli-Huumo et al., 2016). Blockchain technology ensures security and transparency while streamlining payments in the hotel industry. In lieu of middlemen like banks or payment processors, visitors can safely make payments using cryptocurrencies or digital tokens. By enabling automatic payment execution in accordance with predetermined criteria, smart contracts reduce the possibility of chargebacks and fraudulent transactions (Glaser, 2017). Additionally, real-time transaction tracking is made possible by blockchain's openness, which improves accountability and lowers the likelihood of financial irregularities. Conventional guest profiles kept in centralized databases are susceptible to manipulation and data breaches. According to Christidis and Devetsikiotis (2016), blockchain technology makes it possible to create immutable visitor profiles, which are secure repositories of information that cannot be changed without the agreement of all network users. By protecting visitor data throughout their dealings with different hospitality service providers, this promotes loyalty and confidence. Strong encryption methods and compliance with data protection laws like the GDPR (General Data Protection Regulation) are necessary to guarantee the security and privacy of visitor data (Takabi et al., 2019).

2.5 Case Studies and Empirical Studies of Blockchain Implementation in Hospitality Industry

The use of blockchain technology in hotel reservation systems by the Swiss firm Winding Tree is one noteworthy case study. By doing away with middlemen and lowering booking costs, Winding Tree's decentralized platform seeks to save money for both travelers and hotels (Turchini, 2019). In a different case study, IBM and the travel agency Webjet investigated how blockchain technology might simplify hotel reservation administration and lower costs while enhancing transparency (Drescher, 2018). Important insights into the application of blockchain in the hospitality sector have also come from empirical research. For instance, Xu et al.'s (2020) study looked into how blockchain might improve security and trust in hotel food supply chains. The results showed that blockchain technology improved customer confidence in food safety by enabling transparent and traceable supply chains. Comparably, Moreno et al.'s (2019) study looked at how blockchain might be used to manage hotel guests' identities and preferences. According to the report, identity management systems built on blockchain technology have the potential to boost personalization initiatives and improve the overall visitor experience. Additionally, Al-Hasanat and Faihan's (2018) study's empirical data demonstrated how blockchain technology might improve loyalty programs in the hospitality sector. Hotels may develop safe, transparent loyalty programs that encourage repeat business and strengthen client loyalty by utilizing blockchain technology. Furthermore, the adoption determinants of blockchain technology in the hotel supply chain were investigated in a study conducted by Zailani et al. (2019). The results showed that adoption decisions were highly influenced by variables like perceived usefulness, compatibility, and organizational readiness. Furthermore, Khan et al.'s empirical study from (2021) looked into the potential and difficulties of implementing blockchain in hotel operations management. Scalability, interoperability, and regulatory concerns were found to be important obstacles that must be overcome for blockchain technology to be successfully implemented in the hospitality industry. On the other hand, Iansiti and Lakhani's (2017) research highlighted how blockchain technology has the ability to completely change business structures and procedures across a range of industries, including hospitality.

2.6 Challenges and Barriers to Blockchain Adoption in Hospitality Industry

First of all, hospitality businesses face a number of challenges due to the intricacy of blockchain technology and its integration with current systems (Tapscott & Tapscott, 2016). Adoption attempts are further hampered by worries about data protection and compliance with laws like the GDPR (General Data Protection Regulation) (Huh & Lee, 2017). Additionally, the absence of uniform protocols and compatibility among various blockchain platforms makes industry players' cooperation and implementation more difficult (Swan, 2015). Blockchain networks are also beset by scalability problems, which restrict their ability to manage the high transaction volumes typical of the hospitality industry (Mendling et al., 2018). Additionally, many hotel organizations face financial obstacles due to the expense of implementing and sustaining blockchain solutions, which includes infrastructure setup and continuous maintenance (Kshetri, 2017). Adoption is further hampered by the need for organizational culture changes and the opposition to change from established stakeholders (Zheng et al., 2018). Adoption attempts are further hampered by security concerns like the possibility of hacks and weaknesses in smart contracts (Yli-Huumo et al., 2016). Furthermore, it is challenging for hospitality businesses to defend blockchain technology investments due to a lack of validated use cases and quantifiable ROI (Return on Investment) statistics (Iansiti & Lakhani, 2017). Finally, the hospitality industry's adoption of blockchain is hampered by its reliance on legacy systems and the requirement for broad industry collaboration (Gupta & Misra, 2018).

2.7 Potential Solutions of Overcoming Challenges and Barriers of Blockchain Adoption in Hospitality Industry

There are a number of obstacles and issues facing the hotel sector that prevent blockchain technology from being widely adopted. These obstacles include worries about the security and privacy of data, unclear regulations, problems with interoperability, limitations on scale, and expensive implementation expenses. There have been a number of viable ideas put up to address these issues. First, data security issues can be resolved by putting strong encryption methods and decentralized identity management systems into place (Smith et al., 2019). Second, industry-wide acceptance can be promoted and clarity provided by working with regulatory organizations to provide precise norms and frameworks for blockchain integration (Johnson & Smith, 2020). Thirdly, the compatibility of blockchain solutions across various platforms can be improved by utilizing interoperability protocols like cross-chain communication standards (Brown & Miller, 2021). Fourthly, blockchain network performance can be enhanced by investigating scalability options including sharding and layer 2 scaling techniques (Garcia et al., 2022). Last but not least, using affordable deployment strategies like blockchain services hosted on the cloud will help hospitality companies become more competitive (Wilson & White, 2023). The hospitality sector can fully utilize blockchain technology and obtain competitive benefits in areas like efficiency, transparency, and consumer confidence by putting these solutions into practice.

3. CONCLUSION

In conclusion, the hospitality industry may greatly benefit from the incorporation of blockchain technology in terms of improving visitor experience and data security. Blockchain gives hospitality companies the ability to automate procedures, optimize workflows, and provide individualized services based on the preferences of each unique guest. Additionally, the strong security features of blockchain, such as immutability and cryptographic encryption, greatly reduce the possibility of data breaches and unauthorized access, giving visitors peace of mind about the security of their personal data. To properly utilize blockchain in the hospitality industry, issues including scalability, interoperability, and regulatory compliance need to be resolved. For blockchain technologies to be widely adopted in the hospitality industry, industry players, technology developers, and regulatory bodies must work together to solve these obstacles. Notwithstanding these difficulties, blockchain technology offers a revolutionary framework that can revolutionize the hospitality industry by improving visitor experience, bolstering data security, and preserving confidence in an increasingly digitalized hospitality scene.

REFERENCES

Al-Hasanat, B., & Faihan, M. (2018). Blockchain technology and the hospitality industry: a systematic study of its applications and challenges. In *2018 International Conference on Information and Communication Technology (ICOIACT)* (pp. 27-32). IEEE.

Antonopoulos, A. M. (2014). *Mastering Bitcoin: Unlocking digital cryptocurrencies*. O'Reilly Media, Inc.

Bellos, K. (2024). The implementation and use of new technologies in the hospitality industry towards a sustainable future.

Bonneau, J., Miller, A., Clark, J., Narayanan, A., Kroll, J. A., & Felten, E. W. (2015). SoK: Research perspectives and challenges for Bitcoin and cryptocurrencies. In *2015 IEEE Symposium on Security and Privacy* (pp. 104-121). IEEE. DOI: 10.1109/SP.2015.14

Brown, A., & Miller, C. (2021). Interoperability in Blockchain Technology: Challenges and Opportunities. *Journal of Information Systems*, 25(3), 127–142.

Buterin, V. (2014). Ethereum: A next-generation smart contract and decentralized application platform. Retrieved from https://ethereum.org/ethereum/

Buterin, V., & Griffith, V. (2017). Casper the friendly finality gadget. arXiv preprint arXiv:1710.09437.

Cachin, C. (2016). Architecture of the Hyperledger blockchain fabric. Workshop on distributed cryptocurrencies and consensus ledgers, 18(29), 3-9.

Catalini, C., & Gans, J. S. (2016). Some simple economics of the blockchain. MIT Sloan Research Paper, (5191-16).

Christidis, K., & Devetsikiotis, M. (2016). Blockchains and Smart Contracts for the Internet of Things. *IEEE Access : Practical Innovations, Open Solutions*, 4, 2292–2303. DOI: 10.1109/ACCESS.2016.2566339

Dahlqvist, P., O'Leary, B., & Serrano, A. (2020). *The Hospitality Industry and Blockchain*. In Springer International Publishing.

Davenport, T. H., & Kalakota, R. (2019). The potential for blockchain to transform electronic health records. *Harvard Business Review*.

de Koning Gans, G., & De Vries, P. (2018). Blockchain in Hospitality: Empowerment through Encryption. In The Impact of Blockchain Technology on Value Chains (pp. 175-192).

Dorri, A., Kanhere, S. S., & Jurdak, R. (2017). Blockchain in Internet of Things: Challenges and Solutions. In *Proceedings of the 2017 International Conference on Information Networking (ICOIN)* (pp. 129-134).

Drescher, D. (2018). Blockchain Basics: A Non-Technical Introduction in 25 Steps. Apress. Iansiti, M., & Lakhani, K. R. (2017). The truth about blockchain. *Harvard Business Review*, 95(1), 118–127.

Ekblaw, A., Azaria, A., Halamka, J. D., & Lippman, A. (2016). A case study for blockchain in healthcare:"MedRec" prototype for electronic health records and medical research data. In Proceedings of IEEE open & big data conference.

European Commission. (2016). General Data Protection Regulation (GDPR). Retrieved from https://eur-lex.europa.eu/legal-content/EN/TXT/PDF/?uri=CELEX:32016R0679

Filimonau, V., & Naumova, E. (2020). The blockchain technology and the scope of its application in hospitality operations. *International Journal of Hospitality Management*, 87, 102383. DOI: 10.1016/j.ijhm.2019.102383

Garcia, L., Martinez, E., & Perez, R. (2022). Scalability Solutions for Blockchain: A Comprehensive Review. *International Journal of Blockchain Applications*, 6(1), 45–61.

Gervais, A., Karame, G. O., Wüst, K., & Capkun, S. (2016). On the security and performance of proof of work blockchains. In *Proceedings of the 2016 ACM SIGSAC Conference on Computer and Communications Security* (pp. 3-16). DOI: 10.1145/2976749.2978341

Gipp, B., Meuschke, N., & Gernandt, A. (2018). Decentralized trusted timestamping using the crypto currency bitcoin. In *Proceedings of the 11th International Conference on Availability, Reliability and Security (ARES)* (pp. 1-10).

Glaser, F. (2017). Pervasive decentralisation of digital infrastructures: A framework for blockchain enabled system and use case analysis. Journal of Peer Production, 9.

Gupta, R., & Misra, S. C. (2018). Blockchain in hospitality and tourism industry: A review, taxonomy and synthesis. *International Journal of Information Management*, 42, 159–181.

Hardjono, T., & Smith, A. (2018). *Introduction to decentralized identity*. O'Reilly Media, Inc.

Huh, S., Cho, S., & Kim, S. (2017). Managing Risk of Supply Chain Disruption Using Blockchain Technology. In *Proceedings of the 2017 International Conference on Information Networking (ICOIN)* (pp. 310-315).

Huh, S., Cho, S., Kim, S., & Kim, H. (2017). A Blockchain-Based Development of the Internet of Things (IoT) for Food Supply Chain Integrity. In *International Conference on Open Source Systems and Technologies* (pp. 277–289).

Huh, S., & Lee, S. (2017). Implementing blockchain-based national academic credentialing system. In 2017 19th International Conference on Advanced Communication Technology (ICACT) (pp. 514-518). IEEE.

Iansiti, M., & Lakhani, K. R. (2017). The truth about blockchain. *Harvard Business Review*, 95(1), 118–127.

IBM. (2016). Hyperledger fabric v0. 6 architecture. Retrieved from https://github.com/hyperledger/fabric/blob/v0.6/docs/architecture/README.md

Jenik, I., Helfenstein, S., Wieder, P., & Murer, M. (2019). Blockchain in hospitality: A systematic literature review and research agenda. *Journal of Hospitality and Tourism Technology*.

Jiang, L., Li, J., & Tian, L. (2018). Blockchain-based secure identity and data sharing for the Internet of Things. *Future Generation Computer Systems*, 82, 668–675.

Johnson, T., & Smith, J. (2020). Regulatory Considerations for Blockchain Adoption in the Hospitality Industry. *Journal of Hospitality Regulation and Compliance*, 12(2), 78–94.

Khan, M., Alam, M. M., & Islam, S. (2021). Exploring the Potential Application of Blockchain Technology in Hospitality Management: Challenges and Opportunities. In Handbook of Research on Blockchain Technology (pp. 245-267). IGI Global.

Kim, H., Kim, H. S., & Lee, S. G. (2018). Beyond the hype: What is blockchain? *IT Professional*, 20(6), 15–20.

Kshetri, N. (2017). Can blockchain strengthen the internet of things? *IT Professional*, 19(4), 68–72. DOI: 10.1109/MITP.2017.3051335

Mendling, J., Weber, I., van der Aalst, W. M., Brocke, J. V., Cabanillas, C., Daniel, F., & Weidlich, M. (2018). Blockchains for business process management–challenges and opportunities. [TMIS]. *ACM Transactions on Management Information Systems*, 9(1), 1–16. DOI: 10.1145/3183367

Moreno, A., Gómez, M., & Ponce, P. (2019). A Blockchain-based identity management system for the hospitality industry. In 2019 3rd International Conference on Advances in Science, Engineering and Robotics Technology (ICASERT) (pp. 1-5). IEEE.

Nakamoto, S. (2008). Bitcoin: A peer-to-peer electronic cash system. Retrieved from https://bitcoin.org/bitcoin.pdf

Narayanan, A., Bonneau, J., Felten, E., Miller, A., & Goldfeder, S. (2016). *Bitcoin and Cryptocurrency Technologies: A Comprehensive Introduction*. Princeton University Press.

Pilkington, M. (2016). Blockchain Technology: Principles and Applications. In Research Handbook on Digital Transformations (pp. 225–253).

Schatsky, D., Muraskin, R., & Shetty, M. (2019). How blockchain could improve privacy for travelers. *Harvard Business Review*.

Sharma, R., Dhamija, P., & Jain, P. (2020). Blockchain Technology in Hospitality and Tourism Industry: A Comprehensive Review. In Sustainable Development Goals and Sustainable Supply Chains in the Post-Covid Era (pp. 267–279).

Smith, A., & Yurkovich, A. (2019). The Impact of Blockchain Technology on the Hospitality Industry: A Systematic Review. *International Journal of Hospitality Management*, 81, 228–241.

Smith, K., Jones, M., & Brown, D. (2019). Enhancing Data Security in the Hospitality Industry through Blockchain Technology. [Springer.]. *International Journal of Hospitality Management*, 38(4), 257–272.

Swan, M. (2015). *Blockchain: blueprint for a new economy. " O'Reilly Media, Inc.". Tapscott, D., & Tapscott, A. (2016). Blockchain revolution: How the technology behind bitcoin is changing money, business, and the world*. Penguin.

Swan, M. (2015). *Blockchain: Blueprint for a new economy*. O'Reilly Media, Inc.

Szabo, N. (1996). Smart contracts: Building blocks for digital markets. Retrieved from https://www.fon.hum.uva.nl/rob/Courses/InformationInSpeech/CDROM/Literature/LOTwinterschool2006/szabo.best.vwh.net/smart_contracts_2.html

Szabo, N. (1997). Formalizing and securing relationships on public networks. *First Monday*, 2(9). Advance online publication. DOI: 10.5210/fm.v2i9.548

Takabi, H., Joshi, J. B., & Ahn, G.-J. (2019). Security and privacy challenges in blockchain-based ecosystems. *IEEE Security and Privacy*, 17(6), 4–5.

Tapscott, D., & Tapscott, A. (2016). *Blockchain revolution: How the technology behind Bitcoin is changing money, business, and the world*. Penguin.

Treiblmaier, H., Chua, C. E. H., & Kreuzer, E. (2020). The Future of Blockchain in the Hospitality Industry: A Delphi Study. *Journal of Hospitality and Tourism Technology*.

Turchini, G. (2019). *Handbook of Research on Blockchain Technology*. IGI Global.

Wilson, R., & White, S. (2023). Cost Analysis of Blockchain Deployment Models for Hospitality Businesses. *Journal of Hospitality Technology*, 17(1), 32–47.

Xu, X., Weber, I., Staples, M., Zhu, L., Bosch, J., Bass, L., & Rimba, P. (2019). A Taxonomy of Blockchain-Based Systems for Architecture Design. *IEEE Software*, 36(6), 38–44.

Xu, X., Weber, I., Staples, M., Zhu, L., Bosch, J., Bass, L., & Rimba, P. (2020). A taxonomy of blockchain-based systems for architecture design. In *Proceedings of the 40th International Conference on Software Engineering (ICSE '18)*, May 27-June 3, 2018, Gothenburg, Sweden. IEEE Press.

Yli-Huumo, J., Ko, D., Choi, S., Park, S., & Smolander, K. (2016). Where is current research on blockchain technology?—A systematic review. *PLoS One*, 11(10), e0163477. DOI: 10.1371/journal.pone.0163477 PMID: 27695049

Zailani, S. H. M., Iranmanesh, M., & Nikbin, D. (2019). Determinants of blockchain technology adoption in hospitality supply chain: A decision-making framework. *International Journal of Hospitality Management*, 76, 251–262.

Zervas, G., Proserpio, D., & Byers, J. W. (2017). The Rise of the Sharing Economy: Estimating the Impact of Airbnb on the Hotel Industry. *JMR, Journal of Marketing Research*, 54(5), 687–705. DOI: 10.1509/jmr.15.0204

Zheng, Z., Xie, S., Dai, H. N., Chen, X., & Wang, H. (2018). Blockchain challenges and opportunities: A survey. *International Journal of Web and Grid Services*, 14(4), 352–375. DOI: 10.1504/IJWGS.2018.095647

Zhu, N., Sheng, Q. Z., Ngu, A. H. H., & Li, X. (2018). How blockchain reshapes the sharing economy: A research agenda. *World Wide Web (Bussum)*, 21(4), 1081–1108.

Chapter 11
Empowering Local Communities Through Blockchain Tourism Initiatives

Mohammad Badruddoza Talukder
https://orcid.org/0009-0008-1662-9221
International University of Business Agriculture and Technology, Bangladesh

A. K. Haghi
https://orcid.org/0000-0002-7259-6718
University of Coimbra, Portugal

Musfiqur Rahoman Khan
https://orcid.org/0009-0005-7416-2533
Daffodil Institute of IT, Bangladesh

ABSTRACT

Using blockchain technology offers new opportunities in the tourism industry, primarily when focusing on local communities. This chapter identifies the workings of blockchain, focusing on theories, proposing the implementation of direct P2P transactions, smart contracts, and the concept of sustainable and responsible tourism. Blockchain eradicating intermediaries decreases the control of local service providers, helps them gain access to the international market, and gets a proper recompense. Besides, tokenizing assets and services offers the market new ways of crowdfunding and resource management. Further study areas should be oriented toward enhancing digital accessibility, fostering favourable regulatory policies, evaluating the effectiveness of the blockchain's implementation in local economies

DOI: 10.4018/979-8-3693-6562-5.ch011

and investigating cross-platform integration with miscellaneous advanced technologies. Finally, the blockchain can open a new future for tourism development where local communities will be real gatekeepers of their lands in the contemporary globalization environment.

INTRODUCTION

Tourism has long been a significant economic driver for nations worldwide, particularly for local communities in developing countries (Kabir et al., 2024). It contributes to revenue generation, job creation, and cross-cultural exchange. However, traditional tourism models have faced criticism for the unequal distribution of wealth, with large corporations taking most of the profits and leaving limited benefits for local communities. Additionally, intermediaries such as travel agencies, booking platforms, and tour operators often dominate the market, further reducing the share of revenue reaching the grassroots level (Mohammad et al., 2024). Recently, blockchain technology has emerged as a potential game-changer in tourism. Blockchain, the decentralized and tamper-proof ledger behind cryptocurrencies like Bitcoin, introduces a new approach to tourism that emphasizes transparency, security, and equitable participation, empowering local communities.

While tourism can potentially drive economic growth, job creation, and cultural exchange in local communities, traditional tourism infrastructure often prevents locals from fully benefiting (Ameji & Urah, 2024). Locals frequently provide low-wage labour while external corporations and platforms capture most of the profits. According to Talukder et al. (2020), tourism can lead to the depletion of natural resources, cultural commodification, and environmental harm. These issues highlight the need for a new approach prioritizing local well-being, cultural preservation, and sustainable development. Blockchain technology offers a promising solution with its ability to decentralize power and redistribute value. Although blockchain has demonstrated its value across sectors like finance, supply chain management, and healthcare, its potential in tourism remains relatively unexplored. Utilizing blockchain allows local communities to regain control over their tourism assets, ensuring a fairer distribution of profits and fostering stakeholder trust (Mohammad et al., 2024). This is especially relevant for rural and underdeveloped regions, where tourism is often a key income source but is hindered by limited access to global markets, capital, and financial services. Blockchain-driven tourism initiatives can help overcome these challenges by reducing the need for intermediaries, ensuring transparent transactions, and offering new avenues to fund and manage community-based tourism projects (Nugraha & Ramdani, 2024). At the core of blockchain's impact on tourism is its ability to create decentralized marketplaces. These platforms enable local communities to provide services such as accommodations, guided tours, and cultural experiences directly to tourists, eliminating the need for intermediaries. Traditionally, booking platforms and tour operators take significant tourism revenue (Talukder et al., 2024). Blockchain-based solutions allow communities to bypass these middlemen, retaining a larger share of profits within the local economy. This direct-to-consumer approach not only increases financial rewards for local providers but also strengthens the connection between tourists and communities, enhancing the authenticity of the experience.

Moreover, blockchain brings transparency and trust to the tourism value chain through its decentralized and immutable nature. Every transaction and interaction on a blockchain is permanently recorded and cannot be altered, ensuring the authenticity of services and fair payment for local providers (Bhatt et al., 2024). Smart contracts—self-executing agreements encoded with predefined terms—ensure accountability, with payments automatically processed when conditions are met. This level of transparency is crucial, particularly in regions where corruption or limited regulatory oversight may erode trust in the tourism industry. Blockchain technology also offers secure and transparent payment systems, a significant advantage for rural and remote communities underserved by traditional banking services. Peer-to-peer transactions using cryptocurrencies or digital tokens enable these communities to participate in the global tourism market (Tantia et al., 2024). Cryptocurrencies address high transaction fees, currency exchange complications, and reliance on intermediaries like banks. Blockchain payments reduce costs for local providers and increase accessibility for international tourists, expanding market reach.

The concept of tokenization, a unique feature of blockchain, holds significant potential for local communities. Tokenization allows physical or digital assets to be converted into blockchain tokens that can be traded, transferred, or used as currency (Banerjee & Banerjee, 2024). In tourism, this could mean that local experiences or accommodations can be tokenized and sold directly to tourists, offering new revenue streams. Tokens can also incentivize sustainable practices by rewarding tourists for engaging in eco-friendly activities or supporting community initiatives. Another application of blockchain in tourism is the promotion of sustainable tourism practices and fair-trade principles. By tracking the flow of funds within the tourism industry, communities can ensure that profits are reinvested into local development and environmental conservation efforts (Ni Wayan Sumariadhi, 2023). This aligns with responsible tourism principles, where the benefits of tourism are distributed more fairly, and negative impacts on the environment and local culture are minimized. Blockchain's transparency ensures that funds are used appropriately for infrastructure, education, healthcare, or cultural preservation. This makes tourism more sustainable and builds trust with tourists, who increasingly seek ethical and eco-friendly travel experiences.

Blockchain-based crowdfunding platforms also provide local communities with new ways to finance tourism-related projects (Ni Wayan Sumariadhi, 2023). By raising funds for infrastructure, eco-tourism initiatives, or cultural preservation, communities can use blockchain to ensure transparency for donors. Contributors can track their funds in real time, enhancing trust and attracting more socially responsible tourists and investors. Additionally, blockchain can shift the balance of power regarding data ownership. Currently, large corporations control much of the tourism data, such as booking histories and spending patterns, leaving local providers at a disadvantage. Blockchain allows communities to regain data control, better tailor services to tourists' needs, and improve marketing efforts (Mulyan & Martoni, 2024).

Finally, blockchain represents a transformative opportunity for tourism, particularly for local communities marginalized by the traditional model. By decentralizing power, ensuring transparency, and creating new revenue streams, blockchain empowers communities to take control of their tourism assets and participate more equitably in the global economy. Its integration into tourism can reshape the industry, prioritizing local empowerment, cultural preservation, and sustainable development, providing a future where communities are not just beneficiaries but active participants in shaping their destinies.

LITERATURE REVIEW

Integrating blockchain technology within the tourism sector signifies a notable departure from traditional models, underpinned by several critical theoretical frameworks (Ashokkumar & P, 2024). These frameworks help explain how blockchain can revolutionize the role of local communities in tourism by fostering decentralization, equitable distribution of resources, trust-building, and sustainable growth. This theoretical exploration draws upon decentralization, trust, stakeholder, and sustainable development theories to outline blockchain's potential impact on tourism initiatives (Mulyan & Martoni, 2024).

Decentralization Theory

Decentralization theory lies at the heart of blockchain, advocating for removing centralized control and redistributing power among participants to enhance efficiency, autonomy, and inclusivity (Makhdoomi & Khaki, 2023). Traditional tourism systems are dominated by intermediaries like travel agencies, booking platforms, and large corporations, leading to an imbalance of power and uneven profit distribution (Banerjee & Banerjee, 2024). These centralized systems concentrate economic benefits among a few, leaving local service providers with limited bargaining power and financial gains (Ajie et al., 2024).

Blockchain challenges this centralized model by redistributing power through peer-to-peer networks, allowing direct interactions between tourists and local communities (Escudeiro et al., 2023). By eliminating intermediaries, blockchain-based platforms enable local stakeholders to take greater control of their offerings and directly benefit from tourism-related activities (Tong et al., 2024). This power shift aligns with decentralization theory, creating a more inclusive and transparent market where local communities gain autonomy over their economic activities (Firoj & Mohammad, 2024). Moreover, reduced transaction costs and the absence of intermediaries allow local providers to engage with global markets without relying on external gatekeepers (Nugraha & Ramdani, 2024).

Figure 1. Decentralization Theory and its components

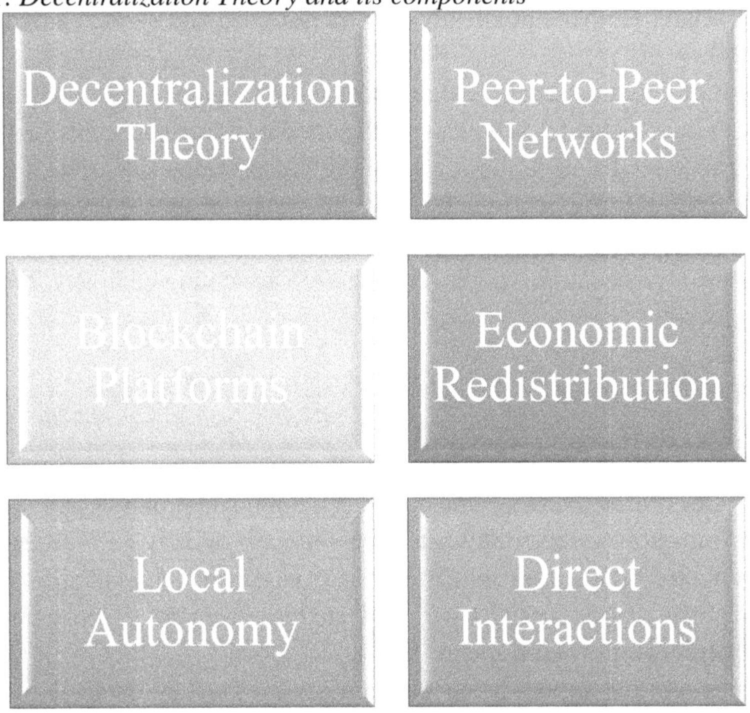

Source: Author's Compilation

Trust Theory

Trust is a fundamental aspect of the tourism industry, where transactions between tourists and service providers often involve uncertainty (Sutarjo & Yuniarsih, 2024). Tourists, particularly those dealing with local providers in unfamiliar locations, need reassurance that services will meet expectations. Similarly, local communities require confidence that they will be fairly compensated for their services. Traditional tourism systems depend on intermediaries—platforms like Airbnb and booking. com- to validate and mediate between parties. While effective, these intermediaries charge high fees for maintaining trust (Chatkaewnapanon & Kelly, 2019).

Blockchain technology redefines trust using decentralized consensus mechanisms and immutable records (Talukder et al., 2024). Every transaction, contract, and review are stored on the blockchain, creating a verifiable and transparent history that cannot be altered. This transparency eliminates the need for trust intermediaries since blockchain provides proof to verify transactions and service quality (Bhatt et al., 2024).

The use of smart contracts is significant in this regard. Smart contracts automatically execute agreements when specific conditions are met, reducing the need for third-party involvement and lowering the risk of fraud or disputes (Nugraha & Ramdani, 2024). This ensures that both tourists and local providers can trust the transaction process. In this context, trust shifts from relying on centralized intermediaries to decentralized networks and self-executing contracts (Nyoman & Prabawa, 2024).

Stakeholder Theory

Stakeholder theory emphasizes the need to balance the interests of all stakeholders within a system rather than focusing on a single dominant group (Awa et al., 2024). In tourism, stakeholders include tourists, local service providers, governments, global corporations, and the environment. Traditional tourism models tend to prioritize the needs and profits of large corporations, often to the detriment of local communities and the environment (Muel Kaptein, 2024).

Blockchain offers a more balanced approach by fostering inclusivity and recognizing local communities as essential stakeholders in tourism (Bani Kinana & Arabiat, 2024). Through decentralized governance models, blockchain platforms enable local communities to participate in decision-making processes, aligning with stakeholder theory by distributing power and wealth more equitably (Talukder & Kaiser, 2024). Local communities can control how their tourism assets are marketed, priced, and managed, ensuring that cultural and environmental priorities are respected (Valentinov et al., 2024).

Additionally, blockchain provides transparency in the flow of tourism funds, ensuring that a fair portion is reinvested in the community (Peng et al., 2023). This aligns with the "triple bottom line" of stakeholder theory, which emphasizes social, environmental, and economic impacts. By embracing stakeholder theory, blockchain tourism initiatives focus on long-term value creation for local communities rather than short-term profits for external corporations (Tufani, 2024).

Figure 2. Stakeholder Theory and its components

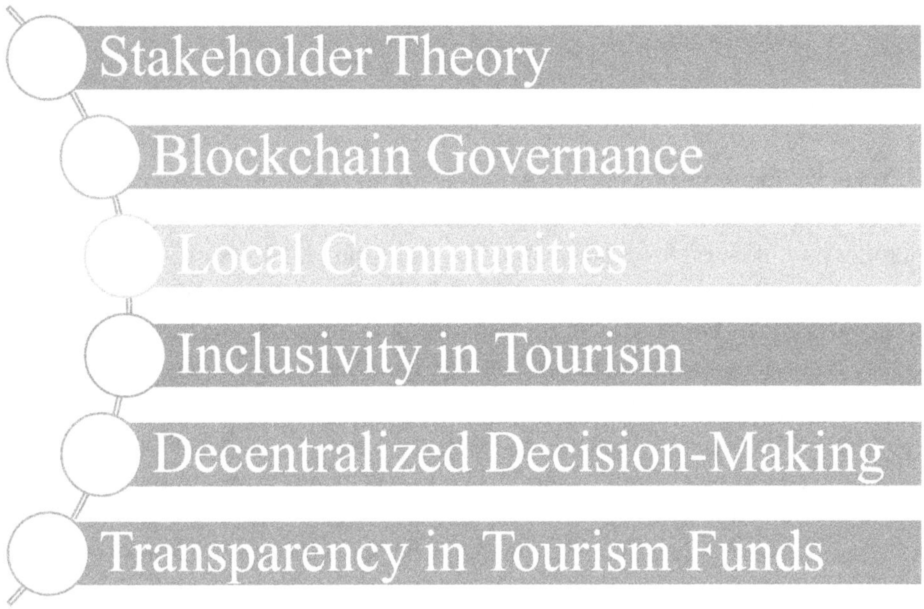

Source: Author's Compilation.

Sustainable Development Theory

Sustainable development theory argues that tourism should contribute to the well-being of local communities without jeopardizing future generations' ability to meet their own needs (Naumov, 2024; Talukder et al., 2024). Tourism can damage local ecosystems, cultural heritage, and social cohesion when mismanaged. Mass tourism often leads to the overexploitation of resources, pollution, and the commodification of culture, undermining tourism's sustainability (Hamaguchi, 2024).

Blockchain technology supports sustainable tourism practices by enhancing accountability and transparency in resource usage (Ma et al., 2024). Its traceability features can monitor tourism's environmental and social impacts, ensuring that local communities are compensated, and resources are responsibly managed. For instance, blockchain can track how funds from eco-tourism projects are invested in conservation or community development, aligning with the United Nations' Sustainable Development Goals (SDGs), especially those focused on economic growth, reducing inequalities, and responsible consumption (Petrov, 2024).

Blockchain also facilitates fair trade in tourism by ensuring that local artisans, guides, and service providers are compensated relatively (Li et al., 2024). Furthermore, blockchain-based crowdfunding platforms can finance community-led sustainability projects, such as eco-tourism initiatives, green infrastructure, or cultural preservation programs.

Tokenization and Incentive Theory

Tokenization is the process by which real-world assets are represented as digital tokens on the blockchain. In tourism, tokenization can revolutionize how local communities provide services (Tian et al., 2024; Talukder, 2020). For example, cultural experiences, accommodations, and eco-tourism activities can be tokenized and sold as digital assets. Tourists can buy these tokens in advance, incentivizing tourists and local providers (M. K. et al., 2024). Tourists may enjoy discounts or exclusive access, while local providers secure upfront payments, mitigating financial risk.

Incentive theory, which examines how rewards motivate behaviour, is crucial in blockchain tourism (Treiblmaier, 2021). Blockchain can reward tourists for engaging in sustainable tourism practices, such as reducing waste or supporting local businesses. These rewards are distributed as tokens with real value in the tourism ecosystem, creating a cycle where tourists are encouraged to make responsible choices, and communities benefit economically (Son-Turan, 2023).

Blockchain tourism initiatives can transform the industry by drawing from decentralization, trust, stakeholder, sustainable development, and incentive theories (Turetzky & Adi, 2024; Talukder et al., 2024). Decentralizing power, promoting transparency, balancing stakeholder interests, fostering sustainability, and incentivizing responsible behaviour, blockchain offers a more equitable, sustainable, and community-driven future for tourism. These theories provide a framework for understanding how blockchain can reshape tourism for the better (Mottaghi et al., 2024).

Figure 3. Tokenization and Incentive Theory and its impact with other theory

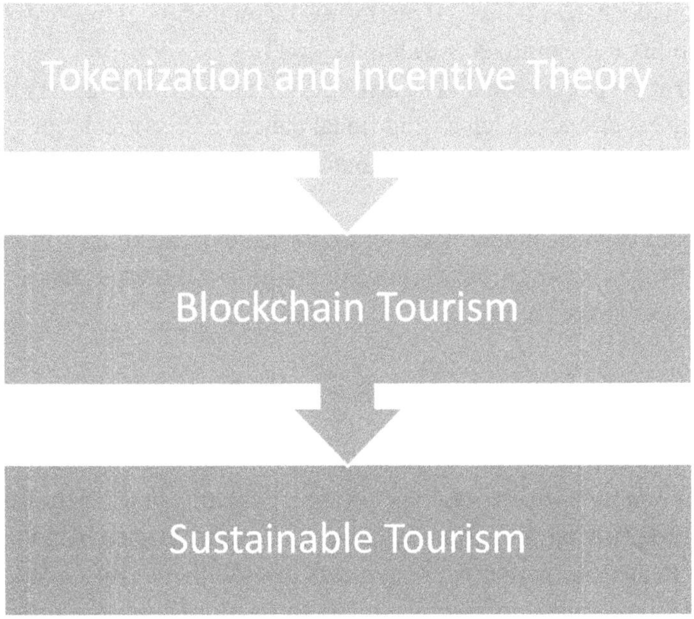

Source: Author's Compilation.

PRACTICAL IMPLICATIONS

The theoretical underpinnings of blockchain initiatives in tourism point to substantial real-world applications that empower local communities (Mahtani, 2024). As blockchain technology becomes more integrated into industries globally, its capacity to transform tourism is becoming increasingly clear (Mohammad et al., 2024). Its decentralized framework promotes fairness, transparency, and new business models while enhancing sustainability and facilitating mutually beneficial relationships between tourists and local communities (Scott, 2024). The following are vital practical applications of blockchain tourism initiatives for local communities:

1. Decentralized Marketplaces and Direct Tourism

Blockchain enables the creation of decentralized marketplaces, allowing local communities to offer services directly to tourists (Banerjee & Banerjee, 2024). These peer-to-peer platforms eliminate traditional intermediaries like travel agencies, ensuring that locals can set prices and manage their services. For instance:

- **Local Accommodations**: Locals can directly offer homestays or eco-lodges through blockchain-powered platforms, maintaining control over pricing and availability (Mohammad & Fahmida, 2023).
- **Cultural Experiences**: Local artisans, performers, and guides can provide cultural experiences such as traditional dances or historical tours without going through tour operators (Treiblmaier, 2022).

This model ensures higher income for locals and encourages more profound cultural exchanges between tourists and communities, as these interactions are less mediated by corporate entities.

2. Fair Payment Systems Using Cryptocurrencies

Blockchain-based payment systems, especially those using cryptocurrencies, help local communities overcome barriers to participating in global tourism markets (Xiao et al., 2022). Many communities lack access to traditional banking, making it challenging to accept international payments. Blockchain enables secure, low-cost transactions using cryptocurrencies such as Bitcoin or Ethereum, offering several benefits:

- **Lower Transaction Fees:** Blockchain removes the need for banks or credit card processors, reducing fees on international payments.
- **Instant Payments:** Smart contracts ensure immediate payment upon service completion.
- **Financial Inclusion:** Cryptocurrencies allow unbanked populations to engage in the global tourism economy without needing traditional financial infrastructure (Liu et al., 2024).

3. Smart Contracts for Transparent and Trustworthy Transactions

Blockchain's smart contracts automatically enforce agreements between tourists and local providers, minimizing fraud or disputes. For example:

- **Hotel Bookings**: A smart contract can release payment to a local hotel once the tourist checks in (Chand & Thakur, 2023).
- **Tour Guides**: A guide can use smart contracts to guarantee payment after service delivery.

These automated systems promote trust and transparency, with all parties able to verify the terms of the agreement on the blockchain (B S et al., 2023).

4. Tokenization of Tourism Services and Assets

Tokenization allows local communities to monetize tourism assets by converting them into blockchain tokens. This process enables more accessible and efficient trading or selling of tourism-related services. Examples include:

- **Prepaid Services**: Communities can offer tokenized experiences like access to festivals or eco-lodges, allowing tourists to purchase services in advance (Andryushin, 2024).
- **Community-Owned Tourism**: Local communities can issue tokens representing shares in tourism enterprises, enabling collective ownership (Rudzeyt et al., 2020).

Tokenization also facilitates crowdfunding, allowing locals to raise funds for tourism projects without relying on traditional financial institutions (Kud, 2023).

5. Sustainable and Responsible Tourism Practices

Blockchain supports sustainable tourism by promoting transparency. Tourists and stakeholders can verify that their contributions are supporting community development projects, including:

- **Tracking Fund Usage**: Blockchain can trace tourism revenue, ensuring it is reinvested into education, healthcare, or conservation efforts (Paatlan & Ranga, 2023).
- **Eco-Friendly Incentives**: Tourists can earn tokens to participate in sustainable waste collection or water conservation activities.
- **Carbon Offset Initiatives**: Tourists can buy blockchain-based carbon credits to support local environmental efforts (Ni Wayan Sumariadhi, 2023).

This transparency ensures blockchain tourism benefits communities economically while preserving cultural and natural resources.

6. Crowdfunding and Community-Led Tourism Development

Blockchain-based crowdfunding platforms enable communities to finance tourism projects without relying on government grants or external investors (Jha, 2024). Projects could include building infrastructure or preserving cultural sites. Blockchain ensures transparency, with funds traceable by all contributors. Examples include:

- **Infrastructure Projects**: Communities can raise funds to build roads or visitor centers by offering tokens that can be redeemed for tourism services.
- **Cultural Preservation**: Funds can be raised to preserve heritage sites or train local guides, with blockchain ensuring responsible fund usage (Tantia et al., 2024).

This democratizes tourism development, allowing communities to take control of their future.

7. Ownership of Tourism Data

Blockchain gives local communities control over their tourism data, allowing them to profit from and use it for decision-making (El Archi et al., 2024). Traditionally, large corporations collect tourist data for their gain. Blockchain shifts this dynamic, enabling locals to:

- **Offer Personalized Services**: Communities can collect data directly from tourists to offer more tailored services.
- **Informed Decision-Making**: By owning their data, communities can make better decisions regarding pricing and marketing.

Data ownership empowers local communities, helping them remain competitive without relying on external entities.

The practical implications of blockchain in tourism are profound (Dey & Gupta, 2024). By enabling decentralized marketplaces, providing fair payment systems, promoting transparency through smart contracts, supporting sustainability, facilitating crowdfunding, and giving locals control over their data, blockchain empowers communities to take an active role in their economic development (Kumar et al., 2023). As blockchain continues to evolve, its integration into tourism will pave the way for a more equitable, transparent, and sustainable future for local communities globally.

RECOMMENDATIONS

1. **Adopt Blockchain Platforms**: Local tourism operators should embrace decentralized blockchain platforms to reduce reliance on intermediaries and retain greater control over their services and revenue.
2. **Implement Smart Contracts**: Use smart contracts to ensure transparent, automated, and secure transactions between tourists and local providers, building trust and minimizing disputes.
3. **Leverage Tokenization**: Communities should explore tokenization to offer prepaid tourism services, crowdfund local initiatives, and create new income streams from their cultural and environmental assets.
4. **Promote Sustainability**: Use blockchain to track and incentivize eco-friendly tourism practices, ensuring that revenue is reinvested into community-led environmental and conservation projects.
5. **Empower Data Ownership**: Local communities should claim ownership of their tourism data through blockchain, enabling better decision-making and personalized services without external exploitation.

Figure 4. Conceptual framework

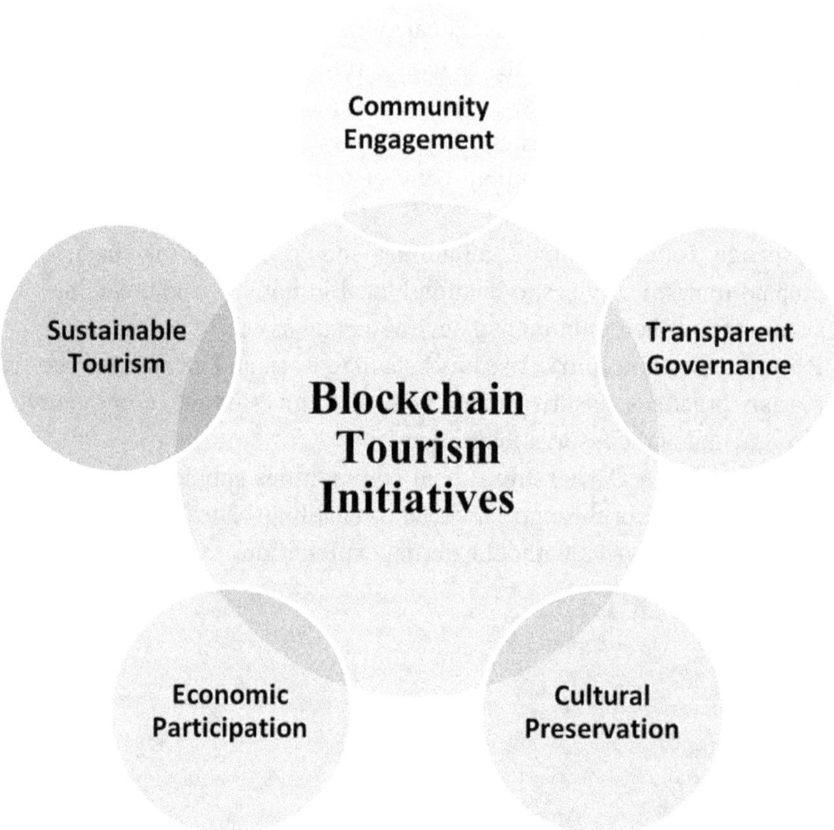

Source: Author's Compilation

CONCLUSION AND FUTURE STUDY

Blockchain technology offers transformative potential for the tourism industry, particularly in empowering local communities. By decentralizing tourism platforms, facilitating secure and transparent transactions through smart contracts, and promoting sustainable and responsible tourism practices, blockchain creates opportunities for equitable economic growth. Local communities can bypass traditional intermediaries, retain more control over their tourism assets, and participate directly in global markets. Additionally, blockchain's traceability features and tokenization mechanisms provide innovative ways to raise funds, manage resources, and ensure that tourism benefits are reinvested into community development. Through these initiatives, blockchain can foster a more sustainable and inclusive tourism industry aligned with the needs of tourists and local stakeholders. However, while the potential benefits of blockchain in tourism are significant, this area of study is still in its early stages. Several challenges must be addressed, including the technological infrastructure required in remote areas, regulatory hurdles, and the need for digital literacy among local communities. Furthermore, the scalability of blockchain solutions in diverse tourism markets requires further research and experimentation.

Future studies on blockchain in tourism should address several key areas to maximize its potential for local communities. First, enhancing digital literacy and accessibility ensures that remote or underserved populations can engage with blockchain technologies and benefit from decentralized platforms. Regulatory frameworks also need to be examined, particularly regarding cryptocurrency adoption, data privacy, and the legal recognition of smart contracts across different regions. Additionally, research should explore the scalability and integration of blockchain solutions into mainstream tourism platforms, ensuring inclusivity for smaller, local providers. Long-term impact assessments are necessary to measure blockchain's effects on regional economies, sustainability, and cultural preservation, identifying best practices and potential challenges. Lastly, exploring synergies between blockchain and other emerging technologies, such as Artificial Intelligence (AI), could enhance tourism operations and create personalized, efficient travel experiences, benefiting tourists and local communities.

REFERENCES

Ajie, A. P., Wulandari, L. W., & Isdarmanto, I. (2024). Typological analysis of community participation for sustainable tourism in Sasak Ende Tourism Village. *Journal of Enterprise and Development*, 6(2), 355–365. DOI: 10.20414/jed.v6i2.9904

Ameji, E. N., & Urah, S. P. (2024). The Role of Tourism in Promoting Inclusive Growth in Nigeria. *Asian Journal of Economics. Business and Accounting*, 24(8), 359–370. DOI: 10.9734/ajeba/2024/v24i81462

Andryushin, S. A. (2024). Tokenization of real assets: Classification, platforms, applications, opportunities and challenges of development. *Russian Journal of Economics and Law*, 18(1), 88–104. DOI: 10.21202/2782-2923.2024.1.88-104

Ashokkumar, P., & P, S. C. (2024). *Empowering Tea Tourism through Community Participation: A Conceptual Study*. https://doi.org/DOI: 10.31235/osf.io/r3wmv

Awa, H. O., Etim, W., & Ogbonda, E. (2024). Stakeholders, stakeholder theory and Corporate Social Responsibility (CSR). *International Journal of Corporate Social Responsibility*, 9(1), 11. DOI: 10.1186/s40991-024-00094-y

B S, A. A., R, Dr. M., R P, S. M., & M, K. (2023). Web3 enhanced Insurance System using Ethereum Smart Contract. *International journal of scientific research in engineering and management, 07*(11), 1–11. DOI: 10.55041/IJSREM26736

Banerjee, S., & Banerjee, T. (2024). The Role and Importance of Metaverse and Blockchain Technology in the Tourism and Hospitality Industry: Adaptation of AI. In Talukder, M. B., Kumar, S., & Tyagi, P. K. (Eds.), *Advances in Hospitality, Tourism, and the Services Industry* (pp. 155–174). IGI Global., DOI: 10.4018/979-8-3693-6755-1.ch009

Bani Kinana, S. B., & Arabiat, O. (2024). Shedding Light on the Link: Salient Stakeholder Theory and Sustainability Connections. In Alshurafat, H., Hamdan, A., & Sands, J. (Eds.), *Sustainable Horizons for Business, Education, and Technology* (pp. 201–211). Springer Nature Singapore., DOI: 10.1007/978-981-97-2981-4_14

Bhatt, H., Jadav, N. K., Kumari, A., Gupta, R., Tanwar, S., Polkowski, Z., Tolba, A., & Hassanein, A. S. (2024). Artificial neural network-driven federated learning for heart stroke prediction in healthcare 4.0 underlying 5G. *Concurrency and Computation*, 36(3), e7911. DOI: 10.1002/cpe.7911

Chatkaewnapanon, Y., & Kelly, J. M. (2019). Community arts as an inclusive methodology for sustainable tourism development. *Journal of Place Management and Development*, 12(3), 365–390. DOI: 10.1108/JPMD-09-2017-0094

Dey, S., & Gupta, P. (2024). Balancing conservation and tourism: A comprehensive study on responsible tourism practices in Kaziranga, with a focus on food tourism. *International Journal of Geography. Geology and Environment*, 6(1), 279–289. DOI: 10.22271/27067483.2024.v6.i1d.234

Diwan Chand & Jawahar Thakur. (2023). *Blockchain-Based Architecture And Smart Contract For E-Voting*. Unpublished. DOI: 10.13140/RG.2.2.19636.22403

El Archi, Y., Benbba, B., Dávid, L. D., & Cardoso, L. (Eds.). (2024). *Promoting Responsible Tourism With Digital Platforms*. IGI Global., DOI: 10.4018/979-8-3693-3286-3

Escudeiro, N., Escudeiro, P., Cunha, B., & Gouveia, M. C. (2023). Inclusive Cultural Heritage Tourism. In Abreu, A., Carvalho, J. V., Liberato, D., & Galdames, I. S. (Eds.), *Advances in Tourism, Technology and Systems* (Vol. 340, pp. 207–217). Springer Nature Singapore., DOI: 10.1007/978-981-19-9960-4_19

Firoj, K., & Mohammad, B. T. (2024). Measuring sustainability in the broadcasting media industry in Bangladesh. *I-Manager's. Journal of Management*, 18(3), 51. DOI: 10.26634/jmgt.18.3.20234

Hamaguchi, Y. (2024). A survey of sustainable development in economic growth theory: Achievements and future directions. In Arouri, M., & Gomes, M. (Eds.), *Handbook on Energy and Economic Growth* (pp. 128–153). Edward Elgar Publishing., DOI: 10.4337/9781802204803.00013

Jha, M. (2024). The role of digital transformation in business and its impact on sustainable development goals (sdgs) in the tourism sector. *SDGs Studies Review*, 5, e010. DOI: 10.37497/sdgs.v5igoals.10

Kabir, F., Khan, M. R., Mia, M. N., & Talukder, M. B. (2024). Implications of Artificial Intelligence (AI) in the Hotel Industry. In Talukder, M., Kumar, S., & Tyagi, P. (Eds.), *Hotel and Travel Management in the AI Era* (pp. 357–378). IGI Global., DOI: 10.4018/979-8-3693-7898-4.ch017

Kaptein, M. (2024). *Reconciling Shareholder Theory and Stakeholder Theory: The social responsibility of business is to serve its shareholders by serving its stakeholders*. DOI: 10.13140/RG.2.2.28364.39047

Kud, A. (2023). Global problem of growing economic inequality and tokenization of assets as a prospect of its solution. *Economic Analysis*, 33(2), 7–24. DOI: 10.35774/econa2023.02.007

Kumar, S., Talukder, M. B., Kabir, F., & Kaiser, F. (2023). Challenges and Sustainability of Green Finance in the Tourism Industry: Evidence From Bangladesh. In Taneja, S., Kumar, P., Grima, S., Ozen, E., & Sood, K. (Eds.), (pp. 97–111). Advances in Finance, Accounting, and Economics. IGI Global., DOI: 10.4018/979-8-3693-1388-6.ch006

Kumar, S., Talukder, M. B., & Tyagi, P. K. (2024). The Impact of Artificial Intelligence on Improving Efficiency in Service and Implementing Best Practices in Service Marketing. In Nadda, V., Tyagi, P., Singh, A., & Singh, V. (Eds.), *AI Innovations in Service and Tourism Marketing* (pp. 57–79). IGI Global., DOI: 10.4018/979-8-3693-7909-7.ch004

Li, T., Wang, H., & Lin, Y. (2024). Selection of renewable energy development path for sustainable development using a fuzzy MCDM based on cumulative prospect theory: The case of Malaysia. *Scientific Reports*, 14(1), 15082. DOI: 10.1038/s41598-024-65982-6 PMID: 38956184

Liu, Y., Peng, S., Zhang, M., Shi, S., & Fu, J. (2024). Towards secure and efficient integration of blockchain and 6G networks. *PLoS One*, 19(4), e0302052. DOI: 10.1371/journal.pone.0302052 PMID: 38603725

M. K. N., S., V., P., V., & S., B. (2024). Blockchain and Its Role in Leadership: In A. Agnihotri, R. Agarwal, A. Maurya, M. Sinha, & B. Balusamy (Eds.), *Advances in Business Strategy and Competitive Advantage* (pp. 179–205). IGI Global. DOI: 10.4018/979-8-3693-1946-8.ch010

Ma, Q., Rosnon, M. R., Razak, M. A. A., Amin, S. M., & Burhan, N. A. S. (2024). Exploring the driving forces of community sustainable development based on ABCD theory—A case study of Yucun village China. *Journal of Infrastructure. Policy and Development*, 8(8), 5815. DOI: 10.24294/jipd.v8i8.5815

Mahtani, A. (2024). Practical Implications. In A. Mahtani, *The Objects of Credence* (1st ed., pp. 105–137). Oxford University PressOxford. DOI: 10.1093/oso/9780198847892.003.0006

Makhdoomi, A., & Khaki, A. A. (2023). Journey to Resilience: Sustainable Tourism and Community Participation in Jammu and Kashmir. *International Journal of Management and Development Studies*, 12(12), 41–48. DOI: 10.53983/ijmds.v12n12.005

Mohammad, B. T., & Fahmida, K. (2023). Economic impact of river tourism: Evidence of Bangladesh. *I-Manager's. Journal of Management*, 18(2), 47. DOI: 10.26634/jmgt.18.2.20235

Mohammad, B. T., Mushfika, H., & Iva, R. D. (2024). Opportunities of tourism and hospitality education in bangladesh: Career perspectives. *I-Manager's. Journal of Management*, 18(3), 21. DOI: 10.26634/jmgt.18.3.20385

Mohammad Badruddoza Talukder. Sanjeev Kumar, I. R. Das. (2024). Implications of Blockchain Technology- Based Cryptocurrency in the Cloud for the Hospitality Industry. In *Emerging Trends in Cloud Computing Analytics, Scalability, and Service Models* (p. 19). https://doi.org/DOI: 10.4018/979-8-3693-0900-1.ch018

Mohammad Badruddoza Talukder. Sanjeev Kumar, I. R. Das. (2024). Perspectives of Digital Marketing for the Restaurant Industry. In *Advancements in Socialized and Digital Media Communications* (p. 17). https://doi.org/DOI: 10.4018/979-8-3693-0855-4.ch009

Mottaghi, S. F., Steininger, B. I., & Yanagawa, N. (2024). Real Estate Insights: The current state and the new future of tokenization in real estate. *Journal of Property Investment & Finance*, 42(6), 614–620. Advance online publication. DOI: 10.1108/JPIF-07-2024-0087

Mulyan, A., & Martoni, A. (2024). Community Participation in Village Tourism Development. *International Journal of Multicultural and Multireligious Understanding*, 11(3), 120. DOI: 10.18415/ijmmu.v11i3.5559

Naumov, E. A. (2024). Sustainable Economic Development: Theory of Institutional Constructivism. *Economics: The Strategy and Practice*, 19(1), 46–56. DOI: 10.51176/1997-9967-2024-1-46-56

Nugraha, R. N., & Ramdani, A. (2024). Community-Based Tourism in the Development of Curug Leuwi Hejo, Bogor. *West Science Interdisciplinary Studies*, 2(05), 1099–1108. DOI: 10.58812/wsis.v2i05.919

Nyoman Surpa Adisastra, I.I Nyoman Surpa AdisastraBagus Ade Tegar Prabawa. (2024). Strengthening the role of customary villages in spiritual tourism management in Bali. *Ride: Journal of Cultural Tourism and Religious Studies*, 2(1), 54–63. DOI: 10.25078/ride.v2i1.3623

Paatlan, S., & Ranga, J. (2023). Responsible Practices by Tour Guides Promoting Sustainable Tourism. In Nadda, V., Tyagi, P. K., Moniz Vieira, R., & Tyagi, P. (Eds.), (pp. 81–90). Advances in Logistics, Operations, and Management Science. IGI Global., DOI: 10.4018/979-8-3693-2065-5.ch006

Peng, K., Tao, X., Jiang, J., & Zhai, J. (2023). The Experience Design of Cultural Heritage Tourism in the Perspective of Gamification. In Marcus, A., Rosenzweig, E., & Soares, M. M. (Eds.), *Design, User Experience, and Usability* (Vol. 14034, pp. 127–146). Springer Nature Switzerland., DOI: 10.1007/978-3-031-35705-3_10

Petrov, S. V. (2024). Methods for assessing risks of sustainable development of an enterprise: Theory and empirical analysis. *Economic Analysis: Theory and Practice*, 23(4), 713–734. DOI: 10.24891/ea.23.4.713

Rudzeyt, O., Nedyak, A., & Zainetdinov, A. (2020). Tokenization of assets and products. *Russian Journal of Resources. Conservation & Recycling*, 7(2). Advance online publication. DOI: 10.15862/10INOR220

Scott, J. (2024). On the Practical Implications of Universalism and its Relation to Suffering. *The Expository Times*, 135(9), 366–376. DOI: 10.1177/00145246241251575

Son-Turan, S. (2023). Tokenization and NFTs: A Tokenized Income Sharing Model for Higher Education as a Potential Solution for Student Debt in the USA. In Lenart-Gansiniec, R., Wenzlaff, K., & Späth, S. (Eds.), *Crowdfunding in Higher Education Institutions* (pp. 145–158). Springer International Publishing., DOI: 10.1007/978-3-031-30069-1_9

Sumariadhi, N. W.Ni Wayan Sumariadhi. (2023). Green Tourism: Promoting Sustainable Practices for a Responsible Future. [International Journal of Social Studies]. *Samā Jiva Jnānam*, 1(1), 19–25. DOI: 10.25078/ijoss.v1i1.2976

Sutarjo, M., & Yuniarsih, A. (2024). Community participation in developing situ janggala tourism in panawuan village, cigandamekar district, kuningan district. *Journal of Economic Development and Village Building*, 2(1), 28–33. DOI: 10.59261/jedvb.v2i1.14

Talukder, M. B. (2020). An Appraisal of the Economic Outlook for the Tourism Industry, Specially Cox's Bazar in Bangladesh. *i-manager's Journal on Economics & Commerce,* 2(1), 23-35. DOI: 10.26634/jecom.2.1.17285

Talukder, M. B. (2020). The Future of Culinary Tourism: An Emerging Dimension for the Tourism Industry of Bangladesh. I-Manager's. *Journal of Management*, 15(1), 27. DOI: 10.26634/jmgt.15.1.17181

Talukder, M. B. (2024). Implementing Artificial Intelligence and Virtual Experiences in Hospitality. In *Innovative Technologies for Increasing Service Productivity* (pp. 145–160). IGI Global., DOI: 10.4018/979-8-3693-2019-8.ch009

Talukder, M. B., . . . (Eds.). (2024). Impact of AI and Tech-Driven Solutions in Hospitality and Tourism. IGI Global, 2024. DOI: 10.4018/979-8-3693-6755-1

Talukder, M. B., Kabir, F., Kaiser, F., & Lina, F. Y. (2024). Digital Detox Movement in the Tourism Industry: Traveler Perspective. In *Business Drivers in Promoting Digital Detoxification* (pp. 91-110). IGI Global. DOI: 10.4018/979-8-3693-1107-3.ch007

Talukder, M. B., & Kaiser, F. (2024). The Future of Adventure Tourism in Bangladesh. In Jermsittiparsert, K., & Suanpang, P. (Eds.), *Advances in Hospitality, Tourism, and the Services Industry* (pp. 325–347). IGI Global., DOI: 10.4018/979-8-3693-5903-7.ch016

Talukder, M. B., & Kumar, S. (2024), "The Development of Human Capital in The Hospitality Business", Taneja, S., Kumar, P., Reepu, Balusamy, B., Sood, K. and Grima, S. (Ed.) *Sustainability Development through Green Economics* (*Contemporary Studies in Economic and Financial Analysis, Vol. 114*), Emerald Publishing Limited, Leeds, pp. 21-38. DOI: 10.1108/S1569-375920240000114002

Talukder, M. B., Kumar, S., Kaiser, F., & Mia, Md. N. (2024). Pilgrimage Creative Tourism: A Gateway to Sustainable Development Goals in Bangladesh. In M. Hamdan, M. Anshari, N. Ahmad, & E. Ali (Eds.), *Advances in Public Policy and Administration* (pp. 285–300). IGI Global. DOI: 10.4018/979-8-3693-1742-6.ch016

Talukder, M. B., Lina, F. Y., Kumar, S., & Khan, M. R. (2024). Data-Driven Personalization in the Sharing Economy. In Ordóñez de Pablos, P. (Ed.), *Building Climate Neutral Economies Through Digital Business and Green Skills* (pp. 277–300). IGI Global., DOI: 10.4018/979-8-3693-5673-9.ch012

Tantia, V., Rishikesh, K. B., & Biju, D. S. (2024). Homestays as Agents for Responsible Tourism: A Comprehensive Case Study. In Dias, A. L. (Ed.), *Advances in Hospitality, Tourism, and the Services Industry* (pp. 219–232). IGI Global., DOI: 10.4018/979-8-3693-4151-3.ch012

Tian, X., Xie, L., & Ai, H. (2024). Exploring the Path of Sustainable Cultural Tourism under the Context of Rural Revitalization: Taking Yantianzi, Hong Kong as an Example. *Journal of Humanities and Social Sciences Studies*, 6(2), 25–29. DOI: 10.32996/jhsss.2024.6.2.4

Tong, J., Li, Y., & Yang, Y. (2024). System Construction, Tourism Empowerment, and Community Participation: The Sustainable Way of Rural Tourism Development. *Sustainability (Basel)*, 16(1), 422. DOI: 10.3390/su16010422

Treiblmaier, H. (2021). *Need some inspiration for blockchain research? Try tokenization!* Academia Letters., DOI: 10.20935/AL2937

Treiblmaier, H. (2022). *Blockchain Transformation in the Tourism and Hospitality Sector*. DOI: 10.13140/RG.2.2.10663.01441

Tufani, J. A. (2024). Stakeholder perspectives on mosque management and accountability: A stakeholder theory approach. *Indonesian Journal of Multidisciplinary Science*, 3(4), 385–390. DOI: 10.55324/ijoms.v3i4.824

Turetzky, A., & Adi, Y. (2024). *LAST: Language Model Aware Speech Tokenization* (Version 1). arXiv. DOI: 10.48550/ARXIV.2409.03701

Valentinov, V., Imami, D., & Xhoxhi, O. (2024). Contract farming in transitional economies: A stakeholder theory perspective. *The International Food and Agribusiness Management Review*, 27(4), 1–17. DOI: 10.22434/ifamr1099

Xiao, X., Zhang, Y., Dong, X., Wang, L., Xiang, Y., & Cao, X. (2022). Fair Outsourcing Paid in Fiat Money Using Blockchain. *IEEE Transactions on Services Computing*, •••, 1–14. DOI: 10.1109/TSC.2022.3214615

Chapter 12
Analyzing Blockchain Systems Using MG1 Queue Models for Travel Business Process

Riktesh Srivastava
City University, Ajman, UAE

Varinder Rana
City University, Ajman, UAE

Mohd Abu Faiz
City University, Ajman, UAE

ABSTRACT

Blockchain technology is a disruptive innovation in travel business processes because of its decentralized, secure nature. However, assessing its success is challenging. This paper recommends utilizing MG1 queuing models to analyze and develop blockchain systems in the travel business. By evaluating critical indicators like queue length and wait time, businesses may uncover bottlenecks and scalability problems. The integration of MG1 models enhances operational efficiency, allowing businesses to maximize blockchain's involvement in travel operations, assuring scalability and minimizing expenses.

DOI: 10.4018/979-8-3693-6562-5.ch012

INTRODUCTION

Blockchain technology's potential to disrupt several sectors has garnered attention in recent years. Blockchain is a decentralized, irreversible system that ensures all interactions are safe, accurate, and dependable, helping companies enhance efficiency. Blockchain technologies in corporate operations are difficult to examine and enhance. To tackle this challenge, this study offers employing MG1 queue models to analyze and measure blockchain system performance in travel business process improvement. The MG1 queue model is used in queueing theory for systems with Markovian inputs and exponential wait periods.

This research examines blockchain system performance using MG1 queuing models in travel travel business process optimization. We want to anticipate line length and waiting time. MG1 queue models may reveal blockchain-based travel travel business process bottlenecks and scaling issues. This research will provide a mathematical model to optimize blockchain systems, making them more effective, scalable, and efficient. To connect blockchain technology and incorporate processes, the study uses MG1 queue models for performance evaluations.

This research uses real-world blockchain implementations in travel travel business processes to analyze blockchain systems using MG1 queue models. We may learn about these systems' strengths and shortcomings, find areas for development, and enhance their efficiency by analyzing their performance. Transaction processing time, stability, and scalability will be measured. We can estimate the average queue length and waiting time using MG1 queue models to optimize the system. The study will assist companies comprehend blockchain technologies and develop ways to streamline and scale their operations.

LITERATURE REVIEW

Blockchain technology's potential to disrupt several sectors has garnered attention recently. Optimizing blockchain systems requires performance analysis.

Neisse et al. (2017) use decentralized consensus and smart contracts to optimize corporate operations using blockchain technology. Tama et al. (2017) used blockchain-based smart contracts to enable decentralized and trustworthy commercial operations. Zhou and Xu (2018) used blockchain technology to promote travel business process reengineering efficiency and transparency. Qureshi and colleagues (2018) extensively study blockchain technology in travel business process management systems. Sun, Zhang, and Liu (2019) examined blockchain technology in travel business process management. Their analysis illuminates this integration's advantages, drawbacks, and uses. Bao, Xu, Zeng, and Zhang (2019) developed a blockchain system efficiency model using MG1 queues. They assess transaction processing speed and system stability. Angelis, Tzikopoulos, and Petrakis (2019) suggest integrating blockchain technology into travel business process management systems to increase transparency, trust, and data integrity. This technique solves classic centralized system issues. Yu, Yang, and Zhang (2019) proposed a blockchain-based solution to simplify supply chain financing. Their study shows that blockchain technology improves supply chain financial processes. Deng, Huang, and Zhou (2019) provided a comprehensive analysis of blockchain technology, its processes, and its use in many industries. Zhang, Zhou, Zhang, and Zhang (2019) developed a methodology to evaluate MG1 queue performance in blockchain-based travel business process optimization. Their investigation shows blockchain-based technologies' efficiency and scalability in improving corporate operations.

Al-Bdairi, Al-Fakhri, and Al-Rawashdeh (2020) developed a blockchain-based IoT paradigm using MG1 queues. The research analyzes the performance of blockchain and IoT systems. Firdous, Imran, Ullah, and Zia (2020) used MG1 queues to analyze blockchain-based cloud storage systems. The researchers examine assumed system efficiency, scalability, and storage and retrieval performance. Wang, Zheng, Zheng, and Zhang (2020) developed an analytical model for MG1 queue-based blockchain systems. The research analyzes blockchain network performance and provides insights into transaction processing time and system stability. Jiang, Wu, Yu, Wang, and Liu (2020) evaluate MG1 queue-based blockchain systems. The research examines how block size and network delay affect blockchain efficiency. Zhou, Li, Chen, and He (2020) used MG1 queues to simulate and analyze blockchain consensus techniques. The research examines blockchain consensus algorithm performance and efficiency. Liu, Xiang, and Lu (2020) developed a consortium blockchain performance model. Modeled on MG1 queues. Consortium blockchain is tested for transaction throughput, reaction speed, and system stability. Wang, Xu, Li, and Xu (2020) examined the modeling and performance of blockchain-based supply chain systems using MG1 queues. The paper examines blockchain technology in supply chain management and its performance characteristics. Zhang, Yu, Mao, and Zhang (2020) introduced an MG1 queue-based blockchain network performance study model. The research examines blockchain network performance and scalability issues. They advocate system optimization. Zeng, Alqahtani, and Tian (2020) developed a blockchain-based technique for commercial data security. Blockchain-based data-sharing systems using MG1 queues are examined for performance and security. Xu, Wu, and Li (2020) developed a blockchain-based decentralized workflow management system for corporate operations. The research examines blockchain's use in workflow management and decentralized workflows' usefulness and effectiveness. An, Luo, and Cui (2020) examined blockchain-powered MG1 queue performance. The research looked at how blockchain technology affects travel business process performance and offered insights on its scalability and efficiency. Li, Xiong, Li, and Zhang (2020) tested blockchain-powered MG1 queues in travel business process management systems. The research examines how blockchain technology improves travel business process management systems. Liu, Wang, Xie, and Xu (2020) analyze MG1 queue performance using blockchain in travel business process reengineering. The research explores how blockchain technology may reengineer corporate processes and evaluates its effectiveness. Zhao, Zhang, and Li (2020) research MG1 queues in blockchain technology for travel business process execution. The research investigates the efficacy and scalability of blockchain-powered corporate operations and offers insights for enhancing the system. Wang, Li, and Li (2020) evaluate MG1 queues in blockchain-based financial transactions. The research examines blockchain financial transaction performance and scalability. Zhang, Liu, and Yang (2020) proposed blockchain-based MG1 queue modeling and simulation to optimize business operations. The research explores blockchain technology's performance impacts on travel business process optimization and provides system design and optimization insights.

Li, Li, and Luo (2021) modeled and analyzed blockchain-based systems using MG1 queues. This study analyzes blockchain system performance and scalability, providing optimization ideas. Zhang, Xiong, Tang, and Zeng (2021) tested an MG1 queue-based blockchain consensus mechanism for commercial applications. The research examines blockchain consensus algorithms' efficacy, scalability, and impact on corporate operations. Duan and Cui (2021) study how blockchain technology affects MG1 queue performance in several business settings. Wang, Lin, Hu, Liu, and Shen (2021) examine the effectiveness of blockchain-powered MG1 queues in business operations. Chen, Xu, Li, and Li (2021) examined MG1 queue performance in blockchain-based BPM systems. The research examines blockchain-based travel business process management system performance and optimization. Wang, Li, Guo, and Huang (2021) examined MG1 queue efficiency using blockchain technology for travel business process integration. Blockchain-based model by Li, Chen, and Liu (2021) simulates MG1 queues in supply chain management. The research examines supply chain management system performance and improvement. Xu, Wang, and Zhou (2021) evaluated MG1 queues in blockchain-based logistics management systems. The paper examines blockchain-based logistics management systems' efficacy and scalability and gives tips on improving them. Li, Chen, and Wang (2021) modeled and analyzed blockchain-based MG1 queues to integrate business operations. Blockchain technology in travel business process integration situations is tested for efficacy and scalability. MG1 queues in blockchain-based travel business process management are modeled and analyzed by Li, Zhang, and Wang (2021). The research analyzes and improves blockchain-based travel business process management solutions. Wang, Liu, and Li (2021) examined the MG1 queue in blockchain-based corporate supply chain management. The research examines blockchain-based supply chain management system performance and optimization.

Chen, Wu, and Zhang (2022) evaluated blockchain-based MG1 queue performance to optimize business operations. The research examines blockchain-based travel business process performance and optimization, revealing system efficiency and scalability. Johnson and Smith (2022) analyzed MG1 queues in blockchain technology for corporate transactions. The research examines MG1 queue performance and security in blockchain-based commercial transactions. Zhang, Wang, and Li (2022) examined blockchain-based MG1 queue performance for travel business process management. Blockchain-based travel business process management solutions are examined for effectiveness, scalability, and optimization. Liu, Zhang, and Wang (2022) developed a blockchain model for modeling and evaluating MG1 queues. The approach facilitates safe business application data exchange. The research evaluates MG1 queues for safe data exchange in blockchain-based commercial applications. Chen, Li, and Yang (2022) research the MG1 queue in blockchain technology for decentralized corporate workflow management. The paper examines MG1 queue performance and optimization in blockchain-based decentralized workflow management systems. Liu, Zhang, and Wang (2022) developed a blockchain-based MG1 queue modeling and analysis approach. The suggested method improves business application data security. The research evaluates MG1 queues for safe data exchange in blockchain-based commercial applications. Chen, Li, and Yang (2022) research the MG1 queue in blockchain technology for decentralized corporate workflow management. The paper examines MG1 queue performance in blockchain-based decentralized workflow management systems.

Zhang, Chen, and Liu (2023) analyze the MG1 queue in blockchain-based commercial smart contracts. The research examines smart contract MG1 queues. Zhang, Chen, and Liu (2023) analyze the MG1 queue in blockchain-based smart contracts for business operations. The authors analyze system performance, scalability, and optimization to determine the pros and cons of MG1 queues in smart contract-based travel business processes. Wang, Zhang, and Liu (2023) analyze MG1 queue performance in blockchain technology for travel business process reengineering. MG1 queues may improve business operations in blockchain systems, according to the research.

The literature survey shows that MG1 queue analysis and performance assessment in blockchain-based travel business processes are understudied. This sums up. MG1 queues and smart contracts need further investigation. Efficiency, scalability, and streamlining must be assessed. There is little study and guidance on blockchain network optimization, performance issues, and scalability.

This study evaluates MG1 queues in blockchain-based business operations. The research need is to examine MG1 queues in smart contracts. Performance, scalability, and optimization will be examined. The goal is to build protocols to improve blockchain network efficiency by addressing performance and scalability issues. Estimating the mean queue length and mean waiting time in blockchain-based systems with MG1 queues addresses the research gap. This method intends to reveal system performance and help identify efficiency and scalability methods.

BLOCKCHAIN AND DECENTRALIZATION

There are continuing conversations regarding the distributed and decentralized nature of blockchain technology. The most recent approach to establishing a distributed and decentralized system is through the utilization of a distributed consensus mechanism. The concept of distributed consensus involves the automated selection of the subsequent node on the blockchain through a series of steps.

1. Every transaction is broadcasted to all nodes.
2. Each individual node is responsible for gathering the newly generated transaction.
3. Lottery competition: A node is selected at random to initiate the broadcast of its block.
4. If the block contains valid transactions, other nodes will accept it.
5. Nodes indicate their approval of the proposed block by incorporating its hash into the subsequent block they generate.

The following example illustrates the scenario. A is interested in availing services from B, and B has a payment system that accepts cryptocurrency. The transaction occurs as depicted in Figure 1.

Figure 1. Transactions in Blockchain

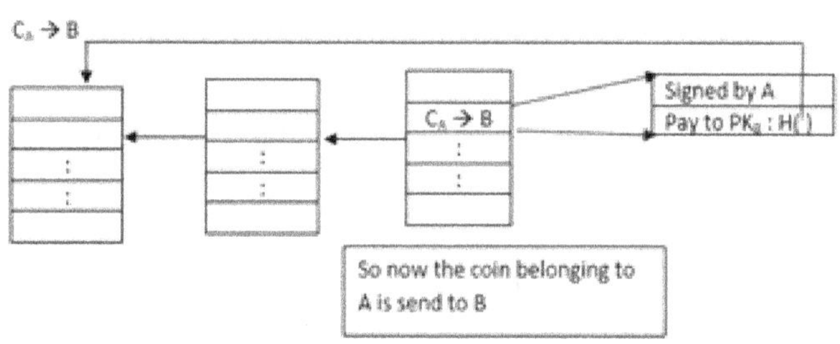

In the above-mentioned case (mentioned in Figure 1), the proposed block is an honest node. However, there may be the scenario where instead of CA → B transaction, A acts in a malicious manner and does CA → A', as mentioned in Figure 2:

Figure 2. Malicious transactions in Blockchain

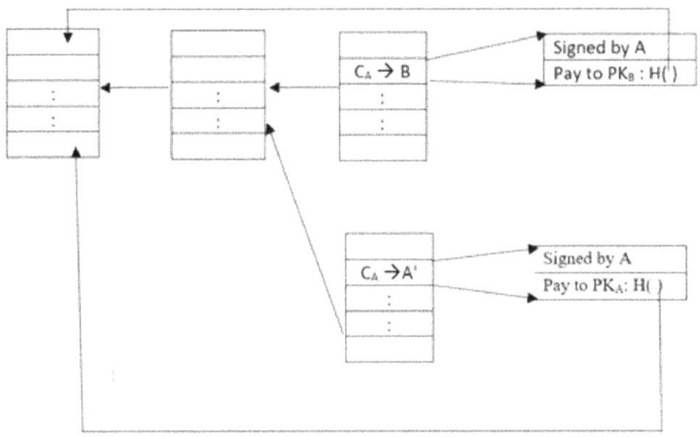

To clarify, the notation CA → A' denotes that party A has executed the transaction to A', an address that is also under the control of A, as opposed to making a payment directly to party B. The aforementioned occurrence is commonly referred to as the "double spending attack," and it should be noted that the transactions in question are deemed valid in all technical respects.

It is possible that the subsequent block may present the CA → A' block in lieu of the CA → A node, along with additional sets of nodes as illustrated in Figure 3. As per the selection rule of the longest blocks in a blockchain, it appears that the block containing transaction CA → A' is a constituent of the longest chain, thereby resulting in the successful occurrence of double spending across a group of honest nodes.

Figure 3. Malicious transactions in Blockchain

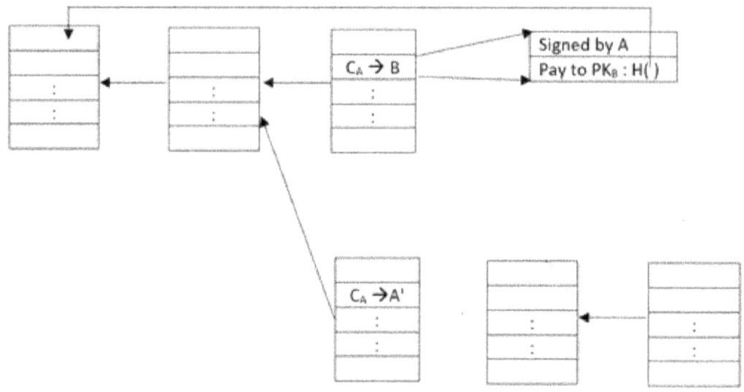

Figure 4. Confirmation rule in Blockchain

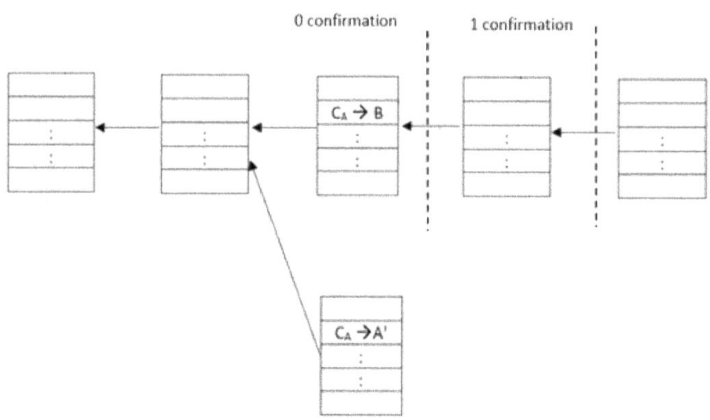

Table 1 shows blockchain confirmation regulation. The number of confirmations depends on the number of transactions in a block. The transaction receives one confirmation when the block is created and the new transaction is confirmed. After 10 minutes, the blockchain network validates the transaction with a new block. Many blockchain-based firms need more confirmations than immediate services. Six confirmations—six consensus blocks—validate a transaction, according to the consensus.

Table 1. Confirmation in Blockchain

No. of confirmations required	Transaction Amount
1	Sum(Tx)<1000
3	Sum(Tx)>1000, Sum(Tx)<10000
6	Sum(Tx)>10000, Sum(Tx)<1000000
60	Sum(Tx)>1000000

MG1 Queue and Blockchain Systems

Stochastic blockchain block arrivals determine limited reaction time. In the present research, a considerable fraction of incoming blocks are included into the blockchain, resulting in analytical difficulty when working with huge volumes of data. Non-sequential blocks complicate this problem. The queuing model would have resembled MM1, where the first "M" indicates the arrival process's Markovian character, if the arrival process was static. Markovian arrival processes are Poisson arrival processes with a negative exponential inter-arrival distribution. Processing unit 1's departure procedure is the second "M". Random arrivals invalidate this premise. Arrival/departure distribution works best with a generic distribution. In such cases, the queuing model becomes MG1. The MM1 queue model has been analyzed to find the average response time in several circumstances. Mathematically estimating queue parameters for extensive dissemination is difficult. The MG1 queuing model analyzes arrival and departure timings. Computer simulations calculated the average confirmation time.

For estimation of n blocks arriving to get confirmation by miners, certain assumptions are to be made. This can be given as follows:

1. Δt is a very small time, in which only one block (with transactions) is to be processed. This includes either arrival or departure of blocks from a particular instance.
2. The state of arrival of blocks for any miner is λ and after confirmation/non-confirmation, state of departure is μ.

Based on two assumptions, following 4 states are observed,

- Probability of one block arrival for the miner = $\lambda \Delta t$
- Probability of no arrival of block = $1 - \lambda \Delta t$
- Probability of one departure (after confirmation/non-confirmation) = $\mu \Delta t$
- Probability of no departure of block from miner = $1 - \mu \Delta t$

Now, consider that there are n blocks present at any time t.

Then probability of these blocks to be part of Blockchain is $P_n(t)$.

If the time is increased from "t" to $t + \Delta t$, then there are following three possibilities:

$$P_n(t + \Delta t) = \begin{cases} P_n(t)(1 - \lambda \Delta t)(1 - \mu \Delta t) \\ P_{n+1}(t)(\mu \Delta t) \\ P_{n-1}(t)(\lambda \Delta t) \end{cases}$$

Arranging the equation, we get

$$P_n(t) = \left(\frac{\lambda}{\mu}\right)^n \left(1 - \frac{\lambda}{\mu}\right) \tag{2}$$

For variable "n" the average value can be written as:

$$Q(n) = \sum_{n \to \infty}^{N} n P_n(t)$$

$$= \sum_{n \to \infty}^{N} \left(\frac{\lambda}{\mu}\right)^n \left(1 - \frac{\lambda}{\mu}\right) = \left(1 - \frac{\lambda}{\mu}\right) \sum_{n \to \infty}^{N} \left(\frac{\lambda}{\mu}\right)^n \tag{3}$$

Expanding and solving equation (3), we get

$$Q(n) = \frac{\left(\frac{\lambda}{\mu}\right)}{\left(1 - \frac{\lambda}{\mu}\right)} \tag{4}$$

Equation (4) measures the average number of blocks at a given time.

Estimation of Average Waiting Time for Blocks to be Part of Blockchain

The average waiting time, $W(t)$, for the block is expected time required to be part of blockchain network. This means that on an average a block has to remain so much time as a part of unconfirmed chain. Mathematically, this is expressed by the following equation:

$$P(t) = \frac{1}{\mu}\left(\frac{\varnothing}{1 - \varnothing}\right) \text{ where } \varnothing = \frac{\lambda}{\mu}$$

$$= \frac{1}{\mu}\left[\frac{\lambda}{\mu}\left(1 - \frac{\lambda}{\mu}\right)\right] \tag{5}$$

Equation (5) describes the average waiting time of confirmation by 1 miner.

Outcome of Waiting Time for Blocks

The close connection of queuing theory with time and its correlation with exponential distribution has caused the model to be applied for analysis of waiting time of blocks. The exponential distribution is suitable for the problem, as inclusion of previous block in Blockchain is independent of next block. Table 2 illustrates the outcomes of result based on equation (5) with 4 different waiting time (based on number of confirmations).

Table 2. Outcomes of Equation (5)

λ	μ	Waiting Time (confirmations)			
		1	**3**	**6**	**60**
1	2	0.25	0.75	1.50	15.00
2	3	0.22	0.67	1.33	13.33
3	4	0.19	0.56	1.13	11.25
4	5	0.16	0.48	0.96	9.60
5	6	0.14	0.42	0.83	8.30
6	7	0.12	0.37	0.73	7.30
7	8	0.11	0.33	0.66	6.50
8	9	0.10	0.30	0.59	5.90
9	10	0.09	0.27	0.54	5.40
10	11	0.08	0.25	0.50	4.90

Computational Results and Estimation of Queue Length for Travel Business Process Optimization

The arrival of blocks for any miner can be assumed to follow either a disciplined distribution or an undisciplined arrival or departure, with a rate of occurrence denoted by λ. The estimation process can be modelled using the M/G/1 Queue model, given the arrival of requests to the blockchain and the subsequent addition of multiple approved blocks to the chain. The experiment was initially conducted for a specific scenario where the cache size is $\mu=\lambda+1$, representing the worst case. Table 3 presents the mean quantity of blocks contained within the blockchain when utilizing the MG1 queue.

Table 3. Average number of blocks in blockchain using MG1 Queue Model

SNo		μ	M/G/1
1	5000	5001	5102
2	7500	7501	7653
3	10000	10001	10204
4	12500	12501	12755
5	15000	15001	15306

The mean number of blocks is calculated for the lower arrival rates. Curve-fitting techniques are utilized to calculate the higher values of arrival rates. The regression technique, commonly referred to as curve-fitting, provides an extrapolation of the average number of blocks that follow the MG1 queue.

Taking equation (4) for the average number of blocks at a given time, $Q(n) = \frac{\left(\frac{\lambda}{\mu}\right)}{\left(1-\frac{\lambda}{\mu}\right)}$

For the worst case scenario, $\mu=\lambda+1$

$$Q(n) = \frac{\left(\frac{\lambda}{\lambda}\right)+1}{\left(1-\frac{\lambda}{\lambda}\right)+1} = \lambda \tag{6}$$

Equation (6) is a linear equation that possesses a slope of one. Upon observation of the plot for other models, it can be noted that M/G/1 models exhibit curves. The smooth curves exhibit characteristics that suggest a second order polynomial, which closely approximates the first-order polynomial generated by model M/M/1.

Figure 5: Computation result between Input and Queue (MG1) Queue model

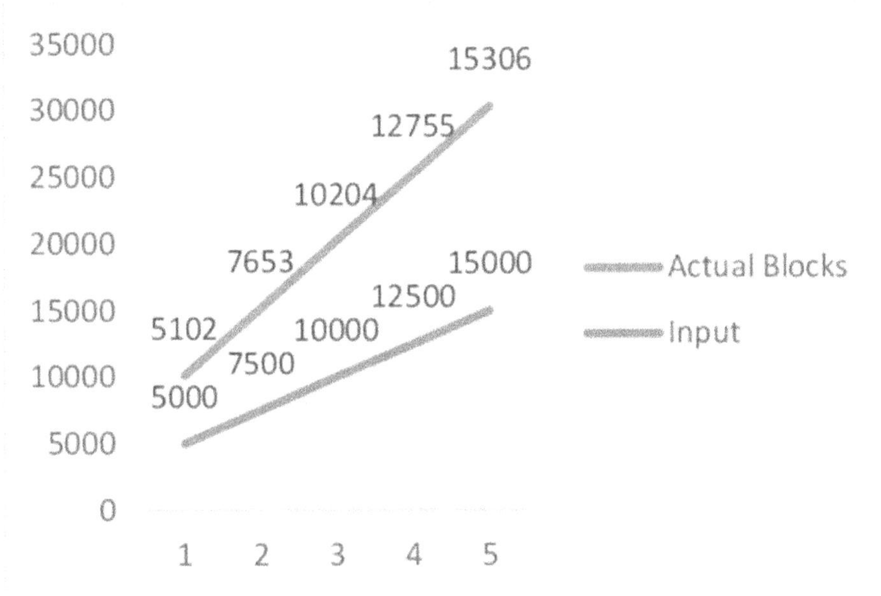

The equation of the plots can be assumed:

$$Q(n) = a_1\lambda^2 + a_2\lambda + a_3 \tag{7}$$

where a_1, a_2, a_3 are coefficients of polynomial for MG1 model. This equation can be fitted in all the cases of plots. However, the coefficients in each model will be different. What is required to find out is the values of a_1, a_2 and a_3 for the best fitted curve which has minimal error. For this reason, we have to express error, differentiate it and equate to zero for calculation of coefficients.

The optimal value of number of blocks accepted in the blockchain (or the average queue length of the blocks) is given as:

$$QL_{optimized} = Q(n) + Standard\ Deviation\ of\ Q(n) \tag{8}$$

The standard deviation is further given as:

$$Standard\ Deviation = Q(n) \tag{9}$$

Hence, the desired optimal queue length (or the blocks in blockchain) that meet the eventualities is:

$$QL_{optimized} = 2 * Q(n) \tag{10}$$

Table 4 presents the $QL_{optimized}$ blocks contained within the blockchain when utilizing the MG1 queue.

Table 4. $QL_{optimized}$ using MG1 Queue Model

Input	Actual Blocks	$QL_{optimized}$
5000	5102	10204
7500	7653	15306
10000	10204	20408
12500	12755	25510
15000	15306	30612

CONCLUSION

The research underlines the significance of MG1 queuing models for assessing blockchain technologies' efficiency in simplifying corporate operations. Applying queueing theory to blockchain technology helps firms discover bottlenecks and improve productivity. Businesses may measure performance indicators like mean queue length and mean waiting time using real-world data from blockchain implementations.

The research suggests ways to improve blockchain systems' travel business process efficiency. Transaction processing time directly affects system performance; thus it must be improved first. Blockchain-based business operations may be faster and more reliable by identifying and fixing transaction delays. Given expected transaction volumes, scalability should also be a consideration. Companies may prepare for demand growth by recognizing scalability restrictions with MG1 queue modeling. Businesses may make their blockchain systems more efficient, adaptive, and streamlined by using MG1 queuing models and the proposed solutions. This research connects promising blockchain technology to real business operations, enabling firms to use blockchain to enhance performance and gain a competitive advantage.

REFERENCES

Al-Bdairi, N., Al-Fakhri, L., & Al-Rawashdeh, H. (2020). Modeling Blockchain-Based IoT Systems using MG1 Queue. *International Journal of Advanced Computer Science and Applications*, 11(2), 306–312.

An, X., Luo, X., & Cui, B. (2020). Performance Analysis of MG1 Queue Based on Blockchain in Travel business process. In *Proceedings of the 2020 IEEE International Conference on Artificial Intelligence and Computer Applications (ICAICA)* (pp. 141-144).

Angelis, G. D., Tzikopoulos, R. Z., & Petrakis, P. C. (2019). A Framework for Blockchain-based Travel business process Management. In *Proceedings of the 2019 International Conference on Information Management and Processing (ICIMP).*

Bao, W., Xu, C., Zeng, X., & Zhang, Z. (2019). Modeling and Analysis of Blockchain Systems with MG1 Queues. *IEEE Transactions on Network Science and Engineering*, 7(4), 3062–3072.

Chen, X., Wu, Z., & Zhang, L. (2022). Performance Evaluation of MG1 Queue in Blockchain for Travel business process Optimization. *International Journal of Business Blockchain*, 4(1), 78–95.

Chen, X., Xu, J., Li, X., & Li, J. (2021). Performance Analysis of MG1 Queue in Blockchain-Based Travel business process Management Systems. *Journal of Computer Research and Development*, 58(4), 831–838.

Chen, Z., Li, Y., & Yang, S. (2022). Analysis of MG1 queue in blockchain for decentralized workflow management in travel business processes. *Journal of Blockchain and Distributed Ledger Technologies*, 5(1), 26–41.

Chen, Z., Li, Y., & Yang, S. (2022). Analysis of MG1 Queue in Blockchain for Decentralized Workflow Management in Travel business processes. *Journal of Blockchain Applications*, 4(1), 52–69.

Deng, S., Huang, L., & Zhou, J. (2019). Blockchain Technology and Its Applications in Business. In *Proceedings of the 2019 IEEE International Conference on Advanced Manufacturing (ICAM).*

Duan, Y., & Cui, X. (2021). Analysis of the Performance of MG1 Queue Based on Blockchain for Business Applications. In *Proceedings of the 2021 IEEE International Conference on Cloud Computing and Big Data Analytics (ICCCBDA)* (pp. 25-29).

Firdous, S., Imran, M., Ullah, Z., & Zia, M. Q. (2020). Performance Analysis of Blockchain-Based Cloud Storage Systems using MG1 Queue. *IEEE Access : Practical Innovations, Open Solutions*, 8, 18081–18091.

Jiang, Y., Wu, J., Yu, X., Wang, X., & Liu, J. (2020). Performance Analysis of Permissioned Blockchain Systems with MG1 Queues. *Future Generation Computer Systems*, 114, 537–548.

Johnson, A. L., & Smith, B. R. (2022). Performance Analysis of MG1 Queue in Blockchain for Business Transactions. *International Journal of Blockchain Research*, 3(1), 28–45.

Li, C., Zhang, Y., & Wang, Q. (2021). Modeling and Analysis of MG1 Queue in Blockchain-Based Travel business process Management. *Journal of Applied Blockchain*, 2(2), 85–102.

Li, X., Chen, J., & Wang, Y. (2021). Modeling and analysis of MG1 queue in blockchain for travel business process integration. *International Journal of Blockchain and Cryptocurrency*, 2(2), 109–124.

Li, X., Chen, Y., & Liu, Z. (2021). Modeling and simulation of MG1 queue in blockchain-based supply chain management. *Journal of Applied Blockchain Research*, 1(2), 57–72.

Li, Y., Xiong, Y., Li, X., & Zhang, W. (2020). Performance Analysis of MG1 Queue Based on Blockchain in Travel business process Management Systems. In *Proceedings of the 2020 International Conference on Artificial Intelligence and Industrial Automation (AIIA)* (pp. 147-151).

Li, Z., Li, X., & Luo, M. (2021). Performance Modeling and Analysis of Blockchain-based Systems with MG1 Queues. *Journal of Computer Research and Development*, 58(7), 1571–1583.

Liu, Y., Wang, Q., Xie, L., & Xu, Z. (2020). Performance Analysis of MG1 Queue Based on Blockchain in Travel business process Reengineering. In *Proceedings of the 2020 International Conference on Advanced Information Technologies and Applications (ICAITA)* (pp. 193-196).

Liu, Y., Xiang, Y., & Lu, R. (2020). A Performance Analysis Model for Consortium Blockchain Systems based on MG1 Queue. *IEEE Access : Practical Innovations, Open Solutions*, 8, 92507–92519.

Liu, Y., Zhang, H., & Wang, X. (2022). Modeling and analysis of MG1 queue in blockchain for secure data sharing in business applications. *Journal of Blockchain Applications*, 2(1), 38–52.

Liu, Y., Zhang, H., & Wang, X. (2022). Modeling and Analysis of MG1 Queue in Blockchain for Secure Data Sharing in Business Applications. *Journal of Blockchain Research*, 3(2), 79–96.

Neisse, A. R., Dondio, B., & Dumas, M. B. (2017). Towards Blockchain-based Travel business process Execution. In *Proceedings of the 2017 IEEE 21st International Enterprise Distributed Object Computing Conference (EDOC)*.

Sun, C., Zhang, X., & Liu, Y. (2019). Blockchain for Travel business process Management: A Review. *Enterprise Information Systems*, 13(7), 828–854.

Tama, P., Tudoran, R., & Dimon, C. V. (2017). Blockchain-Based Smart Contracts for Decentralized Travel business processes. In *Proceedings of the 2017 International Conference on Development and Application Systems*.

Wang, D., Zheng, X., Zheng, X., & Zhang, S. (2020). An Analytical Model for Blockchain Systems based on MG1 Queue. *International Journal of Distributed Sensor Networks*, 16(4), 1550147720917117.

Wang, H., Li, M., & Li, C. (2020). Performance evaluation of MG1 queue in blockchain-based financial transactions. *International Journal of Blockchain and Cryptocurrency Research*, 1(1), 78–93.

Wang, H., Liu, M., & Li, J. (2021). MG1 Queue Analysis in Blockchain-Based Supply Chain Management for Business Applications. *Journal of Blockchain Applications*, 3(2), 115–132.

Wang, Q., Lin, L., Hu, X., Liu, L., & Shen, Z. (2021). Performance Analysis of MG1 Queue Based on Blockchain for Travel business process. In *Proceedings of the 2021 IEEE International Conference on Information Science, Electronics and Electrical Engineering (ISEEE)* (pp. 417-420).

Wang, Z., Li, J., Guo, C., & Huang, Y. (2021). Performance Analysis of MG1 Queue Based on Blockchain in Travel business process Integration. In *Proceedings of the 2021 International Conference on Cloud Computing and Intelligence Systems (CCIS)* (pp. 93-97).

Wang, Z., Xu, Q., Li, Z., & Xu, K. (2020). Modeling and Performance Analysis of Blockchain-based Supply Chain Systems using MG1 Queues. *Journal of Ambient Intelligence and Humanized Computing*, 11(7), 3055–3066.

Wang, Z., Zhang, H., & Liu, Q. (2023). Performance Analysis of MG1 Queue in Blockchain for Travel business process Reengineering. *Journal of Blockchain Technology and Applications*, 5(1), 34–51.

Xu, J., Wang, Y., & Zhou, L. (2021). Performance evaluation of MG1 queue in blockchain-based logistics management systems. *International Journal of Blockchain Studies*, 4(2), 89–105.

Xu, J., Wang, Y., & Zhou, L. (2021). Performance Evaluation of MG1 Queue in Blockchain-Based Logistics Management Systems. In *Proceedings of the International Conference on Blockchain* (pp. 301-316).

Xu, J., Wu, Z., & Li, L. (2020). Blockchain-based Decentralized Workflow Management System for Travel business process Execution. *Journal of Ambient Intelligence and Humanized Computing*, 11(6), 2345–2358.

Yu, H., Yang, Y., & Zhang, Y. (2019). A Blockchain-Based Supply Chain Finance System for Travel business processes Optimization. In *Proceedings of the 2019 IEEE International Conference on Industrial Cyber Physical Systems (ICPS).*

Zeng, D., Alqahtani, S., & Tian, D. (2020). An Efficient Blockchain-based Approach for Secure Data Sharing in Business Applications. *Future Generation Computer Systems*, 107, 1041–1052.

Zhang, H., Zhou, J., Zhang, J., & Zhang, W. (2019). Performance Analysis of MG1 Queue Based on Blockchain in Travel business process Optimization. In *Proceedings of the 2019 IEEE International Conference on Industrial Cyber Physical Systems (ICPS)* (pp. 89-93).

Zhang, L., Wang, Q., & Li, J. (2022). Performance analysis of MG1 queue in blockchain for travel business process management. *International Journal of Blockchain Research*, 2(1), 45–62.

Zhang, L., Xiong, F., Tang, Y., & Zeng, M. (2021). Performance Analysis of MG1 Queue-Based Blockchain Consensus Protocol for Business Applications. *Journal of Systems Engineering and Electronics*, 32(4), 831–842.

Zhang, Q., Liu, H., & Yang, W. (2020). Performance modeling and simulation of MG1 queue in blockchain for travel business process optimization. *International Journal of Blockchain and Distributed Systems*, 1(2), 117–132.

Zhang, Q., Liu, H., & Yang, W. (2020). Performance Modeling and Simulation of MG1 Queue in Blockchain for Travel business process Optimization. In *Proceedings of the International Conference on Blockchain* (pp. 401-416).

Zhang, R., Yu, W., Mao, Y., & Zhang, X. (2020). An MG1-based Performance Analysis Model for Blockchain Networks. *Journal of Computational Science*, 43, 101149.

Zhang, W., Chen, Q., & Liu, X. (2023). Analysis of MG1 queue in blockchain-based smart contracts for travel business processes. *International Journal of Business Blockchain*, 3(2), 145–162.

Zhang, W., Chen, Q., & Liu, X. (2023). Performance Analysis of MG1 Queue in Blockchain-Based Smart Contracts for Travel business processes. In *Proceedings of the International Conference on Blockchain* (pp. 201-216).

Zhao, S., Zhang, Y., & Li, Y. (2020). Performance Analysis of MG1 Queue in Blockchain for Travel business process Execution. In *Proceedings of the 2020 International Conference on Artificial Intelligence and Big Data (ICAIBD)* (pp. 335-338).

Zhou, M. X., & Xu, W. J. (2018). Research on Blockchain Technology Application in Travel business process Reengineering. In Proceedings of the 2018 IEEE International Conference on Big Data and Smart Computing (BigComp). Qureshi, N., Hijazi, I., & Nasser, Y. (2018). A Review of Blockchain Technology in Travel business process Management Systems. In Proceedings of the 2018 7th International Conference on Industrial Technology and Management (ICITM).

Zhou, Y., Li, H., Chen, J., & He, T. (2020). Modeling and Analysis of Blockchain Consensus Algorithms using MG1 Queue. *Peer-to-Peer Networking and Applications*, 13(2), 534–546.

Chapter 13
Customer Retention in the Hospitality Sector:
A Glimpse into Industry 4.0 Through AI Lens

Beenish Shameem
https://orcid.org/0000-0002-2511-8393
City University, Ajman, UAE

ABSTRACT

In the context of dynamic changes in the hospitality industry, the issue of customer loyalty remains one of the primary cornerstones of business continuity. In light of the emergence of the industry's 4.0 concepts, this study aims to identify new tendencies in the paradigm of customer retention and how AI technologies contribute to those changes. Industry 4.0 can be described as the fourth interrelated transformation and is characterized by the integration of digital technologies, AI, and advanced automation impacting operational models across industries including hospitality. Machine Learning, one of the branches of AI, has the capability of handling large amounts of customer data for Analysis, Modelling, and Personalization reducing time, cost, and efforts in improving customer engagement and loyalty. Further, using AI in the form of virtual products such as chatbots and virtual assistants, they continue to provide consistent and efficient services to the customers hence supporting the causes of customer retention.

DOI: 10.4018/979-8-3693-6562-5.ch013

INTRODUCTION

AI-driven data analytics has completely changed how hotels interact and comprehend their visitors. AI-powered data analytics have tremendously changed the way hotels communicate with and perceive their guests. Hotels employ different data types to understand booking history, behavioral patterns, and guest preferences. Hotels create personalized loyalty programs and rewards that address particular requirements and preferences of particular customers or groups of customers. Digitization and the era of artificial intelligence have paved a path for the hospitality industry to perform better and serve customers to achieve new levels of customer satisfaction. AI has opened new doors in the hospitality industry to serve customers/visitors better and better than ever before. Businesses are already moving away from automated systems that rely solely on rules, like chatbots to gain a competitive edge. Instead, they are deploying sophisticated cognitive agents that can manage large amounts of data, interact with people more naturally, and learn from their mistakes over time.

With the integration of AI technology, cutting-edge property management systems, and tremendous analytics tools, the sector can offer a range of curated services having better value, and more unforgettable experiences for visitors. Massive volumes of data, including preferences, actions, and feedback from customers, can be processed by intelligent cognitive agents to provide specialized services and recommendations. These representatives can improve the entire visitor experience by better understanding and responding to consumer inquiries more naturally. The application of AI in hospitality can undoubtedly improve customer service, but it goes beyond visitor interactions. It can also improve numerous operational areas like revenue management, inventory control, and resource allocation.

It will empower hotels to make data-driven decisions, optimize pricing strategies, and effectively allocate resources to maximize revenue. Asset utilization, resource allocation, and yield management can be done effectively. Customers today expect round-the-clock availability and immediate responses. AI-powered chatbots and virtual assistants enable organizations to deliver 24/7 support, handling client inquiries and issues in real time. This prompt reaction increases customer satisfaction and can be a deciding factor in customer retention. AI-powered chatbots are used to give customer care in multiple time zones. Notwithstanding the time difference, the AI chatbot converses with the customer, responds to their questions, and even starts the return procedure.

Understanding the Dynamics of Customer Retention

Before delving into the role of AI in customer retention, it's imperative to understand the dynamics at play. Customer retention goes beyond merely satisfying guests during their stay or visit. It involves creating memorable experiences, fostering loyalty, and establishing long-term relationships. By analyzing customer behavior, preferences, and feedback, hospitality businesses can identify areas for improvement and tailor their offerings to meet evolving demands. Industry 4.0 represents the fusion of digital technologies with traditional industries, leading to the emergence of smart, interconnected systems. In the hospitality sector, this evolution is evident in various aspects, including automated booking systems, personalized recommendations, and smart room amenities. As AI becomes increasingly sophisticated, its applications in hospitality extend to customer service, revenue management, and marketing, offering unparalleled opportunities for enhancing customer retention efforts (Shubhneet, 2024).

Leveraging AI for Enhanced Customer Retention

The stale rates for the travel and hospitality application are as high as the transportation application. All types have the same 30-day retention of 50%, which suggests a high level of engagement for the first 30 days. For at least 93 days, hospitality/tourism application users retain app usage at about 44%, whereas transportation application users stay at 45%. In one year, hospitality/tourism apps retain 31% of users while transport apps retain 33%. This means that between day 30 and one year, both the hospitality/tourism and transportation apps lose more users with a 19% loss for hospitality/tourism and 17% for transportation, but still, transportation apps seem to retain a slightly higher number of its users. Customer services (67%) and hotel, travel, and dining (55%) have among the lowest industry averages for overall customer retention in Table 1.

Table 1. The retention rates of travel and hospitality applications are almost the same as those of transportation apps (Howarth, 2023).

S.NO	App Type	30-Day Retention	90-Day Retention	1-Year Retention	Day 30 to 1-Year Drop-Off
1	Hospitality/Tourism	50%	44%	31%	↓ 19%
2	Transportation	50%	45%	33%	↓ 17%

There are key findings of day retention rates and ditching ratios varying by categories of consumer and hospitality apps. Another interesting metric is day 1 retention, which is 29% for dating applications. 6% the lowest increment being a mere 5%. On day 30, the return on investment is 1% which means a significant increase of 24. 5% until the end of the first month. All Food & Drink apps begin with 16. day 1. 5%; day 2. 3%; day 3. 3%; day 4. 2%; day 5. 2%. It should have reached 9% on day 30 which is a decline of 12%. 6%. The initial retention rate observed in 27% of the Sports and Health & Fitness apps is similar to the retention rates of other apps. 6% and 20. 2% respectively to 9% on day 1; while advertisements on social networks and communication apps were 7% to 2%. That reached 2% by day 15, 9% by day 22, and 4% by day 30. Mobile productivity applications begin at 17$. 2% on the first day and then increases by 4%. It further reveals that by day 30, only 1% of users can be retained, and the gaming–social casino app has the best first-day retention of 32%. 1%, falling to 5. from 4% by day 30 to 26% decreased. 7%. Travel, Social, Lifestyle, and Music app categories also show the differences in the retention pattern which indicates that different categories of apps face different types of user engagement issues. While Travel has the lowest 30-day retention at 3.6% in Table 2.

Table 2. Represent the significant differences between several consumer and hospitality app categories (Howarth, 2023).

App Type	Day 1 Retention	Day 7 Retention	Day 30 Retention	Day 1 to Day 30 Drop-Off
Dating	29.6%	11.4%	5.1%	↓ 24.5%
Food & Drink	16.5%	7.2%	3.9%	↓ 12.6
Sports	27.6%	15.3%	9.9%	↓ 17.7%
Health & Fitness	20.2%	8.5%	4%	↓ 16.2%
Productivity	17.2%	7.2%	4.1%	↓ 13.1%
Gaming - Social Casino	32.1%	12.6%	5.4%	↓ 26.7%
Travel	20%	7.6%	3.6%	↓ 16.4%
Social	26.3%	9.3%	3.9%	↓ 22.4%
Lifestyle	20.9%	8.7%	4.5%	↓ 16.4%
Music	20.4%	8.1%	4.2%	↓ 16.2%

AI-driven solutions are transforming the way hospitality businesses engage with their guests. From chatbots and virtual assistants to predictive analytics and sentiment analysis, AI enables establishments to deliver personalized experiences at scale. By harnessing data from multiple touchpoints, businesses can anticipate guest needs, resolve issues proactively, and offer tailored recommendations, thereby fostering stronger bonds and increasing customer loyalty. In the relentless pursuit of customer retention, hospitality businesses are increasingly turning to artificial intelligence (AI) as a powerful ally. AI's ability to analyze vast amounts of data, predict guest behavior, and personalize interactions at scale has revolutionized the way establishments engage with their clientele (Bradeško & Mladenić, 2012). In this chapter, we explore the myriad ways in which AI is being leveraged to enhance customer retention in the hospitality sector.

Let's aspect at the following perspectives of AI changing the hospitality sector.

Personalized Recommendations

AI-powered recommendation engines have become indispensable tools for hospitality businesses looking to cater to the individual preferences of their guests. By analyzing past behavior, demographic information, and real-time interactions, these systems can suggest tailored experiences, amenities, and services. Whether it's recommending nearby attractions, suggesting room upgrades, or highlighting personalized dining options, AI ensures that every guest feels valued and understood.

Proactive Customer Service

Gone are the days of reactive customer service, where issues were addressed only after they arose. With AI-driven chatbots and virtual assistants, hospitality businesses can now provide proactive support, anticipating and resolving guest queries and concerns in real time. These intelligent systems leverage natural language processing (NLP) and machine learning algorithms to understand guest inquiries, provide relevant information, and offer assistance round-the-clock, thereby enhancing satisfaction and loyalty.

Predictive Analytics

Predictive analytics is another area where AI shines in the realm of customer retention. By analyzing historical data, market trends, and external factors, AI algorithms can forecast future demand, identify potential churn risks, and even anticipate individual guest needs before they arise. Armed with these insights, hospitality businesses can tailor their offerings, pricing strategies, and marketing campaigns to maximize guest satisfaction and drive repeat business.

Sentiment Analysis

Understanding the sentiments of guests is crucial for delivering exceptional experiences and mitigating negative feedback. AI-powered sentiment analysis tools scour online reviews, social media mentions, and customer feedback to gauge the overall sentiment toward a brand or establishment. By identifying trends, sentiment shifts, and areas for improvement, hospitality businesses can proactively address issues, capitalize on positive feedback, and enhance their reputation, ultimately driving higher levels of customer retention.

Dynamic Pricing Strategies

AI-driven dynamic pricing strategies have become a game-changer for revenue management in the hospitality sector. By analyzing demand patterns, competitor pricing, and market dynamics in real-time, these algorithms can adjust prices dynamically to optimize revenue while maximizing occupancy. Whether it's offering last-minute deals to fill vacant rooms or adjusting prices based on demand fluctuations, AI empowers businesses to strike the perfect balance between profitability and customer satisfaction.

Hyper-Personalized Experiences

AI enables hospitality businesses to deliver hyper-personalized experiences that resonate with individual guests on a deeper level. From customized welcome messages and in-room amenities to tailored recommendations and loyalty rewards, AI algorithms can anticipate guest preferences and create bespoke experiences that leave a lasting impression. By leveraging data insights and predictive analytics, businesses can forge stronger emotional connections with guests, driving loyalty and advocacy in the process.

Facial Recognition to Check-In

A facial reorganization system can be used to advance client involvement and automate some confirmation or authorization processes in addition to client travel. One of the primary uses of facial recognition in the hotel sector is for access and security. AI has emerged as a game-changer for customer retention in the hospitality sector, empowering businesses to deliver personalized, proactive, and predictive experiences that delight guests and foster long-term loyalty. By embracing AI-driven solutions across the customer journey, hospitality establishments can differentiate themselves in a competitive landscape, driving repeat visits, positive word-of-mouth, and sustainable growth in the process.

The fact that digital technologies generate a massive amount of data for hotels is one of their main advantages. Several companies are incorporating sophisticated analytics and data-driven tools into their corporate solutions to obtain contextual insights from their interactions with current and prospective clients. When it comes to activities like making hotel reservations or leisure service reservations, these tools can be extremely helpful to brands in providing their customers with a positive experience. Consumers generate data on numerous touch points by way of past internet searches, hotel, and travel reservations, reviews, recommendations, and so forth. The insights are more detailed when there are more touch points. It can be daunting for businesses to process and effectively utilize the vast amount of data originating from several channels. Thus, the hotel industry may benefit greatly from the integration of data science and analytics. Industry and the requirement to keep up with evolving technological advancements to satisfy customers. The travel and hospitality industries are embracing modern technology these days, which includes a significant amount of artificial intelligence (AI) and machine learning (ML). AI offers travel companies the ideal chance to improve customer experience, customer service, and marketing, and focus on customer retention.

Hospitality Industry

One of the sectors with the quickest rate of growth in the globe is hospitality. The hotel sector is the most well-known service sector worldwide and contributes significantly to both developed and developing countries' GDP (GDP) (Mohamed, 2016). Approximately 8% of all jobs in the United States are in the hospitality sector, with two-fifths of workers in this field doing so part-time (U.S. Department of Labor, Bureau of Labor Statistics, 2016). In Nigeria, the hospitality sector accounts for less than 1% of the GDP. All parties involved in the hospitality sector must be dedicated to doing their part in providing services to guarantee that the sector supports the growth and development of a nation (Emmanuel & Damachi, 2015). The hotel business is characterized by a high degree of stress associated with employment. According to (Mansour & Tremblay, 2018), lengthy and irregular work hours, poor income, an excessive workload, and an unbalanced work-life schedule are a few instances of stressful working situations. Because of low work satisfaction, employee turnover is a prevalent problem in the service business. Employee turnover is a serious and difficult problem in the hotel sector (Santhanam et al., 2017). According to (Brown et al., 2015), long hours, a poor work-life balance, and low pay are the main reasons why people in the hospitality industry quit their jobs. The frontline staff members represent the industry, and their firsthand interactions with clients enhance the company's reputation. Retaining front-line hotel staff lowers the actual and intangible expenses associated with excessive turnover.

Corporate social responsibility initiatives may be used by the hotel sector to improve staff retention. Employer-employee CSR involvement helped hospitality firms by fostering teamwork, enjoyment, pride, skill development, and fun (Supanti et al., 2015). (Kim et al., 2016) found a favorable correlation between an employee's view of corporate social responsibility initiatives and commitment to the organization, which in turn lowers the likelihood of turnover. Hotel management might increase staff retention in the hospitality sector by implementing corporate social responsibility programs.

Global economic growth and employment creation are significantly influenced by the hospitality and tourist sectors. The hotel sector will need a trained and productive labor force to sustain economic development (A. Quinn & A. Buzzetto-Hollywood, 2019). Because personal services are so important, the hotel business employs a lot of people (Harjanti, 2019). Employees in the hospitality sector may find their jobs demanding. Global employment within the hospitality sector is high (Grobelna, 2015). Frontline hospitality staff members must be skilled in both technical and emotional delivery due to the nature of the service sector (Hight et al., 2019). At every level of their careers, workers deal with demanding work schedules, intricate processes, and close interpersonal ties. Employees must be adaptable to service clients with varying demands while minimizing mistake rates.

Challenges and Ethical Considerations

While the integration of artificial intelligence (AI) holds immense promise for enhancing customer retention in the hospitality sector, its adoption is not without challenges and ethical considerations. In this chapter, we explore the obstacles that hospitality businesses may encounter as they navigate the AI landscape and discuss the importance of addressing ethical concerns to ensure responsible implementation.

Data Privacy and Security

One of the foremost challenges facing AI adoption in hospitality is the issue of data privacy and security. As businesses collect and analyze vast amounts of guest data to drive personalized experiences, concerns arise regarding the protection of sensitive information. Hospitality establishments must prioritize data security measures, implement robust encryption protocols, and adhere to stringent regulatory frameworks such as GDPR (General Data Protection Regulation) to safeguard guest privacy and earn their trust.

Algorithmic Bias and Fairness

AI algorithms are only as unbiased as the data they are trained on, raising concerns about algorithmic bias and fairness. In the context of customer retention, biased algorithms could lead to discriminatory outcomes, such as preferential treatment based on demographic factors or past behavior. Hospitality businesses must strive for transparency and fairness in their AI-driven systems, regularly auditing algorithms for biases, and implementing safeguards to ensure equitable treatment for all guests.

Displacement of Human Workers

The increasing automation enabled by AI has sparked fears of job displacement among hospitality workers. While AI-driven solutions can enhance efficiency and productivity, they must complement, rather than replace, human labor. Hospitality businesses should invest in reskilling and upskilling initiatives to empower their workforce with the digital skills needed to thrive in an AI-powered environment. Moreover, they must foster a culture of collaboration between humans and machines, recognizing the unique strengths that each brings to the table.

Over-Reliance on Automation

Another challenge associated with AI adoption is the risk of over-reliance on automation, leading to a loss of the human touch and empathy. While AI can streamline processes and optimize operations, it cannot replicate the warmth and empathy of human interaction. Empathy is the core centrist of hospitality operations. Hospitality businesses must strike a delicate balance between automation and human engagement, leveraging AI to enhance, rather than detract from, the guest experience. This entails identifying touchpoints where human interaction is irreplaceable and ensuring that AI augments, rather than replaces these interactions.

Ethical Use of Guest Data

The ethical use of guest data is paramount in the age of AI-driven personalization. Hospitality businesses must obtain explicit consent from guests before collecting their data and communicating how it will be used. Moreover, they must ensure transparency and accountability in their data practices, allowing guests to access, modify, or delete their information upon request. By fostering a culture of trust and transparency, hospitality establishments can cultivate stronger relationships with their guests, driving loyalty and retention in the process.

Management Practices for Compatibility with Industry 4.0

The several management practices for compatibility with Industry 4.0 are.

Management Practices for Industry 4.0

It is evident from previous literature that to thrive in an Industry 4. 0 environment, organisations must consider training, learning, knowledge management, and innovation capability (Lasi et al., 2014; Shamim et al., 2016). This can be on matters of cyber-physical systems (computer networks, embedded actuators, sensors, and other related equipment), differentiation, product or service reengineering, or effectiveness and efficiency of the supply chain. To maintain smartness, innovative capacity, and performance, organizations require creative and innovative staff, who are willing and able to operate in smart unpredictable, and competitive environments such as the industry 4. 0. To such a development of the workforce according to the requirements and conditions of Industry 4. 0 there must correspond suitable management practices (Limna, 2023). In a broader perspective, management can be defined as the accomplishment of organizational goals through people though the task is not very simple. The reality of the organizational environment means that the practices of management should be adjusted to the environment and the purposes of organizational management. Thus, in the context of this study, the learning, knowledge management, and innovation capability of Industry 4. 0's environment are the broader outcomes (Nov & Ye, 2008; Yi & Hwang, 2003) related to the technology acceptance, for example, digital improvements and the integration of CPS. It is quite logical that modern organizations responded to Industry 4. 0 are experiencing many social, technological, and economic issues. To overcome these challenges, there is a call for dynamic capabilities and innovative employees.

This study develops its reasoning on the premise that the environment of Industry 4. 0 is dynamic and unpredictable, a situation that demands a higher level of technology embrace for digital improvements and CPS incorporation ARY; and that technology embrace can be driven by a specific degree of learning, efficient knowledge management, and innovativeness, both within the individual actor and the organization. This phenomenon is presented in Figure 1.

Figure 1. Represent the conceptual framework

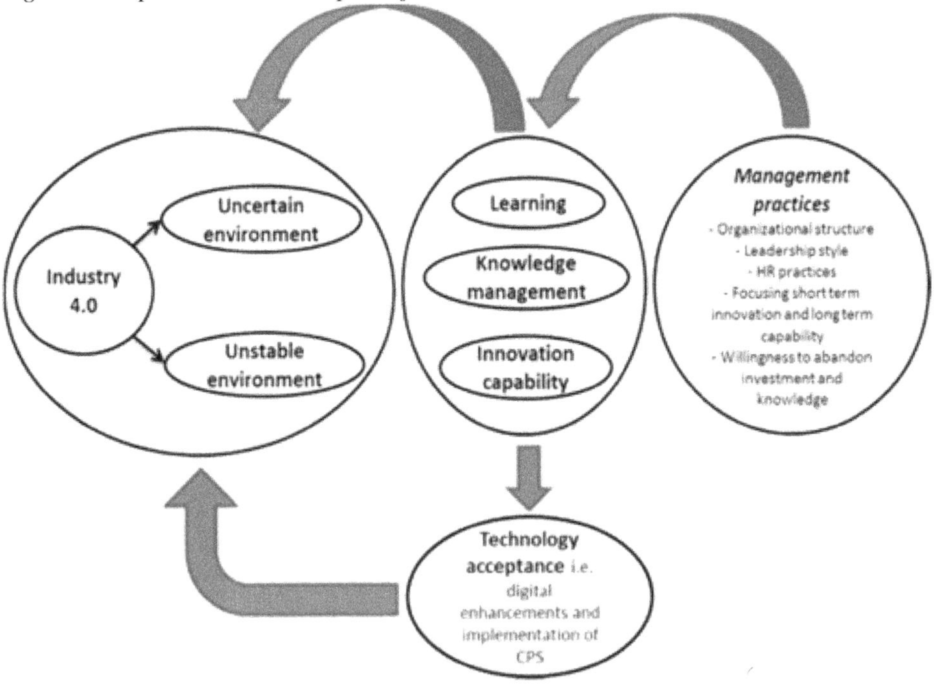

(Shamim et al., 2017).

Thus, the purpose of the study is to recommend managerial strategies that are more suited for learning as well as the knowledge management and innovation capacities of both businesses and their personnel. Let's go over these management strategies below.

Organizational Structure

As for the case where changes are very frequent the organizational structure could work as a useful tool to foster the climate for innovation and learning (Van Der Sluis, 2004). While there are variations in the degree of organization of the organization, it is possible to speak about an organic design of an organization and a mechanistic organizational design on a broader scale (Daft, 2008). Some of the mechanistic design features include that the task is limited to being specialized; authority is concentrated and the decision-making process also; rules and policies tend to be more formal; communication is more structured and occurs from the top down; there are numerous hierarchical levels and many levels of authority. Such types of systems are better suited in conditions where the changes are not very often, the environment is more stable. It also implies that such types of organizational designs are not fit for an Industry 4. 0 environment because the environment is characterized by the absence of stability. Indeed, the organizational structure required for Industry 4. 0 may not be fully formal; may not prefer strict rules and policies; decentralized; the employees empowered; work in teams and flatten communication structure with more horizontal communications. Organization structure to support innovation capability in the environment Can be better aligned with an organic structure.

Leadership Style

Leadership is best described as the ability to lead and enable others. They have labeled it as implementation intentions that are inspiring, motivating, and providing direction towards attaining the intended objectives. This paper agrees with the situational theories that claim that organizational leadership goals as well as behavioral output from the employees can be attained by employing the correct leadership style provided the situation (House, 1971; Shamim et al., 2016). The significance of leadership can also be observed in industry for instance Apple Inc. is among the most intelligent firms and in many instances it was attributed to the leadership ability of Steve Jobs rather than technical knowledge. He understood that an employee can only give their best if they are happy and motivated to do their job (Isaacson, 2012; Shah & Mulla, 2013). This means that implementing the right type of leadership changes depending on the needs and circumstances of Industry 4. 0 can go a long way to enhancing innovations and learning in an organization both from the organizational perspective and the employee level.

Human Resource Practices

In an organizational setting, to attain organizational goals, it is necessary to foster the desirable skill, capacity, disposition, and conduct among the workforce of an organization. An organization's human resource (HR) practices are argued to be one of the biggest influences on the capability, skill, attitude, and behavior of those in the workplace. Consequently, managers who wish to improve learning, knowledge management, innovativeness, and technology acceptance, must ensure that their HR strategy reflects these. Appropriate work and employment practices for knowledge workers can create a substantive competitive advantage in a knowledge economy. Key activities in human resource management include staffing, training, performance evaluation and review, work design, and compensation (Chen & Huang, 2009; Collins & Clark, 2003). Thus, for organizations to attain the concept of Industry 4. 0 effectively, it is required that appropriate HR practices that support learning and innovations in the organizations are developed.

Long-Term Capabilities and Short-Term Innovations

Nowadays, due to advanced technologies, and political, social, and economic shifts, the environment in industry 4. 0 is very unpredictable and dynamic. It is important in such an environment that normal projects are expected to have a shorter developmental time. In addition to these short-term focused activities, organizations also cannot afford to be blinded by the long-term view because it is important as well. It was also observed that innovations in this kind of environment do not have a long life Expectancy. So, innovations should be admitted as an organizational practice, whereby creating more extensive dynamic capabilities in the long term for both the organization and its employees is necessary. This can be achieved through the implementation of the right management tools based on the dynamics of the unfolding situation (Lee & Kelley, 2008). Transforming the organization and the employees to be adaptive to the change is critical in the implementation of Industry 4. 0, which can be achieved through short-term innovations and long-term capabilities.

AI in Clinical Decision-Making

This section examines how artificial intelligence (AI) is changing the field of medical diagnosis and treatment via its sophisticated learning and processing capabilities. Healthcare workers now have access to technologies that provide deeper insights into patient data thanks to the use of AI. This results in more precise diagnosis and successful treatment strategies. We're going to examine three important factors. Case studies of AI in identifying conditions like diabetes and cancer, AI algorithms for diagnosis and prognosis, and AI's function in the expanding area of customized medicine.

AI Algorithms for Diagnosis and Prognosis

AI algorithms are providing new insights into healthcare and are becoming a significant part of illness diagnosis and prediction. Large volumes of medical data are analyzed by these algorithms to find connections and patterns that may be missed by human examination. AI systems, for example, may go through genetic data, radiographic pictures, and patient histories in oncology to find cancer early (Hosny et al., 2018). Similarly, by examining ECG patterns and other vital indicators, AI models are used in the area of cardiology to forecast heart attacks and strokes (Kagiyama et al., 2019). AI's capacity to learn and grow is one of its main advantages in diagnosis. These algorithms improve in predicting accuracy and diagnostic precision as more data is fed into them. This is essential for treating chronic and complicated illnesses when prompt action and early identification may save lives (Bardhan et al.,

2020). Furthermore, AI has a similarly revolutionary impact on prognosis (Fahad Binhowemel et al., 2023; Huang et al., 2020). Artificial intelligence (AI) may predict probable consequences by examining trends in illness development, which allows healthcare workers to plan and take preventive action. This is especially crucial for long-term conditions like diabetes, where AI can forecast future risks including kidney failure or eyesight loss by tracking changes in blood sugar levels, lifestyle choices, and treatment outcomes over time (Guan et al., 2023). Machine learning, deep learning, and natural language processing are the three main categories of AI algorithms; each has particular advantages and uses.

Machine Learning (ML).

Machine learning algorithms are not specifically coded for a job; instead, they learn from data to produce predictions or judgments (Waring et al., 2020). The development of prediction models for patient outcomes based on historical data in the healthcare industry has been made possible by supervised learning algorithms (Eloranta & Boman, 2022). Contrarily, unsupervised learning is used to find patterns or clusters in data, which is helpful in the identification of new disease subtypes (Eloranta & Boman, 2022). Personalized therapy optimization may benefit from reinforcement learning, which teaches computers to make judgments via trial and error (Eloranta & Boman, 2022).

Deep Learning (DL).

Deep learning, a kind of machine learning, analyses complicated data structures by using neural networks with numerous layers hence the term "deep." Convolutional Neural Networks (CNNs) are very useful for identifying illnesses from medical pictures such as MRIs and X-rays because of their exceptional performance in processing imaging data (Sarvamangala & Kulkarni, 2022). With their advantages and uses in image analysis, classification, and graph data processing, some more sophisticated CNN designs include Residual Networks (ResNet), Inception, Visual Geometry Group (VGG), and Graph Convolutional Networks (GCNs) (Y. Yang et al., 2021). Recurrent neural networks (RNNs), which are renowned for their capacity to manage sequential data, are used in the analysis of time-series data, including physiological signals obtained during patient monitoring, to forecast changes in health or consequences over an extended period (Rim et al., 2020). For example, utilizing polysomnography data, Long Short-Term Memory (LSTM) networks a complex variation of RNNs have been widely used in the identification of sleep pane (Bahrami & Forouzanfar, 2022).

Natural Language Processing (NLP)

NLP algorithms provide computers with the ability to comprehend and interpret spoken language. NLP is utilized in the healthcare industry to extract relevant data from unstructured data sources, such as clinical notes or the research literature, supporting prognosis estimates and diagnostic procedures alike (Zhou et al., 2024). The GatorTron is an example of such a language model. The large-scale Transformer-based NLP model is specifically designed for the healthcare industry (X. Yang et al., 2022). Electronic health records are interpreted and analyzed using the Transformer architecture, which is well-known for its effectiveness in managing sequence-to-sequence operations and its capacity to handle big datasets. GatorTron, a very sophisticated model for extracting and comprehending complicated medical information from unstructured data sources, has 8.9 billion parameters and has been trained on over 90 billion words of clinical literature. AI algorithms offer a paradigm change in our knowledge of and approach to treating health and illness; they are more than merely useful tools for accurate diagnosis and prognosis. Further illustrating AI's significant influence on clinical decision-making, the next paragraphs will provide more in-depth analyses of certain case studies in addition to the role of AI in customizing medical treatment.

Case Studies of AI in Detecting Diseases

Numerous case studies have shown how AI may be used to accurately diagnose and identify illnesses like diabetes, cancer, and other serious ailments early on. This chapter looks at a few noteworthy instances to show how AI technology is advancing the area of illness detection.

Cancer Detection

The early identification of cancer is one of the most innovative uses of AI. One noteworthy case study uses deep learning algorithms to analyze mammograms and diagnose breast cancer. Studies have shown that artificial intelligence (AI) can, often more accurately than conventional techniques, recognize patterns in mammography pictures that are suggestive of malignant growth. Google Health developed an AI model, according to noteworthy research that was published in the journal Nature (X. Yang et al., 2022). After being trained on a big dataset of mammograms, this model proved to be more precise than human radiologists in identifying breast cancer. The AI system demonstrated a decrease in false negatives and positives, which are critical components in the diagnosis of cancer. Because early identification of breast cancer may significantly improve prognosis and treatment results, this advancement in AI technology is important.

Diabetes Management

The use of AI in diabetes management and detection, especially with the use of machine learning algorithms, represents a major advancement in healthcare. Numerous studies have shown that these algorithms are capable of analyzing patient data to predict the start, progression, and consequences of diabetes.

In one study, the eight diabetes complications metabolic syndrome, dyslipidemia, neuropathy, nephropathy, diabetic foot, hypertension, obesity, and retinopathy were predicted and categorized using several supervised classification algorithms (Jian et al., 2021). The dataset used in this research has 79 input variables, including demographic data gathered from 884 patients and test results. The models' performance was assessed based on their accuracy and F1 score, with maximum scores of 97.8% and 97.7%, respectively. Random forest (RF), Adaboost, and XGBoost outperformed the other classifiers. This great degree of precision indicates how machine learning may be used to accurately forecast the consequences of diabetes.

A further study examined how well machine learning algorithms might anticipate problems and inadequate glucose control in individuals with nonadherent type 2 diabetes (Fan et al., 2021). Of the 800 type 2 diabetes patients whose data were utilized in this real-world investigation, 165 of them satisfied the inclusion requirements. Prediction models were created using a variety of machine learning methods, and the area under the curve was used to measure the predictive performance. The models have shown great efficacy in predicting a range of sequelae, including diabetic nephropathy, neuropathy, angiopathy, and eye disease, with the highest performance scores being 85.9%, 88.9%, 83.2%, and 90.2%.

Heart Disease Prediction

AI-based heart disease prediction is a major development in cardiovascular healthcare. This program aims to predict the onset of cardiac disease as well as its severity, which is important information for managing and treating the condition effectively.

A novel study in this field examined a prediction model based on machine learning that can classify cardiac disease in both binary and multivariate ways (Yuan et al., 2022). The Fuzzy-GBDT model combines a gradient-boosting decision tree with fuzzy logic to reduce data complexity and enhance prediction accuracy. The model also uses a bagging strategy to prevent overfitting, which improves the model's capacity to categorize the severity of heart disease. The model's assessment findings indicate that it can forecast cardiac illness with great accuracy and stability, suggesting that it might be a useful tool in the medical field.

A novel healthcare system that uses ensemble deep learning in conjunction with feature fusion techniques is presented in another fascinating work (Ali et al., 2020). The shortcomings of conventional machine learning models, which have trouble handling high-dimensional datasets, are intended to be addressed by this method. This is accomplished by merging sensor data with electronic health records to provide a more comprehensive dataset for the prediction of cardiac disease. This dataset is streamlined by the system utilizing the information gain approach, which reduces computational complexity by concentrating on the most important attributes. This model's use of conditional probability for accurate feature weighting is a crucial component that improves the system's overall performance. This ensemble deep-learning approach outperformed previous models and demonstrated its effectiveness in predicting heart disease with an impressive accuracy of 98.5%.

CONCLUSION

In conclusion, while AI offers unprecedented opportunities for enhancing customer retention in the hospitality sector, its adoption must be accompanied by careful consideration of the challenges and ethical considerations at play. By prioritizing data privacy, addressing algorithmic bias, empowering human workers, avoiding over-reliance on automation, and ethically managing guest data, hospitality businesses can harness the power of AI to deliver exceptional experiences while upholding the highest standards of integrity and responsibility. AI integration in customer service drives improved customer service interaction products and solutions. Virtual agents and chatbots help customers be attended to immediately and their complaints solved in the blink of an eye, thus enhancing the value of purchasing a product. It is also evident that this round-the-clock availability is significantly helpful in achieving higher customer satisfaction and retention. Moreover, the issues of ethics related to the use of AI are also a vital factor that should not be taken lightly. The protection of customer data and the explanation of the AI-based decisions taken are essential for the building of trust and the application of the rules of data protection in the field of AI. It will therefore be vital to witness a balance between innovation and responsibility in the development of AI in this hospitality sub-sector.

REFERENCES

Ali, F., El-Sappagh, S., Islam, S. M. R., Kwak, D., Ali, A., Imran, M., & Kwak, K. S. (2020). A smart healthcare monitoring system for heart disease prediction based on ensemble deep learning and feature fusion. *Information Fusion*. https.// DOI: 10.1016/j.inffus.2020.06.008

Bahrami, M., & Forouzanfar, M. (2022). Sleep Apnea Detection from Single-Lead ECG. A Comprehensive Analysis of Machine Learning and Deep Learning Algorithms. *IEEE Transactions on Instrumentation and Measurement*. https.//DOI: 10.1109/TIM.2022.3151947

Bardhan, I., Chen, H., & Karahanna, E. (2020). Connecting systems, data, and people. A multidisciplinary research roadmap for chronic disease management. In *MIS Quarterly. Management Information Systems*. https.//DOI: <ALIGNMENT. qj></ALIGNMENT>10.25300/MISQ/2020/14644

Bradeško, L., & Mladenić, D. (2012). A Survey of Chatbot Systems through a Loebner Prize Competition. *Proceedings of Slovenian Language Technologies Society Eighth Conference of Language Technologies, 2*(January 2012), 34–37. http.//nl.ijs .si/isjt12/proceedings/isjt2012_06.pdf

Brown, E. A., Thomas, N. J., & Bosselman, R. H. (2015). Are they leaving or staying. A qualitative analysis of turnover issues for Generation Y hospitality employees with a hospitality education. *International Journal of Hospitality Management*. https.// DOI: 10.1016/j.ijhm.2015.01.011

Chen, C. J., & Huang, J. W. (2009). Strategic human resource practices and innovation performance - The mediating role of knowledge management capacity. *Journal of Business Research*. https.//DOI: 10.1016/j.jbusres.2007.11.016

Collins, C. J., & Clark, K. D. (2003). Strategic human resource practices, top management team social networks, and firm performance. The role of human resource practices in creating organizational competitive advantage. In *Academy of Management Journal*. https.//DOI: 10.2307/30040665

Daft, R. L. (2008). *Organization Design and Theory*.

Eloranta, S., & Boman, M. (2022). Predictive models for clinical decision making. Deep dives in practical machine learning. *Journal of Internal Medicine, 292*(2), 278–295. https.//DOI: 10.1111/joim.13483

Emmanuel, I. E., & Damachi, G. U. (2015). *Employees' Participation in Decision Making and the Hospitality Industry in Nigeria. An Investigative Study of Selected Hotels in the Federal Capital Territory*. Academic Journal of Economic Studies.

Fahad Binhowemel, S., Alfakhri, M. O., Alreshaid, K. M., & Alyani, A. M. (2023). The Role of Artificial Intelligence in Diabetes Research, Diagnosis and Prognosis. A Narrative Review. [http.//www.jhidc.org/]. *Journal of Health Informatics in Developing Countries*, 17(2), 2023.

Fan, Y., Long, E., Cai, L., Cao, Q., Wu, X., & Tong, R. (2021). Machine Learning Approaches to Predict Risks of Diabetic Complications and Poor Glycemic Control in Nonadherent Type 2 Diabetes. *Frontiers in Pharmacology*. https.//DOI: 10.3389/fphar.2021.665951

Grobelna, A. (2015). Intercultural Challenges Facing the Hospitality Industry. Implications for Education and Hospitality Management. *Journal of Intercultural Management*. https.//DOI: 10.1515/joim-2015-0023

Guan, Z., Li, H., Liu, R., Cai, C., Liu, Y., Li, J., Wang, X., Huang, S., Wu, L., Liu, D., Yu, S., Wang, Z., Shu, J., Hou, X., Yang, X., Jia, W., & Sheng, B. (2023). Artificial intelligence in diabetes management. Advancements, opportunities, and challenges. In *Cell Reports Medicine*. https.//DOI: 10.1016/j.xcrm.2023.101213

Harjanti, D. (2019). Burnout and Employee Performance in Hospitality Industry. The Role of Social Capital. *Jurnal Teknik Industri*. https.//DOI: 10.9744/jti.21.1.15-24

Hight, S. K., Gajjar, T., & Okumus, F. (2019). Managers from "Hell" in the hospitality industry. How do hospitality employees profile bad managers? *International Journal of Hospitality Management*. https.//DOI: 10.1016/j.ijhm.2018.06.018

Hosny, A., Parmar, C., Quackenbush, J., Schwartz, L. H., & Aerts, H. J. W. L. (2018). Artificial intelligence in radiology. *Nature Reviews Cancer, 18*(8), 500–510. https.//DOI: 10.1038/s41568-018-0016-5

House, R. J. (1971). A Path Goal Theory of Leader Effectiveness. *Administrative Science Quarterly*. https.//DOI: 10.2307/2391905

Howarth, J. (2023). *Average Customer Retention By Industry*. https.//explodingtopics.com/blog/customer-retention-rates

Huang, S., Yang, J., Fong, S., & Zhao, Q. (2020). Artificial intelligence in cancer diagnosis and prognosis. Opportunities and challenges. In *Cancer Letters*. https.//DOI: 10.1016/j.canlet.2019.12.007

Isaacson, W. (2012). *Real Leadership Lessons*. https.//hbr.org/2012/04/the-real-leadership-lessons-of-steve-jobs

Jian, Y., Pasquier, M., Sagahyroon, A., & Aloul, F. (2021). A Machine Learning Approach to Predicting Diabetes Complications. *Healthcare, 9*(12), 1712. https.// DOI: 10.3390/healthcare9121712

Kagiyama, N., Shrestha, S., Farjo, P. D., & Sengupta, P. P. (2019). Artificial Intelligence. Practical Primer for Clinical Research in Cardiovascular Disease. *Journal of the American Heart Association, 8*(17). https.//DOI: 10.1161/JAHA.119.012788

Kim, J., Song, H. J., & Lee, C. K. (2016). Effects of corporate social responsibility and internal marketing on organizational commitment and turnover intentions. *International Journal of Hospitality Management*. https.//DOI: 10.1016/j.ijhm.2016.02.007

Lasi, H., Fettke, P., Kemper, H. G., Feld, T., & Hoffmann, M. (2014). Industry 4.0. *Business and Information Systems Engineering, 6*(4), 239–242. https.//DOI: 10.1007/s12599-014-0334-4

Lee, H., & Kelley, D. (2008). Building dynamic capabilities for innovation. An exploratory study of key management practices. *R and D Management*. https.//DOI: 10.1111/j.1467-9310.2008.00506.x

Limna, P. (2023). Artificial Intelligence (AI) in the Hospitality Industry. A Review Article. *International Journal of Computing Sciences Research*. https.//DOI: 10.25147/ijcsr.2017.001.1.103

Mansour, S., & Tremblay, D.-G. (2018). Work–family conflict/family–work conflict, job stress, burnout and intention to leave in the hotel industry in Quebec (Canada). moderating role of need for family friendly practices as "resource passageways." *The International Journal of Human Resource Management, 29*(16), 2399–2430. https.//DOI: 10.1080/09585192.2016.1239216

Mohamed, L. M. (2016). Assessing the effects of transformational leadership. A study on Egyptian hotel employees. *Journal of Hospitality and Tourism Management*. https.//DOI: 10.1016/j.jhtm.2016.04.001

Nov, O., & Ye, C. (2008). Personality and technology acceptance. Personal innovativeness in IT, openness and resistance to change. *Proceedings of the Annual Hawaii International Conference on System Sciences*. https.//DOI: 10.1109/HICSS.2008.348

A. Quinn, K., & A. Buzzetto-Hollywood, N. (2019). Faculty and Student Perceptions of the Importance of Management Skills in the Hospitality Industry. *Interdisciplinary Journal of E-Skills and Lifelong Learning*. https.//DOI: 10.28945/4198

Rim, B., Sung, N. J., Min, S., & Hong, M. (2020). Deep learning in physiological signal data. A survey. In *Sensors (Switzerland)*. https.//DOI: 10.3390/s20040969

Santhanam, N., Kamalanabhan, T. J., Dyaram, L., & Ziegler, H. (2017). Impact of human resource management practices on employee turnover intentions. Moderating role of psychological contract breach. *Journal of Indian Business Research*. https.// DOI: 10.1108/JIBR-10-2016-0116

Sarvamangala, D. R., & Kulkarni, R. V. (2022). Convolutional neural networks in medical image understanding. a survey. In *Evolutionary Intelligence*. https.//DOI: 10.1007/s12065-020-00540-3

Shah, T., & Mulla, Z. R. (2013). Leader Motives, Impression Management, and Charisma. A Comparison of Steve Jobs and Bill Gates. *Management and Labour Studies*. https.//DOI: 10.1177/0258042X13509736

Shamim, S., Cang, S., Yu, H., & Li, Y. (2016). Management approaches for Industry 4.0. A human resource management perspective. *2016 IEEE Congress on Evolutionary Computation, CEC 2016*. https.//DOI: 10.1109/CEC.2016.7748365

Shamim, S., Cang, S., Yu, H., & Li, Y. (2017). Examining the feasibilities of Industry 4.0 for the hospitality sector with the lens of management practice. *Energies*. https.//DOI: 10.3390/en10040499

Shubhneet. (2024). *Automation in the Hospitality Sector*. https.//indiaai.gov.in/article/ai-and-automation-in-the-hospitality-sector

Supanti, D., Butcher, K., & Fredline, L. (2015). Enhancing the employer-employee relationship through corporate social responsibility (CSR) engagement. *International Journal of Contemporary Hospitality Management*. https.//DOI: 10.1108/IJCHM-07-2014-0319

Van Der Sluis, L. E. c. (2004). Designing the workplace for learning and innovation . Organizational factors affecting learning and innovation. *Development and Learning in Organizations. An International Journal*. https.//DOI: 10.1108/14777280410554942

Vieira, S., Pinaya, W. H. L., & Mechelli, A. (2017). Using deep learning to investigate the neuroimaging correlates of psychiatric and neurological disorders. Methods and applications. In *Neuroscience and Biobehavioral Reviews*. https.//DOI: 10.1016/j.neubiorev.2017.01.002

Waring, J., Lindvall, C., & Umeton, R. (2020). Automated machine learning. Review of the state-of-the-art and opportunities for healthcare. In *Artificial Intelligence in Medicine*. https.//DOI: 10.1016/j.artmed.2020.101822

Yang, X., Chen, A., PourNejatian, N., Shin, H. C., Smith, K. E., Parisien, C., Compas, C., Martin, C., Costa, A. B., Flores, M. G., Zhang, Y., Magoc, T., Harle, C. A., Lipori, G., Mitchell, D. A., Hogan, W. R., Shenkman, E. A., Bian, J., & Wu, Y. (2022). A large language model for electronic health records. *Npj Digital Medicine*. https.//DOI: 10.1038/s41746-022-00742-2

Yang, Y., Zhang, L., Du, M., Bo, J., Liu, H., Ren, L., Li, X., & Deen, M. J. (2021). A comparative analysis of eleven neural networks architectures for small datasets of lung images of COVID-19 patients toward improved clinical decisions. *Computers in Biology and Medicine*. https.//DOI: 10.1016/j.compbiomed.2021.104887

Yi, M. Y., & Hwang, Y. (2003). Predicting the use of web-based information systems. Self-efficacy, enjoyment, learning goal orientation, and the technology acceptance model. *International Journal of Human Computer Studies*. https.//DOI: 10.1016/S1071-5819(03)00114-9

Yuan, X., Chen, J., Zhang, K., Wu, Y., & Yang, T. (2022). A Stable AI-Based Binary and Multiple Class Heart Disease Prediction Model for IoMT. *IEEE Transactions on Industrial Informatics*. https.//DOI: 10.1109/TII.2021.3098306

Zhou, B., Yang, G., Shi, Z., & Ma, S. (2024). Natural Language Processing for Smart Healthcare. *IEEE Reviews in Biomedical Engineering, 17*, 4–18. https.//DOI: 10.1109/RBME.2022.3210270

Chapter 14
Decentralized Fundraising:
A Web3 Crowdfunding Platform With Blockchain Integration

Rasmita Kumari Mohanty
https://orcid.org/0000-0002-5828-5649
VNR Vignana Jyothi Institute of Engineering and Technology, India

Talluri Aruna Sri
VNR Vignana Jyothi Institute of Engineering and Technology, India

V. Manjula
Vallurupalli Nageswara Rao Vignana Jyothi Institute of Engineering and Technology, India

Gopisetty Rathnamma
GITAM University, India

ABSTRACT

This chapter introduces a Web3 crowdfunding platform with blockchain integration, enabling decentralized fundraising campaigns and offering an intuitive user experience. The platform includes MetaMask for wallet interface, Solidity for creating and deploying smart contracts, and efficient Ethereum transaction network connectivity. The platform uses the transparency, security, and decentralization of blockchain to transform conventional fundraising. With a user-friendly layout and dynamic user interface, users can establish and take part in fundraising campaigns that are driven by smart contracts. Users may securely link their wallets, manage funds, and sign transactions using the platform's seamless integration of the well-

DOI: 10.4018/979-8-3693-6562-5.ch014

known Ethereum wallet extension MetaMask. To manage wallets, the platform also interfaces with MetaMask, enabling a speedy and secure exchange of Ethereum. Solidity-written smart contracts enforce campaign-specific rules and streamline the contribution-handling process.

1. INTRODUCTION

In this Project 'Crafting the Future of CrowdFunding; Web3, Block chain, MetaMask' The building and deployment of a Web3 crowdfunding platform with block chain integration is intended to revolutionize the current crowd funding scene. This initiative seeks to transform the way fundraising campaigns are carried out by fusing an attractive design with cutting-edge blockchain technology. The user experience for crowd funding is about to be completely reimagined with the addition of technologies like MetaMask pairing for safe wallet management, interaction with smart contracts, and seamless Ethereum transfers across the blockchain network. Smart contracts will automate critical campaign operations using Solidity code, assuring efficiency and transparency in money distribution. This project embodies the fusion of cutting-edge technology, decentralized principles, and design aesthetics to provide a revolutionary Web3 crowdfunding platform.

The future of crowd funding for major projects lies at the intersection of innovation and decentralization, where Web3, blockchain technology, and MetaMask converge to redefine the fundraising landscape. Traditional crowd funding platforms face inherent limitations, including centralization risks, opacity, and inefficiencies. In response, this transformative approach leverages cutting-edge technologies to overcome these challenges and unlock a new era of transparent, secure, and inclusive funding. At its core, this envisioned system employs smart contracts on a decentralized blockchain network, ensuring tamper-resistant record-keeping and automating crucial aspects of project funding. Users interact seamlessly through Web3 protocols, utilizing the MetaMask wallet as a gateway to decentralized applications. The integration of tokenization standards allows for fractional ownership, enhancing liquidity and democratizing access to major projects.

This paradigm shift embraces decentralized identity solutions, real-time data oracles, and scalable architectures to create a robust ecosystem. By prioritizing user-friendly interfaces and stringent security measures, this crowdfunding model aims to empower backers, foster global participation, and provide a transparent avenue for major project financing. In crafting this future, we envision not just a crowdfunding platform but a catalyst for innovation, where the principles of decentralization and blockchain technology reshape the dynamics of project funding on a global scale.

2. BACKGROUND

There are many factors that determine the feasibility to use Web3, blockchain or MetaMask for major projects crowdfunding. Assess technical concerns including that of blockchain scalability and interconnection. Anticipate regulatory risks and remain compliant. Examine quality of end-user experience, barriers to adoption and ultimately security assurance. This will give a good review for you on the strength of taking such an approach in your crowdfunding program.

2.1 Organizational Feasibility

A feasibility study on revolutionizing conventional crowdfunding via Web3, Blockchain technology, and MetaMask platforms in major construction projects entails numerous intricate analyzes. Start by assessing scalability, risks, the extent of simplicity or complexities that will accompany its integration into existing technologies platforms. Perform check on the installed equipment and requirement for re-training if necessary. Make sure you stay on the right side of your local regulations and therefore be a law-abiding organization as this will help mitigate any forms of legal risks.

What can be done to ensure that it is usable by potential users? How much does a possible user need to understand to be able to use it and what does he or she need that knowledge for? Finally, the management should consider setting up the cost for establishment and regular expenses leading to revenues generated extra. Through partnering, one ensures that the project undertaken in the block-chain setting is feasible and sustainable. Moreover, the organization's flexibility should be measured through assessing their impact on routine and identifying if refinement is necessary. Be honest with stakeholders and open as possible when disclosing information to them if you want trust and acceptance of your ideas. Finally, it is essential to carry out a comprehensive feasibility study which describes the likelihood of organizing large-scale projects under the web 3, the blockchain and MetaMask technologies perspective but also taking into account issues associated with institutions, other actors, etc.

2.2 Economic Feasibility

Meta mask Crowdfunding on web3, blockchain will determine all the costs and benefits involved in developing it. The first tranche includes investments such as development, blockchain infrastructure, and integration. Subsequently, running operations would incur spending that focuses mainly on upkeep, security, and scalability. Do not overcompensate these added advantages by exploring other means of revenues such as transaction charges and tokenization strategies.

These will serve to reduce the transaction costs and increase liquidity which in turn can enlarge the gro up of investors. However, you should think about the effect on existing revenue streams, and how many years it will take to become self-financing. Management of expectation involves having straight talks with stakeholders. Such dynamic Web3 and blockchain technologies environment can allow for an innovative strategic management of the project financial matters which could maintain the sustainability of the crowdfunding campaign.

2.3 Behavioral Feasibility

Evaluation of the behavioral viability of shaping the future of major projects crowdfunding via Web3, blockchain, and MetaMask. Inform the user about the advantages of decentralization, openness, and anti-fraud measures to foster confidence.

Think of the learning curve associated with MetaMask and blockchain and how it will impact the entry barrier. Assess user's inclination towards a decentralized/blockchain-supported crowdfunding system. Emphasize on user-oriented characteristics for instance user friendly interfaces and easy navigation to stimulate acceptance. Education and supportive initiatives geared towards resolving resistance to changes in the user community.

Interact with early adopters and get advice on how to modify the platform as per their needs. Evaluate its effect on users' behavior related to engagement, input, as well as interaction inside a distributed crowdfunding system. When it comes to winning people over and making them comfortable with this platform in a world where web3 and blockchain technologies are developing fast, the initiative needs to consider issues surrounding usability while also emphasize on issues that relate to behavioral factors such as experience.

3. LITERATURE SURVEY

(Fauziah, Latifah, Omar, Khoirunisa, & Millah, 2020) analysed success factors for crowdfunding campaigns, categorized them into project-related and campaign-related factors, and compared them across different crowdfunding types. It identified key factors for specific campaigns and discussed their impact on success.The paper acknowledges the hybrid security token model's existence but lacks a detailed analysis of regulatory challenges and implications for blockchain-based crowdfunding.

Success factors like registration, presale, and location are not specific to blockchain-based crowdfunding, and a comprehensive analysis of team size is lacking.

(Gururaj, Janhavi, Holla, Kumar, Bhumika, & Goundar, 2021) highlights blockchain's role in enhancing crowdfunding security and efficiency while emphasizing the importance of project attributes like duration, funding goal, and category for crowdfunding success. The paper lacks an examination of potential drawbacks and regulatory issues in implementing blockchain-based decentralized crowdfunding. Additionally, it overlooks scalability concerns and the impact on user experience, focusing solely on the benefits of security and transparency.

(Zhu & Zhou, 2016) developed a blockchain-based crowdfunding system using Ethereum smart contracts, demonstrating increased transparency and reduced information asymmetry; however, it observed slower transaction speeds. The system utilized independent modules, Ethereum's Solidity language, MetaMask for user interaction, and Infula for Ethereum connectivity. Further research is needed to enhance user experience and expedite Ethereum transfers in the system, addressing challenges such as slow transactions, usability barriers for non-blockchain users, and unexplored smart contract token controls.

(Mohanty, Sahoo, & Kabat, 2023) Comparative analysis demonstrates Bit Fund's superior performance over other methods, offering transparency and security through blockchain's tamper-proof recording of project transactions and outcomes, security, and efficiency, while emphasizing the importance of project attributes like duration, funding goal, and category for crowdfunding success. The paper neglects to address potential drawbacks, such as blockchain's evolving nature and reliance on active participant engagement in decentralized crowdfunding.

(Mohanty, Sahoo, & Kabat, 2022) introduces a crowdfunding technique using Ethereum, an open-source, public blockchain-based platform, and Solidity for smart contract functionality. Two smart contracts are developed: a generator contract for new campaigns and a campaign contract for managing funds. The campaign manager can generate payment requests and transfer funds to sellers after approval. Web3.js and Ganache command line interfaces are also mentioned for interaction with remote nodes. The paper lacks a detailed analysis of potential drawbacks and challenges of implementing a decentralized crowdfunding platform using blockchain technology.

(Mohanty, Sahoo, & Kabat, 2024) presents FundDapp, a blockchain-based decentralized crowdfunding web app, showcasing secure donations and unique features through Object-Oriented Analysis and Design methodology. The paper discusses limitations of FundDapp, including the requirement of MetaMask for transactions, absence of a search bar, and inability to edit comments, while not extensively exploring additional

(Mohanty, Sahoo, & Kabat, 2023) explores the conceptual map, research issues, and technical opportunities of decentralized AI and edge intelligence. It evaluates complementarity and meta-synthesis between centralized and decentralized AI, focusing on properties, characteristics, pros, and cons. The paper also highlights the integration of CeAI and DeAI in complex AI systems and intelligent problem-solving, highlighting the potential for creating a smart metaverse. The paper mentions that it is not possible to discuss all the functions and research issues of device- edge-cloud hybrid data-sharing edge AI systems due to space limitations and refers interested readers to other works by Cao on X-interactions, X-complexities, and X-intelligences in complex systems and their data science and AI-driven solutions.

(Mohanty, Motupalli, Manju, Gangappa, Gouthami, & Mounika, 2023) investigates Web3 frameworks, decentralized identity, Oracle services, tokenization, and consensus mechanisms. This work aims to provide insights into how technology shapes the evolution and applications of smart contracts, aiding researchers, and practitioners in leveraging their potential across industries. The paper lacks a descriptive review of the applicability of smart contracts in securing the Internet and IoT. The paper does not address the lack of standards in smart contracts, which is a major challenge faced by companies seeking to use blockchain-enabled smart contracts

(Mohanty, Kumar, Padmaja, & Prashanthi, 2024) explores how blockchain technology can address issues in Chinese equity crowdfunding, suggesting secure stock registration, simplified transactions, and improved corporate governance. Blockchain's power and resource-intensive nature is a drawback, while the complexity of existing equity registration and limited capability of crowdfunding platforms hinder efficient equity trading.

(Mohanty & Jyothi, 2015) provides a brief overview of the most important discrepancies between Hyperledger Fabric and Ethereum distributed ledger technologies (DLT). The paper only provides a brief overview of the discrepancies between Hyperledger Fabric and Ethereum distributed ledger technologies, without analysis.

4. EXISTING SYSTEM

The existing system for crowdfunding major projects typically relies on centralized platforms, often characterized by intermediary involvement, limited transparency, and higher transaction costs. These platforms use traditional payment gateways, causing delays and inefficiencies in fund transfers. Trust is established through centralized authorities, and project backers may face obstacles due to geographical restrictions and lengthy verification processes.

In contrast, crafting the future of crowdfunding using Web3, blockchain, and MetaMask envisions a decentralized model. Blockchain ensures transparency, traceability, and reduced fraud risk by recording transactions on a tamper-resistant ledger. Smart contracts, a key feature of blockchain, automate fund transfers and project milestones, streamlining the process. MetaMask, as a Web3 wallet, empowers users to interact seamlessly with decentralized applications, providing a user-friendly gateway to the blockchain.

This transformative approach aims to democratize fundraising, allowing global participation without intermediaries. Backers can contribute with cryptocurrencies, and tokenization facilitates the representation of project shares. The potential benefits include increased accessibility, lowered costs, and a more inclusive and efficient crowdfunding ecosystem, shaping a future where decentralization and blockchain technology redefine the dynamics of major project funding.

By combining and analyzing these data points, an IoT device can be uniquely identified within a given network or ecosystem. This identification process enables security measures, device management, and data analysis in IoT deployments.

4.1 Definitions

Some key definitions related to Crowd Funding using Web3, MetaMask.

1. **Crowdfunding:** The practice of funding a project or venture by raising small amounts of money from many people, typically via the internet.
2. **Web3:** A term used to describe the next evolution of the internet, characterized by decentralized protocols and technologies such as blockchain, smart contracts, and decentralized applications (DApps).
3. **MetaMask**: A popular cryptocurrency wallet and gateway to the Ethereum blockchain, allowing users to interact with Ethereum DApps directly from their web browser.
4. **Blockchain:** A distributed ledger technology that records transactions across multiple computers in a way that is transparent, secure, and immutable.
5. **Smart Contracts:** Self-executing contracts with the terms of the agreement directly written into code. They automatically execute and enforce the terms of an agreement when predefined conditions are met.
6. **Decentralized Finance (DeFi):** A term used to describe financial services built on blockchain technology that aims to make financial services more accessible, transparent, and inclusive by eliminating intermediaries.

7. **Tokenization:** The process of representing real-world or digital assets as tokens on a blockchain. Tokens can represent ownership rights, access to services, voting power, and more.
8. **Ethereum:** A decentralized platform that enables the creation and execution of smart contracts and decentralized applications (DApps) through its blockchain.
9. **Decentralized Autonomous Organization (DAO):** An organization represented by rules encoded as a computer program that is transparent, controlled by organization members, and not influenced by a central government.
10. **Immutable Ledger:** A ledger or record of transactions that cannot be altered or deleted once they have been confirmed and added to the blockchain, providing a tamper-proof and auditable history of transactions.

4.2 System Architecture

Figure 1. System architecture

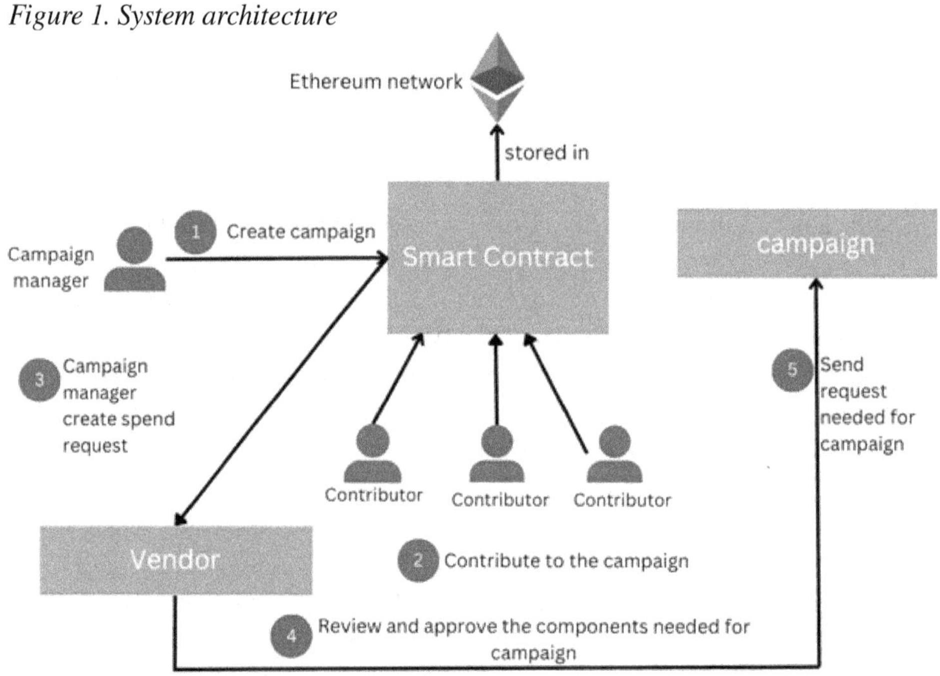

The system architecture Fig:1 shows the future of crowdfunding, leveraging Web3, blockchain, and MetaMask for major projects, is designed to be decentralized, transparent, and secure. Here's a concise overview:

1. **Smart Contracts:** Utilize blockchain's smart contracts to automate project milestones, fund transfers, and token issuance. These self-executing contracts enhance transparency and eliminate the need for intermediaries.
2. **Blockchain Network:** Implement a decentralized blockchain network to store and secure transaction data. This ensures an immutable ledger, reducing fraud risks and providing a transparent record of all crowdfunding activities.
3. **Web3 Integration:** Integrate Web3 protocols to enable seamless interaction with decentralized applications (DApps). This empowers users, allowing them to connect their MetaMask wallets to participate in crowdfunding directly from their browsers.
4. **Tokenization Standards:** Apply blockchain tokenization standards (e.g., ERC-20) to represent project shares as digital assets. This facilitates fractional ownership, enhancing liquidity and opening up new possibilities for backers.
5. **Decentralized Identity:** Implement decentralized identity solutions to enhance user privacy and security. This ensures that participants maintain control over their personal information during crowdfunding activities.
6. **Oracles for Real-World Data:** Use oracles to fetch real-world data (e.g., project progress, external market conditions) and feed it into smart contracts, enhancing the accuracy and relevance of project milestones.
7. **Scalability Solutions:** Integrate scalability solutions such as layer 2 solutions or sidechains to address potential congestion and high transaction costs associated with the main blockchain network.
8. **User Interface (UI) Design:** Develop an intuitive user interface that seamlessly integrates MetaMask functionality, allowing users to easily navigate the crowdfunding platform and interact with smart contracts.
9. **Interoperability:** Ensure interoperability with other blockchain networks and financial systems to enhance accessibility and promote a more interconnected crowdfunding ecosystem.
10. **Security Protocols:** Implement robust security protocols, including encryption and multi-signature wallets, to safeguard user funds, smart contracts, and sensitive data from potential threats. This comprehensive system architecture aims to redefine crowdfunding, providing a secure, transparent, and inclusive environment for major project financing.

4.3 Functional Requirements

Functional requirements for a crowdfunding website utilizing Web3, MetaMask, and blockchain technology:

1. **User Registration and Authentication:** Users should be able to register and authenticate their accounts securely using MetaMask and verify user identities through MetaMask's authentication mechanism.
2. **Project Creation and Management:** Allow users to create crowdfunding projects, specifying project details such as funding goal, description, and duration and implement project management features for project owners to update project details and communicate with backers.
3. **Contribution Processing:** Enable backers to contribute funds to projects securely using MetaMask and blockchain transactions and display real-time updates of contributions and funding progress.
4. **Smart Contract Integration:** Implement smart contracts to govern crowdfunding campaigns, ensuring transparency and automated execution of rules and define smart contract functionalities for managing fund transfers, project milestones, and dispute resolution.
5. **Tokenization and Reward Distribution**: Tokenize project ownership or rewards using blockchain tokens and automate token distribution to backers based on predefined rules or project milestones.
6. **Decentralized Governance:** Implement decentralized governance mechanisms, allowing stakeholders to participate in decision-making processes and enable voting on project proposals, funding allocation, or project updates.
7. **Transparency and Auditability**: Provide transparent access to project information, funding details, and transaction history on the blockchain and ensure all project-related actions are recorded immutably on the blockchain for auditability.
8. **Notifications and Communication**: Send notifications to project owners and backers regarding project updates, milestones, and important events and facilitate communication between project owners and backers through messaging or comment features.
9. **Security Measures**: Implement robust security measures to protect user accounts, transactions, and sensitive data and utilize encryption and secure coding practices to prevent unauthorized access and data breaches.
10. **User Interface and Experience**: Design an intuitive and user-friendly interface accessible via web browsers and MetaMask extension and ensure responsive design for seamless user experience across different devices and screen sizes.
11. **Testing and Quality Assurance**: Conduct thorough testing of the crowdfunding platform to ensure functionality, security, and performance and perform testing on different browsers and devices to ensure compatibility.
12. **Documentation and Support**: Provide comprehensive documentation and user guides for using the crowdfunding platform and offer customer support channels for addressing user inquiries, issues.

4.4 Non- Functional Requirements

Non- functional requirements for a crowdfunding website utilizing Web3, MetaMask and Blockchain Technology.

1. **Performance:** Ensure fast loading times and responsiveness of the website, even during peak traffic periods. Optimize blockchain interactions and smart contract executions to minimize latency and improve user experience.
2. **Scalability:** Design the platform to handle a growing number of users, projects, and transactions without compromising performance. Implement scalable architecture and infrastructure to accommodate increased demand.
3. **Security:** Employ industry-standard security practices to protect user accounts, private keys, and sensitive data. Utilize secure coding practices and regularly audit smart contracts for vulnerabilities and implement measures to prevent common blockchain attacks such as replay attacks, front-running, and phishing.
4. **Reliability**: Ensure high availability and reliability of the platform to minimize downtime and disruptions. Implement redundancy and failover mechanisms to mitigate the impact of system failures.
5. **Privacy:** Respect user privacy by minimizing the collection and exposure of personally identifiable information. Encrypt sensitive data and communication channels to protect user confidentiality.
6. **Regulatory Compliance:** Comply with relevant legal and regulatory requirements, such as anti-money laundering (AML) and know your customer (KYC) regulations. Implement features for identity verification and compliance monitoring as necessary.
7. **Interoperability:** Ensure compatibility with different blockchain networks, wallets, and decentralized applications (DApps) to maximize interoperability. Support multiple cryptocurrencies and token standards to accommodate diverse user preferences.
8. **Usability:** Design an intuitive and user-friendly interface that is accessible to users with varying levels of technical expertise. Provide clear instructions and guidance for using MetaMask and interacting with blockchain features.
9. **Maintainability:** Structure the codebase and architecture in a modular and maintainable manner to facilitate future updates and enhancements. Document code, APIs, and system architecture to aid in troubleshooting and maintenance.
10. **Monitoring and Logging:** Implement monitoring and logging mechanisms to track system performance, user activity, and security events. Use analytics tools to gather insights into user behavior and platform usage for optimization purposes.

4.5 System Analysis

Figure 2. System analysis

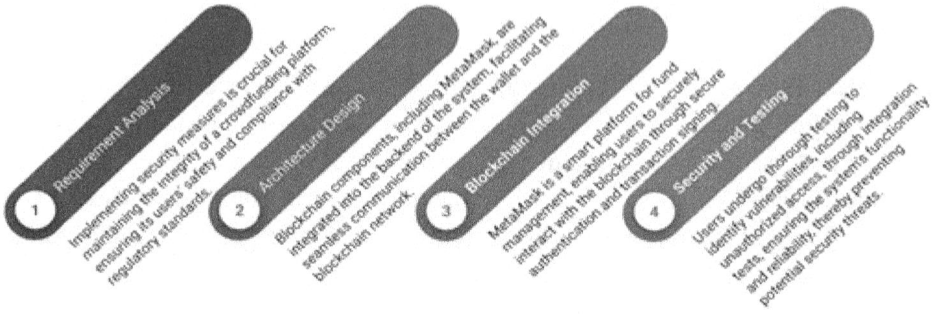

A system analysis of a crowdfunding website using Web3, MetaMask, and blockchain involves gathering requirements, defining use cases, and designing a data model shown in Fig 2. This involves interviews with stakeholders to understand their needs and objectives, identifying functional and non-functional requirements, and analysing each use case to identify actors, goals, and steps involved. The data model should represent the relationships between different entities and define their attributes and constraints.

The system's architecture includes frontend, backend, and blockchain components, with appropriate technologies and frameworks for development. The system's interaction with the frontend user interface, backend servers, MetaMask wallet, and blockchain network is defined. A suitable blockchain platform like Ethereum is chosen for smart contract deployment. Smart contracts are developed to govern crowdfunding campaigns and manage project funds. Security measures are implemented to protect user accounts and sensitive data. The system's scalability and performance are assessed, with smart contract code optimized to minimize latency and improve system responsiveness.

4.6 Software Requirement Specification

Workplace for Development

Visual Studio Code: The compugter has to have the most recent version of Visual Studio Code (VS Code) installed. A code editor that is both lightweight and flexible, VS Code is compatible with a wide range of programming languages and frameworks.

Extensions

1. **Solidity Extension:** For Solidity support, install Juan Blanco's "Solidity" extension or one similar to it. Code completion, syntax highlighting, and other Solidity development-specific capabilities are provided by this extension.
2. **HTML/CSS/JavaScript Extensions**: Install extensions to enable the languages of HTML, CSS, and JavaScript. With the addition of code formatting, syntax highlighting, and other crucial web development tools, these additions improve the coding experience.
3. **Install the "Live Server"**: This extension or a comparable program to observe a real-time preview of web construction. This extension improves the development workflow by enabling developers to rapidly observe changes in the browser and run a local development server.
4. **Install the "Debugger for Chrome"**: This extension to enable the debugging of JavaScript code. With the help of this plugin, developers may efficiently troubleshoot web applications by being able to debug client-side JavaScript code that is executing in the Chrome browser directly from within Visual Studio Code.

4.7 Compiler for Solidity

Install the Solidity compiler (solc) as a local dependency inside the project or as a global installation. In order to translate Solidity smart contracts into bytecode that can be implemented on Ethereum or other blockchains that are compatible, the Solidity compiler is required. For improved version control and compatibility, developers can opt to include solc as a local dependency within their project or install it globally using npm or yarn.

Developers can build up a stable working environment in Visual Studio Code for Solidity code execution and web development by adhering to these software needs and configurations. This facilitates effective and productive software development workflows.

5. PROPOSED SYSTEM

Figure 3. Methodology

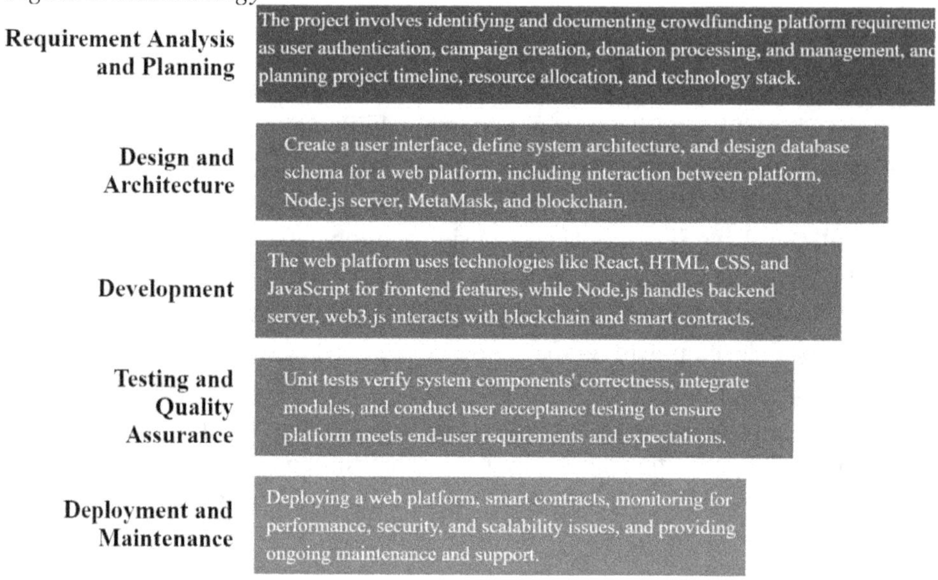

Implementation

1. **User Authentication Setup:** Begin by implementing a stable authentication mechanism to ensure secure access to the platform. Consider using industry-standard methods such as OAuth or JSON Web Tokens (JWT) for user authentication. This mechanism will allow users to securely log in to the platform, ensuring that only authorized individuals can create campaigns or donate to existing ones.
2. **Campaign Creation Form:** Develop a user-friendly form within the React application to enable users to input essential campaign parameters. These parameters may include the campaign title, a descriptive outline of the campaign's purpose, the target funding amount in cryptocurrency, the campaign duration in days, and an optional image for visual appeal. Utilize HTML and CSS to design the form, ensuring an intuitive and visually appealing interface for users to input campaign details.
3. **Backend Integration:** Establish communication between the React application and a Node.js backend server. Utilize web3.js libraries to facilitate interaction with the deployed smart contract on the blockchain, initially targeting the Goerli test network for development purposes. This integration ensures seamless data

transmission between the frontend and backend components of the platform, enabling efficient handling of campaign creation requests and interactions with the blockchain.

4. **Smart Contract Development:** Develop a smart contract function responsible for creating campaigns on the blockchain. This function should accept the campaign parameters provided by the user through the React application and securely store this information on the blockchain. Additionally, incorporate validation logic within the smart contract to ensure that the target funding amount and campaign duration fall within reasonable limits, enhancing the integrity and reliability of the crowdfunding process.
5. **Confirmation and Visibility:** Upon successful creation of a campaign, provide confirmation to the user on the platform. Additionally, make the newly created campaign visible to other users browsing for funding opportunities. Display pertinent details such as the campaign name, target amount, funding progress, remaining duration, and an optional campaign image. This visibility fosters transparency and encourages user engagement with active campaigns.
6. **Campaign Management Features:** Implement features to empower campaign creators to manage their campaigns effectively. Allow creators to view detailed campaign information, potentially update campaign parameters, and communicate updates or progress to donors through the platform. Integrate functionalities such as editing campaign details and posting campaign updates to facilitate efficient campaign management and donor engagement.
7. **Smart Contract Functionality:** Enhance the smart contract with functionality to track campaign duration autonomously. Continuously monitor the blockchain to determine if a campaign has reached its predefined end date. If the campaign expires, execute a scheduled event within the smart contract to automatically close the campaign, prevent further contributions, and initiate payment processing based on the campaign's funding goals. This autonomous functionality ensures the integrity and efficiency of campaign management on the platform.
8. **Donation Process:** Enable users to contribute to campaigns that resonate with them by implementing a streamlined donation process. Incorporate a "Donate" button on the campaign page, triggering a pop-up window within the React application. This pop-up window should seamlessly connect to the platform using web3.js libraries and MetaMask, leveraging the user's MetaMask wallet for cryptocurrency transactions.

Facilitate secure transfer of cryptocurrency from the donor's MetaMask wallet to the specific smart contract associated with the target campaign, ensuring transparency and trust in the donation process.

9. **Transaction Recording and Confirmation:** Record donation transactions securely on the blockchain, making them immutable and transparent. Provide donors with confirmation of their valid donations and update cryptocurrency balances in their MetaMask wallets accordingly. This transparent recording of transactions enhances trust and accountability within the crowdfunding ecosystem, fostering donor confidence and participation.
10. **Real-time Updates:** Automatically update the campaign page on the platform to reflect increased revenue through dynamic elements such as a development bar. This real-time feedback mechanism provides users with instant visibility into the progress of campaigns, encouraging continued engagement and participation. Implementing real-time updates enhances user experience and fosters a sense of community and collaboration within the crowdfunding platform.

By following these implementation steps in Fig:3, you can create a robust and user-friendly crowdfunding platform that leverages blockchain technology to enhance security, transparency, and efficiency in fundraising campaigns.

5.1 Functionalities

The functionalities are categorized into six steps and they are:

1. **User Authentication and Campaign Creation:**
    - Users log in using authentication mechanisms like OAuth or JWT.
    - Upon login, users are directed to the campaign creation form within the React application.
    - The form allows users to input campaign parameters such as title, description, target funding amount, duration, and optional image. Users submit the form, triggering backend integration with the Node.js server.
2. **Backend Integration and Smart Contract Deployment:**
    - The Node.js server interacts with web3.js libraries to communicate with the blockchain network.
    - Upon receiving campaign data from the React application, the Node.js server deploys a smart contract on the blockchain. The smart contract function for creating a campaign is invoked, passing along the supplied information and securely storing it on the blockchain.
    - The smart contract validates the entered data, ensuring the target amount and duration are within reasonable limits.
3. **Campaign Confirmation and Visibility:**
    - Upon successful campaign creation, users receive confirmation on the platform.

- The newly created campaign becomes visible to other users browsing for funding opportunities.
- The platform displays a listing of active campaigns with details like name, target amount, funding progress, duration, and optional campaign image.
- Campaign creators can view their campaign information, potentially update details, or engage with donors through the platform.

4. **Smart Contract Functionality for Campaign Management:**
    - The smart contract continuously monitors campaign duration on the blockchain.
    - If a campaign reaches its predefined end date, the smart contract executes a scheduled event.
    - This event closes the campaign, prevents further contributions, and initiates payment processing based on the funding goals.
    - Users browsing for campaigns can choose to donate to causes that resonate with them.
5. **Donation Process and Transaction Recording:**
    - Users click the "Donate" button on the campaign page, triggering a pop-up window within the React application.
    - The pop-up window connects to the platform using web3.js libraries and MetaMask with the user's MetaMask wallet.
    - Users confirm their donations, securely transferring cryptocurrency from their MetaMask wallet to the specific smart contract associated with the campaign.
    - Donation transactions are recorded securely on the blockchain, making them irrevocable and transparent.
6. **Real-Time Updates and User Feedback:**
    - The platform automatically updates the campaign page to reflect increased revenue through dynamic elements like a development bar.
    - This real-time feedback mechanism provides users with instant visibility into campaign progress.
    - Donors receive confirmation of their valid donations and updated cryptocurrency balances in their MetaMask wallets.
    - These functionalities enhance user experience, trust, and engagement within the crowdfunding platform.

By implementing these functionalities in a step-by-step manner, the crowdfunding platform can provide a seamless and transparent experience for users, creators, and donors alike.

6. CONCLUSION AND FUTURE SCOPE

The integration of blockchain technology within the Web3 crowdfunding platform represents a significant leap forward in the realm of decentralized fundraising. By leveraging the transparency, security, and decentralization inherent to blockchain, the platform offers a robust and user-friendly experience for campaign creators and contributors alike. The seamless integration of MetaMask ensures that users can easily and securely manage their funds, while the Solidity-based smart contracts enforce campaign rules and streamline the contribution process. This innovative approach not only enhances the efficiency of fundraising but also builds trust among users by ensuring that all transactions are transparent and immutable. The successful deployment and rigorous testing of both the front-end and back-end components underscore the platform's reliability and security, making it a valuable tool in the growing landscape of decentralized applications.

Looking ahead, the Web3 crowdfunding platform has the potential to evolve further and integrate additional features that enhance user engagement and broaden its applicability. Future developments could include the incorporation of multi-chain support, enabling users to conduct fundraising campaigns across different blockchain networks, thereby increasing flexibility and reach. Moreover, integrating advanced analytics and machine learning algorithms could provide deeper insights into fundraising patterns and campaign performance, helping users to optimize their strategies. Another promising direction is the implementation of decentralized identity solutions to enhance user verification and security. Additionally, expanding the platform's functionality to support tokenized assets and non-fungible tokens (NFTs) could open new avenues for creative and innovative fundraising methods. These advancements would not only solidify the platform's position in the decentralized finance (DeFi) ecosystem but also contribute to the broader adoption of blockchain technology in various sectors.

REFERENCES

Fauziah, Z., Latifah, H., Omar, X., Khoirunisa, A., & Millah, S. (2020). Application of blockchain technology in smart contracts: A systematic literature review. [ATT]. *Aptisi Transactions on Technopreneurship*, 2(2), 160–166. DOI: 10.34306/att.v2i2.97

Gururaj, H. L., Janhavi, V., Holla, A. M., Kumar, A. A., Bhumika, R., & Goundar, S. (2021). Decentralised application for crowdfunding using blockchain technology. *International Journal of Blockchains and Cryptocurrencies*, 2(1), 68–82. DOI: 10.1504/IJBC.2021.117809

MOHANTY, R. K., & JYOTHI, N. (2015). A Secured Framework for Protecting Sensitive Information from Unauthorized Users.

Mohanty, R. K., Kumar, A. P., Padmaja, R., & Prashanthi, V. (2024). Deep Learning for Analyzing User and Entity Behaviors: Techniques and Applications. In *Consumer and Organizational Behavior in the Age of AI* (pp. 219-250). IGI Global.

Mohanty, R. K., Motupalli, R. K., Manju, D., Gangappa, M., Gouthami, B., & Mounika, G. (2023, December). Energy-Efficient Cluster Based Routing Protocol to Enhance the Lifetime of Wearable Wireless Body Area Networks (WBAN). In *2023 OITS International Conference on Information Technology (OCIT)* (pp. 71-76). IEEE. DOI: 10.1109/OCIT59427.2023.10431071

Mohanty, R. K., Sahoo, S. P., & Kabat, M. R. (2022, October). A Survey on Emerging Technologies in Wireless Body Area Network. In *2022 13th International Conference on Computing Communication and Networking Technologies (ICCCNT)* (pp. 1-5). IEEE.

Mohanty, R. K., Sahoo, S. P., & Kabat, M. R. (2023). Sustainable remote patient monitoring in wireless body area network with Multi-hop routing and scheduling: A four-fold objective based optimization approach. *Wireless Networks*, 29(5), 2337–2351. DOI: 10.1007/s11276-023-03276-x

Mohanty, R. K., Sahoo, S. P., & Kabat, M. R. (2023, June). A Network Reliability based Secure Routing Protocol (NRSRP) for Secure Transmission in Wireless Body Area Network. In *2023 8th International Conference on Communication and Electronics Systems (ICCES)* (pp. 663-668). IEEE.

Mohanty, R. K., Sahoo, S. P., & Kabat, M. R. (2024). Thermal-energy-efficient-secured-link reliable and delay-aware routing protocol (TESLDAR) for wireless body area networks. *International Journal of Computers and Applications*, 1-13. IEEE. (2021, June 25). Hyperledger, Ethereum, and blockchain technology: A short overview.

Zhu, H., & Zhou, Z. Z. (2016). Analysis and outlook of applications of blockchain technology to equity crowdfunding in China. *Financial Innovation*, 2(1), 1–11. DOI: 10.1186/s40854-016-0044-7

Chapter 15
Decentralized Identity Verification:
Revolutionizing Travel Documentation

Asmita Manna
Pimpri Chinchwad College of Engineering, India

Rohini Yogesh Sarode
https://orcid.org/0009-0006-4557-3429
Pimpri Chinchwad College of Engineering, India

Rachana Yogesh Patil
Pimpri Chinchwad College of Engineering, India

Manjiri R. Ranjanikar
Pimpri Chinchwad College of Engineering, India

ABSTRACT

With the advent of e-tourism services, airlines, hotels, and other hospitality-related enterprises are able to attract global customers. Therefore, a smart and efficient decentralized identity management system integrated with document management is the need of the hour. In this chapter, a blockchain and decentralized identifier-based system is proposed that will enable the service requesters to verify the identity and authenticity of the documents by exploiting the on-chain and off-chain data; making the process safe, reliable, and hassle-free. A model called Self-Sovereign-Identity (SSI) is employed in this work to develop a decentralized application that is secure, transparent, and user-centric. To ease the storage issues, the InterPlanetary File System (IPFS) is used for storing the DID (Decentralized Identifiers) documents

DOI: 10.4018/979-8-3693-6562-5.ch015

and Verifiable Credential certificates. In addition to the proposed model, a few case studies are provided for in-depth analysis of the concepts. This chapter also discusses the practical challenges while implementing the system and future prospects.

1. INTRODUCTION

The travel and tourism industry is one of the first industries to adopt digitization to its core; however, the passport, VISA, and immigration documents verification process still more or less depends on paper documents, leading travelers to wait in long queues at the immigration counters to complete the verification formalities. Moreover, the COVID-19 outbreak has highlighted the importance of paperless and contactless e-services, especially for identity verification (Dabban, Abdullahi, Adepoju, & Ojerinde, 2023). Paper documentation has few more challenges as well.

The immigration process is complex and depends heavily on manual intervention as the passport is a physical entity (Chiller-Glaus, Schwaninger, & Hofer, 2007). A passport must be presented at all entry and exit points along with other travel documents like Visa and Immigration stamps, resulting in similar verification being done manually at multiple checkpoints. This screening and immigration stamping often exhaust individuals because of long checkpoint queues. If some documents are misplaced in a foreign land, it is a reason for huge anxiety for an individual (Tamrakar, Ekberg, & Asokan, 2011). The process of obtaining duplicate documents is tedious and challenging due to the lack of verification opportunities. Manual processes are generally cumbersome resulting in longer delays. Currently, each country maintains its own databases of information on all travelers, and there is hardly any smooth channel across all countries for sharing that information. Passport and VISA frauds are also not that uncommon, where people try to assume the identity of a deceased individual or produce fake supporting documents. As immigration officers rely on the information produced before them and cannot access an individual's past travel history, documentation fraud may go unnoticed, as furnishing fabricated documents would be easier. With respect to these challenges, it can be understood that a cross-national secured digital framework where all past records are conserved in a tamper-proof way is the need of the hour for identity verification (Murtagh, Gatersleben, & Uzzell, 2012).

The digital solution should not only cater to the needs of the countries but also should provide privacy protection to every individual. The credentials should be verified for identity as well as context information in such a way that there will be no need of any additional personal data. The Verifiable Credential should form a portable and verifiable entity that provides complete authority to the data owner (Stockburger, Kokosioulis, Mukkamala, Mukkamala, & Avital, 2021). Therefore, the proposed solution should be based on a trustworthy decentralized architecture which will allow authorities to issue verifiable credentials to travelers that can be shared and verified at all immigration checkpoints. Blockchain-based architecture is best suited for this type of application as being a decentralized, unchangeable, and trustworthy distributed ledger, it ensures the integrity of identification when recording transactions (Banerji, Rashideh, Arora, & Pratihari, 2021). Not only the authorities will benefit, but also the users will be empowered to manage their credentials on their smartphone using an encrypted digital wallet, giving them a choice over what they share, with whom, and for what reason (Li, He, Liang, & Jiang, 2021).

This chapter proposes a blockchain-based Digital Identifier framework comprising Self Sovereign Identity and InterPlanatory File System. The chapter is organized as follows. The second section discusses the current scenario of decentralized identity verification in travel and tourism, third section proposes a Self Sovereign Identity and Interplanetary File System based system framework, fourth section provides case studies of digital passport verification and the fifth section concludes the chapter by discussing the challenges and future prospects.

2. ROLE OF DECENTRALIZED IDENTITY VERIFICATION TO OVERCOME THE CHALLENGES OF TRADITIONAL IDENTITY MANAGEMENT SYSTEM

2.1 Evolution of DID

Figure 1. Evolution timeline of DID

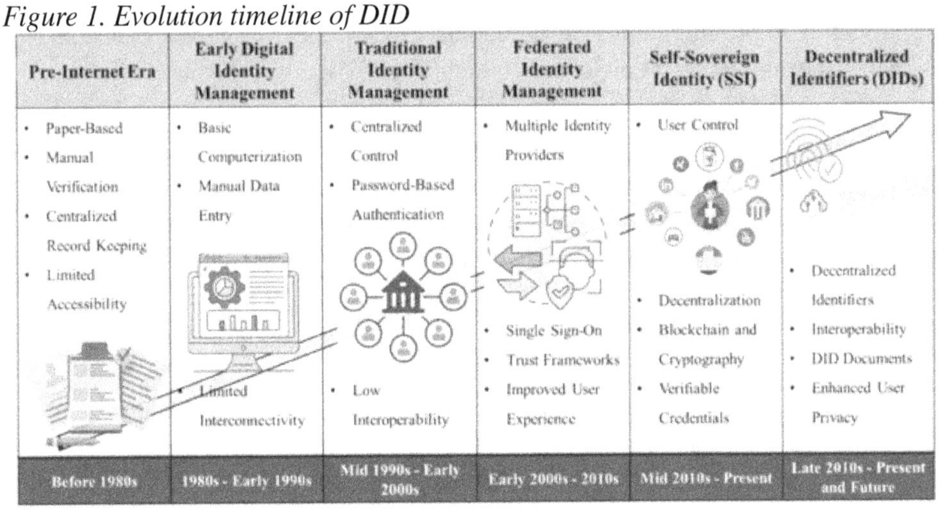

Before the advent of the internet and digital technologies, identity management up to the 1980s relied on manual, paper-based systems. Centralized record-keeping by government agencies and large institutions was common, with verification processes heavily dependent on physical documents such as birth certificates and driver's licenses (Lampropoulos & Denazis, 2011). This approach limited accessibility and increased susceptibility to fraud due to the labor-intensive nature of in-person verification.

The transition to digital identity management from 1980 to the early 1990s marked a shift towards basic computerization. Organizations began moving from manual record-keeping to early computer systems. However, these systems were rudimentary and often involved manual data entry. Interconnectivity between different systems was limited, which hindered seamless authentication processes across various platforms (Zhu & Badr, 2018).

From the mid-1990s to the early 2000s, traditional identity management systems emphasized centralized control and relied heavily on password-based authentication (Kuperberg, 2019). Organizations adopted centralized directories like LDAP and Microsoft Active Directory for managing user identities within their networks. However, this centralized approach led to security vulnerabilities, such as weak passwords, and low interoperability between different systems managed by separate organizations.

The early 2000s to 2010s saw the emergence of federated identity management, which facilitated integration across multiple identity providers and services using standardized protocols such as SAML and OAuth. This approach enabled single sign-on capabilities, allowing users to authenticate once and access various applications and services across different domains without repeated logins. Trust frameworks were established to ensure secure transactions and data sharing among trusted parties, significantly improving both security and user experience (Naik & Jenkins, 2017).

Since the mid-2010s, Self-Sovereign Identity (SSI) has transformed identity management by prioritizing user control, decentralization, and verifiable credentials. In SSI architectures, users manage their identities and attestations through distributed ledgers, typically leveraging blockchain technology (Preukschat & Reed, 2021). This decentralized approach eliminates the need for traditional registration authorities by anchoring each user's identity to a unique identifier tied to a public key through asymmetric cryptography. Verifiable claims are stored off-chain for privacy and selectively shared with relying parties based on established trust relationships via the blockchain (Der, Jähnichen, & Sürmeli, 2017).

Decentralized Identifiers (DIDs), introduced since the late 2010s, have further advanced identity management by enhancing user privacy and self-sovereignty. DIDs are random public strings mapped to decentralized registries, coupled with securely held private information by the DID owner. This architecture allows users to construct ownership proofs using their private data, which are verified against public registry entries (Mahamuni et al., 2022a). Complementing DIDs, Verifiable Credentials (VCs) include claims issued to holders, linked to public registry data and private holder information, enabling proof of claim ownership while safeguarding privacy through selective disclosure. These technologies empower individuals to control their identity data persistently and portably across platforms, ensuring interoperability and allowing for user-managed updates without reliance on third parties. They prioritize user consent and minimal disclosure, offering robust privacy protections in digital interactions (Mahamuni et al., 2022b). This is depicted in Figure 1.

Table 1. Evolution of DID

Identity Management Method	**Year**	**Authentication Methods**	**Interoperability**	**Privacy and Control**	**User Experience**	**Security**
Pre-Internet Era	Before 1980	Physical documents; manual verification	Limited, fragmented	Centralized control; limited user control	Labor-intensive; prone to errors and fraud	Vulnerable to document forgery and theft
Early Digital Identity	1980s - Early 1990s	Basic computer systems; manual data entry	Limited interconnectivity	Centralized control; limited user autonomy	Improved efficiency with digital records	Vulnerable to early cyber threats
Traditional Identity Management	Mid-1990s - Early 2000s	Passwords; LDAP, Active Directory	Low interoperability	Centralized control; dependency on providers	Improved usability with network directories	Vulnerable to password attacks, insider threats
Federated Identity	Early 2000s - 2010s	SAML, OAuth; Single sign-on (SSO)	Improved with standards	Trust frameworks; reduced password fatigue	Enhanced user convenience with SSO	Enhanced security with mutual trust frameworks
Self-Sovereign Identity (SSI)	Mid-2010s - Present	Blockchain-based; Decentralized identifiers	High interoperability	User controls data; selective disclosure	Empowers users with identity ownership	Enhanced security with cryptographic proofs
Decentralized Identifiers (DIDs)	Late 2010s - Present	DIDs; Blockchain-based authentication	High interoperability	Enhanced privacy; self-sovereignty	Enables selective disclosure of claims	Enhanced security with cryptographic proofs

2.2 Working of DID

The Fig. 2 shows Decentralized Identifiers' (DIDs') architecture and operation. Fundamentally, a DID URL—such as did.example.abc123/path/resource—serves as a unique ID in URL form referencing a particular resource. Issued to a DID Controller, this DID URL captures a DID like did.example.abc123. Managing and making changes to the DID Document, the DID Controller—an entity with change capabilities—referrals to the DID Subject, the entity identified by the DID (e.g., a person or company) (Dib & Toumi, 2020).

Figure 2. DID architecture and operation

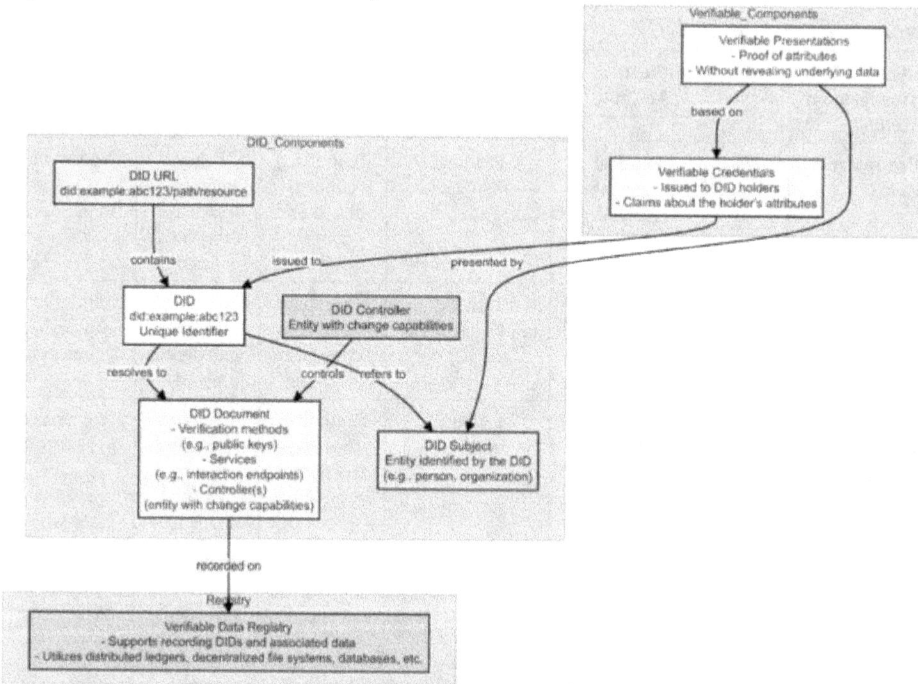

Crucially including public keys, services (such interaction endpoints), and controller(s) information, the DID Document is a component with verification mechanisms. Resolving the DID to get required verification and service data depends on this paper. Establishing the relationship between the identifier and the entity it stands for, the DID Controller exercises control over the DID Document and refers to the DID Subject (Luecking, Fries, Lamberti, & Stork, 2020). Using distributed ledgers, distributed file systems, databases, and such technologies, this entire configuration is logged on a Verifiable Data Registry, therefore supporting the recording of DIDs and related data.

Verifiable Credentials are granted to DID holders on the other side of the building. These credentials constitute the foundation for Verifiable Presentations and assert the holder's qualifications. Verifiable Presentations give evidence of characteristics, therefore enabling the DID bearer to deliver verified information without revealing underlying facts. This method guarantees that DIDs are scattered and safe, thereby facilitating interaction and verification in a way that respects digital identity management and privacy (Goodell & Aste, 2019).

2.3 Resilience and Availability of Blockchain Network

The thorough architecture and processes shown in Figure 3 guarantee the resilience and continued running of blockchain systems. Decentralization, Fault Tolerance, Immutability and Security, Network Resilience, and Availability makes of five primary areas. Every part defines the particular characteristics that support the blockchain's capacity to sustain data integrity, resist errors, and offer great availability.

Blockchain technology is mostly based on decentralization; the distributed ledger is a fundamental aspect. By replicating this ledger throughout several network nodes, one depends less on a single point of failure. Furthermore used are consensus systems like as Proof of Work (PoW) and Proof of Stake (PoS) to get nodes in agreement on the blockchain's condition. These systems guarantee consistency and integrity of data via the network even in the presence of maybe hostile individuals (Bakre, Patil, & Gupta, 2017).

Byzantine fault tolerance and redundancy help one to reach fault tolerance. The design of the blockchain network consists on several nodes carrying copies of the blockchain data, therefore guaranteeing ongoing operation even in the case of individual node faults. Byzantine fault tolerance improves this even further by letting the network run as expected even in cases of certain nodes acting maliciously or unpredictably, hence preserving the security and stability of the network.

Important qualities of blockchain systems are immutability and security. Every block is linked to its predecessor using cryptographic hash, thus changing the data is computationally impossible. This guarantees imutability and integrity of the blockchain. Smart contracts also play a big part since they let self-executing agreements come forth. These agreements ensure that transactions are carried out as planned and lower the possibility of human error or manipulation by automatically enforcing and executing terms contained into code without the requirement of intermediaries.

Social Media Platform The peer-to peer (P2P) network structure, whereby nodes interact directly with one another, strengthens resilience. This enhances the robustness of the network by removing reliance on a central server. The network's self-healing capacity lets it easily bounce back from node breakdowns. Other nodes can take over when a node fails, and the failing node can resynchronize with the network upon recovery so reducing disturbance and preserving continuous functioning.

Blockchain networks' worldwide accessibility and continuous functioning help to provide a major benefit—availability. Globally distributed nodes guarantee great availability, therefore making the network always available. Designed to run around-the-clock without fail, the blockchain offers consumers and apps a strong and dependable foundation. This ongoing process guarantees that the network stays accessible and functional around-the-clock, therefore supporting different use cases needing continuous connectivity.

Figure 3. Resilience and availability of blockchain network

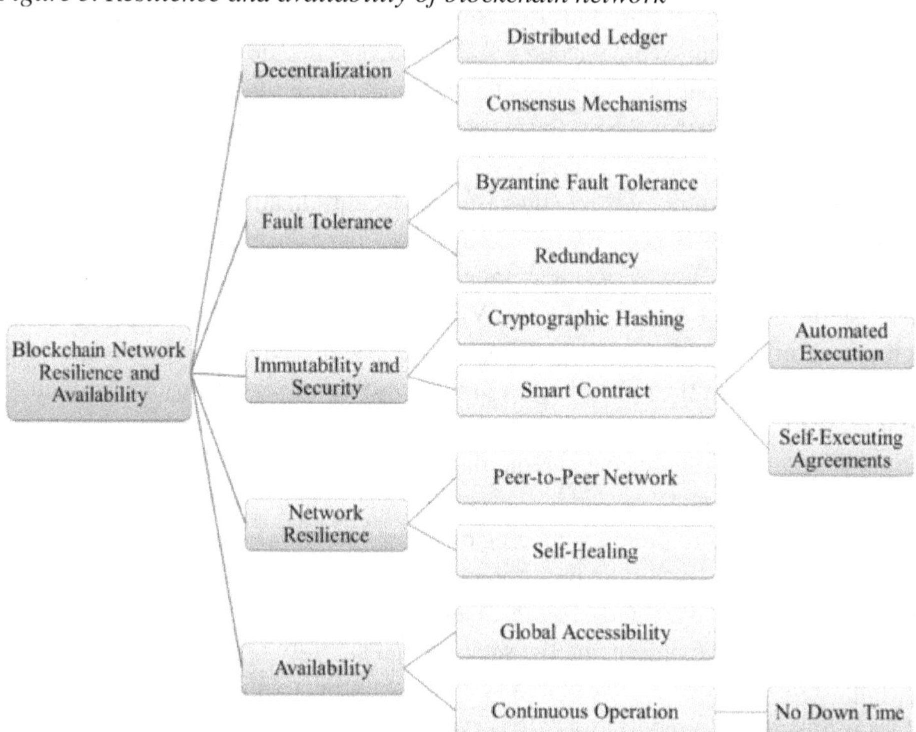

3. PROPOSED SYSTEM USING DID

3.1 Self-Sovereign Identity

Self-sovereign identity (SSI) is a decentralized identity management model that enables individuals to have complete control over their personal information and digital identity. In an SSI system, individuals can create and manage their own digital identity, which is secured using cryptography and blockchain technology.

SSI allows individuals to selectively disclose their personal information and control who has access to it, rather than relying on third-party organizations to manage their identity. This can help to reduce the risk of identity theft, data breaches, and other forms of digital fraud, as well as protect individuals' privacy and personal autonomy.

In an SSI system, individuals typically create a unique digital identity, which is verified by a network of trusted validators using decentralized identity protocols. Once verified, the individual's identity can be stored on a decentralized ledger or other distributed data store, such as a blockchain. The individual then controls access to their identity information and can selectively disclose it to third parties as needed, such as when applying for a job, opening a bank account, or using an online service. Overall, self-sovereign identity represents a significant shift away from centralized identity models, and has the potential to improve privacy, security, and personal autonomy in the digital age.

There are three main pillars of self sovereign identity as shown in Figure 4: a. Verifiable Credentials, b. Blockchain, c. Decentralized Identifiers.

Figure 4. Pillars of self sovereign identity

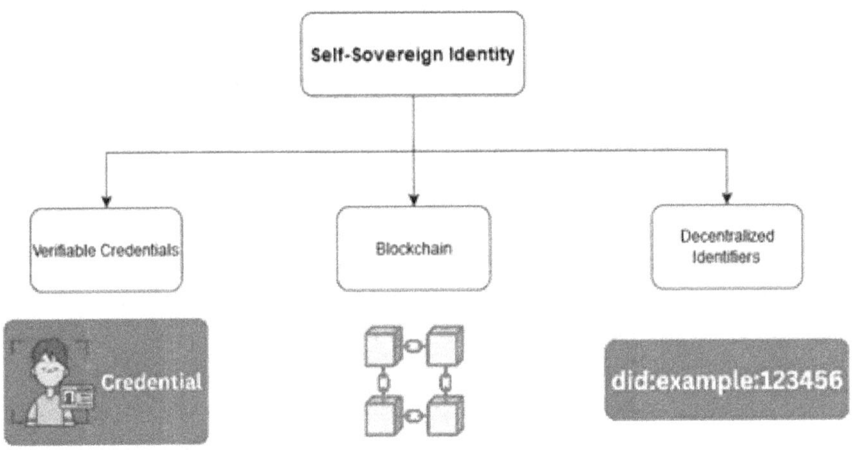

In our proposed system we recommend to use self sovereign identity for traveller to create and use their identities with access control. We recommended to use IPFS to store DIDs by combining IPFS with blockchain network. These three pillers works together to provide a secured and immutatble identity management system for the traveller.

3.1.1 Verifiable Credential Identities

Verifiable Credentials (VCs) (Chadwick et al., 2019) are digital credentials that represent information about an individual, organization, or thing, that can be cryptographically verified. VCs are a form of digital identity that can be shared and trusted across different platforms and organizations. They can be issued by trusted entities, such as governments or educational institutions, and can contain information such as qualifications, certifications, or personal attributes. Together, DID and Verifiable Credentials (Sedlmeir, Smethurst, Rieger, & Fridgen, 2021) enable secure, private, and trusted interactions between entities on the internet without the need for a centralized identity provider. DID provides a unique identifier that can be used to store and manage VCs, while VCs provide a trusted way to represent and share identity information.

In our proposed system following components are included with verifiable credentials to manage the identity of a person.

1. **Identity Creation:** An individual initiates their SSI journey by creating a decentralized identifier (DID), which is a unique identifier linked to their cryptographic keys. This process ensures that the identity is tamper-proof and can be verified independently.
2. **Verifiable Credentials:** Credentials such as passports, driver's licenses, and other identity documents are issued as verifiable credentials. These credentials are cryptographically signed by issuers (e.g., governments, airlines) and can be stored in the individual's digital wallet.
3. **Issuer Verification:** Issuers digitally sign credentials using their private keys. These credentials are then stored in the individual's digital wallet, associated with their DID, which is stored on IPFS.
4. **Presentation:** When needed, the individual can present these verifiable credentials to verifiers (e.g., airlines) without revealing unnecessary personal information. The verifier can independently verify the credentials against the issuer's public key and the integrity of the blockchain or decentralized ledger where the credentials are stored.

3.1.1.1 Workflow of Verifiable Credentials

a) **Issuance:** A trusted issuer creates a VC using a digital signature that links the credential to the individual's identity. The VC can include information such as the person's name, date of birth, education, or professional certification. The transaction is recorded on chain but any personal information is not stored on chain.
b) **Storage:** Verifiable credentials in an SSI system are typically stored on a digital wallet that is under the control of the identity holder. These digital wallets can be software applications that run on a user's device.
c) **Verification:** A verifier who wants to confirm the authenticity of a VC can request access to the blockchain. They can use the DID to retrieve the VC and verify the digital signature to ensure that the credential is valid and has not been tampered with. If the verification is successful, the verifier can trust the information in the VC and make a decision based on it.
d) **Revocation:** In some cases, a VC may need to be revoked if it is no longer valid or has been compromised. The issuer can publish a revocation notice on the blockchain, which will be accessible to anyone who tries to verify the credential. Once a VC has been revoked, it can no longer be used for verification.

3.1.2 InterPlanetary File System

The primary underlying issue with research data sharing is researchers' fear of data misuse and misinterpretation. This is because, in the context of trust, which the research community is gradually coming to understand, data sharing approaches are still in their infancy. Many solutions are put up to address this problem, such as controlling access to the data rather than granting unrestricted access to it and protecting each person's identity. These solutions, however, are unable to provide digital data immutability, trust, or traceability with relation to data utilization (Nyaletey et al., 2019).

The overabundance of data is stored on cloud servers, which are centralized authorities. A single point of failure is just one of the many risks connected to a central authority. Data backups are provided by third parties to prevent such mishaps. The introduction of a blockchain to give trust and transparency eliminates the need for third parties in the development of a trust-based business. With the use of decentralized storage, data can be independently stored as a distributed ledger across several network nodes. The network nodes' limited processing and storing capacity is the issue. A peer-to-peer architecture known as the interplanetary file system (IPFS) is modified for this use. Since it handles content addressing, there is no chance of a single point of failure. Data is kept on the decentralized IPFS network, which guarantees its availability.

IPFS is widely utilized as a framework for data sharing storage. Its high availability and strong performance are offset by its inability to trace authentication or access, which makes authorship and unauthorized access difficult to look into. In this concept, IPFS incorporates a blockchain. Metadata generated by file actions, like adding or reading a file, is recorded on the blockchain.

The blockchain is responsible for storing and managing the metadata of the data. Figure 5 shows an overview of the architecture of working of blockchain with IPFS

Figure 5. Architecture diagram

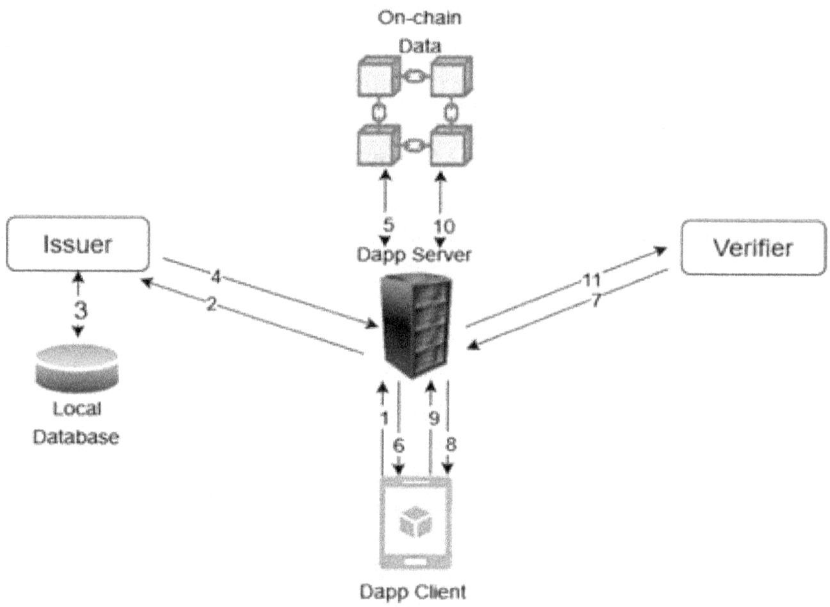

3.1.3 Decentralised Identity Creation (DID)

In our proposed system we have four main components in the architecture diagram of our system as shown in the figure 2. Steps for the flow of the DIDs and working of the architecture is as mentioned below.

I. User creates a DID and shares DID along with claims to Issuer via Dapp Server
II. Dapp server forwards the request to appropriate Issuer

III. Issuer checks the provided information against local database
IV. If correct, Issuer creates Verifiable Credential(VC) and signs the VC
V. Server creates an entry on-chain, using issuer's key-pair
VI. Notification is sent to Dapp client, in order to import the credential
VII. Verifier requests credentials from Dapp Client
VIII. Dapp server forwards the request to Dapp Client
IX. Dapp Client gives access to credentials
X. Dapp server checks against on-chain data
XI. If found correct forwards the information to verifier

3.1.4 Decentralised Identity Creation (DID)

DID stands for "Decentralized Identifier". It is a globally unique identifier that is not controlled by any central authority or organization. A decentralized identifier (DID) is a pseudo-anonymous identifier for a person or company. DIDs are designed to give individuals and entities control over their digital identity and enable secure and private interactions on the internet. They are used in decentralized systems like blockchain and distributed ledger technologies to enable self-sovereign identity [22]. Each DID is secured by a private key. Only the private key owner can establish that they own or control their identity. One person can have many DIDs, which limits the extent to which they can be tracked across the multiple activities in their life. For instance, a person could have one DID associated with a gaming platform, and a separate one with their credit reporting platform.

Each DID is often associated with a series of verifiable credentials (attestations) issued by other DIDs, that verifies to specific characteristics of that DID (such as age, diplomas, pay-slips, location). These credentials are cryptographically signed by their issuers, which allow DID owners to store these credential themselves as an alternative to a single profile provider.

Example. "did.example.1234xyzdefghijklmnopqrstvwabc"

The string "did" is the scheme, striing "example", is the DID method, "1234xyzdefghijklmnopqrstvwabc" is the DID method Specific string.

A DID is recorded on the public ledger along with a DID document that includes the network addresses for interaction, the public key for the DID, and any additional public credentials that the identity owner wants to share with the public. By managing the corresponding private key, the identity owner can exert authority over the DID document in this way.

In our system the DIDs are created and stored on the IPFS for further usage with blockchain when and wherever required by any individual or an authorised entity such as government or airlines. Once the DIDs are used or accessed the blockchain creates a transaction and the record will be permanently stored and immutable beacause of the blockchain network.

3.1.5 Proposed System for a Travel

The proposed idea can be implemented further for checking identity to verify traveller for booking tickets with security and more efficiently by using SSI based digital identities (Querido, 2020).

1. **Booking and Check-In:** Individuals can use their SSI-based digital identities to book flights and check-in securely. They present their verifiable credentials (e.g., passport, visa) digitally to the airline.
2. **Security and Efficiency:** Airlines can verify the authenticity of these credentials quickly and securely using decentralized verification methods, reducing fraud and improving the efficiency of check-in processes.
3. **Privacy and Data Minimization:** SSI ensures that individuals only share necessary information (e.g., proof of identity and ticket validity) without disclosing unnecessary personal details, enhancing privacy protection.
4. **Resilience and Interoperability:** SSI systems built on DIDs and IPFS are interoperable across different platforms and services, providing a seamless experience for travelers across various airlines and travel agencies.

Figure 6. Sequence of actions by system and users

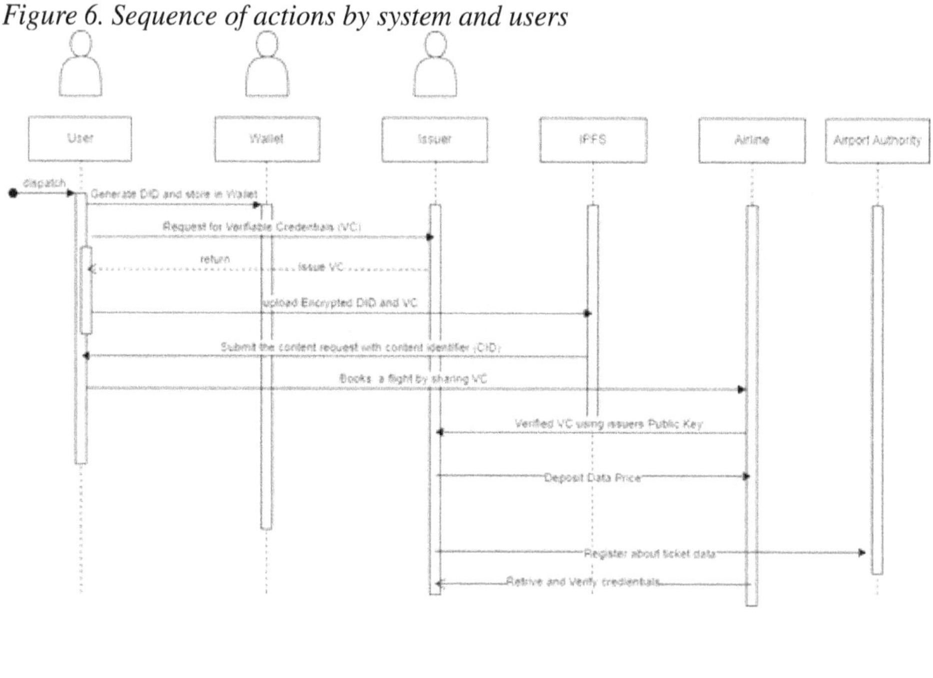

This sequence diagram in figure 6, illustrates a process where a user generates a decentralized identifier (DID) and uses verifiable credentials (VC) to book a flight. The interaction involves various participants. User, Wallet, Issuer, IPFS (InterPlanetary File System), Airline, and Airport Authority. Here's a step-by-step explanation.

1. User.
   - Generate DID and store in Wallet. The user generates a decentralized identifier (DID) and stores it in their digital wallet.
   - Request for Verifiable Credentials (VC). The user requests verifiable credentials from the issuer through the wallet.
2. Wallet.
   - Forward VC Request to Issuer. The wallet forwards the user's request for verifiable credentials to the issuer.
3. Issuer.
   - Issue VC. The issuer creates and issues the verifiable credentials.
   - Return VC to Wallet. The issuer sends the verifiable credentials back to the user's wallet.
4. Wallet.
   - Upload Encrypted DID and VC to IPFS. The wallet uploads the encrypted DID and verifiable credentials to the InterPlanetary File System (IPFS).
5. User.
   - Submit Content Request with Content Identifier (CID). The user submits a request containing the content identifier (CID) of the uploaded data to the airline.
6. Airline.
   - Verify VC using Issuer's Public Key. The airline retrieves and verifies the verifiable credentials using the issuer's public key.
   - Deposit Data Price. The airline deposits the data price for accessing the ticket information.
   - Register Ticket Data. The airline registers the ticket data with the airport authority.
7. Airport Authority.
   - Retrieve and Verify Credentials. The airport authority retrieves and verifies the credentials as needed.

4. CASE STUDIES

A self-sovereign identity-based digital identity verification system can enable travellers to walk through international borders seamlessly without any hassles. Some countries are taking the initiative of launching Decentralized Identifier to provide a seamless experience across borders. Some notable pilot projects are discussed below.

4.1 European Union's European Self-Sovereign Identity Framework (Essif, 2024)

This is a notable initiative by EU launched around the year 2020 for facilitating the citizens with better identity management where the control over the digital identity solely lies with the data-owner. The ESSIF is a use case of the European Blockchain Service Infrastructure (EBSI), which is a cooperative program by twenty-seven European Union member states, Norway, and Liechtenstein. This framework aims to empower the citizens to access healthcare, education, and employment across the borders of all participating nations. EBSI has been establishing various network of distributed nodes across Europe and experimenting with use cases in different service areas that use self-sovereign identity, decentralized identifiers, and verifiable credentials. Out of these use cases, ESSIF is one of the most advanced ones.

The framework consists of three major components. Decentralized Identifier (DID), Verifiable Credentials (VC), and Identity Wallets. DIDs are created and managed by the users without the intervention of any central authority, and the same is stored in the blockchain. As the user is the sole owner and controller of the DID, it ensures the user's privacy. Verifiable Credentials are issued by the trusted and legal authorities and are cryptographically secured against tampering. The VCs can be presented by the user without furnishing any additional personal information for verification purposes. Identity wallets are secure applications that assist users storing, and manage their DID, VC, and other identity-related credentials. Other than these three major components, ESSIF adheres to various standards and protocols to ensure that DIDs and VCs can be used across different systems and services within the EU. The framework also incorporates various advanced cryptographic techniques to comply with GDPR and other regulatory frameworks.

Though the ESSIF is not currently being used directly for travel and tourism purposes, but the same framework can be extended for the same. Regarding tourism, the government authority should issue VC against passport, visa, and other immigration documents.

4.2. Known Traveler Digital Identity Program

Launched in 2018, the Known Traveller Digital Identity (KTDI) (KTDI, 2024) program is an initiative by the World Economic Forum in association with the Canadian Government and the Netherlands government, along with a few private partners like Air Canada, KLM Royal Dutch Airlines, Toronto Airport, and Amsterdam Airport. The main aim of KTDI is to uphold the values and principles of decentralized identity, which embraces the ownership and control of identity.

The base model of DID implementation (World Economic Forum, 2024) consists of four layers, out of which two layers namely DID Networks and DID Communication Protocol are based on cryptographic trust while other two layers namely Credential Exchange, and Governance Frameworks are based on the human trust framework. The layers are developed based on the principles of Digital Identity Creation, Verifiable Credential, and Control over Data Sharing. Travelers create a digital identity with personal information and travel history, securely stored using blockchain technology whereas government authorities issue verifiable credentials comprising of passport information, visa status, and travel history. An issuing authority has the ability to revoke a VC that it had previously issued by modifying the blockchain-based cryptographic accumulator appropriately. Once the VC is obtained, the traveller can present the VCs to relevant authorities and service providers (e.g., airlines, border control) using their digital wallet when required.

DID networks layer is further spilt into two layers. blockchain network and the decentralized identity overlay. In this layer 1, wallets and agents are also implemented for enabling credential exchange. Hyperledger Indy is selected as the decentralized identity platform for the KTDI pilot solution.

The KTDI implementation is still in the early stage. To gain world-wise acceptability, it should adhere to all international standards, open specifications, and incorporate industry best practices. As KTDI is modular, scalable, and secured, it can be a global benchmark for DID based smart tourism.

4.3. South Korea and DID

South Korea is adopting and integrating blockchain technology into various sectors, strongly emphasizing the digital identity solutions. Through various initiatives and regulations, the government has taken significant steps to support and promote DID (Decentralized Identifiers) technology. The key projects are MyID Alliance (MyIDAlliance, 2024), Seoul Blockchain Governance Team, **SK Telecom** etc. MyID Alliance purposes to create a standardized DID framework that allows users to verify their identities securely and seamlessly across different platforms. Seoul Blockchain Governance Team is implementing DID based architecture for improving citizens' life reducing the administrative inefficiencies. SK Telecom's DID based mobile identification verification system allows the users to access various online and offline services by verifying their identities. Once these use cases are successful, South Korea may move for DID based smart tourism as well.

4.4. Singapore and Smart Immigration System

Starting in 2024, Singapore's Changi airport has initiated a Smart Immigration system (Chen, 2023) based on biometric data which enables the users completing immigration in no time. Though the system does not use DID as of now, it may incorporate the same in the near future.

From the above case studies, it is understood that the combination of DID, VC and blockchain can build an efficient smart travel and tourism authentication service where all the past history of a traveler will be stored in an immutable ledger, providing the opportunity to verify it in a swift way. As the DID itself is the identifier for an individual, no additional personal data is required for the verification. For example, if any traveller is applying for visa by providing their DID in any consulate, the consulate can issue a Verifiable Credential against that. The tourist can now present the same for accessing hotel services or some internal permit if required. The entire process will be smooth and time-saving.

5. CHALLENGES IN IMPLEMENTATION

From the case studies provided in the previous section, it is well perceived that SSI and IPFS based Decentralized Identification Verification comes with multiple virtues making the work of the individual travellers, immigration officers, and national intelligence agencies easier. However, as the system is still in its infancy, it also has multiple shortcomings which are to be overcome while implementing the system. Let's analyze these challenges one by one.

a) **Standardization and Seamless Integration:** Although some of the organizations like W3C have tried to standardize the implementation of DID and VC, many challenges related to the standardization of protocols and contents are there. As of now, DID specifications have different formats, different set of information, and different versioning methodology resulting in obstacles in integration of different systems. Not only that, many legacy systems may refuse to provide signed verifiable credentials which will make the integration with the legacy system strenuous.

b) **Willingness of different Governments:** Whenever it is expected that different nations should come together and share the database, there will be lots of challenges due to the varied rules and regulations of different countries. Unless a standard regulation like GDPR comes into action, it will be difficult to implement cross-national solution.
c) **Accountability:** The core principle of DID is to ensure individuals' privacy, which sometimes conflicts with regulations like Know Your Customer. While implementing the DID, it should be ensured that it adheres to the regulations and screen individuals accordingly.
d) **Privacy:** The implementation should ensure privacy-specific features are incorporated within DID while being compliant with the privacy and security regulations.
e) **Right to be Forgotten:** As transactions can't be removed once placed in a Blockchain, that threatens an individual's right to be forgotten. There should be adequate measures such that the all the stakeholders are provided with the mechanism for revocation of verifiable credentials. Once the VC is removed, the transactions should be masked so that the right to be forgotten is implemented for all practical purposes.
f) **Third-Party DID Management:** If third-party DID management is in place, there should be a proper mechanism to ensure that no DIDs are misused.

To summarize, while the challenges are substantial, it motivates researchers to create a DID framework which are complaint to all rules and regulations and well accepted by all.

6. CONCLUSION AND FUTURE PROSPECTS

In this chapter, a blockchain-based DID architecture is proposed for administering essential travel-related documents like passports, visas, and any other immigration stamping. The proposed solution uses a Self-Sovereign Identity-based Decentralized Identity verification mechanism where the data-owner is the ultimate regulator of their personal data, and the verification can be consummated in a hassle-free way without using any additional personal data.

Therefore, the proposed solution provides complete privacy to an individual and, at the same time, provides a swift, secure, and trustworthy immigration experience. The solution is not only a blessing to an individual but also is beneficial to the government as the complete travel history of individuals will be available in the distributed ledger itself. Access to the complete travel history in a single click will help the issuing authority verify the data conveniently in a streamlined manner.

Moreover, this would assist the national intelligence agencies to track down any shadowy travel of some suspected persons, provided that person is ready to cooperate by providing access to his data.

As discussed in the earlier section, significant challenges may hinder the implementation of DID in real life. However, the researchers can channel their energy to provide better, trustworthy, and regulation-compliant solutions by designing cryptographic or privacy-enhancing protocols.

REFERENCES

Avellaneda, O., Bachmann, A., Barbir, A., Brenan, J., Dingle, P., Duffy, K. H., Maler, E., Reed, D., & Sporny, M. (2019). Decentralized identity. Where did it come from and where is it going? *IEEE Communications Standards Magazine*, 3(4), 10–13. DOI: 10.1109/MCOMSTD.2019.9031542

Bakre, A., Patil, N., & Gupta, S. (2017). Implementing decentralized digital identity using blockchain. *International Journal of Engineering Technology Science and Research*, 4(10), 379–385.

Banerji, D., Rashideh, W., Arora, B., & Pratihari, A. R. (2021). Application potential of Blockchain technologies in the travel and tourism industry. In *Blockchain Applications in IoT Ecosystem* (pp. 289–299). Springer International Publishing. DOI: 10.1007/978-3-030-65691-1_19

Chen, H. 'This world-class airport will soon go passport-free', CNN, September, 2023. https.//edition.cnn.com/travel/article/changi-airport-singapore-passport-free -travel-intl-hnk/index.html#.~.text=Starting%20in%202024%2C%20officials%20 say,passports%2C%20using%20only%20biometric%20data

Chiller-Glaus, S. D., Schwaninger, A., & Hofer, F. (2007, October). Identity verification from photographs in travel documents. The role of display duration and orientation on performance. [). Sage CA. Los Angeles, CA. SAGE Publications.]. *Proceedings of the Human Factors and Ergonomics Society Annual Meeting*, 51(19), 1327–1330. DOI: 10.1177/154193120705101910

Dabban, M.A., Abdullahi, M.B., Adepoju, S.A. and Ojerinde, O.A., 2023. A framework for Identity Verification Management System using Blockchain for International Travel.

David W. Chadwick, Romain Laborde, Arnaud Oglaza, Remi Venant, Samer Wazan, and Manreet Nijjar. Improved identity management with verifiable credentials and FIDO. IEEE Communications Standards Magazine, 3(4).14–20, December 2019.

Der, U., Jähnichen, S., & Sürmeli, J. 2017. Self-sovereign identity $-$ opportunities and challenges for the digital revolution. *arXiv preprint arXiv.1712.01767.*

Dib, O., & Toumi, K. (2020). *Decentralized identity systems. Architecture, challenges, solutions and future directions. Annals of Emerging Technologies in Computing (AETiC).* Print ISSN.

Goodell, G., & Aste, T. (2019). A decentralized digital identity architecture. *Frontiers in Blockchain*, 2, 491305. DOI: 10.3389/fbloc.2019.00017 https.//myidalliance.org/ [Accessed on July 1, 2024]

https.//docs.essif.sk/en/about-essif-framework/ [Accessed on June 30, 2024]

https.//ktdi.org/ [Accessed on June 30, 2024]

https.//www3.weforum.org/docs/WEF_KTDI_Specifications_Guidance_2020.pdf [Accessed on June 30, 2024]

Kuperberg, M. (2019). Blockchain-based identity management. A survey from the enterprise and ecosystem perspective. *IEEE Transactions on Engineering Management*, 67(4), 1008–1027. DOI: 10.1109/TEM.2019.2926471

Lampropoulos, K., & Denazis, S. (2011). Identity management directions in future internet. *IEEE Communications Magazine*, 49(12), 74–83. DOI: 10.1109/MCOM.2011.6094009

Li, J., He, Q., Liang, R., & Jiang, B. 2021. Smart tourism identity authentication service based on blockchain and decentralized identifier. In *Blockchain and Trustworthy Systems. Third International Conference, BlockSys 2021,Guangzhou, China,August 5–6, 2021, Revised Selected Papers 3* (pp. 545-558). Springer Singapore. DOI: 10.1007/978-981-16-7993-3_42

Luecking, M., Fries, C., Lamberti, R., & Stork, W. 2020, May. Decentralized identity and trust management framework for Internet of Things. In *2020 IEEE International Conference on Blockchain and Cryptocurrency (ICBC)* (pp. 1-9). IEEE. DOI: 10.1109/ICBC48266.2020.9169411

Mahamuni, N., Nikam, H., Pattewar, G., Loka, O., & Patil, R. 2022, September. Management of IoT devices data security using blockchain and proxy re-encryption algorithm. In *International Conference on Emerging Technologies and Intelligent Systems* (pp. 551-558). Cham. Springer International Publishing.

Mahamuni, N., Pattewar, G., Nikam, H., Loka, O., & Patil, R. 2022, September. A blockchain and proxy re-encryption based approach for IoT data security. a review. In *International Conference on Emerging Technologies and Intelligent Systems* (pp. 587-595). Cham. Springer International Publishing.

Murtagh, N., Gatersleben, B., & Uzzell, D. (2012). Multiple identities and travel mode choice for regular journeys. *Transportation Research Part F: Traffic Psychology and Behaviour*, 15(5), 514–524. DOI: 10.1016/j.trf.2012.05.002

Naik, N., & Jenkins, P. 2017, May. Securing digital identities in the cloud by selecting an apposite Federated Identity Management from SAML, OAuth and OpenID Connect. In *2017 11th International Conference on Research Challenges in Information Science (RCIS)* (pp. 163-174). IEEE.

Naz, Muqaddas, et al. "A secure data sharing platform using blockchain and interplanetary file system." Sustainability 11.24 (2019). 7054.

Nyaletey, E., "BlockIPFS-blockchain-enabled interplanetary file system for forensic and trusted data traceability." *2019 IEEE International Conference on Blockchain (Blockchain)*. IEEE, 2019. DOI: 10.1109/Blockchain.2019.00012

Preukschat, A., & Reed, D. (2021). *Self-sovereign identity*. Manning Publications.

Querido, P. C. Blockchain Based Identity Management and Ticketing for MaaS. MS thesis. Universidade de Lisboa (Portugal), 2020.

Johannes Sedlmeir, Reilly Smethurst, Alexander Rieger, and Gilbert Fridgen. Digital identities and verifiable credentials. Business &amp Information Systems Engineering, 63(5).603–613, October 2021.

Stockburger, L., Kokosioulis, G., Mukkamala, A., Mukkamala, R. R., & Avital, M. (2021). Blockchain-enabled decentralized identity management. The case of self-sovereign identity in public transportation. *Blockchain.Research and Applications*, 2(2), 100014. DOI: 10.1016/j.bcra.2021.100014

Tamrakar, S., Ekberg, J. E., & Asokan, N. 2011, October. Identity verification schemes for public transport ticketing with NFC phones. In *Proceedings of the sixth ACM workshop on Scalable trusted computing* (pp. 37-48). DOI: 10.1145/2046582.2046591

Zhu, X., & Badr, Y. 2018, July. A survey on blockchain-based identity management systems for the Internet of Things. In *2018 IEEE International Conference on Internet of Things (iThings) and IEEE Green Computing and Communications (GreenCom) and IEEE Cyber, Physical and Social Computing (CPSCom) and IEEE Smart Data (SmartData)* (pp. 1568-1573). IEEE. DOI: 10.1109/Cybermatics_2018.2018.00263

Chapter 16
Enhancing Guest Experience in Hospitality Through Blockchain Technology

Gaurav Bathla
https://orcid.org/0000-0002-6992-811X
CT University, India

Ashish Raina
https://orcid.org/0000-0001-5812-5920
CT University, India

Varinder Singh Rana
https://orcid.org/0000-0001-6158-9195
City University, Ajman, UAE

Subhashish Mishra
https://orcid.org/0009-0000-8402-4154
State Institute of Hotel Management, Gujrat, India

ABSTRACT

The integration of blockchain technology into the hospitality industry represents a significant opportunity to enhance operational efficiency and improve guest experiences. Blockchain, a decentralized digital ledger offers transparency in security and immutability of data making it well-suited for applications in hospitality. The chapter explores various applications of blockchain technology in hospitality including booking and reservation systems, payment solutions, identity verification, supply chain management, loyalty programs and guest reviews. By leveraging blockchain

DOI: 10.4018/979-8-3693-6562-5.ch016

hospitality businesses can streamline processes, reduce costs and provide more personalized services to guests. However, the adoption of blockchain in hospitality also presents challenge including technical scalability issues, regulatory uncertainties and integration complexities. Collaborative efforts between industry stakeholders, technology providers and regulatory bodies will be essential in overcoming these challenges and unlocking the transformative power of blockchain in hospitality.

1. INTRODUCTION

In recent years, the hospitality industry has witnessed significant advancements in technology, reshaping the way businesses operate and interact with guests. One such technology that has gained considerable attention is blockchain. Blockchain, initially introduced as the underlying technology behind Bitcoin, has evolved beyond cryptocurrency and found applications across various industries, including hospitality.

Consumers' ever-shifting expectations and technological developments propel the hospitality industry into a state of perpetual flux. Within the hospitality and tourism industry, a tourist product is typically made up of a variety of different elements. These components could either be material or immaterial in nature. For instance, in a particular location there may be several different suppliers that contribute to the creation of services (Singh & Bathla 2023).

The hotel industry is just one of several that has seen blockchain technology's revolutionary impact in recent years. Guests' experiences, operations, and data integrity may all be improved with the use of blockchain technology, which is renowned for its decentralised and secure nature. Stakeholders that want to stay competitive and enhance service quality must understand the possibilities of blockchain in this context.

The primary purpose of this chapter is to critically review the application of blockchain technology in the hospitality industry, with a specific focus on enhancing guest experiences. This review will explore how blockchain can be integrated into various aspects of hospitality services, the benefits it brings, and the challenges faced in its implementation. By examining current uses, potential benefits, and future trends, this review aims to provide a comprehensive understanding of blockchain's impact on the hospitality industry.

1.1. Overview of Blockchain Technology

Definition and Key Concepts

To prevent tampering with the record of transactions without affecting the blocks that follow it and the network's consensus, blockchain technology uses several computers to create a distributed digital ledger (Zheng et al., 2017). This makes sure that the data kept on the blockchain is secure, transparent, and unchangeable.

According to Mukta (2023), key concepts of blockchain technology include:

- **Blocks:** The fundamental units of a blockchain, which contain a list of transactions. Each block is linked to the previous one through a cryptographic hash.
- **Decentralization:** Unlike traditional centralized databases, a blockchain is maintained by a network of nodes (computers) that work together to validate and record transactions.
- **Consensus Mechanisms:** Protocols used to achieve agreement on the blockchain's state across all nodes. Common mechanisms include Proof of Work (PoW) and Proof of Stake (PoS).
- **Cryptographic Hashing:** A process that converts an input into a fixed-size string of characters, which appears random. Each block contains the hash of the previous block, ensuring the integrity of the chain.
- **Smart Contracts:** Self-executing contracts with the terms of the agreement directly written into code. They automatically enforce and execute the contract when predefined conditions are met.

1.2 Evolution of Blockchain

Zheng et al. (2017) state that a new age of online reservations and bookings began with the advent of e-Tourism and the commercialization of the Internet in the 1990s. Furthermore, Katschnig (2022) added that the hospitality business has developed into one that heavily depends on information and communication technology, being an information-intensive sector.

Blockchain technology has evolved through several stages:

- **Blockchain 1.0 (Cryptocurrency):** The introduction of Bitcoin in 2009 by an anonymous person or group known as Satoshi Nakamoto marked the first application of blockchain technology. Bitcoin aimed to create a decentralized digital currency, free from government control.

- **Blockchain 2.0 (Smart Contracts):** Ethereum, introduced in 2015 by Vitalik Buterin, expanded blockchain's capabilities beyond cryptocurrency. Ethereum's platform allowed for the creation and execution of smart contracts, enabling decentralized applications (dApps).
- **Blockchain 3.0 (Scalability and Interoperability):** Current developments focus on improving scalability, interoperability, and usability of blockchain technology. Projects like Polkadot and Cardano aim to connect different blockchains and enhance transaction throughput (Forsström, 2018).
- **Blockchain 4.0 (Integration with Industry):** The latest stage involves integrating blockchain technology with various industries, including finance, supply chain, healthcare, and hospitality. This phase emphasizes practical applications and user-friendly interfaces to bring blockchain to mainstream use.

1.3 Types of Blockchain: Public vs Private

Sri and Bhaskari (2018) state that public and private blockchain networks are the two most common kinds, and each has its own set of advantages and disadvantages.

Public Blockchains

- **Definition:** Open and permissionless networks where anyone can join and participate. Examples include Bitcoin and Ethereum.
- **Characteristics:**
  Decentralized and distributed across a vast network of nodes.
  High transparency, as all transactions are visible to anyone on the network.
  Security through consensus mechanisms like PoW and PoS, making it difficult to alter past transactions.
- **Use Cases:** Cryptocurrencies, decentralized finance (DeFi), and public smart contract platforms.

Private Blockchains

- **Definition:** Restricted and permissioned networks where only authorized participants can join and transact. Examples include Hyperledger and Corda.
- **Characteristics:**
  Centralized to some extent, with control resting with a single organization or a group of entities.

Enhanced privacy, as transaction details are only accessible to authorized participants.

Faster transaction processing due to the limited number of nodes and absence of complex consensus mechanisms.

- **Use Cases:** Enterprise applications, supply chain management, and internal organizational processes.

Sarma (2019) explains that both public and private blockchains offer distinct advantages and can be chosen based on the specific needs and objectives of the application within the hospitality industry or any other sector.

1.4 Blockchain in the Hospitality Industry

Current Uses and Applications

Blockchain technology is being explored and adopted in various aspects of the hospitality industry, aiming to improve efficiency, transparency, and customer satisfaction. Here are some notable applications (Gupta, 2018):

Booking and Reservation Systems: Blockchain can streamline the booking process by creating a decentralized and transparent system for reservations. According to Dhiraj et al. (2023), this eliminates the need for intermediaries, reducing costs and potential errors. It also ensures that booking details are secure and tamper-proof.

Payment Solutions: Blockchain facilitates secure and efficient payment processing. Cryptocurrencies and blockchain-based payment systems can offer lower transaction fees, faster processing times, and enhanced security compared to traditional payment methods.

Identity Verification: Blockchain can improve the check-in process through secure and verifiable digital identities. Guests can have their identities verified quickly and securely, enhancing convenience and reducing the risk of fraud.

Supply Chain Management: Hotels and restaurants can use blockchain to track and verify the origins and quality of their supplies. Zielińska (2020) states that this ensures transparency and accountability in sourcing, contributing to better quality control and trust among customers.

Loyalty Programs: Blockchain can revolutionize loyalty programs by creating a unified and secure platform for rewards. Guests can earn, manage, and redeem loyalty points across various properties and services seamlessly.

Guest Reviews and Feedback: Blockchain ensures the authenticity of guest reviews by preventing fraudulent entries. Authentic reviews are crucial for maintaining trust and credibility in the hospitality industry.

Potential Benefits

Blockchain technology offers several significant benefits to the hospitality industry, including:

Enhanced Security: The decentralized and encrypted nature of blockchain ensures that data is secure and resistant to hacking. This is particularly important for protecting sensitive guest information and transaction details.
Increased Transparency: Blockchain's immutable ledger provides transparency in transactions and operations. This builds trust among guests and stakeholders, as they can verify the authenticity of transactions and reviews.
Cost Efficiency: By eliminating intermediaries and reducing transaction fees, blockchain can lower operational costs. This is especially beneficial in booking and payment processes, where third-party fees can be substantial.
Improved Efficiency: Automation of processes through smart contracts can streamline operations, reduce administrative overhead, and minimize errors. Yele and Litoriya (2024) state that this leads to a more efficient and responsive service delivery.
Better Customer Experience: Enhanced security, transparency, and efficiency contribute to a superior guest experience. Quick check-ins, secure payments, and trustworthy reviews create a positive and seamless experience for guests.

Case Studies and Examples

Tyan et al. (2021) note that several hospitality companies have started integrating blockchain technology into their operations, demonstrating its practical benefits:

TUI Group: The global travel and tourism company uses blockchain for managing its inventory, aiming to eliminate intermediaries and improve efficiency. TUI's private blockchain helps streamline internal processes and enhance data security.
Winding Tree: This decentralized travel marketplace uses blockchain to connect travel service providers directly with consumers, reducing the role of intermediaries. By leveraging blockchain, Winding Tree aims to lower costs and improve the booking experience. (Kopanaki et al., 2021)

LockTrip: A blockchain-based hotel booking platform that offers reduced prices by eliminating commissions. LockTrip uses its own cryptocurrency to facilitate transactions, ensuring lower fees and faster payments.
Trippki: A blockchain-based rewards program that allows guests to earn tokens for staying at participating hotels. These tokens can be used for future bookings or traded, creating a flexible and transparent loyalty system (Sarnacchiaro et al., 2024).

1.5 Enhancing Guest Experience through Blockchain

Figure 1. Role of blockchain in hospitality industry for enhancing guest experience

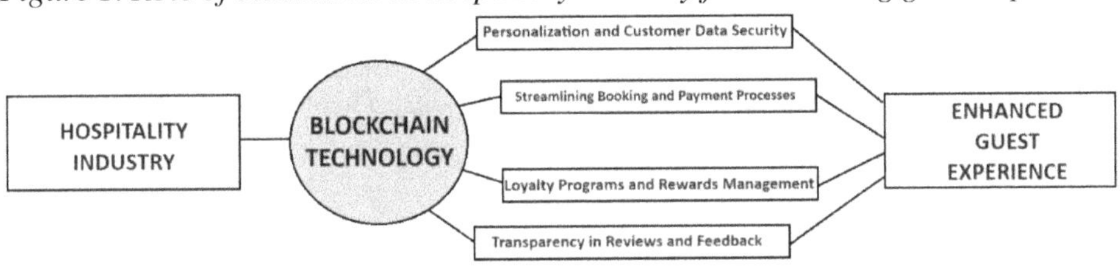

Personalization and Customer Data Security

Pradhan et al. (2023) suggest that blockchain can significantly enhance personalization in the hospitality industry by securely managing and utilizing guest data. According to Prados-Castillo et al. (2023), with blockchain, hotels can create detailed and secure guest profiles that include preferences, past stays, and feedback. This data can be used to tailor services and offers to individual guests, improving their overall experience. Importantly, blockchain ensures that this data is stored securely and accessed only with proper authorization, addressing privacy concerns.

Streamlining Booking and Payment Processes

Blockchain can streamline the booking and payment processes by creating a transparent and efficient system. Smart contracts can automate booking confirmations and payments, reducing the time and effort required from both guests and service providers. Barik et al. (2023) state that blockchain-based payment systems, including cryptocurrencies, offer fast and secure transactions with lower fees, enhancing the overall convenience for guests.

Loyalty Programs and Rewards Management

Traditional loyalty programs often suffer from fragmentation and inefficiencies. Blockchain can create a unified and transparent platform for managing loyalty programs. Guests can easily earn, manage, and redeem rewards across various properties and services, creating a seamless experience (Ebarefimia, 2017). The security and transparency of blockchain ensure that loyalty points are accurately tracked and managed, reducing the risk of fraud and errors.

Transparency in Reviews and Feedback

Guest reviews play a crucial role in the hospitality industry, influencing booking decisions and reputations. Blockchain can enhance the credibility of reviews by ensuring their authenticity. By storing reviews on an immutable ledger, blockchain prevents the manipulation or falsification of feedback. This builds trust among potential guests, knowing that the reviews they read are genuine and reliable (Maythu et al., 2024).

2. LITERATURE REVIEW

Khanna et al. (2020) investigate the potential uses of blockchain technology in the hospitality industry, focusing on its main applications. They argue that blockchain technology has the potential to revolutionize the hospitality industry in various aspects, including operational efficiency, income generation, security, and privacy. The study explores these possibilities by introducing the concept of blockchain and its potential applications in the hotel industry, followed by an examination of current literature and case studies. Through an integrated evaluation of key contributions to the literature on blockchain technology and the hospitality industry, the article presents a comprehensive overview. It discusses recent developments in the field and their potential uses in the hospitality industry, thus contributing to the broader understanding of blockchain's implications in the sector.

Cobanoglu et al. (2021) propose a decentralized verification mechanism that guarantees that reviews only originate from actual guests and visitors, which could significantly aid in the prevention of fraudulent reviews. They suggest that the irreversible and visible data on the Blockchain ensures the authenticity of reviews. Additionally, they highlight the role of smart contracts, which allow individuals to rate and evaluate a restaurant, hotel, or airline only once they have genuinely experienced their services.

Dogru et al. (2018) suggest that while blockchain technology is still in its early stages, it has the potential to greatly benefit the hospitality industry, including restaurants, hotels, airlines, and travel agencies. They argue that by leveraging this technology, these firms might enhance their service quality, client pleasure, and profitability. Additionally, they propose that members of the hospitality industry as a whole stand to gain from blockchain technology's widespread adoption. The authors highlight the various ways in which the hospitality industry may leverage blockchain technology, which they discuss in the subsequent sections.

Nguyen et al. (2023) investigate the present and future applications of blockchain technology in the Asian hospitality and tourist sector. They shed light on the advantages and disadvantages of this technology and explore its benefits, including decentralization, auditability, and persistency. Additionally, they discuss the various uses of blockchain technology, such as in the cryptocurrency industry, the Internet of Things (IoT), financial services, and public services. The study suggests that blockchain technology has the potential to transform the way the Asian hospitality industry functions. The report concludes with suggestions on where the Asian hotel and tourist industry may utilize blockchain technology in the future, thus offering insights into its potential impact and opportunities for innovation in the sector.

Fernández (2022) highlights the growing interdependence between blockchain technology and the hospitality industry, despite appearing unrelated from an outside perspective. They emphasize the vast opportunities that modern technology presents in the hotel industry, ranging from increased efficiency and ease of operations to enhanced privacy and security. The author notes that more businesses, particularly larger ones, are increasingly incorporating blockchain into their operations across multiple sectors. However, they also acknowledge that blockchain technology is still in its early stages, with plenty of uncharted territory to explore, leading to some flaws and significant opportunities for further development and improvement.

Das (2023) conducts a study that delves into the significant influence of technology on hotel management and visitor experience, a subject of considerable interest in modern hospitality research. The primary objective is to investigate the various ways in which technological developments are reshaping hotel guest services and operational efficiency. The research highlights the growing dependence of the hospitality industry on technology and the evolving expectations of guests, emphasizing the importance of understanding these changes in the market. It elucidates how technology contributes to improving service quality, customization, and convenience. One of the major findings of the study is the positive association between technology integration and enhanced operational efficiency in hotels. The study further reveals how modern technology has revolutionized hotel operations, making processes more convenient for visitors, with examples including digital check-in/out, mobile key access, and online reservation systems.

Krietemeyer (2019) outlines the purpose of their thesis, which is to understand, from the perspective of channel management experts and others in a similar field, what blockchain hotel booking platforms are and how they are altering the hotel booking environment. The literature suggests that blockchain-based booking systems have the potential to eliminate middlemen, particularly Online Travel Agencies (OTAs), by offering a comparable booking experience without the associated commission costs. However, it is noted that the internet booking sector is often considered to have minimal space for new entrants, presenting a challenge for the adoption and success of blockchain-based booking platforms in this competitive market.

2.1 Challenges and Limitations

The integration of blockchain technology into the hospitality industry represents a significant opportunity to enhance operational efficiency and improve guest experiences. Current applications of blockchain in hospitality encompass various areas such as booking and reservation systems, payment solutions, identity verification, supply chain management, loyalty programs, and guest reviews. These applications leverage blockchain's decentralized and transparent nature to streamline processes, increase security, and foster trust among stakeholders. For instance, blockchain can automate booking confirmations and payments through smart contracts, ensuring faster and more secure transactions. Tepe (2020) highlights that moreover, blockchain-based loyalty programs offer guests a unified platform to earn, manage, and redeem rewards across different properties and services. However, Ghazaleh & Zabadi (2021) point out that despite the promising benefits, the adoption of blockchain in hospitality faces several challenges, including technical scalability, regulatory compliance, integration with existing systems, and initial investment costs. Nonetheless, strategic implementation and collaboration with tech partners can help overcome these challenges and unlock the full potential of blockchain technology in revolutionizing the hospitality industry. As blockchain technology continues to evolve and address these challenges, it is poised to become an essential tool for hospitality businesses seeking to stay competitive and deliver exceptional guest experiences.

2.2 Future Trends and Opportunities

The future of blockchain in the hospitality industry is poised to be shaped by several emerging trends and technologies. Önder & Gunter (2022) highlight the significant trend of integrating blockchain with the Internet of Things (IoT), which can create more efficient and automated systems such as smart rooms and automated check-ins. According to Hochschwarzer (2019), by leveraging IoT devices with blockchain's secure and transparent framework, hotels can enhance operational efficiency and provide a seamless experience for guests.

Furthermore, Rana et al. (2022) points out that the combination of artificial intelligence (AI) and blockchain holds promise for advancing data analysis and personalization. AI can analyze vast amounts of data stored on blockchain to gain deeper insights into guest preferences and behaviors, allowing for more personalized services and improved customer satisfaction.

Moreover, the development of decentralized applications (dApps) tailored to hospitality can offer innovative solutions for booking, payments, and rewards, creating new ways for guests to interact with services.

Balasubramanian et al. (2022) suggest that as blockchain technology continues to mature, its adoption in the hospitality industry is expected to grow. Increased awareness of blockchain's benefits will drive more hospitality businesses to explore and implement the technology. Advances in blockchain scalability, such as sharding and layer 2 solutions, will address current limitations and make it more feasible for high-volume applications. Regulatory clarity around blockchain and cryptocurrencies will also encourage adoption by providing businesses with the confidence needed to navigate compliance challenges.

Looking ahead, Dutta et al. (2020) predicts several trends in the future landscape of blockchain in hospitality. The widespread use of blockchain-based payments will offer guests more payment options as cryptocurrency adoption grows. Enhanced guest personalization will be achieved through secure and comprehensive guest profiles enabled by blockchain, leading to tailored experiences. Moreover, blockchain will facilitate the creation of unified loyalty programs that span multiple brands and services, enhancing guest engagement and retention.

3. CONCLUSION

Blockchain technology holds significant potential to transform the hospitality industry by enhancing security, transparency, and efficiency. Early applications demonstrate its ability to streamline booking and payment processes, improve guest personalization, and create unified loyalty programs. However, challenges related to scalability, integration, and regulation must be addressed to fully realize its benefits. Overcoming these obstacles requires a concerted effort from industry stakeholders, technology providers, and regulatory bodies to create a supportive environment for blockchain adoption.

The adoption of blockchain technology can lead to a more secure, efficient, and guest-centric hospitality industry. As blockchain technology matures and overcomes current limitations, it will become a vital tool for hospitality businesses seeking to enhance their competitive edge and provide superior guest experiences. Innovations such as smart contracts and decentralized applications will further drive the utility of blockchain, enabling more sophisticated and seamless interactions between guests and service providers.

Blockchain technology represents a promising innovation for the hospitality industry, offering numerous benefits that can significantly enhance guest experiences and operational efficiency. While challenges remain, continued advancements and strategic implementation will pave the way for a more secure, transparent, and efficient hospitality landscape. As the industry adapts to these changes, the potential for blockchain to revolutionize hospitality becomes increasingly apparent, positioning it as a cornerstone of future advancements and guest satisfaction.

The widespread adoption of blockchain in hospitality could also foster more collaborative and interconnected industry ecosystems. By facilitating seamless data sharing and transaction processing across different entities within the industry, blockchain can help create integrated networks of hotels, service providers, and travel platforms. This interconnectedness can enhance the overall guest journey, from initial booking to post-stay engagement, ultimately driving higher levels of satisfaction and loyalty. Moreover, the standardization of blockchain protocols and best practices will be essential in ensuring interoperability and maximizing the benefits of this transformative technology across the global hospitality sector.

REFERENCES

Balasubramanian, S., Sethi, J. S., Ajayan, S., & Paris, C. M. (2022). An enabling Framework for Blockchain in Tourism. *Information Technology & Tourism*, 24(2), 165–179. DOI: 10.1007/s40558-022-00229-6

Barik, K., Misra, S., Ray, A. K., & Sukla, A. (2023). A blockchain-based evaluation approach to analyse customer satisfaction using AI techniques. *Heliyon*, 9(6), e16766. DOI: 10.1016/j.heliyon.2023.e16766 PMID: 37292278

Cobanoglu, C. Dr. Seden Dogan, Dr. Katerina Berezina, & Dr. Galen Collins. (2021). Blockchain in the Hospitality and Tourism Industry. *Hospitality and Tourism Information Technology*. https://scholarcommons.usf.edu/m3publishing/vol17/iss9781732127593/

Das, P. (2023). Technology and Guest Experience: Innovations Reshaping Hotel Management. *International Journal for Multidimensional Research Perspectives*, 1(3), 76–95.

Dhiraj, A., Kumar, S., Rani, D., Grima, S., & Sood, K. (2023). Blockchain Payment Services in the Hospitality Sector: The Mediating Role of Data Security on Utilisation Efficiency of the Customer. *Data*, 8(8), 123. Advance online publication. DOI: 10.3390/data8080123

Dogru, B. T., Mody, M., Leonardi, C., Dogru, T., Mody, M., & Leonardi, C. (2018). Blockchain Technology & its Implications for the Hospitality Industry. *Boston Hospitality Review*, (Winter), 1–12.

Dutta, P., Choi, T., Somani, S., & Butala, R. (2020). Since January 2020 Elsevier has created a COVID-19 resource centre with free information in English and Mandarin on the novel coronavirus COVID- 19. The COVID-19 resource centre is hosted on Elsevier Connect, the company ' s public news and information. *Transportation Research*, 4(1), 1–33.

Ebarefimia, S. (2017). Impact Of Blockchain Technology In Enhancing Customer Loyalty Programs In Airline Business. *International Journal of Innovative Research and Advanced Studies*, 4(6), 257–263. http://www.ijiras.com/2017/Vol_4-Issue_6/paper_44.pdf

Fernández, A. S. (2022). *BACHELOR ' S THESIS Blockchain in the hospitality industry : Identifying main applications Blockchain in the hospitality industry : Identifying main applications Antonio Salamanca Fernández Bachelor ' s Thesis Faculty of Tourism University of the Balearic Islands.*

Forsström, S. (2018). Blockchain. *Research Reports (Montgomery)*, (December), 1–12.

Ghazaleh, M. A., & Zabadi, A. M. (2021). BlockChain (BC) Upending Customer Experience: Promoting a New Customer Relationship Management (CRM) Structure Using Blockchain Technology (BCT). *Journal of Management and Sustainability*, 11(1), 203. DOI: 10.5539/jms.v11n1p203

Gupta, M. (2018). Blockchain for Hospitality. *John Wiley & Sons. Inc*, 2, 44.

Hochschwarzer, D. (2019). *Impact factors on the adoption of Blockchain Technology in the Hotel In-dustry*. 206. https://www.modul.ac.at/uploads/files/Theses/Master/Grad_2019/David_Hochschwarzer_-_no_sig.pdf

Katschnig, M. (2022). *The impact of blockchain technology on hotel booking systems. May.*

Khanna, A., Sah, A., Choudhury, T., & Maheshwari, P. (2020). Blockchain Technology for Hospitality Industry. *Lecture Notes in Business Information Processing*, 402(November), 99–112. DOI: 10.1007/978-3-030-63396-7_7

Kopanaki, E., Stroumpoulis, A., & Oikonomou, M. (2021). The Impact of Blockchain Technology on Food Waste Management in the Hospitality Industry. *ENTRENOVA - ENTerprise REsearch InNOVAtion, 7*(1), 428–437. DOI: 10.54820/CQRJ6465

Krietemeyer, M. (2019). *Blockchain Technologies' Influence on Hotel Bookings.*

Maythu, Y., Kwok, A. O. J., & Teh, P. L. (2024). Blockchain technology diffusion in tourism: Evidence from early enterprise adopters and innovators. *Heliyon*, 10(2), e24675. DOI: 10.1016/j.heliyon.2024.e24675 PMID: 38304774

Mukta, S. N. (2023). *Blockchain Technology : An Overview Blockchain Technology : An Overview Shamima Nasrin Mukta Assistant Professor Department of Humanities. March.*

Nguyen, T. T., Truong, T. T., & Da Nguyen, L. T. (2023). Blockchain in Hospitality and Tourism: A Game-Changer for Asian Markets. *International Journal of Research Publication and Reviews*, 4(6), 3209–3213. DOI: 10.55248/gengpi.4.623.46183

Omar, I. A., Hasan, H., Jayaraman, R., Salah, K., Omar, M., Dhabi, A., Emirates, U. A., Science, C., Dhabi, A., & Emirates, U. A. (2019). *Using blockchain technology to achiece sustainabilty in the hospitality industry by recuing food waste.*

Önder, I., & Gunter, U. (2022). Blockchain: Is it the future for the tourism and hospitality industry? *Tourism Economics*, 28(2), 291–299. DOI: 10.1177/1354816620961707

Pradhan, B., Roy, M., & Bhatia, S. (2023). Enhancing Tourists' Satisfaction Through Blockchain Technology. *PUSA Journal of Hospitality and Applied Sciences*, 9(2), 37–47. DOI: 10.48165/pjhas.2023.9.2.5

Prados-Castillo, J. F., Torrecilla-García, J. A., Andraz, G., & Guaita Martínez, J. M. (2023). Blockchain in Peer-to-Peer Platforms: Enhancing Sustainability and Customer Experience in Tourism. *Sustainability (Basel)*, 15(22), 15968. DOI: 10.3390/su152215968

Rana, R. L., Adamashvili, N., & Tricase, C. (2022). The Impact of Blockchain Technology Adoption on Tourism Industry: A Systematic Literature Review. *Sustainability (Basel)*, 14(12), 7383. Advance online publication. DOI: 10.3390/su14127383

Sarma, R. (2019)... *Study Paper on Security Aspects of Blockchain.*, 6(3), 104–107.

Sarnacchiaro, P., Luongo, S., Sepe, F., & Della Corte, V. (2024). The role of blockchain technology in the tourism industry: Analyzing the factors affecting its adoption. *Quality & Quantity*, 0123456789. Advance online publication. DOI: 10.1007/s11135-024-01836-7

Singh, A., & Bathla, G. (2023). Fostering Creativity and Innovation: Tourism and Hospitality Perspective. In Embracing Business Sustainability Through Innovation and Creativity in the Service Sector (pp. 70-83). IGI Global.

Sri, P. S. G. A., & Bhaskari, D. L. (2018). A study on blockchain technology. *International Journal of Engineering and Technology(UAE)*, 7, 418–421. DOI: 10.14419/ijet.v7i2.7.10757

Tepe, Y. (2020). *Decentralisation of hotel and tourism industry : Effects of blockchain technology in hotel booking systems*. 1–109.

Tyan, I., Yagüe, M., & Guevara-Plaza, A. (2021). Blockchain adoption in tourism:Grounded theory-based conceptual model. *Ara: Revista de Investigación En Turismo*, 10(1), 68–89. DOI: 10.1344/ara.v10i1.32819

Yele, S., & Litoriya, R. (2024). Blockchain-based secure dining: Enhancing safety, transparency, and traceability in food consumption environment. *Blockchain: Research and Applications*, 100187(2), 100187. Advance online publication. DOI: 10.1016/j.bcra.2023.100187

Zheng, Z., Xie, S., Dai, H., Chen, X., & Wang, H. (2017a). An Overview of Blockchain Technology: Architecture, Consensus, and Future Trends. *Proceedings - 2017 IEEE 6th International Congress on Big Data, BigData Congress 2017, October*, 557–564. DOI: 10.1109/BigDataCongress.2017.85

Zheng, Z., Xie, S., Dai, H., Chen, X., & Wang, H. (2017b). An Overview of Blockchain Technology: Architecture, Consensus, and Future Trends. *Proceedings - 2017 IEEE 6th International Congress on Big Data, BigData Congress 2017, July*, 557–564. DOI: 10.1109/BigDataCongress.2017.85

Zielińska, A. (2020). Application possibilities of blockchain technology in the energy sector. *E3S Web of Conferences, 154*. DOI: 10.1051/e3sconf/202015407003

Chapter 17
Exploring the Growing Threat of Cyber Risks and Vulnerabilities in the Hospitality Industry

Priya Harit
Lovely Professional University, India

Amrik Singh
https://orcid.org/0000-0003-3598-8787
Lovely Professional University, India

Kritika Agrawal
Institute of Hotel Management Catering Technology and Applied Nutrition, Chennai, India

Devangana Verma
Institute of Hotel Management, Ahmedabad, India

Gaurav Bathla
https://orcid.org/0000-0002-6992-811X
CT University, India

Ashish Raina
https://orcid.org/0000-0001-5812-5920
CT University, India

ABSTRACT

This chapter discussed the necessity of strong protective measures and the inherent challenges of cybersecurity in the hospitality sector. As hotels increasingly rely on digital systems to import guest experiences, they become prime targets for cybercriminals. The chapter lists major cyber threats and highlights their influence on customer confidence and financial stability. These threats include malware, phishing, Distributed Denial of Service (DDoS) attacks, and insider threats. It also addresses the human factor in cybersecurity. By examining the case studies of notable breaches impacting companies such as Marriott, IHG, and Hilton, the chapter offers valuable insights into the comprehensive cybersecurity strategies that include risk assessment, employee training, and the adoption of established

DOI: 10.4018/979-8-3693-6562-5.ch017

frameworks. Cybersecurity awareness can strengthen the defence, safeguard sensitive data, and guarantee long term sustainability of the hospitality industry with leveraging cutting edge technologies.

INTRODUCTION

The hospitality industry, an interconnected world encompassing hotels, resorts, and other lodging services, increasingly depends on digital systems to manage operations and enhance guest experiences. In an era where information is a cornerstone of competitive advantage, understanding the importance of cybersecurity is more crucial than ever for industry stakeholders. (Jack Holdsworth, 2017) As businesses collect and store immense volumes of sensitive customer information, from financial details to personal identification, the repercussions of data breach. Almost all companies have undergone a digital shift to find new ways to use data, innovate, retain talent, and generate revenue.

The rapid digitization of the hospitality sector has introduced numerous opportunities for enhancing the customer experience and operational efficiencies. (Gabriel Raicu, 2022) With the integration of advanced technologies such as mobile check-ins, online booking systems, and Internet of Things (IoT) devices, the guest experience is more convenient and personalized. However, this increased digitization concurrently elevates organizations' risk landscape, placing immense pressure on them to implement strong cybersecurity measures. (Chen & Fiscus, 2018) As technology advances, so too do the tactics of cybercriminals, underscoring the critical need for businesses to remain vigilant and proactive in safeguarding their data. (Jack Holdsworth, 2017)

Statistics illustrate the alarming state of cybersecurity in the hospitality sector. Reports indicate that nearly 31% of hospitality providers have experienced data breaches, with basic web attacks affecting around 90% of breaches related to guest information (Chen & Fiscus, 2018). Moreover, incidents of ransomware—a frequently employed tactic by cybercriminals to extort businesses—can severely disrupt operations, particularly in establishments reliant on seamless access to their IT systems for customer service. In an industry where customer trust is paramount, these breaches can not only result in immediate financial repercussions but can also lead to a long-term decline in guest loyalty and brand integrity. (Jack Holdsworth, 2017)

Data breaches are a significant threat across industries globally, and hotels are particularly at risk due to the vast amount of personal information they handle from guests and customers. Hackers can steal a wide range of sensitive data from hotels, including email addresses, home addresses, and credit card information.

A data breach occurs when private or confidential information is unintentionally or intentionally exposed to an untrusted environment. Essentially, it happens when unauthorized individuals access or transfer data. This breach can involve various types of sensitive information, such as financial details like credit card or bank information, personal health information (PHI), personally identifiable information (PII), corporate trade secrets, or intellectual property. Typically, data breaches involve the compromise of files, documents, and other sensitive materials. (LUDYNIA, 2024)

While the financial penalties for data breaches are substantial, they are not the only concern for hotels. A security breach can severely damage a hotel's reputation, leading to public distrust. Many travelers report that they are less likely to book with a company that has experienced a data breach.

Criminals use anonymity, distance, and speed to commit crimes over the internet, making cybercrime more accessible and raising cyber-risks. Interpol considers cybercrime as a rapidly expanding criminal activity. Cybercriminals have become increasingly adept at crafting convincing scams, leveraging social engineering tactics to manipulate targets into divulging personal and financial information. Additionally, the use of compromised POS systems—where card data is intercepted during transactions—has been highlighted as a significant risk, emphasizing vulnerabilities in third-party vendors that cater to these operational needs. (LUDYNIA, 2024)

Furthermore, the difficulties related to physical security should not be disregarded. Businesses frequently depend on a variety of networked systems to provide customer service, which may unintentionally result in the creation of numerous potential exposure points. Unsecured Wi-Fi networks, inadequate staff training regarding cyber hygiene, and a lack of awareness about the proper handling of sensitive data all contribute to an environment ripe for cyber infiltration (Blanco, 2024). Hotel staff, often untrained in identifying cybersecurity threats, can unwittingly become a weak link in an organization's defense strategy, highlighting the importance of investing in comprehensive training programs and awareness initiatives. (Blanco, 2024)

Unsecured wireless networks, insufficient cyber hygiene training for employees, and ignorance of appropriate methods for handling confidential information all create an atmosphere that is highly susceptible to cyber intrusion. (Aryee, 2020) Hotel employees might unintentionally become a weak point in an organization's defensive strategy since they are frequently unskilled in spotting cybersecurity threats. This emphasizes the significance of funding thorough training programs and awareness activities.

The financial implications of data breaches extend beyond immediate remediation costs, potentially involving substantial fines, litigation, and lost revenue due to brand reputation damage. Companies like Marriott and Hilton have faced significant fallout from breaches, exemplifying the costs associated with data loss and compromised customer trust. (Blanco, 2024) The potential for increased regulatory scrutiny and pressure to comply with evolving data protection laws adds yet another layer of complexity for hospitality businesses attempting to navigate this landscape.

To mitigate these multifaceted risks, organizations must adopt a holistic approach to cybersecurity that encompasses not only technological upgrades but also comprehensive risk management strategies. This includes the implementation of robust firewalls, intrusion detection systems, and regular software updates to enhance network defenses. (Gabriel Raicu, 2022)Additionally, establishing well-defined incident response plans and employee training programs can prepare hospitality businesses to swiftly respond to cyber incidents, minimizing the potential for damage.

Investing in cyber insurance is another proactive measure that can help shield businesses from the financial fallout associated with data breaches. (Gabriel Raicu, 2022) Cyber insurance can provide coverage for remediation costs, legal fees, and penalties stemming from a breach, making it an essential component of a comprehensive risk management strategy. Moreover, as hospitality organizations continue to expand their digital footprints, ongoing vigilance and adaptation to emerging threats will be paramount in maintaining resilience against cybercrime. As the hospitality industry continues to evolve and recover from recent challenges, including those posed by the global pandemic, the potential for cyber threats will only increase. (Jack Holdsworth, 2017) Stakeholders must understand that cybersecurity is a collective responsibility, necessitating cooperation across all organizational levels and collaboration with technology experts to create a secure environment. By making cybersecurity a priority and integrating it into their operational culture, businesses can safeguard their assets, maintain their reputations, and build customer trust in our increasingly interconnected and digital world.

In conclusion, cybersecurity's significance in the hospitality industry is paramount. With an ever-growing and evolving range of threats, stakeholders must stay alert and proactive. Investing in cybersecurity not only safeguards sensitive customer data but also strengthens the overall integrity and long-term sustainability of hospitality operations as they face a complex array of risks.

LITERATURE REVIEW

While cybercrime has existed since the invention of computers, the types of attacks and crimes have evolved with technology. The most prevalent security assaults include hacking, technology theft, and fraud, although other types of attacks may also occur. (C. & Demicco, 2007)The hospitality sector has been a popular target for cyberattacks because to its reliance on digital systems for reservations guest management, and internal operations. This literature study examines the importance of cybersecurity in the hotel industry, diving into the numerous problems it confronts and the solutions used to manage such risks. The hospitality business includes hotels, restaurants, and travel agencies, all of which rely largely on technology for operational efficiency and guest service. Loyalty schemes at hotels make them more vulnerable to security assaults due to increased access to consumer data. Loyalty schemes expose the personal information of hospitality guests and consumers to greater risks. (Shabani & Munir, 2020)

In today's digital era, the hospitality industry depends more than ever on advanced technologies to elevate guest experiences and optimize operations. (Wynn & Lam, 2023) However, this growing dependence has also made hospitality businesses more susceptible to cyber threats. The intersection of technology and hospitality has created an attractive target for cybercriminals, highlighting the need for a deep understanding of the cybersecurity issues that affect this sector. (B.P. Aniruddha Prabhu, 2023) The industry is broad, spanning large multinational hotel chains to smaller independent operators, each facing distinct cybersecurity challenges and vulnerabilities.

Cybersecurity is crucial in the hospitality industry due to the large volumes of sensitive data it generates, including guests' personal information, payment details, and proprietary business data. Data breaches can have devastating consequences, not only for the businesses involved but also for the guests whose information is exposed. (Wynn & Lam, 2023) Research indicates that the hospitality sector is experiencing a growing number of data breaches and cyber-attacks, underscoring the urgent need for robust cybersecurity practices to protect sensitive information and uphold customer trust. (Jack Holdsworth, 2017)

Furthermore, customer expectations have evolved, with guests becoming more aware of their right to data protection. A data breach can severely tarnish a hotel's reputation, resulting in a loss of customer loyalty and significant financial setbacks. Studies indicate that the financial impact of data breaches on hospitality businesses is substantial, encompassing damage control costs, customer compensation, and regulatory fines. As a result, a proactive approach to cybersecurity is no longer optional but essential for maintaining competitiveness in the market. (Chen & Fiscus, 2018)

The hospitality industry encounters several challenges in establishing effective cybersecurity measures. A significant challenge is the integration of complex information systems and technologies, which often lack sufficient security safeguards. (O'Connor & Murphy, 2004) The swift adoption of cloud computing, mobile applications, and the Internet of Things (IoT) has opened new avenues for cyberattacks. For example, cloud computing enables hotels to store vast amounts of data off-site, which can lead to vulnerabilities if robust security protocols are not implemented.

Additionally, many hospitality organizations continue to rely on outdated systems that frequently miss essential security updates and patches. These legacy systems can serve as entry points for cybercriminals seeking to exploit vulnerabilities for malicious purposes. The challenge is compounded by the integration of various technologies without strong cybersecurity measures. Often, different systems—such as booking platforms and payment systems—fail to communicate effectively, creating gaps in security coverage that can be exploited by attackers.

Another major challenge in cybersecurity is the human factor. Employees often unintentionally create security risks due to negligence or a lack of awareness about cybersecurity protocols. In the hospitality industry, frontline staff have access to sensitive customer data, and without rigorous training programs, they may inadvertently cause data breaches through their actions. Implementing comprehensive cybersecurity training that emphasizes the importance of data protection is essential to reducing human errors that could compromise security.

Moreover, understanding the psychological aspects of guests is vital for effective cybersecurity strategies. Many customers remain skeptical about the online security measures employed by hospitality businesses. Therefore, hotels must go beyond securing their systems; they must also ensure that customers feel confident in the safety of their data. This involves being transparent about the measures taken to protect guest information and actively building trust with customers through clear communication and assurance.

Compliance with data protection regulations is another critical challenge for the hospitality industry. With stringent laws like the General Data Protection Regulation (GDPR) and various local data protection regulations, hotels and related businesses must adhere to these standards to avoid severe penalties and damage to their reputation. Many organizations in the hospitality sector may lack the expertise or resources needed to navigate these complex regulations, which can result in non-compliance and the associated risks.

COMMON CYBER SECURITY THREATS IN HOSPITALITY SECTOR

Organizations that use IT are subject to a variety of security risks and attacks. Common risks include viruses, internal network assaults, laptop theft, spoofing, unauthorized insider access, outside attacks, and denial of service. Information security attempts to increase revenue and minimize harm from security attacks. (Rusch, 2003)Cybersecurity threats can be broadly categorized into various types, including network attacks, malware, phishing, and insider threats. Each of these threats poses unique challenges and can inflict varying degrees of damage to hospitality businesses. With the growing sophistication of cybercriminals, the hospitality sector must remain vigilant against these evolving threats. The hospitality sector is vulnerable to various cybersecurity threats that can compromise guest data and disrupt services. Here are some prevalent threats:

1. Hotel Malware

Malware, or malicious software, is designed to infiltrate and damage computer systems and networks. In the hospitality sector, malware can compromise point-of-sale (POS) systems, allowing cybercriminals to gain access to sensitive credit card information and other confidential data. Once malware is installed, it can spread rapidly and cause significant operational disruptions. (Fragniere & Yagci, 2021) The impact of malware extends beyond immediate financial losses; it can significantly damage a hotel's reputation and customer trust. In the event of a data breach, for example, customers may hesitate to book accommodations or share personal information, leading to reduced business. Additionally, the costs associated with recovery and legal ramifications can burden hospitality providers, underscoring the need for preventive measures. It is perhaps the most common and the most dangerous of online security threats, due to its diversity.

Table 1. Officially, Malicious Software and malware consist of many different types of potential threats to hotel technology. (Aryee, 2020) These include:

Viruses	**A computer virus will infect files on your system, just like a virus you might contract, and then spread in an uncontrolled way, finally crippling the machine if not treated. Viruses are malicious programs that attach themselves to legitimate files and applications, causing harm when activated. In the hospitality context, viruses can corrupt critical reservation systems, leading to operational delays and financial loss. Protecting against viruses requires regular updates to antivirus software and user education about the risks of downloading unverified attachments or software.**
Trojans	Trojans disguise themselves as legitimate software to trick users into installation. Once activated, they can create backdoors for attackers, allowing unauthorized access to sensitive hotel management systems and customer databases. This data compromise can lead to identity theft or financial fraud. Implementing strict software vetting processes and monitoring network activity are effective measures against Trojan infections.
Ransomware	This malware locks your computer, encrypts data, and demands a ransom for decryption, disrupting operations. Ransomware is one of the most formidable forms of malware affecting the hospitality industry. It encrypts files and demands a ransom for their decryption, often leading to service outages and loss of customer trust. Affected businesses may find themselves unable to process reservations or payments, resulting in significant operational challenges and economic damages. Prominent cases have highlighted the vulnerability of hotels and resorts to ransomware attacks, emphasizing the need for comprehensive backup and incident response strategies.
Spyware	Spyware is designed to lurk in the background of your system, hiding, and taking note of what you do online. It will look for passwords, and collect sensitive data, such as credit card information and personal details. Spyware secretly gathers information from a user's system without their knowledge, which is particularly concerning given the hospitality industry's reliance on customer data. (Fragniere & Yagci, 2021) It can track keystrokes or monitor online activities, potentially exposing sensitive customer information like credit card details. Preventing spyware infections involves deploying robust security software and conducting regular audits of system activity.
Worms	Worms are like viruses but can spread independently across networks without needing a host program. They exploit vulnerabilities in network protocols, making them particularly dangerous in interconnected systems common in hotels and resorts. A successful worm attack can overwhelm network resources, leading to significant downtime4. Regular system updates and network monitoring are crucial measures to mitigate this risk.
Adware	Displays unwanted ads or pop-up windows, but it may also provide an avenue for other malware to enter. Adware automatically serves advertisements to users, often degrading system performance and user experience. (Fragniere & Yagci, 2021) While less harmful than other types of malware, excessive adware can distract staff and customers alike, impairing business operations. Maintaining clean software environments through regular maintenance and using adware removal tools can help mitigate these risks.

2. Phishing Attacks

A type of social engineering technique that poses a significant threat to the hospitality industry. These attacks involve tricking individuals into divulging sensitive information, such as login credentials, credit card numbers, or personal data, which can have devastating consequences, including data breaches, financial loss, operational disruption, and reputational damage. To mitigate the risk of phishing attacks, hospitality companies must prioritize employee education and awareness, implement robust security measures, and regularly review and update their cybersecurity protocols.

Table 2. By taking a proactive and multi-layered approach to phishing prevention, hotels and resorts can protect their guests, employees, and reputations from the devastating consequences of these attacks.

	Types of Phishing Attacks
Email Phishing	Fraudulent emails that appear to be from a legitimate source, such as a hotel's reservation system or a popular online travel agency
Spear Phishing	Targeted attacks on specific individuals, such as hotel managers or IT personnel
Whaling	Phishing attacks targeting high-level executives, such as CEOs or CFOs.
Smishing	Phishing attacks via SMS or text messages
Vishing	Phishing attacks via voice calls

Consequences of Phishing Attacks in Hospitality

- **Data Breaches**: Phishing attacks can lead to data breaches, compromising sensitive guest data and resulting in reputational damage.
- **Financial Loss:** Phishing attacks can result in financial loss, either through fraudulent transactions or the cost of responding to a data breach.
- **Operational Disruption**: Phishing attacks can disrupt hotel operations, causing delays and impacting the guest experience.
- **Regulatory Penalties**: Phishing attacks can result in regulatory penalties for non-compliance with data protection regulations.

3. DDoS (Distributed Denial of Service) Attacks

A Distributed Denial of Service (DDoS) attack involves overwhelming a target website or network with massive amounts of traffic from numerous internet-connected devices. This flood of traffic renders the site or network inaccessible to legitimate users, causing service disruptions and potentially damaging the targeted organization's reputation. The hospitality industry is particularly susceptible to DDoS attacks due to its dependence on online systems for reservations, payments, and customer feedback. When these services are disrupted, it can severely affect customer experience and harm the business's reputation. Hotels are highly vulnerable to DDoS (distributed denial of service) assaults. These assaults can bring down the whole hotel chain's website by overwhelming it with traffic sources. DDoS attacks hotels' various systems. All of the system's devices may be utilized to deliver pulses that deactivate them. DDoS attacks can make a website, application, or network resource unavailable.

Table 3. DDoS attacks can result in significant financial losses due to downtime and lost productivity.

	Types of DDoS attacks
Volumetric attacks	Overwhelming the targeted system with a high volume of traffic
Protocol attacks	Exploiting weaknesses in network protocols to consume system resources
Application attacks	Targeting specific applications or services to disrupt their functionality

Defending Against DDoS Attacks

DDoS assaults are prevented using a mix of standard security measures, a well-prepared response plan, a strong anti-DDoS architecture, adherence to network and application security best practices, and frequent system upgrades and patches. Implementing these methods can considerably improve defenses against DDoS assaults while also ensuring the resilience and availability of online services. Some of practices to protect from DDoS attacks are:

- **Monitor Network Traffic:** Regularly monitor network traffic to detect unusual patterns.
- **Keep Software Up-To-Date:** Ensure that software and systems are up-to-date with the latest security patches.

- **Use Secure Protocols:** Use secure communication protocols such as HTTPS and SFTP.
- **Implement Rate Limiting:** Limit the rate of traffic to prevent overwhelming your systems.

4. Insider Threats

Insider threats refer to security risks originating from within an organization, often perpetrated by employees or contractors. In the hospitality sector, insiders may intentionally or unintentionally compromise data security through negligence or malicious intent. Ensuring that staff are trained in cybersecurity protocols is crucial for minimizing the risk posed by insider threats. While external cyber threats provide considerable hurdles, insider risks remain an important concern in the hotel industry. Insider risks are staff members or individuals with authorized access to hotel systems and data who may abuse their privileges, either purposefully or accidentally, resulting in data breaches or other security issues. To limit the risk of insider attacks, hotels should impose rigorous access controls, provide regular employee training, and monitor user activity. Furthermore, building a strong culture of cybersecurity knowledge and responsibility inside the company improves the overall security posture of hotels.

5. Credential Theft

Credential theft is a growing concern in the hospitality sector, particularly as many organizations utilize cloud-based services. Cybercriminals may attempt to steal login credentials through various means, such as phishing emails or exploiting weak passwords. (Fragniere & Yagci, 2021) Once access is gained, cybercriminals can move laterally within systems and cause widespread damage.

RECENT HOTEL SECURITY BREACHE INCIDENTS

Marriott Hotel Security Breach

One of the biggest data security breaches in recent memory, the Marriott data breach exposed weaknesses in data management procedures and impacted hundreds of millions of people. In 2018, Marriott announced that hackers had attempted to access its Starwood Hotels & Resorts Worldwide guest reservation database. Further investigation revealed unauthorized access to the system as far back as 2014, two years before Marriott acquired Starwood. The metrics and statistics related to this breach shed light on its scope, consequences, and the necessity of strong cybersecurity defenses.

Up to 327 million of the approximately 500 million guest records that were exposed in the breach included at least one piece of personally identifiable information (PII), such as names, addresses, and email addresses. The breach started in 2014, meaning that the data was available for use for roughly four years before it was found in September 2018. This extended exposure exposes serious shortcomings in early detection and security protocols. A variety of sensitive information types were included in the exposed data. Interestingly, it has been reported that approximately 22 million credit card numbers and expiration dates were accessed; however, many of these records were encrypted. Furthermore impacted were private data like passport numbers and reservation specifics. After the breach, Marriott was hit with severe financial consequences that were projected to cost hundreds of millions of dollars. These included possible legal fees, regulatory fines, and reputational harm. Numerous regulatory agencies, including the UK Information Commissioner's Office, opened investigations into the breach and had the potential to impose sizable fines under the GDPR.

IHG Security Breach

The InterContinental Hotels Group (IHG) data breach in 2016 regarded as a major event in the hospitality sector, with valuable cybersecurity lessons for businesses and customers alike. The impact of the hack on consumer confidence, business standing, and financial ramifications emphasizes the need for improved data security protocols and potent crisis management techniques in order to lessen the fallout from such incidents. In 2016, IHG experienced a cyberattack that compromised over 1,000 properties, attributed to malicious software targeting the organization's point-of-sale systems. (Panai) This breach is notable for affecting a large number of customers and leading to significant concerns regarding the security of personal and financial information. The breach primarily involved the theft of credit card information and personal data of customers who had stayed at the affected hotels6. According to reporting, the incident raised alarm regarding the industry's vulnerability to cyberattacks, as various major hotel chains, including Hilton and Hyatt, have also faced similar threats. As with many data breaches, the financial repercussions for IHG included legal fees, potential fines, and a decline in consumer trust, which could affect future revenues. Research indicates that companies often see a drop in stock prices following a significant breach announcement, which could lead to long-term economic consequences for the affected organization. The impact on consumer trust can be particularly damaging; studies show that customers are concerned about their data being adequately protected. The breach likely influenced IHG's customer retention and acquisition strategies, with loyalty among customers of hospitality brands being significantly affected following data breach incidents. In response to the breach, IHG, like many organizations affected by cybersecurity incidents, likely enhanced its security measures and adopted a comprehensive crisis communication strategy to address customer concerns and rebuild trust. This situation emphasizes the need for continual investment in cybersecurity and risk management, as breaches are becoming increasingly common and costly within the hospitality sector.

Hilton Hotel Security Breach

The data breach at the Hilton Hotel is a noteworthy event that brings to light the data security vulnerabilities that big players in the hospitality industry face. The hack not only had serious financial repercussions but also sparked doubts about consumer confidence and the effectiveness of cybersecurity safeguards. When Hilton Hotels revealed a data breach affecting its payment processing systems in 2017, the company came under intense scrutiny. Cybercriminals were able to obtain access to hotel payment systems without authorization, which could have compromised thousands of visitors' credit or debit card information. (Panai)The hack, which involved malware placed on payment terminals, showed how even well-known companies can become targets of crafty cyberattacks. An estimated 356,000 credit card numbers were impacted by the hack, according to reports. This event was part of a larger series of related attacks that targeted hospitality businesses because they regularly deal with private financial information. Customers were not the only ones affected by the breach; the hotel chain's operations were severely disrupted. The financial repercussions of the breach were substantial. In 2017, Hilton faced a cumulative fine of approximately $700,000 due to non-compliance with data protection laws. These penalties stem from the hotel chain's failure to take adequate measures to protect customer data, which subsequently eroded consumer trust and led to a decline in revenue. As a result of the breach, Hilton was subjected to scrutiny from regulatory bodies, which emphasized the necessity for organizations to bolster their data protection protocols. The incident served as a catalyst for discussions around the need for stricter regulations governing data privacy and cybersecurity in the hospitality sector. In the wake of the breach, Hilton enhanced its cybersecurity framework. This included investing in advanced security measures such as encryption of payment transactions, more rigorous monitoring of payment systems, and comprehensive employee training programs regarding data security. These steps were aimed at preventing future incidents and restoring customer confidence in the brand.Strong cybersecurity measures are imperative, and the Hilton data breach provides an important case study for the hospitality industry. In order to preserve customer confidence and adhere to legal requirements, it underscores the possible consequences of insufficient data protection and stresses that hospitality organizations need to give financial and personal information security top priority. This event serves as a reminder of both the dynamic nature of cyber threats and the value of taking preventative measures to protect sensitive data.

Wyndham Hotel Security Breach

Wyndham Hotels experienced a significant data breach that spanned from 2008 to 2010, affecting approximately 600,000 customer payment card records. The attack was characterized by multiple incursions into their networks, resulting in unauthorized access to sensitive customer data, including credit card information and personal identifiable information (PII).The breach was facilitated through a combination of SQL injection and other cyber-attack techniques. Cybercriminals exploited vulnerabilities in Wyndham's computer systems, demonstrating that the hotel chain's existing security measures were insufficient to protect sensitive data from sophisticated threats. As a result of the breach, customers faced potential fraud and identity theft issues. In addition to credit card information, the exposed data contained the names, addresses, and contact information of a large number of customers. This caused guests to have serious concerns about their financial security and privacy.Wyndham faced legal actions from various parties, including customers and financial institutions. A landmark case regarding the Federal Trade Commission's (FTC) jurisdiction over cybersecurity practices in the hospitality industry resulted from the FTC's intervention as well, which claimed that Wyndham's security measures were insufficient. The Wyndham Hotel breach exemplifies the importance of robust cybersecurity policies and practices. Organizations, particularly in the hospitality industry, must prioritize the implementation of comprehensive security measures, employee training, and adherence to compliance regulations to mitigate the risk of future breaches.

Expedia Security Breach

The Expedia security breach occurred when the personal information of a substantial number of customers was exposed. Unauthorized access to customer data, including names, email addresses, and reservation details, was the source of this incident, which may have far-reaching effects on those who were impacted. While exact numbers concerning the total records breached may vary, the incident affected a large number of users, raising alarms regarding the precautions in place for safeguarding sensitive information. Such incidents are indicative of broader trends where personal data vulnerabilities are exploited across various industries. The unauthorized access was caused in part by monitoring systems that were not up to date and outdated security protocols, according to investigations into the breach. Legacy systems that are vulnerable to hacks present a challenge to many businesses, including Expedia.

In the aftermath of the breach, Expedia took steps to mitigate the damage, including notifying affected customers and enhancing security protocols. This response is critical in maintaining consumer trust and minimizing the impact of the breach. The Expedia breach serves as a cautionary tale for companies regarding the importance of robust cybersecurity measures. Organizations must continuously evolve their security practices and educate employees to prevent future incidents

CONCLUSION

The future of cybersecurity in the hospitality sector is closely linked to ongoing digital transformation. As the industry adopts new technologies, its cybersecurity frameworks must evolve accordingly. Emerging technologies like artificial intelligence (AI) and machine learning are anticipated to significantly enhance security measures. AI can facilitate advanced threat detection and automate responses to incidents by identifying anomalous behavior in real-time and assessing risks more quickly than traditional methods. Additionally, block chain technology has the potential to secure data transactions by creating tamper-proof records, which can strengthen trust and security in hospitality services.

Protecting sensitive guest data is paramount, as breaches can severely damage a company's reputation and finances. Addressing the unique cybersecurity challenges faced by the hospitality sector—such as technological vulnerabilities, the human factor, and regulatory compliance—is essential for maintaining a competitive edge in the rapidly evolving digital landscape. The successful integration of innovation and security will ultimately determine the hospitality industry's ability to thrive amidst growing cyber threats.

While the hospitality sector has made progress in recognizing the importance of cybersecurity, continuous efforts are crucial to fostering a culture of security awareness and proactive risk management. By strengthening their cybersecurity measures, hospitality businesses can protect their operations and maintain customer trust, laying the foundation for resilience in an increasingly digital future.

As technology advances to improve guest's experiences in the hospitality industry, cybersecurity is critical. A comprehensive cybersecurity strategy including network security, regulatory compliance, and employee training in order to safeguards sensitive data and preserves operational integrity.

In addition to reducing risks, hotels and resorts can improve their reputation as secure locations by implementing proactive cybersecurity measures. The ability of the industry to adjust to new difficulties while maintaining the safety and privacy of its visitors will ultimately determine its future.

REFERENCES

Aniruddha Prabhu, B. P. R. D. (2023). A study of the challenges faced by the hotel sector with regards to cyber security. In R. D. B.P. Aniruddha Prabhu, *Automation and Computation* (p. 11).

Aryee, D. (2020). *Cybersecurity Threats to The Hotel Industry and Mitigation Strategies*. Utica College. Retrieved from https://www.proquest.com/openview/64221b72cf1d4d9a39a0a17cbe763b25/1?pq-origsite=gscholar&cbl=18750&diss=y

Blanco, M. (2024, FEBURARY 14). Cyber Security Is Awakening as Key Concern for Hoteliers. Retrieved from https://www.costar.com/article/804855050/cyber-security-is-awakening-as-key-concern-for-hoteliers

C., C., & Demicco, F. (2007). To Be Secure or Not to Be: Isn't This the Question?A Critical Look at Hotel's Network Security. *International Journal of Hospitality & Tourism Administration, 8*(1), 43-59. DOI: 10.1300/J149v08n01_03

Chen, H. S., & Fiscus, J. (2018). The inhospitable vulnerability: A need for cybersecurity risk assessment in the hospitality industry. *Journal of Hospitality and Tourism Technology*, 9(2), 223–234. Advance online publication. DOI: 10.1108/JHTT-07-2017-0044

Fragniere, E., & Yagci, K. (2021). Key Terms: a Glimpse Into the World of Cyber-Attacks. In E. Fragniere, & K. Yagci, *Network & cyber security in Hospitality and Tourism* (p. 23). South Florida: USF M3 Publishing. doi:https://www.doi.org/10.5038/9781732127593

Gabriel Raicu, A. R. (2022, DECEMBER 20). CYBERSECURITY STRATEGIES IN INDUSTRY 4.0. *International Journal of Modern Manufacturing Technologies*. DOI: 10.54684/ijmmt.2022.14.3.233

Jack Holdsworth, E. A. (2017). An Effective Immersive Cyber Security Awareness Learning Platform for Businesses in the Hospitality Sector. DOI: 10.1109/REW.2017.47

LUDYNIA. A. (2024). *Cybersecurity in the Hospitality Industry.* Shiji Group. Retrieved from https://www.hospitalitynet.org/news/4120586.html

O'Connor, P., & Murphy, J. (2004). Research on information technology in the hospitality industry. *International Journal of Hospitality Management*, 23(5), 473–484. Advance online publication. DOI: 10.1016/j.ijhm.2004.10.002

Panai, E. (n.d.). A Cyber Security Framework for Independent Hotels. Retrieved from https://www.researchgate.net/profile/Enrico-Panai/publication/325780143_A_Cyber_Security_Framework_for_Independent_Hotels/links/5b235fe2aca272277fb0f8ee/A-Cyber-Security-Framework-for-Independent-Hotels.pdf

Rusch, J. (2003). Computer and Internet Fraud: A Risk Identification Overview. *Computer Fraud & Security*, 2003(6), 6–9. DOI: 10.1016/S1361-3723(03)06008-1

Shabani, N., & Munir, A. (2020). *A Review of Cyber Security Issues in.* doi:DOI: DOI: 10.1007/978-3-030-52243-8_35

Wynn, M., & Lam, C. (2023). Digitalisation and IT Strategy in the Hospitality Industry. *Systems*, 11(10), 501. Advance online publication. DOI: 10.3390/systems11100501

Chapter 18
Crypto Travel and Its Future Implications

Edmund Christopher
https://orcid.org/0000-0001-8803-5539
City University, Ajman, UAE

ABSTRACT

The advent of the realm of cryptocurrency has undoubtedly emancipated a single turn in the domain of outweighing sectors and its stride had shed its limelight over travel as well. The chapter delves into examining the domineering scope of travel accelerated by blockchain technology and digital currencies. Addition to the discussion regarding its potentiality superseding innovation, the chapter denounces the foregrounds that hamper the adoption of wide spread crypto travel these include regulatory uncertainty, scalability problem and concerns regarding volatility and legal compliance all of which must be taken in to account to drastically render upon block chain technology in the travel sector. Ranging from the expansion of tokenized Loyalty program to the disclosure of decentralized travel market places and the incorporation of virtual reality experiences, the possibilities of innovations are thoroughly breath taking.

INTRODUCTION

'Crypto Travel' a developing concept uses cryptocurrencies as a main source for money transfers in the travel business. Blockchain technology ensures the safe and effective way of money transfers for tourists. As digital currencies are widely

DOI: 10.4018/979-8-3693-6562-5.ch018

accepted, cryptocurrencies have changed the plans, booking and experience of the tourists.

The launch of cryptocurrency leads to a great progress in the many industries especially tourism. The 'crypto travel' highlights the function of Bitcoin, Ethereum and other altcoins in the travel business. It also includes booking travel, lodging and making transactions for facilities and good and mode of transportation.

1. Financial Transactions that are Decentralized:

   Replacement of Mediators: Transactions done through banks and other transaction processors requires additional charges. The development of cryptocurrency results in cost – effective and fast transactions.

   International Availability: With Cryptocurrency cross-border travel is uncomplicated. Travelers with the use of digital wallets can exchange money anywhere in the world.
2. Privacy and Security:

   Security: Blockchain technology with encryption techniques assures an improved degree of security for travelers. Fraudulent and theft possibilities are considerably low.

   Fortification: Compared to conventional payment methods, Cryptocurrency offers a great deal of privacy comparing traditional transactions. In this process transactions are done in unspecified methods thus protecting travelers personal and financial status.
3. Convenience and Efficiency:

   Immediate Transactions: In Cryptocurrencies immediate transactions takes place eradicating the waiting period common with conventional payment methods.

   Lower Charges: Generally, Traditional payment options for foreign transactions are high whereas in cryptocurrencies, the transaction costs are low.
4. Crypto-Friendly Locations and Facilities:

   Travel organizations and Platforms: Cryptocurrency payments are accepted in booking platforms and many other travel firms. It provides an entire package from travel, lodging to rent cars and holiday packages.

   Spot: Digital currencies are widely accepted in more establishments, hotels, and various tourist spots. Eventually, some nations and towns are revolving into crypto-friendly travel spots. As part of the growing trend of cryptocurrency travel, these spots are often promoted.
5. Smart Contracts and Bitcoin Applications:

Smart Contracts: The contracts have the terms programmed straight into the code can make things easier for number of travel-related tasks. As a result, it reduces the risks of human error and consecutively increase the production by programming tasks like insurance rights, loyalty programs, and booking confirmations.

Bitcoin for Travel Services: Bitcoin enhances the assurance and transparency. It is used to regulate traveler IDs, the traceability of luggage, and confirm the validity of travel valuations.

6. Effect on the Experience of Traveling:

Personalized Travel: Cryptocurrency and blockchain technology can offer more customized travel experiences tailored to client's preferences, increasing fulfillment levels overall.

Expansion and Connection: The crypto travel movement promotes invention in the tourism industry and builds a sense of community among tech-savvy tourists. This crypto travel movement will give rise to brand-new, innovative travel experiences and services.

The idea of "crypto travel" is set to develop the way financial transactions are made in the travel industry. Cryptocurrencies and blockchain technology, benefit travelers with increased security, privacy, efficiency, and convenience.

Importance of the Study

Knowledge on crypto travel is significant in today's world for several reasons:

1. Technological Innovation and Advancement:

Technology Development: The travel business needs to remain competitive and applicable as technology advances quickly. Advancement of blockchain technology and cryptocurrencies have the potential to entirely change how people travel.

Generating Innovation: Utilizing cryptocurrencies in travel promotes the progress of new services, products, and business models that advance the traveler experience.

2. Economic Efficiency and Cost Reduction:

Cost - Effective: Transactions that are facilitated by several middlemen in the traditional financial systems charges a fee. With the use cryptocurrency, travel can be cost-effective.

Eradicating Currency Exchange costs: Travelers must pay large sum of money while exchanging currencies. In cryptocurrency, these costs are eliminated, providing travelers abroad a more affordable choice.

3. Enhanced Security and Privacy

Enhanced Security: Blockchain technology's enhanced security lower the possibility of fraud and cyberattacks, which are common in traditional financial systems.

Privacy: With encryption technology cryptocurrency provide travelers with increased privacy.

4. International Financial Inclusion and Accessibility

Worldwide Acceptance: Cryptocurrencies can be used anywhere in the world as it is not bound to national currencies or financial systems. This worldwide acceptance of cryptocurrency is especially convenient for tourists visiting several nations.

Financial Services: To indulge more people in the global travel, cryptocurrencies provide financial services to people who are underbanked or unbanked.

5. Regulatory and Compliance Awareness

Navigating boundaries: To sustain amenability and prevent legal complications, travelers and businesses must be aware of the restrictions that countries and regulatory organizations are developing for the use of cryptocurrencies.

Evolving Future Policies: To adhere to the practical laws and proper usage of digital currency it is significant to be fully informed about the evolving future policies about cryptocurrency in travel sector.

6. Consumer Demand and Market Trends:

Fulfilling Demands: Customers prefer the use of cryptocurrencies when they travel. To enhance the market function and satisfy the customer needs it is important for the industries to have the better understanding of the demands.

Market Trends: Investigating customer behavior with a focus on cryptocurrency travel trends supports firms foresee and adjust to shifting customer preferences.

II SCOPE AND OBJECTIVES OF THE CHAPTER

Scope of the Chapter

This chapter objective is to broadly explore the connection of cryptocurrency and travel, encircling its historical development, current trends, advantages, risks, and future.

It also digs into how cryptocurrencies are connected to various aspects of travel including booking, payments, security, and overall travel experiences. Additionally, the chapter study the regulatory setting affecting the adoption of cryptocurrencies in the travel sector.

Objectives of this Chapter

1. Historical Context and Evolution:
   - o Deliver an ancient outline of cryptocurrency, sketching its growth.
   - o Discover the improvement mileposts of crypto travel.
2. Current Adoption and Practices:
   - o Examine the existing acceptance of cryptocurrency by travel companies and endpoints.
   - o Recognize and define facilities and terminuses that are crypto-friendly.
3. Benefits Analysis:
   - o Assess the profits of expending cryptocurrency for travel, containing cost competence, safety, confidentiality, and global availability.
   - o Explain how crypto travel can soften currency exchange disputes.
4. Challenges and Risks:
   - o Categorize regulatory, security, and usability tasks related with crypto travel.
   - o Investigate the effect of cryptocurrency price instability on the travel industry.
5. Future Implications and Trends:
   - o Forecast technological encroachments and evolving drifts in crypto travel.
   - o Measure the possible long-term bearings of crypto travel on the travel industry and regulatory site.
6. Technological Integration:
   - o Discover how blockchain, AI, IoT, and smart contracts enrich the crypto travel involvement.
   - o Focus positive applications and lessons learned from everyday uses.
7. Case Studies and Real-World Applications:
   - o Contemporary thorough case studies of businesses and destinations positively leveraging cryptocurrency.
   - o Converse future projects and creativities in the crypto travel sector.
8. Conclusions and Recommendations:
   - o Abridge key visions from the chapter.
   - o Offer commendations for travelers, travel companies, and policymakers on implementation and piloting the dominion of crypto travel.
   - o By speaking these notions, this chapter targets to afford a comprehensive understanding of crypto travel, its current implication, and its prospective to shape the future of the travel industry.

III THE EVOLUTION OF CRYPTOCURRENCY

History and Development: A Brief History of Cryptocurrency and Its Evolution

The evolution of cryptocurrency grants an attractive journey, bridging from its theoretical beginnings to its present position as a transformative financial.

Discovering this history suggests important intuitions into the rise of crypto travel and its impending future waves.

Early Concepts and Precursors

During the 1980s, David Chaum, a cryptographer, initiated DigiCash, an early recapitulation of electronic currency that employed cryptographic methods to augment privacy and security in digital transactions. Despite meeting business hindrances that led to its subsequent demise, DigiCash recognized an initial agenda for consequent encroachments in digital currencies.

Cryptographers Nick Szabo and Wei Dai put out ideas for regionalized digital currencies in the late 1990s, called Bit Gold and B-Money, correspondingly. Significant concepts like proof-of-work and decentralized consensus were offered by these theories, and they would later play a vital role in the progress of cryptocurrencies.

The Birth of Bitcoin

A paper entitled "Bitcoin: A Peer-to-Peer Electronic Cash System" was issued in October 2008 by an individual or group going by the pseudonym Satoshi Nakamoto. In order to aid secured, exposed, and unalterable transactions, this paper presented a dispersed digital money that sorts practice of blockchain technology.

On January 3, 2009, Nakamoto effectively quarried the inaugural block of the Bitcoin blockchain, authoritatively starting the Bitcoin network. Throughout its early stages, Bitcoin fascinated largely to cryptography fanatics and supporters of decentralized economics. The first known real-world transaction using Bitcoin took place in 2010 when programmer Laszlo Hanyecz substituted 10,000 BTC for two pizzas, showcasing the currency's practicality for day-to-day transactions.

Bitcoin originated to increase acceptance as a substitute to conservative financial systems as more individuals renowned its potential. Primary adopters and originators played key roles in intensifying the linkage, augmenting its safety and usability over time.

Expansion and Diversification

After Bitcoin's upsurge, a flood of different cryptocurrencies, labelled altcoins, arrived the arcade. Litecoin, familiarized by Charlie Lee in 2011, meant to develop upon Bitcoin's swiftness and adeptness. Ripple, propelled in 2012, engrossed on enabling fast and cost-effective international money transfers through blockchain technology.

Every altcoin fetched exclusive features and innovations, elevating the cryptocurrency ecosystem. Ethereum, for example, hosted smart contracts and decentralized applications (dApps), while Monero highlighted radical privacy features.

In 2015, Vitalik Buterin formed Ethereum, a non-central area that pushed the boundaries of blockchain technology past just digital currency. Ethereum transformed the industry by presenting smart contracts, contracts that implement themselves based on circumstances programmed directly into the blockchain, allowing a broad spectrum of applications (dApps).

Ethereum also forged the creation of ERC-20 tokens, which abridged the enlargement of

new cryptocurrencies and projects on its stage. This encroachment flashed the appearance of Initial Coin Offerings (ICOs) as a prevalent fundraising method for blockchain-based transactions.

Mainstream Recognition and Adoption

As cryptocurrencies turn out to be more standard, they started to gainer considerable media attraction. Ratifications from high-profile individuals, celebrity investments, and stories of substantial investment returns all fuelled growing public interest in the sector.

Financial institutions, technology companies, and governments arose to identify the importance of cryptocurrencies. This recognition aggravated high investment, research and upgrading efforts in the sector.

Governments and regulatory sectors universally started to introduce plans to observe the usage, with the development of cryptocurrencies. These rules focussed on securing customers, diminish illegal practices and spread the usage of cryptocurrencies into the larger ecosystem. Originations in rules have aided cryptocurrency projects to agree to their protocols and safety measures, thereby initiating a constructed and firm environment.

Current Trends and Future Directions

1. DeFi and Decentralized Finance:

Decentralized Finance (DeFi) has painted a noteworthy style within the kindom of cryptocurrency. In order to intimate clear and inclusive ecosystem, monetary amenities such as loaning, borrowing and trading straightforwardly, using smart contracts and blockchain technology have been intimidated by DeFi. Even though it puts forward innovative economic aids, it also has few disadvantages including privacy problems and ambiguous regulations. It is still continuing to evolve, with continuous efforts to collaborate truthfulness and threat control measures.

2. NFTs and Digital Assets:

NFTs are recent trends that widespread significant digital properties including digital art, collectibles and various other digital properties. NFTs provide authoritative ownership and attribution which paves way for artists and creators by using blockchain technology. NFTs and digital possessions are presently arranging their practices from art and collectibles into games, computer generated real estates and knowledgeable asset.

3. Integration with Traditional Finance:

Huge monetary companies and firms are initiating cryptocurrency usage into their daily practices recently. This embraces companies implementing Bitcoin as part of their balance sheets, banks providing cryptocurrency services, and investment firms familiarizing cryptocurrency funds. There are current determinations to link traditional financial systems with digital currencies, stressing interoperability, scalability, and manageable interfaces.

4. Sustainability and Environmental Impact:

The ecological effects of cryptocurrency excavating, mainly for Bitcoin, have flickered concerns regarding energy use and availability. Creativities are happening to craft more energy efficient mechanisms, like proof-of-stake, to tackle these problems. The cryptocurrency civic is dynamically pursuing means to enrich sustainability within the industry, such as accepting renewable energy sources and supportive eco-friendly wits.

In conclusion, the fruition of cryptocurrency is clear by momentous highlights,

From its cryptographic roots to the upswing of Bitcoin and the spread of altcoins, the cryptocurrency setting has incessantly grown, lashing technical progressions and altering the financial sector. Accepting this history is decisive for gaining the recent state of crypto travel and antedating its forthcoming suggestions.

IV KEY CRYPTOCURRENCIES IN TRAVEL

Overview of Major Cryptocurrencies Used in the Travel Industry

The travel industry has embraced various cryptocurrencies, each offering unique features that enhance the travel experience. Here are some of the major cryptocurrencies widely used in travel:

1. Bitcoin (BTC):
   - o **Pioneer and Market Leader:** Bitcoin, as the pioneering and most renowned cryptocurrency, continues to lead as the foremost choice in digital currency for travel-related transactions due to its widespread acceptance.
   - o **Adoption by Travel Services:** Many travel agencies, airlines, hotels, and online booking platforms have incorporated Bitcoin into their payment options. Examples include Expedia and CheapAir, both of which have seamlessly integrated Bitcoin payments into their systems.
   - o **Worldwide Acceptance:** International travelers consider Bitcoin as convenient payment option for its worldwide recognition and acceptance.
2. Ethereum (ETH):
   - o **Smart Pacts and dApps:** Ethereum's blockchain enable inventive solutions in the travel industry like automated booking systems and loyalty programs through smart pacts and decentralized applications (dApps)
   - o **ERC-20 Tokens:** Using Ethereum platform, numerous projects and services within the travel industry generate their own tokens, taking benefit of its robust ecosystem.
3. **Travel Facilities:** Websites like Travala.com accepts Ethereum payments. ETH enables travelers to book hotels,flights, and other services.
4. Litecoin (LTC):
   - o **Quick Transactions:** Travelers consider Litecoin as an attractive option for travel payments for its faster transaction times and lower fees compared to Bitcoin.
   - o **Commercial Adoption:** Litecoin's speed and efficiency are beneficial for quick bookings and payments. Considering this, numerous travel companies including airlines and booking platforms adopted Litecoin payment.
5. Ripple (XRP):
   - o **Trans-national Payments:** Ripple enables quick and low-cost transnational money transfers. It is helpful for global travel.

- o **Corporations with Financial Institutions:** Ripple's corporations with financial organizations and banks strengthen its reliability and integration into the conventional financial system. This partnership supports its application within the travel industry.

6. Binance Coin (BNB):
    - o **Travel Rebates:** Binance is a prominent cryptocurrency exchange. Users paying with Binance Coin obtains discounts on travel services. Travelers can use these discounts to book flights, hotel, and rental cars. It is accessible through platforms such as Travala.com.
    - o **Usefulness within Binance Ecosystem:** BNB's usefulness within the Binance ecosystem outspreads to travel services. It further provides benefits to travelers using this platform.
7. Bitcoin Cash (BCH):
    - o **Low Charge and Quick Transactions:** Bitcoin Cash was established to tackle Bitcoin's scalability tests. Bitcoin Cash offers low charge and quick transactions, making it advantageous for payments related to travel.
    - o **Commercial Acceptance:** Numerous travel merchants adopt Bitcoin Cash. Thus, making it a viable choice for travelers looking for economical transactions.
8. Stablecoins (e.g., USDT, USDC):
    - o **Stability:** To ensure the price stability, stablecoins like Tether (USDT) and USD Coin (USDC) are linked to fiat currencies. Travelers can make use of it to avoid the price fluctuations associated with other cryptocurrencies.
    - o **Extensive Use:** Numerous travel platforms accept stablecoins. It ensures transactions free from the volatility risks of other cryptocurrencies.

Blockchain Technology

Description of Blockchain Technology and Its Significance to Crypto Travel

Blockchain is the underlying technology behind cryptocurrencies. It offers a decentralized, secure, and transparent technique of recording transactions. Blockchain's relevance to crypto travel lies in its capability to discourse some key challenges in the travel industry.

1. Decentralization:

- o **No Chief Authority:** Blockchain functions on a decentralized network of nodes. Thus, it eliminates the need for chief authority. This decentralization strengthens the sanctuary and flexibility of the system and reduces the risk of single points of disaster.
- o **Person to Person Transaction:** Travelers have the chance to directly involve in person-person transactions. Bypassing intermediaries this approach lowers transaction costs and improves overall productivity.

2. Security and Transparency:
   - o **Absolute Record:** Blockchain hold an absolute record of all transactions. To ensure the veracity and sanctuary of the data, a transaction recorded cannot be altered.
3. Clearness:

   To provide the findability and clearness of the data, Blockchain publicly display all the transactions to prevent fraud and build trust among users.
4. Smart Contracts:
   - o **Computerized Implementation:** Smart contracts execute code-defined terms. It is computerized and work automatically upon meeting conditions and less dependence, or intermediaries. It also lowers the probability of human error.
   - o **Claims in Travel:** Smart contracts can mechanize numerous tasks including insurance claims, booking confirmations and loyalty programs within the travel sector. To simplify and advance the payment procedure smart contract can initiate payment to a hotel upon a traveller's check-in.

4. Reduced Costs and Increased Efficiency:
   - o **Subordinate Transaction Fees:** Compared to traditional payment procedure Blockchain transactions are cost-effective. As it involves no intermediaries it charges no extra fees.
   - o **Quick Transactions:** As Blockchain technology allows quick transaction it decreases the waiting time for travelers.
5. Global Accessibility:
   - o **Indefinite Transactions:** Blockchain allows travelers to use digital wallets anywhere in the world enabling indefinite transactions, without the need for currency exchange.
   - o **Financial Insertion:** Blockchain technology broadens the participation in the travel economy by extending financial insertion to unbanked and underbanked populations.
6. Enhanced Customer Experience:
   - o **Customisation and Trustworthiness:** To provide the tailored services and rewards to users, Blockchain firmly secure traveler preferences, loyalty points, and customized offers to enhance the experience.

- **Confidence and Validity:** Blockchain improve the confidence and reduce the risk of con through authentic verification of travel reviews, service quality, and traveler identities.

7. Innovative Applications:
   - **Distributed Travel Platforms:** With distributed travel platforms, Blockchain connect travelers straight with service workers, reducing price and enhancing transparency.
   - **Tokenized Facilities:** Blockchain provides travel facilities to users through tokens. Using this tokenized facility users can book flights, accommodations, arranging local tours and experiences. It enables travelers to utilize these facilities effortlessly.

Blockchain technology brings noteworthy advantages to the travel platforms. It offers safe, transparent, and effective transactions. Blockchain technology's integration with smart contracts and decentralized applications improves the travel experience by allowing automatic processes and enhanced transparency. Cryptocurrencies and blockchain receive wider acceptance on the travel sector. Therefore, the blockchain technology is poised to expand, fostering innovation and driving transformative variations.

V KEY CRYPTOCURRENCIES IN TRAVEL

Current State of Crypto Travel

With the incorporation of cryptocurrency, the landscape of travel has seen a momentous shift from a niche concept into a growing sector. It is determined by the rising acceptance of digital currencies, the need for greater security and cost-effective payment options. With the advent of technology, numerous travel sectors started approving cryptocurrency payments. Blockchain technology's integration in travel services, marks a new era in the travel industry.

1. Growing Acceptance and Integration:
   - **Majority Adoption:** As many travel sectors accept cryptocurrencies, it allows travelers to use digital currencies for a variety of expenses, from booking flights and hotels to paying for local transportation and banqueting.
2. Crypto-Specific Travel Sector:

Users paying with Binance Coin receive discounts on travel services on websites like Travala.com. These discounts apply to flights, lodgings, and rental cars.

3. Advantages for Travellers:

   Cost Efficacy: Cryptocurrencies incur lower transaction fees comparing traditional payment methods. It makes international travel affordable.

   - o **Global Accessibility:** Digital currencies operate beyond national borders, eliminating the need for currency exchange and its associated costs.
   - o **Enhanced Security:** Blockchain technology provides strong security features, reducing the risk of fraud and ensuring the integrity of transactions.

4. Challenges and Limitations:
   - o **Volatility:** The significant fluctuation in cryptocurrency values can affect the cost of travel services, posing a challenge for users.
   - o **Regulatory Uncertainty:** The regulatory environment for cryptocurrencies varies widely across different countries, leading to uncertainty for both travelers and businesses.

     Adoption and Awareness: Despite the growing use of cryptocurrencies, many travelers and travel businesses are still not well-versed in digital currencies and blockchain technology.

Enhanced education and awareness are necessary to promote wider acceptance.

Implementation by Travel Companies

Many travel companies have started accepting cryptocurrency payment identifying the benefits. List of travel companies that have incorporated cryptocurrency payment systems are mentioned below:

1. Expedia:
   - o **Collaboration with Travala:** To allow cryptocurrency payments Expedia, a leading online travel booking platform, partners with Travala.com. Bitcoin, Ethereum and other cryptocurrencies lets the travelers to pay for hotels and accommodations.
2. Travala.com:
   - o **Inclusive Crypto Travel Platform:** A prominent travel booking platform Travala.com takes over 30 cryptocurrencies, including Bitcoin, Ethereum, Litecoin and Binance Coin. To provide a seamless experi-

ence for cryptocurrency users, travala.com supports bookings for hotels, flights, and activities.
   - **Collaboration and Development:** With the aim to expands its positioning and offerings in the travel sector, Travala.com has formed associations with chief travel brands for a seamless experience.
3. CheapAir:
   - **Initial Adopter:** CheapAir.com was one among of the first travel companies to take Bitcoin for flight bookings. ChearAir.com in its cryptocurrency payment options has included Ethereum, Litecoin and Dash
   - **Crypto Rewards:** CheapAir provides rewards and discounts to travelers choosing this payment method.
4. AirBaltic:
   - **Airline Incorporation:** A Latvian airline, AirBaltic, was a pioneer in offering a Bitcoin payment option for flight bookings. This airline incorporated cryptocurrency payments into its booking system, allows direct Bitcoin payments on its website.
5. LOT Polish Airlines:
   - **Increasing Payment Options:** LOT Polish Airlines allows travelers to book flights using Bitcoin payment option providing an alternative payment options.
6. Bitcoin.travel:
   - **Crypto – Exclusive setting:** Bitcoin.travel takes cryptocurrencies for flight bookings, lodgings, and car rentals. Bitcoin.travel focuses exclusively on crypto payments, catering to the crypto community.
7. Alternative Airlines:
   - **Various Payment Options:** An online travel agency, Alternative Airlines, takes various cryptocurrencies, including Bitcoin, Ethereum, Dash, and Monero, for flight bookings. Alternative Airlines different payment options have made it a prominent choice among crypto enthusiasts.
8. Destinia:
   - **Universal acceptance:** Destinia takes Bitcoin payment options for hotel bookings, flight tickets, and car rentals. It has extended its global customer base and reach by incorporating cryptocurrency payments.
9. More Stays:
   - **Vacation Rentals:** More Stays lets customers book for vacation rentals with Bitcoin and other cryptocurrencies. It caters to tourists looking for alternative payment methods and accommodations.
10. ABitSky:

- o **Complete Services:** ABitSky travel agency takes Bitcoin payment method for booking flights, car rentals, lodgings, and other travel services. The wide acceptance of crypto-friendly policies makes it a suitable choice for tourists.

Above examples shed light on the adoption of cryptocurrency in various travel sector highlighting the different payment options and flexibility for tourists who prefer digital currencies. Many travel industries have incorporated digital currencies into their payment mode making it a convenient option for tourists. Digital currency payment system offers noteworthy advantages, including low costs, universal acceptance, and improved security. Although, the cryptocurrency payment sector undergoes challenges such as price instability, regulatory doubts, and the need for wider acceptance and responsiveness. The increasing cryptocurrency usage and blockchain technology in the travel forum is increasing, promoting further inventions and additions inside the companies.

Crypto-Friendly Destinations

The growth in cryptocurrency usage enlarge, various universal endpoints are welcoming cryptocurrency users majorly, which paves way for the travellers to use their digital possessions for numerous aids. The listed below are some of the crypto-friendly destinations:

Tokyo, Japan:

- **Wide Acceptance**: Tokyo is a major city to use cryptocurrency. Numerous companies, consisting hotels, restaurants and retail shops, admit Bitcoin and other cryptocurrencies. Travellers find it easy to convert their digital belongings to money because of various cryptocurrency ATMs and it also aids usability.
- **Tech-Savvy Culture**: Japan's high technological sight and helpful guideline ecosystem boosts its status as a crypto-friendly destination. Cryptocurrency fans find the place suitable because of its technology and invention.

Zurich, Switzerland:

- **Crypto Valley**: Zurich is a main place under the "Crypto valley" of Switzerland, well-known for its developments in blockchain and cryptocurrency. Variety of business in Zurich admits cryptocurrency and it also plays a vital role in encouraging startups and businesses, making a healthier ecosystem.

- **Regulatory Support**: The advanced outline in Switzerland highlights Zurich's charm to cryptocurrency fans, thus it is considered a main place for crypto travellers.

Ljubljana, Slovenia:

- **Bitcoin City**: Ljubljana is known for "Bitcoin City," a huge shopping area. Most of the shop owners admit Bitcoin in this city, creating it an important crypto community and they often conduct events and conferences.
- **Widespread Adoption:** Routine transactions using cryptocurrency is made possible in Ljubljana, creating it an awaiting area for crypto travellers.

Miami, USA:

- **Crypto Capital:** Miami is evolving as a weighty area for cryptocurrency and blockchain technology. The city conducts yearly meetings on Bitcoin and also possesses various businesses, incorporating wealthy hotels and real estate companies that admit cryptocurrency.
- **Government Support:** The national government encourages cryptocurrency making it a crypto-friendly nation.

Singapore:

- **Financial Hub:** Singapore, welcomes cryptocurrency and blockchain technology with open hands, and it also serves as world monetary spot. Almost every companies admit cryptocurrencies, aided by a user-friendly rules.
- **Innovation and Investment**: Singapore is a key area for crypto business, since it pulls blockchain innovation and investment and draws startups and entrepreneurs from all around the world towards it, and strongly confirms its status.

Amsterdam, Netherlands:

- **Crypto-Friendly Businesses**: Amsterdam's crypto- friendly creations include cafes, bars, and hotels. It is also provided with abundant cryptocurrency ATMs and conducts blockchain programmes often.
- **Progressive Attitude**: Amsterdam's continuous development on technology and innovation makes it a perfect destination for cryptocurrency fans.

San Francisco, USA:

- **Tech Epicenter:** San Francisco, situated at the heart of the tech production, holds maximum attraction of companies that admit cryptocurrency. It is also heaven for various blockchain startups and conducts trade programmes.

- **Innovative Culture:** San Francisco's invention aids in large usage and assimilation of cryptocurrency across various areas.

Prague, Czech Republic:

- **Crypto Hub:** Prague is recognized for its bouncy crypto community and a flood of companies that admit cryptocurrency transactions. It is also provided with abundant cryptocurrency ATMs and conducts blockchain programmes often.
- **Historical Significance**: Prague's well-known historical significance and its modern crypto-friendly ecosystem define it as significant and attractive spot for nomads.

Traveller Demographics

For personalized services, a keen knowledge about the demographic profile of the crypto travellers is needed. Below given data defines the authentic demographic profile of crypto and marketing travelers:

Age:

- **Young Adults**: Young adults aged 18-25 are majorly crypto travellers. They easily familiarise to new technologies including cryptocurrency due to their inborn nature.
- **Early Adopters**: These travellers tend to stay updated to recent trends and they are early adopters.

Gender:

- **Male Dominance**: In the recent days, women tend to maintain the rapport with men who mainly uses crypto technology.
- **Increasing Diversity**: A sophisticated demographic profile is created while initiating multiplicity and incorporation inside the crypto community.

Income Level:

- **Middle to High Income:** The crypto travellers' income level ranges from middle to high allowing them to finance in cryptocurrencies and meet the expense of intercontinental travel.
- **Investment Mindset:** Crypto travellers see their digital belongings as an investment and are willing to spend that for travel and other practises.

Education:

- **Well-Educated:** A considerate portion of crypto travellers are well-educated, with many holding college degrees or higher.

- **Continuous Learners**: Crypto travellers are likely to engage in continuous learning and staying updated on blockchain technology and cryptocurrency regulations.

Tech-Savvy:

- **Comfort with Technology**: they are usually well versed in managing various applications, technology and digital platforms which helps them in planning their trips and managing their crypto assets.
- **Early Technology Adopters**: This often opens to new innovations and adoptions in the technology before it becomes conventional.

Geographic Distribution:

- **Urban Residents**: Crypto travellers are mostly urban residents with better access to technology, financial services and high travel plans.
- **Global Citizens**: Crypto travellers frequently travelling for business and leisure purposes consider themselves as global citizens.

Case Studies

In the travel industry, companies and destinations utilizing crypto provide insights into the practical applications with detailed case studies and benefits of cryptocurrency.

Three case studies listed below are:

Travala.com:

- **Overview:** Travala.com is a chief blockchain-based travel booking mode that admits over 30 different cryptocurrencies, including Bitcoin, Ethereum, and Binance Coin. An array of travel services are provided by the platform including flights, hotels, and activities.
- **Business Model:** Travala.com provides a devolved travelling experience by powering blockchain technology. The platform offers competitive prices, transparency, and secure transactions through smart contracts.
- **Impact:** The platform has seen significant growth since its launch. Cryptocurrency payments scheme has been received positively by variety of people gaining a global recognition. Its partnership with major travel brands has boosted its popularity and the exclusive offers for crypto payments is also a reason for its popularity.

CheapAir:

- **Overview**: One of the first in the industry to accept Bitcoin for flight bookings is CheapAir.com, an online travel agency. Ethereum, Litecoin, and Dash have also been included in its cryptocurrency payment options.

- **Business Model:** CheapAir.com integrates cryptocurrency payments through an easily accessible process. The company offers a faultless experience for travellers looking to pay with digital currencies and also ensures flexibility and convenience.
- **Impact**: CheapAir.com's is considered as a forerunner in the adoption of cryptocurrency in the travel industry. The company's assurance to offering assorted payment options has appealed a loyal customer base. CheapAir.com has also emerged with idea to reward for crypto payments, attracting more travellers to use crypto currency.

Zurich, Switzerland:

- **Overview:** Zurich is a major city within Switzerland's "Crypto Valley," a region known for its blockchain and cryptocurrency invention. The city is like a paradise to numerous businesses that accept cryptocurrency and hosts various blockchain-related events.
- **Crypto Integration:** In Zurich, Cryptocurrencies are widely used by travellers to pay for services such as hotel stays, shopping and dining. The regulatory guidelines of the city in encouraging crypto further paves way for innovation and adoption.
- **Impact:** Crypto travellers' popular destination is made due to Zurich's embrace of cryptocurrency. The city's integration of cryptocurrency has made a huge impact into everyday transactions, enhancing the travel experience, providing convenience and implementing a technology forward environment. Tourists and businesses who are interested in blockchain technology are being attracted by Zurich's reputation as a growing crypto-friendly destination.

The progress of crypto travel is obvious by the growing reception of cryptocurrencies by travel companies and the advent of crypto-friendly destinations. The demographic contour of crypto travellers is branded by young, tech-savvy individuals with a strong inclination towards economic technology. Case studies of companies like Travala.com and CheapAir, as well as destinations like Zurich, validate the profits and increasing influence of cryptocurrency in the industry of travel. The imminence of crypto travel promotes further invention and alteration, aligning digital currencies an imperative part of worldwide travel ecosystem.

VI BENEFITS OF CRYPTO TRAVEL

Cost Efficiency: Reducing Costs for Travelers Using Crypto Currency

Lower Transaction Fees:

- **Traditional Payment Methods**: Travellers who are making transactions through credit cards and bank transfers for international payments, require high transaction fees and it add up significantly while making multiple transactions abroad.
- **Cryptocurrency Transactions:** Cryptocurrency transactions, including Bitcoin and Ethereum require lower fee compared to traditional payment methods, especially for international transactions.

Case Studies:

- **Example**: A traveller saved over 10% using Bitcoin in transaction fee compared to credit card transaction fee, while booking a hotel in Europe.
- **Another Example**: A digital nomad working from different countries found out that using crytocurrency instead of traditional payments methods saved upto 15% in their entire transaction fee.

Elimination of Currency Exchange Fees

- **Currency Exchange Hassles**: Conversion from local currency to foreign currency generally attracts fees and adverse exchange rates at banks and the booths where currency is exchanged.
- **Cryptocurrency as a Universal Currency**: Cryptocurrency like Bitcoin can be used all over the world without the need to exchange it to foreign currency, thus it saves extra exchange fees.

Traveler Testimonials

Example: A habitual traveler uses Bitcoin instead of currency found it very useful and under budget.

Reduced Costs for Businesses

- **Merchant Fees:** Traditional payment methods accept 2-3% of payment for transaction fees, wherein cryptocurrency transactions processing fee is as low to 1% in Business transactions.

- **Savings Passed to Consumers:** The saved fee in transactions through cryptocurrency usage is passed to consumers in the form of savings and discount in Business.

Case Studies

- **Example**: A hotel chain witnessed increase in bookings from tech-savvy travellers after implementing 5% discount for those who use cryptocurrency during payment.
- **Security and Privacy**: Enhanced Security and Privacy Features of Cryptocurrency Transactions

Enhanced Security Features

- **Blockchain Technology**: The decentralized nature and cryptographic techniques of cryptocurrencies and blockchain makes it secure.
- **Secure Transactions:** Fraudulent actions which lead to lose in money during credit card payments can be eliminated through cryptocurrency transactions, which are free from fraud and chargebacks.
- **Real-World Examples**: A travel agency observed notable decrease in fraudulent incidents, through usage of blockchain, which in turn improved their overall customer trust.

Privacy Benefits

- **Anonymity and Pseudonymity**: Higher degree of anonymity is offered in cryptocurrency compared to traditional payment methods. Though the transaction details are public, the identity of the individual is not directly linked with their personal information, making it pseudonymous.
- **Protection of Personal Information:** Travellers' personal information remain disclosed while using cryptocurrency. Since cryptocurrency does not require sharing sensitive details, thereby minimizing identity theft.
- **Privacy-Focused Cryptocurrencies:** Certain cryptocurrencies, like Monero and Zcash, are designed precisely to enhance discretion and offers features like hidden transaction amounts and addresses.

Traveler Experiences

- **Example**: Travelers who are concerned with their privacy opt to Monero, where their transaction details remain confidential.

- **Global Accessibility**: Ease of Accessing and Using Cryptocurrency Worldwide Borderless Transactions
- **Global Reach:** Cryptocurrencies can be used anywhere in the world and it only requires access to internet, making them user-friendly for international travellers.
- **Availability:** Cryptocurrencies can be accessed 24/7, unlike the traditional system which limit the travellers from transactions with regard to banking hours and holidays.

Case Examples: By using Bitcoin, a traveller found it convenient to pay for his services in various countries without the need for multiple bank accounts or carrying huge amount of cash.

Growing Acceptance

- **Increasing Number of Merchants**: The increasing number of merchants worldwide accepting cryptocurrencies, from hotels and airlines to restaurants and retail stores, makes it easier for travellers to utilize their digital assets.
- **Cryptocurrency ATMs:** The increasing number of cryptocurrency ATMs in major cities and travel destinations enables travellers to conveniently convert their crypto into local currency as required.

Traveler Testimonials

- **Example:** An explorer who used cryptocurrency ATMs in cities like Tokyo and Amsterdam appreciated the accessibility of converting crypto to local currency on the fly.
- **Eliminating Currency Exchange Issues**: How Crypto Can Eliminate the Hassle of Currency Exchange

Avoiding Exchange Rate Fluctuations

- **Stable Value Transfers**: Cryptocurrency usage also helps in avoiding the unpredictable hike in exchange rates while converting the currencies. When stablecoins pegged to major currencies, cryptocurrency offers stable value transfer.
- **Predictable Spending**: It also helps the travellers in planning their trips without worrying about currency exchange rates.

Traveler Testimonials

Example: A traveler using a stablecoin pegged to the US dollar realized that it was much easier and it barely affects the exchange rates.

Simplifying Financial Management

- **Single Currency for Multiple Countries**: Single cryptocurrency is used in various countries that avoid the rate of exchange fee and the need to convert the currency.
- **Ease of Transactions**: Payment through cryptocurrency is convenient and it also eliminates the risk of carrying different currencies and cash in person.

Traveler Experiences

Example: Digital nomads traveling across Europe found it handy to use Ethereum for their needs, lessening the need to exchange of currency and for simpler financial management.

The benefits of crypto travel are multi-layers, including cost efficiency, higher security and privacy, easy accessibility around the world, decreasing the currency exchange issues. These advantages are recognized by business people and travellers and the use of cryptocurrency among them has been increased and is still growing, making way for effortless, efficient and secured travel experience.

VII CHALLENGES AND RISKS

Regulatory Issues: Regulatory Challenges Facing Crypto Travel

Diverse Regulatory Landscape

- **Varying Regulations**: Various countries have varied approaches to cryptocurrencies ranging from ban to strict rules and regulations or welcoming charter.
- **Compliance Challenges**: Travel companies and platforms face various encounters with the changing regulatory requirements across territories.

Case Examples

Example: A travel reservation platform had to join its crypto payment option in selected countries due to regulatory uncertainties and compliance disputes.

Legal Uncertainty

- **Unclear Legal Status:** Cryptocurrencies regularly exist in an indeterminate territory in many provinces, leading to vagueness for trades and nomads.
- **Impact on Adoption**: Legitimate ambiguity can avert businesses from accommodating cryptocurrencies and travellers from expending them due to fright of legal concerns.
- **Regulatory Updates**: It is tougher for travel platforms and individuals to keep themselves informed about the regulatory informs about crypto tradition.

Compliance Burden

KYC/AML Requirements: Know Your Customer (KYC) and Anti-Money Laundering (AML) policies add additional problems on businesses that offer crypto services.
Cost of Compliance: Startup companies, small business and travel agencies may find it difficult since the compliance measures can be costly and onerous.
Industry Advocacy: Involvement of industry associations and advocacy might narrow the crypto regulations.

Volatility of Cryptocurrency: The Impact of Cryptocurrency Price Volatility on Travel

Price Fluctuations

- **High Volatility**: Instability in price is a backdrop for cryptocurrencies and values vary over short period of time.
- **Impact on Travel Budgets**: Fluctuations in price of cryptocurrencies makes it hard for the travellers to decide their budget beforehand.
- **Mitigation Strategies**: Price fluctuations may be reduced by immediately converting the crypto to flat currency or by using stablecoins.

Financial Risk

- **Currency Conversion Risks**: Conversion of crypto to flat currency might lead to financial loss among the nomads under uncertain situations.

- **Planning and Hedging**: Wanderers have to plan in advance to elude contact to crypto unpredictability by intensifying their expense and financial mechanisms.

Business Implications

- **Revenue Management:** Businesses need to bend in order to face price fluctuations by depicting pricing tactics or implementing equivocation tool.
- **Customer Expectations:** It is vital in upholding trust among the customers, when it comes to crypto usage since the price is wavering.
- **Security Concerns**: Potential Security Risks Associated with Using Cryptocurrency

Cybersecurity Threats

- **Hacking and Fraud**: Permanence in blockchain technology in Cryptocurrency transactions lead to fraudulent and hacking activities.
- **Protecting Private Keys**: To prevent unauthorized access and theft it is necessary for the users to protect their private keys and wallets.
- **Education and Awareness**: Awareness and education of cybersecurity practices should be provided to travellers to implement safe crypto transactions and to eliminate security challenges.

Phishing and Scams

- **Social Engineering**: A sum of crypto users are under phishing threats as hackers try to trick them into providing their private keys or passwords.
- **Scam ICOs and Projects**: Tourists who spend in travel-based Initial Coin Offerings (ICOs) or projects should be watchful enough not to be victim to scams.

Regulatory Compliance

- **Compliance Risks**: Non-defiance with such regulatory needs like KYC/AML obligations can have legal and monetary concerns for travelers and business bodies involved.
- **Legal Frameworks**: Loyalty to sturdy safety practices, guidelines and plans, can help diminish chances of security breaks as well as build trust in crypto transactions.

- **Acceptance and Usability**: Challenges Related to the Widespread Acceptance and Usability of Cryptocurrency

Limited Acceptance

- **Merchant Adoption**: In the developing cryptocurrency forum, a bulk of companies especially SMEs do not agree cryptos for transactions.
- **Geographical Variations**: The usage of cryptocurrency among the tourists is based on the accepting policies of various countries, which affects the travellers frequently.
- **Incentivizing Adoption**: To reach mass acceptance; organizations can be driven by factors like information and establishment of incentives, clarity on regulatory necessities.

Usability Issues

- **User Experience**: Conventional users might be dispirited from partaking if complications such as wallet management and transaction handling remain unsettled.
- **User Education**: By teaching people on the advantages of cryptos while at the same time providing user friendly interfaces that also enable easy adoption by travellers enhances its growth rate.
- **Infrastructure Development**: For example, buying crypto ATMs or payment gateways could make cryptocurrencies more usable by travelers or more accessible from them.

Currency Conversion Challenges

- **Conversion Services**: The limited availability and high fees associated with converting cryptocurrencies to fiat currency can make them less user-friendly for those who want to travel.
- **Cross-Border Payments**: To enable the seamless cross-border payments with the use of digital currencies, there must be found a way around regulatory, technical and liquidity obstacle
- **Future Trends:** Innovations in blockchain technology and financial services are expected to address usability issues and enhance the acceptance of cryptocurrencies in the travel industry.

Today crypto travel has many advantages such as cost efficiency, better security, worldwide access and simplified forex but it is not without its own set back such as price volatility, legal uncertainty, acceptance and security threats. This will involve collaborations between various stakeholders including technology providers, regulators, travel companies among others that will result in an all-secure transaction environment that is efficient for cryptos on traveling business grounds. As regulations change and new technologies emerge however these horizons will open up further possibilities for travelers across the globe.

VIII FUTURE IMPLICATIONS OF CRYPTO TRAVEL

Technological Advancements: How Future Technological Advancements May Impact Crypto Travel?

Blockchain Innovations

- **Scalability Solutions**: Future developments in blockchain technology, such as Layer 2 solutions and sharding can potentially improve business and reduce costs associated with crypto travel.
- **Interoperability**: Wider reception and interoperability of various blockchain networks can potentially ease cross-border payments and hence increase the utility of cryptocurrencies for travelers.
- **Smart Contracts**: Using smart contracts in travel bookings can automate processes such as ticketing, accommodation booking, loyalty programs etc.

Privacy Enhancements

- **Privacy Coins**: On-going development on privacy-centric cryptocurrencies can provide even more private options in order to protect the confidentiality of one's transactions while traveling.
- **Zero-Knowledge Proofs**: The adoption of zero-knowledge proofs and other privacy-preserving technologies can greatly improve security and anonymity when making transactions using cryptocurrencies during travel.

User Experience

- **Enhanced Wallet Solutions**: One of them would be the enhancement of the crypto wallets and payment interfaces which can be employed by a traveler.

- **Integration with Travel Apps**: Even extending the crypto payment option in the most popular travel applications or related platforms may also assist the travelers to arrange their travels in cryptocurrencies.

Predicted Trends: Emerging Trends in Crypto Travel

Increased Merchant Adoption

Expansion of Crypto-Friendly Businesses: A projection sees more businesses within the travel sector, such as airlines, accommodations, and logistical facilitators, incorporating cryptocurrency payment systems, influenced by burgeoning user demand and the strategic benefits.

Diverse Cryptocurrency Acceptance: Anticipated is a broader spectrum of accepted cryptocurrencies extending beyond Bitcoin and Ether, addressing the varied preferences and financial strategies of travelers.

Integration of Decentralized Finance (DeFi)

- **DeFi Applications in Travel:** The application of decentralized financial systems may produce novel fiscal services within the travel sphere, including decentralized borrowing for travel-related costs and blockchain-based loyalty initiatives.
- **Travel NFTs:** Arrangement of travel-specific non-fungible tokens (NFTs) for altered travel know-hows, virtual trips, and collectibles are used to know the experience of travel and how it is retained.

Global Travel Accessibility

- **Financial Inclusion**: Cryptocurrencies inherits the capability to increase monetary incorporation by widening banking abilities to unbanked geographies in separated areas.
- **Borderless Payments:** The evolution in cryptocurrency-based international payment ways could lead to disseminate the old-fashioned travel needs, and also helps in unhindered world travel.

Impact on the Travel Industry: Probable Lasting Impacts on the Travel Industry

Disintermediation

- **Direct Peer-to-Peer Transactions**: By using cryptocurrency tends to direct transaction between one person to another without the involvement of banks and payment sources.
- **Marketplace Disruption**: Traditional travel booking may face struggle due to the transparency in crypto using platforms through blockchain technology.

Customer Empowerment

- **Ownership of Data**: Travellers are empowered to control and monetize their personal data, enhancing trust and transparency in travel transactions by adopting decentralized identity solutions and data ownership models.
- **Customized Travel Experiences**: Cryptocurrencies and blockchain enable personalized travel experiences based on preferences and historical data of transactions of the traveller.

Sustainability Initiatives

Green Blockchain Solutions: Eco-friendly blockchain technology and carbon-neutral cryptocurrency enable viable tourism practices and alley environmental impact of travel.

Transparency in Supply Chains: Blockchain-enabled supply chain transparency could verify supportable practices in travel accommodations, transportation, and tourism activities.

Future Regulatory Landscape: Predictions on How Regulations Might Evolve Regulatory Clarity

Standardized Guidelines: There is a need for the regulatory authorities to develop permanent guidelines and outlines to make sure the legal status of cryptocurrencies and alleviate regulatory uncertainties for travel companies and consumers.

Compliance Requirements: In order to address the risks in crypto transactions in travel, enhanced KYC/AML regulations and consumer protection measures could be introduced.

Global Coordination

- **International Collaboration:** To promote an environment for global crypto travel, there should be increased international collaboration among the regulatory bodies, who could harmonize the regulations among various nations.
- **Adaptive Policies**: Stable frameworks have to be initiated in order to maintain the consumer rights and to safe guard financial stability in blockchain and cryptocurrencies.
- Innovation Support
- **Regulatory Sandboxes**: Supervisory sandboxes and pilot programs may be created to encourage innovation in blockchain and crypto technologies, allowing the companies to test the solutions within the travel industry.
- **Stakeholder Engagement**: Continued dialogue between regulators, industry stakeholders, and technology developers could shape future guidelines that balance innovation with directing compliance in crypto travel.

The future of crypto travel would be influenced by technological developments, trends, impacts on the travel industry in the long run and changing regulations. With the development of blockchain technology and a higher level of acceptance for cryptocurrencies, travelers and travel companies will benefit from improved efficiency, transparency. and global connection within the digital world. Therefore, to take advantage of the opportunities as well as overcome the obstacles that crypto travel poses in several upcoming years, stakeholders need to have proper preparations.

Integration with Other Technologies AI and Crypto Travel

1. **Customized Suggestion**

- **AI Algorithms**: Artificial intelligence can provide personalized travel references based on each person's comforts and pecuniary limits by inspecting traveler favorites, transaction history, and social media data.
- **Incorporation of Crypto Wallets**: AI-driven travel stands can suggest the prime cryptocurrency wallets and payment modes based on the needs of passengers, user experience advancement.

2. **Predictive Analytics**

- **Demand Prediction**: Travelers can refurbish the rating stratagems and inventory management by using AI powered prophetic analytics to calculate travel demand patterns on historical data and market trends
- **Innovative Pricing:** AI algorithms can enhance income and effectiveness by regularly altering crypto travel rates in real-time subject to the supply and demand dynamics.

3. **Customer Service Automation**

- **Chatbots and virtual assistants:** AI-driven chatbots can rapidly help travelers using cryptocurrency with probes concerning payments, informs reservations, and travel tips
- **Natural Language Processing**: Integration of natural language processing (NLP) award artificial intelligence (AI) to understand and respond to demands in a multiplicity of languages from tourists, growing user commitment and accessibility.
- **IoT and Blockchain**: Integration of Internet of Things (IoT) with Blockchain Technology in Travel

4. **Enriched Travel Security**
    - o **IoT Devices**: IoT devices such as biometric scanners and smart locks can be merged with blockchain based identity verification systems through which security and check-in protocols for crypto travellers can be improved.
    - o **Indelible Records**: IoT-generated data may be securely kept on blockchain's irreversible ledger, assuring the precision and rightfulness of data pertaining to traveler actions and communications.

5. **Smart Travel Infrastructure**

- **Block Chain**: IoT sensors assimilated into lodging and transportation establishments have the capacity to recruit smart contracts centered on scheduled parameters. Instances of these conditions contain mechanized check-ins, room alterations, and car rentals, all of which are made potential by cryptocurrency payments.
- **Innovative Processes**: Blockchain allowed IoT networks can make the most of resource consumption and functioning competence in travel services, decreasing expenses and refining service delivery for cryptocurrency travelers.

6. **Supply Chain Transparency**

- **Tracking**: Concurrent tracking and traceability of luggage and items across the travel supply chain can be simplified by the permutation of IoT sensors and blockchain technology. This enriches clearness and drops the chance of burglary or damage.
- **Payments:** IoT-enabled devices have the skill to robotically twitch cryptocurrency payments when predetermined necessities are encountered. This makes transactions stress-free and protects money on administrative overhead for travel-related jobs.

Smart Contracts: Use of Smart Contracts in Travel Bookings and Services

1. Automated Booking Processes
    - **Centralized Booking Platforms**: Digital contracts may streamline the crypto travel services reservation and authorization procedure.
    - **Transaction**: Smart contracts have the facility to purpose as security agents, keeping cryptocurrency payments in sustention until certain requirements are fulfilled, such customer gratification or service transfer.
2. Loyalty Programs and Rewards
    - **Tokenized Loyal Points:** Crypto travelers can earn loyalty points and recompenses through smart contracts, which offer easy refurbishment and cross-partner and environment transferability.
    - **Distributing Rewards Transparently**: Fair loyalty points, confidence development and interaction between policy givers and crypto users are guaranteed by blockchain-based smart contracts.
3. Dispute Resolution
    - **Automated Conflict Solution**: Code-encoded smart bonds have the skill to include pre-established clash determination procedures, permitting for the automatic intervention and expenditure of discrepancies between businesses and service providers.
    - **Permanent Records**: The purity of blockchain technology guarantees reasonable and liability in cryptocurrency travel transactions by proposing an auditable track of contracts and transaction history.

Conclusion

Blockchain technology combined with artificial intelligence, the Internet of Things (IoT), and smart contracts has the capability to significantly improve crypto travel experiences, accelerate operations, and enhance security and transparency in the travel sector. These technologies have the capacity to completely change how travelers use loyalty programs, handle payments, and interact with travel agencies as they develop and combine. The travel ecosystem's stakeholders ought to investigate and welcome these technical developments in order to seize fresh chances for uniqueness and innovation in the coin travel sector.

REAL-WORLD APPLICATIONS

Examples of Successful Implementations of Crypto Travel

1. Travel Booking Platforms:
    - o **Expedia**: In 2014 the International online travel booking platform Expedia started taking Bitcoin payments. This payment served as an additional and alternative method for tech-savvy tourists.
    - o **TravelbyBit**: TravelbyBit, a travel booking platform allows tourists to book flights, hotels and tours through crypto payment using cryptocurrencies like Bitcoin and Ethereum. It aims for easy travel arrangements for crypto enthusiasts.
2. Airlines and Hospitality:
    - **LOT Polish Airlines**: In 2015, LOT Polish Airlines was among the first airlines to use the Bitcoin payment method for flight tickets. LOT Polish Airlines dives into the emerging cryptocurrency market aimed at providing alternative payment options for tourists.
    - **Kessler Collection:** To provide ease and flexibility payment option for tourists familiar with crypto payment, Kessler Collection, a luxury hotel group in the United States, collaborated with BitPay to accept Bitcoin and Bitcoin Cash payments.
3. Tourism and Activities:

    DubaiCoin: Dubai, famous for its innovative approaches to tourism and technology, unmasked the cryptocurrency DubaiCoin as a means of payment. The Dubai Coin payment method can be used for a range of city services, including travel-related events and attractions.

    - **Crypto Destinations**: With a cryptocurrency payment mode, this company offers a variety of vacation moments, from lavish retreats to daring excursions. It increases accessibility for travelers using cryptocurrencies all around the world.

Case Studies

1. Consumer Demand and Adoption:
    - **Market Division**: Active applications of cryptocurrencies have confirmed that a group of customers encompassed of tech-savvy tourists and cryptocurrency enthusiasts are ready to practice cryptocurrencies to sort travel preparations.

- **Education and Awareness**: To accept and shape assurance in the travel division, it is essential to educate both travelers and travel contractors about the benefits and usage of cryptocurrency payments.

2. Operational Considerations:
   - **Interaction Problems**: As cryptocurrency payment choices are developing, they comprise firm technical interaction with existing payment systems and stand by regulatory agreement to diminish the early functioning glitches.
   - **Customer Help**: Confirming a great user understanding entails contribution focused customer help for cryptocurrency transactions, containing debugging, and answering questions about payments.
3. Risk Management:
   - **Turbulence Prevention**: For companies that offer bitcoin payment selections, it is important to have measures in place to lower the effect of price precariousness on pricing and financial solidity.
   - **Security Systems**: In order to shield customer trust and safe their funds it is critical to expand cybersecurity actions to safeguard against possible hazards related with cryptocurrency transactions, such as fraud and hacking.

Upcoming Projects and Initiatives in Crypto Travel

1. Expansion of Cryptocurrency Acceptance:
   - **Global Adoption**: In a struggle to aid a larger custom of bitcoin users universally, travel agencies, hotels, and airlines are continuing to rise their reception of cryptocurrencies.
   - **New Cryptocurrencies:** Provision for newer cryptocurrencies outside of Bitcoin and Ethereum is being presented. This replicates altering consumer tastes and technological improvements within the cryptocurrency industry.
2. Integration with Blockchain Solutions:
   - o **Bitcoin-Based Loyalty Programs:** Consuming blockchain-based technology, decentralized loyalty programs and incentives systems are being shaped to mend client preservation in the travel industry.
   - o **Applications of Smart Contracts**: Using smart contracts to automate payment, scheduling, and dispute resolution procedures will upturn usefulness and availability in travel-related happenings.
3. Regulatory Developments:

- **Clarity:** Maintaining up to date on changes to the law and modifying regulations to guarantee that the tourism industry abides by the new rules regulating cryptocurrency transactions.
- **Industry Collaboration**: To create best practices and standards for the safe and long-term expansion of crypto travel initiatives, industry players, regulatory agencies, and technology providers should collaborate.

The routine uses of cryptocurrency travel display noteworthy progress in integrating cryptocurrencies into customary travel amenities, motivated by active efforts, deep insights, and adventurous plans for the upcoming. Stakeholders can use these visions as the crypto travel network matures to take gain of commercial possibilities, solve practical issues, and lead the way in mounting cutting-edge solutions that will entirely alter the travel industry. Through collaboration, revolution, and regulatory conformity, the travel sector may fully apply cryptocurrencies to expand passenger experiences and stimulus the direction of worldwide tourism in the future.

Conclusion

Blockchain technology combined with artificial intelligence, the Internet of Things (IoT), and smart contracts has the capability to significantly improve crypto travel experiences, accelerate operations, and enhance security and transparency in the travel sector. These technologies have the capacity to completely change how travelers use loyalty programs, handle payments, and interact with travel agencies as they develop and combine. The travel ecosystem's stakeholders ought to investigate and welcome these technical developments in order to seize fresh chances for uniqueness and innovation in the coin travel sector.

CONCLUSION

Summary

1. Introduction to Crypto Travel:

    Definition and Context: Crypto travel denotes to the habit of digital currencies, such as Bitcoin and Ethereum, to book flights, hotels and other travel-related services.

    Expansion: Tech-savvy tourists regarding for more financial secrecy and other payment choices have taken an attraction to the impression.
2. Benefits of Crypto Travel:

Savings: Transaction costs linked to traditional payment systems and currency exchange fees can be curtailed by using cryptocurrencies.

Cybersecurity and Privacy: Blockchain technology's heightened security features allow the travelers to transact in a private and secure manner.

Worldwide Availability: Cryptocurrencies permit easy international money transmissions and financial addition for tourists from all over the domain.

Removal of Currency Exchange: Crypto bids flawless and operative payment options rejecting payments allied with currency exchange.

3. Challenges and Risks:

Regulation Problems: A multiplicity of frequently varying regulations present qualms for travelers and compliance disputes for travel organizations.

Flexibility of Cryptocurrency: Price variations have an impression on travelers' and travel industry businesses' financial scheduling and costing.

Privacy Issues: Intimidations like fraud and hacking focus the requirement of strong cybersecurity resistances and user alertness campaigns.

Approval and Interface: The wide-ranging use of cryptocurrencies in travel is hindered by merchants' limited reception and usability hitches.

4. Future Implications:

Technological Developments: Smart contracts, AI, and the Internet of Things are working to develop the efficacy, safety, and personalized travel experiences for cryptocurrency.

Projected Trends: The prospect of cryptocurrency travel is being molded by budding merchant adoption, DeFi integration, and eco-friendly travel strategies.

Impact on Travel Industry: The travel industry is suffering noteworthy transformation due to features such as disintermediation, client empowerment, and sustainability edges.

Future Regulatory Landscape: Stimulating a setting that is encouraging to cryptocurrency travel obliges universal partnership, regulatory clarity, and support for innovation.

5. Integration with Other Technologies:

AI and Crypto Travel: AI expands user knowledge in cryptocurrency transactions by means of computerized customer support, predictive analytics, and custom-made recommendations.

IoT and Blockchain: Incorporation enriches supply chain transparency, active efficacy, and security in the tourism industry.

Smart Contracts: By systematizing loyalty platforms, booking procedures, and dispute resolution, crypto travel transactions become more effectual and reliable.

6. Practical Implementations:

    Effective Implementations: To attract to tech-savvy tourists, travel agencies, airlines, and lodging providers have incorporated cryptocurrencies.
    Lessons Learned: When laying crypto travel resolutions into exercise, it's critical to deliberate consumer education, operational preparedness, and risk management techniques.
    Future Projects: New projects target to advance blockchain technology, enlarge the adoption of cryptocurrencies, and convert varying legal environments in the travel sector.

Future of Crypto Travel

Crypto travel has a hopeful future that might absolutely modify the travel sector. As customer prejudices and technological development move forward to alter the areas, the way passengers plan, enjoy, and pay for their journeys will be substantially persuaded by cryptocurrencies and blockchain technology. A safe, energetic, and comprehensive crypto travel ecosystem is possible by the stakeholder committee and adaptable tricks, even though there may exist unfavourable regulations and security danger. Life-long allowance and transnational travel connection is made possible by the collaboration of cryptocurrencies, IoT, and AI. It will further initiate innovation and strengthen proficiencies with smart contracts.

Recommendations for Travelers, Travel Companies, and Policymakers

1. For Travelers:

    Being Aware: Observing keenly on the advantages and side effects of crypto travel and look deeper into the security and customer safety.
    Financial Planning: It is necessary to look into the instable cryptocurrency values, and hold on to various payment options while planning for trips.
    Secure Practices: Using promising wallets and forums for cryptocurrency transactions, and have private keys and individual information secure.

2. For Travel Companies:

    Integration: Admit cryptocurrency as a payment option in order to attract the crypto travellers and inherit benefits.

Operational Readiness: To agree easy cryptocurrency transactions and rejuvenate customer feedback, leads to firm system and consumer funding possessions.

Compliance and Security: Strengthened cybersecurity measures and providing translucent regulations help in maintaining trust of customers who use cryptocurrencies and trail legal necessities.

3. For Policymakers:

Regulatory Clarity: To stabilize the framework that takes care of consumer rights and monetary stability while imbibing reconstruction.

International Cooperation: To join hands with worldwide partners to regularize cryptocurrency laws, increase intercontinental trade, and the tourism industry's long-term development.

Innovation Support: To aid studies, pilot programs, and industry partnerships that disclose the assistance of blockchain technology and cryptocurrencies among tourists and development in the base of the travel society.

Conclusion

Motivated by customer yearning for digital solutions, legislative changes, and technology improvements, crypto travel denotes an advancement in the way travel transactions are carried out and practiced. Through solving obstacles, taking opportunities, and promoting cooperative initiatives, stakeholders may practice the innovatory impending of cryptocurrencies to inaugurate a travel ecosystem that is more inclusive, real, and long-lasting. Proactive involvement, creativity, and ethical management will be central in modeling a future where crypto travel mends experiences, lifts connectedness, and authorizes travelers.

REFERENCES

Antonopoulos, A. M. (2014). *Mastering Bitcoin: Unlocking digital cryptocurrencies*. O'Reilly Media.

Böhme, R., Christin, N., Edelman, B., & Moore, T. (2015). Bitcoin: Economics, technology, and governance. *The Journal of Economic Perspectives*, 29(2), 213–238. DOI: 10.1257/jep.29.2.213

Brown, J. R., & Floros, J. D. (2021). The emergence of cryptocurrency in tourism: A systematic review. *International Journal of Contemporary Hospitality Management*, 33(6), 1896–1927. DOI: 10.1108/IJCHM-01-2020-0108

Buterin, V. (2014). A next-generation smart contract and decentralized application platform: Ethereum. White paper. https://ethereum.org/en/whitepaper/

Cheah, E. T., & Fry, J. (2015). Speculative bubbles in Bitcoin markets? An empirical investigation into the fundamental value of Bitcoin. *Economics Letters*, 130, 32–36. DOI: 10.1016/j.econlet.2015.02.029

Deutsche Bank Research. (2020). Imagine 2030: Crypto's tipping point. Deutsche Bank. https://www.dbresearch.com/PROD/RPS_EN-PROD/PROD0000000000503192/Imagine_2030:_Crypto%27s_tipping_point.pdf

Fanning, K., & Centers, D. P. (2016). Blockchain and its coming impact on financial services. *Journal of Corporate Accounting & Finance*, 27(5), 53–57. DOI: 10.1002/jcaf.22179

Faria, J. R., & Vilela, A. S. (2020). Corporate social responsibility and the telecommunication sector: A systematic review. *Telematics and Informatics*, 49, 101366. DOI: 10.1016/j.tele.2020.101366

Gans, J. S., & Halaburda, H. (2018). Some economics of private digital currency. *The Journal of Economic Perspectives*, 31(4), 3–22. DOI: 10.1257/jep.31.4.3

Giudici, G., & Adhami, S. (2020). Decentralized finance (DeFi) and the future of banking. *Journal of Corporate Finance*, 67, 101876. DOI: 10.1016/j.jcorpfin.2020.101876

Grigg, I. (2005). Triple entry accounting. Ian Grigg. https://iang.org/papers/triple_entry.html

Gupta, A., Kondeti, S., & Deka, G. C. (2021). Blockchain technology and applications: A bibliometric study. *Journal of Industrial Integration and Management*, 6(4), 481–503. DOI: 10.5267/j.jiim.2020.11.006

Hileman, G., & Rauchs, M. (2017). Global cryptocurrency benchmarking study. Cambridge Centre for Alternative Finance. https://www.jbs.cam.ac.uk/faculty-research/centres/alternative-finance/publications/global-cryptocurrency/

Hoffmann, K., Ivanova, M., & Kubicek, B. (2020). The potentials of blockchain technology for governance. *Policy and Internet*, 12(3), 310–327. DOI: 10.1002/poi3.231

Karame, G. O., & Androulaki, E. (2016). Two Bitcoins at the price of one? Double-spending attacks on fast payments in Bitcoin. In *Proceedings of the 2012 ACM conference on Computer and communications security* (pp. 906-917). ACM. DOI: 10.1145/2976749.2978392

Khanna, V., & Sultania, A. (2021). Blockchain technology in travel and tourism: A systematic review. *Tourism Management Perspectives*, 37, 100796. DOI: 10.1016/j.tmp.2020.100796

Nakamoto, S. (2008). Bitcoin: A peer-to-peer electronic cash system. Bitcoin.org. https://bitcoin.org/bitcoin.pdf

O'Dwyer, K. J., & Malone, D. (2014). Bitcoin mining and its energy footprint. In Proceedings of the 25th IET Irish Signals & Systems Conference (ISSC 2014) (pp. 280-285). DOI: 10.1049/cp.2014.0699

Pilkington, M. (2015). *Blockchain technology: Principles and applications. Research Handbook on Digital Transformations*. Edward Elgar Publishing.

Ransbotham, S., & Mitra, S. (2018). Blockchain: What does it mean for consumers? *MIT Sloan Management Review*, 59(4), 1–6.

Rosenfeld, M. (2011). Overview of blockchain technology: Architecture and consensus algorithms. In *Financial Cryptography and Data Security* (pp. 507–527). Springer., DOI: 10.1007/978-3-642-19348-4_33

Sharma, R., & Maheshwari, P. (2021). Blockchain technology in supply chain management and business. *Operations and Supply Chain Management: An International Journal*, 14(1), 21–37. DOI: 10.31387/oscm058

Tapscott, D., & Tapscott, A. (2016). *Blockchain revolution: How the technology behind Bitcoin and other cryptocurrencies is changing the world*. Penguin Random House.

Tasca, P., Tessone, C. J., & Schweitzer, F. (2018). The evolution of the Bitcoin economy: Extracting and analyzing the network of payment relationships. *The Journal of Risk Finance*, 19(2), 94–126. DOI: 10.1108/JRF-03-2017-0059

Tschorsch, F., & Scheuermann, B. (2016). Bitcoin and beyond: A technical survey on decentralized digital currencies. *IEEE Communications Surveys and Tutorials*, 18(3), 2084–2123. DOI: 10.1109/COMST.2016.2535718

Yermack, D. (2015). Is Bitcoin a real currency? An economic appraisal. In *Handbook of digital currency: Bitcoin, innovation, financial instruments, and big data* (pp. 31–43). Academic Press. DOI: 10.1016/B978-0-12-802117-0.00002-3

Zohar, A. (2015). Bitcoin: Under the hood. *Communications of the ACM*, 58(9), 104–113. DOI: 10.1145/2701411

Compilation of References

A. Quinn, K., & A. Buzzetto-Hollywood, N. (2019). Faculty and Student Perceptions of the Importance of Management Skills in the Hospitality Industry. *Interdisciplinary Journal of E-Skills and Lifelong Learning*. https.//DOI: 10.28945/4198

Aaron, T. (2020, January 13). Marianna, Sigala. (2020). 2. Road block(chain): Bit(coin)s for tourism sustainable development goals? *Journal of Hospitality and Tourism Technology*, 11(2), 203–222. Advance online publication. DOI: 10.1108/JHTT-05-2019-0069

ABABNEH, M., & ALJARRAH, A. (2024). CYBERSECURITY: MALWARE MULTI-ATTACK DETECTOR ON ANDROID-BASED DEVICES USING DEEP LEARNING METHODS. *Journal of Theoretical and Applied Information Technology*, 102(1).

Abbas, S., Bouazzi, I., Ojo, S., Al Hejaili, A., Sampedro, G. A., Almadhor, A., & Gregus, M. (2024). Evaluating deep learning variants for cyber-attacks detection and multi-class classification in IoT networks. *PeerJ. Computer Science*, 10, e1793. DOI: 10.7717/peerj-cs.1793 PMID: 38259893

Abdalrdha, Z. K., Al-Bakry, A. M., & Farhan, A. K. (2023). A Survey on Cybercrime Using Social Media. *Iraqi Journal for Computers and Informatics*, 49(1), 52–65. DOI: 10.25195/ijci.v49i1.404

Abdulhussein, M. (2024). The Impact of Artificial Intelligence and Machine Learning on Organizations Cybersecurity.

Abebe, R., Barocas, S., Kleinberg, J., Levy, K., Raghavan, M., & Robinson, D. G. (2020, January). Roles for computing in social change. In *Proceedings of the 2020 conference on fairness, accountability, and transparency* (pp. 252-260). DOI: 10.1145/3351095.3372871

Afrifa, S., Varadarajan, V., Appiahene, P., & Zhang, T. (2023). Using Machine Learning to Classify Network Abnormalities into Legitimate or Assault in IoT-based Cyber Physical System. *Sensors and Electronic Instrumentation Advances*, 150.

AJ, B., & Kaythry, P. (2023). A Review of Deep Learning Strategies for Enhancing Cybersecurity in Networks.

Ajie, A. P., Wulandari, L. W., & Isdarmanto, I. (2024). Typological analysis of community participation for sustainable tourism in Sasak Ende Tourism Village. *Journal of Enterprise and Development*, 6(2), 355–365. DOI: 10.20414/jed.v6i2.9904

Alabdulkreem, E., Alotaibi, S. S., Alamgeer, M., Marzouk, R., Hilal, A. M., Motwakel, A., & Rizwanullah, M. (2023). Intelligent Cybersecurity Classification Using Chaos Game Optimization with Deep Learning Model. *Computer Systems Science and Engineering*, 45(1), 971–983. DOI: 10.32604/csse.2023.030362

Alain, B. (2019). 3. encointer — Local Community Crypto-currencies with Universal Basic Income. arXiv: Cryptography and Security

Alazab, M., Soman, K. P., Srinivasan, S., Venkatraman, S., & Pham, V. Q. (2023). Deep learning for cyber security applications: A comprehensive survey. *Authorea Preprints*.

Al-Bdairi, N., Al-Fakhri, L., & Al-Rawashdeh, H. (2020). Modeling Blockchain-Based IoT Systems using MG1 Queue. *International Journal of Advanced Computer Science and Applications*, 11(2), 306–312.

AL-Dosari, K., Fetais, N., & Kucukvar, M.AL-Dosari. (2024). Artificial intelligence and cyber defense system for banking industry: A qualitative study of AI applications and challenges. *Cybernetics and Systems*, 55(2), 302–330. DOI: 10.1080/01969722.2022.2112539

Al-Hasanat, B., & Faihan, M. (2018). Blockchain technology and the hospitality industry: a systematic study of its applications and challenges. In *2018 International Conference on Information and Communication Technology (ICOIACT)* (pp. 27-32). IEEE.

Ali, B., & Farooq, A. (2023, May). Ensemble Based AI Detector for Cyber Crimes. In *2023 6th International Conference on Electronics Technology (ICET)* (pp. 619-623). IEEE. DOI: 10.1109/ICET58434.2023.10211904

Ali, F., El-Sappagh, S., Islam, S. M. R., Kwak, D., Ali, A., Imran, M., & Kwak, K. S. (2020). A smart healthcare monitoring system for heart disease prediction based on ensemble deep learning and feature fusion. *Information Fusion*. https.// DOI: 10.1016/j.inffus.2020.06.008

Ali, H. H., Naif, J. R., & Humood, W. R. (2024, March). Deep learning algorithms for IoT security (survey). In *AIP Conference Proceedings* (Vol. 2885, No. 1). AIP Publishing.

Ali, M., Shahroz, M., Mushtaq, M. F., Alfarhood, S., Safran, M., & Ashraf, I. (2024). Hybrid Machine Learning Model for Efficient Botnet Attack Detection in IoT Environment. *IEEE Access : Practical Innovations, Open Solutions*, 12, 40682–40699. DOI: 10.1109/ACCESS.2024.3376400

Aljuhani, A., Kumar, P., Alanazi, R., Albalawi, T., Taouali, O., Islam, A. N., & Alazab, M. (2023). A deep learning integrated blockchain framework for securing industrial iot. *IEEE Internet of Things Journal.*

Al-Quayed, F., Ahmad, Z., & Humayun, M. (2024). A situation based predictive approach for cybersecurity intrusion detection and prevention using machine learning and deep learning algorithms in wireless sensor networks of industry 4.0. *IEEE Access : Practical Innovations, Open Solutions*, 12, 34800–34819. DOI: 10.1109/ACCESS.2024.3372187

Alrubayyi, H., Alshareef, M. S., Nadeem, Z., Abdelmoniem, A. M., & Jaber, M. (2024). Security Threats and Promising Solutions Arising from the Intersection of AI and IoT: A Study of IoMT and IoET Applications. *Future Internet*, 16(3), 85. DOI: 10.3390/fi16030085

Alruwaili, F. F. (2023). Optimal hybrid deep learning enabled attack detection and classification in IoT environment. *Computers, Materials & Continua*, 75(1), 99–115. DOI: 10.32604/cmc.2023.034752

Aluri, A., Price, B. S., & McIntyre, N. H. (2019). Using Machine Learning To Cocreate Value Through Dynamic Customer Engagement In A Brand Loyalty Program. *Journal of Hospitality & Tourism Research (Washington, D.C.)*, 43(1), 78–100. DOI: 10.1177/1096348017753521

Ambika, N. (2024). Early Detection of Darknet Traffic in Internet of Things Applications. *Automated Secure Computing for Next-Generation Systems*, 139-153.

Ameji, E. N., & Urah, S. P. (2024). The Role of Tourism in Promoting Inclusive Growth in Nigeria. *Asian Journal of Economics. Business and Accounting*, 24(8), 359–370. DOI: 10.9734/ajeba/2024/v24i81462

Andryushin, S. A. (2024). Tokenization of real assets: Classification, platforms, applications, opportunities and challenges of development. *Russian Journal of Economics and Law*, 18(1), 88–104. DOI: 10.21202/2782-2923.2024.1.88-104

Angelis, G. D., Tzikopoulos, R. Z., & Petrakis, P. C. (2019). A Framework for Blockchain-based Travel business process Management. In *Proceedings of the 2019 International Conference on Information Management and Processing (ICIMP)*.

Aniruddha Prabhu, B. P. R. D. (2023). A study of the challenges faced by the hotel sector with regards to cyber security. In R. D. B.P. Aniruddha Prabhu, *Automation and Computation* (p. 11).

Anis, G. M., Aboutabl, A. E., & Galal, A. (2023). MACHINE LEARNING FOR DETECTING CYBERCRIME IN THE BANKING SECTOR. *Journal of Southwest Jiaotong University*, 58(5).

Antonopoulos, A. M. (2014). *Mastering Bitcoin: Unlocking digital cryptocurrencies*. O'Reilly Media, Inc.

An, X., Luo, X., & Cui, B. (2020). Performance Analysis of MG1 Queue Based on Blockchain in Travel business process. In *Proceedings of the 2020 IEEE International Conference on Artificial Intelligence and Computer Applications (ICAICA)* (pp. 141-144).

Aramonte, S., Huang, W., & Schrimpf, A. (2021). *DeFi risks and the decentralisation illusion*. BIS Quarterly Review.

Aryee, D. (2020). *Cybersecurity Threats to The Hotel Industry and Mitigation Strategies*. Utica College. Retrieved from https://www.proquest.com/openview/64221b72cf1d4d9a39a0a17cbe763b25/1?pq-origsite=gscholar&cbl=18750&diss=y

Ashokkumar, P., & P, S. C. (2024). *Empowering Tea Tourism through Community Participation: A Conceptual Study*. https://doi.org/DOI: 10.31235/osf.io/r3wmv

Attaran, M., & Deb, P. (2018). Machine learning: The new'big thing'for competitive advantage. *International Journal of Knowledge Engineering and Data Mining*, 5(4), 277–305. DOI: 10.1504/IJKEDM.2018.095523

Avellaneda, O., Bachmann, A., Barbir, A., Brenan, J., Dingle, P., Duffy, K. H., Maler, E., Reed, D., & Sporny, M. (2019). Decentralized identity. Where did it come from and where is it going? *IEEE Communications Standards Magazine*, 3(4), 10–13. DOI: 10.1109/MCOMSTD.2019.9031542

Awa, H. O., Etim, W., & Ogbonda, E. (2024). Stakeholders, stakeholder theory and Corporate Social Responsibility (CSR). *International Journal of Corporate Social Responsibility*, 9(1), 11. DOI: 10.1186/s40991-024-00094-y

Awajan, A. (2023). A novel deep learning-based intrusion detection system for IOT networks. *Computers*, 12(2), 34. DOI: 10.3390/computers12020034

Aziz, L. A. R., & Andriansyah, Y. (2023). The Role Artificial Intelligence in Modern Banking: An Exploration of AI-Driven Approaches for Enhanced Fraud Prevention, Risk Management, and Regulatory Compliance. *Reviews of Contemporary Business Analytics*, 6(1), 110–132.

Azjen, I. (1988). *Attitudes, personality and behavior*. Open University Press.

B S, A. A., R, Dr. M., R P, S. M., & M, K. (2023). Web3 enhanced Insurance System using Ethereum Smart Contract. *International journal of scientific research in engineering and management, 07*(11), 1–11. DOI: 10.55041/IJSREM26736

Bachmann, N. M., Drasch, B., Fridgen, G., Miksch, M., Regner, F., Schweizer, A., & Urbach, N. (2022). Tarzan and chain: Exploring the ICO jungle and evaluating design archetypes. *Electronic Markets*, 32(3), 1707–1723. DOI: 10.1007/s12525-021-00463-6

Back, A. (2017). Using Blockchain for Digital Identity & Crypto Assets. Retrieved from medium.com/blockchain-review/self-sovereign-identity-and-the-digitization-of-realworld-assets-738e87dc530c

Bahrami, M., & Forouzanfar, M. (2022). Sleep Apnea Detection from Single-Lead ECG. A Comprehensive Analysis of Machine Learning and Deep Learning Algorithms. *IEEE Transactions on Instrumentation and Measurement*. https.//DOI: 10.1109/TIM.2022.3151947

Baker, D. J., & Robinson, P. H. (Eds.). (2020). *Artificial Intelligence and the Law: Cybercrime and Criminal Liability*. Routledge. DOI: 10.4324/9780429344015

Bakre, A., Patil, N., & Gupta, S. (2017). Implementing decentralized digital identity using blockchain. *International Journal of Engineering Technology Science and Research*, 4(10), 379–385.

Balasubramanian, S., Sethi, J. S., Ajayan, S., & Paris, C. M. (2022). An enabling Framework for Blockchain in Tourism. *Information Technology & Tourism*, 24(2), 165–179. Advance online publication. DOI: 10.1007/s40558-022-00229-6

Banerjee, S., & Banerjee, T. (2024). The Role and Importance of Metaverse and Blockchain Technology in the Tourism and Hospitality Industry: Adaptation of AI. In Talukder, M. B., Kumar, S., & Tyagi, P. K. (Eds.), *Advances in Hospitality, Tourism, and the Services Industry* (pp. 155–174). IGI Global., DOI: 10.4018/979-8-3693-6755-1.ch009

Banerji, D., Rashideh, W., Arora, B., & Pratihari, A. R. (2021). Application potential of Blockchain technologies in the travel and tourism industry. In *Blockchain Applications in IoT Ecosystem* (pp. 289–299). Springer International Publishing. DOI: 10.1007/978-3-030-65691-1_19

Bani Kinana, S. B., & Arabiat, O. (2024). Shedding Light on the Link: Salient Stakeholder Theory and Sustainability Connections. In Alshurafat, H., Hamdan, A., & Sands, J. (Eds.), *Sustainable Horizons for Business, Education, and Technology* (pp. 201–211). Springer Nature Singapore., DOI: 10.1007/978-981-97-2981-4_14

Bao, W., Xu, C., Zeng, X., & Zhang, Z. (2019). Modeling and Analysis of Blockchain Systems with MG1 Queues. *IEEE Transactions on Network Science and Engineering*, 7(4), 3062–3072.

Bao, Y., Hilary, G., & Ke, B. (2022). Artificial intelligence and fraud detection. *Innovative Technology at the Interface of Finance and Operations*, I, 223–247. DOI: 10.1007/978-3-030-75729-8_8

Bardhan, I., Chen, H., & Karahanna, E. (2020). Connecting systems, data, and people. A multidisciplinary research roadmap for chronic disease management. In *MIS Quarterly. Management Information Systems*. https.//DOI: <ALIGNMENT.qj></ALIGNMENT>10.25300/MISQ/2020/14644

Barik, K., Misra, S., Ray, A. K., & Sukla, A. (2023). A blockchain-based evaluation approach to analyse customer satisfaction using AI techniques. *Heliyon*, 9(6), e16766. DOI: 10.1016/j.heliyon.2023.e16766 PMID: 37292278

Barocas, S., Hardt, M., & Narayanan, A. (2023). *Fairness and machine learning: Limitations and opportunities*. MIT Press.

Bashir, I. (2018). *Mastering Blockchain:Distributed Ledger Technology,Decentralization,and Smart Contracts Explained*. Packt Publishing Ltd.

Batwa, A., & Norrman, A. (2021). Blockchain Technology and Trust in Supply Chain Management: A Literature Review and Research Agenda. *OPERATIONS AND SUPPLY CHAIN MANAGEMENT*, 14(2), 203–220. DOI: 10.31387/oscm0450297

Behiry, M. H., & Aly, M. (2024). Cyberattack detection in wireless sensor networks using a hybrid feature reduction technique with AI and machine learning methods. *Journal of Big Data*, 11(1), 16. DOI: 10.1186/s40537-023-00870-w

Bellos, K. (2024). The implementation and use of new technologies in the hospitality industry towards a sustainable future.

Ben, V. (2020). 1. Blockchain in travel. *Journal of Revenue and Pricing Management*, 19(1), 2–6. Advance online publication. DOI: 10.1057/s41272-019-00213-6

Berk, R., Heidari, H., Jabbari, S., Kearns, M., & Roth, A. (2021). Fairness in criminal justice risk assessments: The state of the art. *Sociological Methods & Research*, 50(1), 3–44. DOI: 10.1177/0049124118782533

Berry, L. L. (1983). Relationship marketing. In Berry, L. L., Shostack, G. L., & Upah, G. D. (Eds.), *Emerging Perspectives on Services Marketing*.

Bhatt, H., Jadav, N. K., Kumari, A., Gupta, R., Tanwar, S., Polkowski, Z., Tolba, A., & Hassanein, A. S. (2024). Artificial neural network-driven federated learning for heart stroke prediction in healthcare 4.0 underlying 5G. *Concurrency and Computation*, 36(3), e7911. DOI: 10.1002/cpe.7911

Bhuvaneshwari, A. J., & Kaythry, P. (2023). A Review of Deep Learning Strategies for Enhancing Cybersecurity in Networks: DEEP LEARNING STRATEGIES FOR ENHANCING CYBERSECURITY. [JSIR]. *Journal of Scientific and Industrial Research*, 82(12), 1316–1330.

Bingjie, Liu., William, C., Norman. (2016). 4. Developing a conceptual framework to understand local residents' contribution in online travel communities

Blanco, M. (2024, FEBURARY 14). Cyber Security Is Awakening as Key Concern for Hoteliers. Retrieved from https://www.costar.com/article/804855050/cyber-security-is-awakening-as-key-concern-for-hoteliers

Böhme, R., Christin, N., Edelman, B., & Moore, T. (2015). Bitcoin: Economics, technology, and governance. *The Journal of Economic Perspectives*, 29(2), 213–238. DOI: 10.1257/jep.29.2.213

Bonneau, J., Miller, A., Clark, J., Narayanan, A., Kroll, J. A., & Felten, E. W. (2015). SoK: Research perspectives and challenges for Bitcoin and cryptocurrencies. In *2015 IEEE Symposium on Security and Privacy* (pp. 104-121). IEEE. DOI: 10.1109/SP.2015.14

Bradeško, L., & Mladenić, D. (2012). A Survey of Chatbot Systems through a Loebner Prize Competition. *Proceedings of Slovenian Language Technologies Society Eighth Conference of Language Technologies, 2*(January 2012), 34–37. http.//nl.ijs.si/isjt12/proceedings/isjt2012_06.pdf

Bromberg, D. E., Charbonneau, É., & Smith, A. (2020). Public support for facial recognition via police body-worn cameras: Findings from a list experiment. *Government Information Quarterly*, 37(1), 101415. Advance online publication. DOI: 10.1016/j.giq.2019.101415

Brotcke, L. (2022). Time to assess bias in machine learning models for credit decisions. *Journal of Risk and Financial Management*, 15(4), 165. DOI: 10.3390/jrfm15040165

Brown, E. A., Thomas, N. J., & Bosselman, R. H. (2015). Are they leaving or staying. A qualitative analysis of turnover issues for Generation Y hospitality employees with a hospitality education. *International Journal of Hospitality Management*. https.// DOI: 10.1016/j.ijhm.2015.01.011

Brown, A., & Miller, C. (2021). Interoperability in Blockchain Technology: Challenges and Opportunities. *Journal of Information Systems*, 25(3), 127–142.

Brown, J. R., & Floros, J. D. (2021). The emergence of cryptocurrency in tourism: A systematic review. *International Journal of Contemporary Hospitality Management*, 33(6), 1896–1927. DOI: 10.1108/IJCHM-01-2020-0108

Bui, H. T., Aboutorab, H., Mahboubi, A., Gao, Y., Sultan, N. H., Chauhan, A., Parvez, M. Z., Bewong, M., Islam, R., Islam, Z., Camtepe, S. A., Gauravaram, P., Singh, D., Ali Babar, M., & Yan, S. (2024). Agriculture 4.0 and Beyond: Evaluating Cyber Threat Intelligence Sources and Techniques in Smart Farming Ecosystems. *Computers & Security*, 140, 103754. DOI: 10.1016/j.cose.2024.103754

Bulchand-Gidumal, J. (2020). *Impact of Artificial Intelligence in Travel*. Tourism, and Hospitality., DOI: 10.1007/978-3-030-05324-6_110-1

Buterin, V. (2014). A next-generation smart contract and decentralized application platform: Ethereum. White paper. https://ethereum.org/en/whitepaper/

Buterin, V. (2014). Ethereum: A next-generation smart contract and decentralized application platform. Retrieved from https://ethereum.org/ethereum/

Buterin, V., & Griffith, V. (2017). Casper the friendly finality gadget. arXiv preprint arXiv:1710.09437.

Buttle, F., & Maklan, S. (2015). *Customer Relationship Management: Concepts and Technologies*. Routledge. DOI: 10.4324/9781315764597

C., C., & Demicco, F. (2007). To Be Secure or Not to Be: Isn't This the Question?A Critical Look at Hotel's Network Security. *International Journal of Hospitality & Tourism Administration, 8*(1), 43-59. DOI: 10.1300/J149v08n01_03

Cachin, C. (2016). Architecture of the Hyperledger blockchain fabric. Workshop on distributed cryptocurrencies and consensus ledgers, 18(29), 3-9.

Cao, D. M., Sayed, M. A., Islam, M. T., Mia, M. T., Ayon, E. H., Ghosh, B. P., & Raihan, A. (2024). Advanced Cybercrime Detection: A Comprehensive Study on Supervised and Unsupervised Machine Learning Approaches Using Real-world Datasets. *Journal of Computer Science and Technology Studies*, 6(1), 40–48. DOI: 10.32996/jcsts.2024.6.1.5

Cao, L., Yang, Q., & Yu, P. S. (2021). Data science and AI in FinTech: An overview. *International Journal of Data Science and Analytics*, 12(2), 81–99. DOI: 10.1007/s41060-021-00278-w

Catalini, C., & Gans, J. S. (2016). Some simple economics of the blockchain. MIT Sloan Research Paper, (5191-16).

Catalini, C., & Gans, J. S. (2016). Some Simple Economics of the Blockchain. *National Bureau of Economic Research*. https.//DOI: 10.3386/w22952

Chang, M., Walimuni, A. C. S. M., Kim, M., & Lim, H. (2022a). Acceptance of tourism blockchain based on UTAUT and connectivism theory. *Technology in Society*, 71, 102027. Advance online publication. DOI: 10.1016/j.techsoc.2022.102027

Chaouk, M., Pagliari, R., & Miyoshi, C. (2019). A critical review of airport privatisation in the Kingdom of Saudi Arabia: Case study of Medina Airport. *Case Studies on Transport Policy*, 7(2), 433–442. DOI: 10.1016/j.cstp.2019.02.001

Chatkaewnapanon, Y., & Kelly, J. M. (2019). Community arts as an inclusive methodology for sustainable tourism development. *Journal of Place Management and Development*, 12(3), 365–390. DOI: 10.1108/JPMD-09-2017-0094

Cheah, E.-T., & Fry, J. (2015). Speculative bubbles in Bitcoin markets? An empirical investigation into the fundamental value of Bitcoin. *Economics Letters, 130*, 32-36. https.//DOI: 10.1016/j.econlet.2015.02.029

Chen, C. J., & Huang, J. W. (2009). Strategic human resource practices and innovation performance - The mediating role of knowledge management capacity. *Journal of Business Research*. https.//DOI: 10.1016/j.jbusres.2007.11.016

Chen, H. 'This world-class airport will soon go passport-free', CNN, September, 2023. https.//edition.cnn.com/travel/article/changi-airport-singapore-passport-free-travel-intl-hnk/index.html#.~.text=Starting%20in%202024%2C%20officials%20say,passports%2C%20using%20only%20biometric%20data

Cheng, N. T. Y., Fong, L. H. N., & Law, R. (2021). Mobile payment technology in hospitality and tourism: A critical review through the lens of demand, supply and policy. *International Journal of Contemporary Hospitality Management*, 33(10), 3636–3660. DOI: 10.1108/IJCHM-02-2021-0261

Cheng, X., Liu, S., Sun, X., Wang, Z., Zhou, H., Shao, Y., & Shen, H. (2021). Combating emerging financial risks in the big data era: A perspective review. *Fundamental Research (Beijing)*, 1(5), 595–606. DOI: 10.1016/j.fmre.2021.08.017

Chen, H. S., & Fiscus, J. (2018). The inhospitable vulnerability: A need for cybersecurity risk assessment in the hospitality industry. *Journal of Hospitality and Tourism Technology*, 9(2), 223–234. Advance online publication. DOI: 10.1108/JHTT-07-2017-0044

Chen, I. J., & Popovich, K. (2003). Understanding customer relationship management (CRM): People, process and technology. *Business Process Management Journal*, 9(5), 672–688. DOI: 10.1108/14637150310496758

Chen, X., Wu, Z., & Zhang, L. (2022). Performance Evaluation of MG1 Queue in Blockchain for Travel business process Optimization. *International Journal of Business Blockchain*, 4(1), 78–95.

Chen, X., Xu, J., Li, X., & Li, J. (2021). Performance Analysis of MG1 Queue in Blockchain-Based Travel business process Management Systems. *Journal of Computer Research and Development*, 58(4), 831–838.

Chen, Z., Li, Y., & Yang, S. (2022). Analysis of MG1 queue in blockchain for decentralized workflow management in travel business processes. *Journal of Blockchain and Distributed Ledger Technologies*, 5(1), 26–41.

Chen, Z., Li, Y., & Yang, S. (2022). Analysis of MG1 Queue in Blockchain for Decentralized Workflow Management in Travel business processes. *Journal of Blockchain Applications*, 4(1), 52–69.

Chen, Z., Van Khoa, L. D., Teoh, E. N., Nazir, A., Karuppiah, E. K., & Lam, K. S. (2018). Machine learning techniques for anti-money laundering (AML) solutions in suspicious transaction detection: A review. *Knowledge and Information Systems*, 57(2), 245–285. DOI: 10.1007/s10115-017-1144-z

Chhabra, A. S., Choudhury, T., Srivastava, A. V., & Aggarwal, A. (2017, December). Prediction for big data and IoT in 2017. In *2017 International Conference on Infocom Technologies and Unmanned Systems (Trends and Future Directions) (ICTUS)* (pp. 181-187). IEEE.

Chiller-Glaus, S. D., Schwaninger, A., & Hofer, F. (2007, October). Identity verification from photographs in travel documents. The role of display duration and orientation on performance. [). Sage CA. Los Angeles, CA. SAGE Publications.]. *Proceedings of the Human Factors and Ergonomics Society Annual Meeting*, 51(19), 1327–1330. DOI: 10.1177/154193120705101910

Chohan, M. N., Haider, U., Ayub, M. Y., Shoukat, H., Bhatia, T. K., & Hassan, M. F. U. (2023). Detection of Cyber Attacks using Machine Learning based Intrusion Detection System for IoT Based Smart Cities. *EAI Endorsed Transactions on Smart Cities*, 7(2), e4–e4.

Chowdhury, S., Rodriguez-Espindola, O., Dey, P., & Budhwar, P. (2023). Blockchain technology adoption for managing risks in operations and supply chain management: Evidence from the UK. *Annals of Operations Research*, 327(1), 539–574. DOI: 10.1007/s10479-021-04487-1 PMID: 34629606

Christidis, K., & Devetsikiotis, M. (2016). Blockchains and Smart Contracts for the Internet of Things. *IEEE Access : Practical Innovations, Open Solutions*, 4, 2292–2303. DOI: 10.1109/ACCESS.2016.2566339

Cobanoglu, C. Dr. Seden Dogan, Dr. Katerina Berezina, & Dr. Galen Collins. (2021). Blockchain in the Hospitality and Tourism Industry. *Hospitality and Tourism Information Technology*. https://scholarcommons.usf.edu/m3publishing/vol17/iss9781732127593/

Collins, C. J., & Clark, K. D. (2003). Strategic human resource practices, top management team social networks, and firm performance. The role of human resource practices in creating organizational competitive advantage. In *Academy of Management Journal*. https.//DOI: 10.2307/30040665

Costa, M. B., & Sofikitis, D. (2024). Applying Deep Learning and Data Analytics to identify Malware Attacks.

Cronbach, L. J. (1951). Coefficient alpha and the internal structure of tests. *Psychometrika*, 16(3), 297–334. DOI: 10.1007/BF02310555

Dabban, M.A., Abdullahi, M.B., Adepoju, S.A. and Ojerinde, O.A., 2023. A framework for Identity Verification Management System using Blockchain for International Travel.

Daft, R. L. (2008). *Organization Design and Theory*.

Dahlqvist, P., O'Leary, B., & Serrano, A. (2020). *The Hospitality Industry and Blockchain*. In Springer International Publishing.

Dasari, S., & Kaluri, R. (2024). An Effective Classification of DDoS Attacks in a Distributed Network by Adopting Hierarchical Machine Learning and Hyperparameters Optimization Techniques. *IEEE Access : Practical Innovations, Open Solutions*, 12, 10834–10845. DOI: 10.1109/ACCESS.2024.3352281

Dash, B., Sharma, P., & Ali, A. (2022). Federated learning for privacy-preserving: A review of PII data analysis in Fintech. [IJSEA]. *International Journal of Software Engineering and Its Applications*, 13(4).

Das, P. (2023). Technology and Guest Experience: Innovations Reshaping Hotel Management. *International Journal for Multidimensional Research Perspectives*, 1(3), 76–95.

Das, S., Balmiki, A. K., Mazumdar, K., & Bhowmick, P. (2023). Cyber-Physical Security Issues and Challenges Using Machine Learning and Deep Learning Technologies. In *Artificial Intelligence in Cyber-Physical Systems* (pp. 105–123). CRC Press. DOI: 10.1201/9781003248750-7

Daugherty, P. R., & Wilson, H. J. (2018). *Human+ machine: Reimagining work in the age of AI*. Harvard Business Press.

Davenport, T. H., Harris, J. G., & Kohli, A. K. (2001). How do they know their customers so well? *MIT Sloan Management Review*.

Davenport, T. H., & Kalakota, R. (2019). The potential for blockchain to transform electronic health records. *Harvard Business Review*.

David W. Chadwick, Romain Laborde, Arnaud Oglaza, Remi Venant, Samer Wazan, and Manreet Nijjar. Improved identity management with verifiable credentials and FIDO. IEEE Communications Standards Magazine, 3(4).14–20, December 2019.

de Koning Gans, G., & De Vries, P. (2018). Blockchain in Hospitality: Empowerment through Encryption. In The Impact of Blockchain Technology on Value Chains (pp. 175-192).

Demir, B., & Serkan, A. (2024). Cyber Vigilantes: A Deep Dive into the Art and Science of Digital Defense. *Integrated Journal of Science and Technology, 1*(2).

Demirciftci, T., Chen, C., & Erdem, M. (2020). A tabulation of information technology and consumer behavior in hospitality revenue management research. *Journal of Hospitality and Tourism Technology*, 11(3), 575–587. DOI: 10.1108/JHTT-02-2019-0018

Deng, S., Huang, L., & Zhou, J. (2019). Blockchain Technology and Its Applications in Business. In *Proceedings of the 2019 IEEE International Conference on Advanced Manufacturing (ICAM)*.

Der, U., Jähnichen, S., & Sürmeli, J. 2017. Self-sovereign identity $-$ opportunities and challenges for the digital revolution. *arXiv preprint arXiv.1712.01767.*

Deutsche Bank Research. (2020). Imagine 2030: Crypto's tipping point. Deutsche Bank. https://www.dbresearch.com/PROD/RPS_EN-PROD/PROD0000000000503192/Imagine_2030:_Crypto%27s_tipping_point.pdf

Devan, A. M., Raghul, V., Dhasmana, U., Rath, A., & Jacob, L. (2024). 6 Deep Support Learning Model Decision for Police Investigation. *Artificial Intelligence for Cyber Defense and Smart Policing*, 76.

Dey, S., & Gupta, P. (2024). Balancing conservation and tourism: A comprehensive study on responsible tourism practices in Kaziranga, with a focus on food tourism. *International Journal of Geography. Geology and Environment*, 6(1), 279–289. DOI: 10.22271/27067483.2024.v6.i1d.234

Dhiraj, A., Kumar, S., Rani, D., Grima, S., & Sood, K. (2023). Blockchain Payment Services in the Hospitality Sector: The Mediating Role of Data Security on Utilisation Efficiency of the Customer. *Data*, 8(8), 123. Advance online publication. DOI: 10.3390/data8080123

Dhoni, P., & Kumar, R. (2023). Synergizing generative ai and cybersecurity: Roles of generative ai entities, companies, agencies, and government in enhancing cybersecurity. *Authorea Preprints*.

Dias, S., & Afonso, V. (2021). Impact of Mobile Applications in Changing the Tourist Experience. European Journal of Tourism. *Hospitality and Recreation.*, 11(1), 113–120. DOI: 10.2478/ejthr-2021-0011

Dib, O., & Toumi, K. (2020). *Decentralized identity systems. Architecture, challenges, solutions and future directions. Annals of Emerging Technologies in Computing (AETiC)*. Print ISSN.

din, S. M. U., Sharma, R., Rizvi, F., & Sharma, N. (2024). Detection of botnet in IoT network through machine learning based optimized feature importance via ensemble models. *International Journal of Information Technology, 16*(2), 1203-1211.

Ding, K., Niu, Y., & Choo, W. C. (2023, June 8). The evolution of Airbnb research: A systematic literature review using structural topic modeling. *Heliyon*, 9(6), e17090. DOI: 10.1016/j.heliyon.2023.e17090 PMID: 37484274

Diwan Chand & Jawahar Thakur. (2023). *Blockchain-Based Architecture And Smart Contract For E-Voting*. Unpublished. DOI: 10.13140/RG.2.2.19636.22403

Djenna, A., Barka, E., Benchikh, A., & Khadir, K. (2023). Unmasking Cybercrime with Artificial-Intelligence-Driven Cybersecurity Analytics. *Sensors (Basel)*, 23(14), 6302. DOI: 10.3390/s23146302 PMID: 37514596

Dogru, B. T., Mody, M., Leonardi, C., Dogru, T., Mody, M., & Leonardi, C. (2018). Blockchain Technology & its Implications for the Hospitality Industry. *Boston Hospitality Review*, (Winter), 1–12.

Domínguez Vila, Trinidad & Araújo, Noelia & Brea, José Antonio & Alén, Elisa. (2017). Tourism Search and Metasearch Engines for Online Booking:. .DOI: 10.4018/978-1-5225-1054-3.ch003

Dorri, A., Kanhere, S. S., & Jurdak, R. (2017). Blockchain in Internet of Things: Challenges and Solutions. In *Proceedings of the 2017 International Conference on Information Networking (ICOIN)* (pp. 129-134).

Drescher, D. (2018). Blockchain Basics: A Non-Technical Introduction in 25 Steps. Apress. Iansiti, M., & Lakhani, K. R. (2017). The truth about blockchain. *Harvard Business Review*, 95(1), 118–127.

Duan, J., Kang, L., Chen, Z., Peng, T., & Wang, Y. (2020). A photo-sharing social network based on blockchain technology. *International Journal of Technology Management*, 84(1/2), 70–85. DOI: 10.1504/IJTM.2020.112078

Duan, Y., & Cui, X. (2021). Analysis of the Performance of MG1 Queue Based on Blockchain for Business Applications. In *Proceedings of the 2021 IEEE International Conference on Cloud Computing and Big Data Analytics (ICCCBDA)* (pp. 25-29).

Dudás, G., Boros, L., & Vida, G. (2017). Comparing the temporal changes of airfares on online travel agency websites and metasearch engines. *Tourism (Zagreb)*, 65, 187–203.

Dutta, P., Choi, T., Somani, S., & Butala, R. (2020). Since January 2020 Elsevier has created a COVID-19 resource centre with free information in English and Mandarin on the novel coronavirus COVID- 19. The COVID-19 resource centre is hosted on Elsevier Connect, the company ' s public news and information. *Transportation Research*, 4(1), 1–33.

Ebarefimia, S. (2017). Impact Of Blockchain Technology In Enhancing Customer Loyalty Programs In Airline Business. *International Journal of Innovative Research and Advanced Studies*, 4(6), 257–263. http://www.ijiras.com/2017/Vol_4-Issue_6/paper_44.pdf

Ekblaw, A., Azaria, A., Halamka, J. D., & Lippman, A. (2016). A case study for blockchain in healthcare:"MedRec" prototype for electronic health records and medical research data. In Proceedings of IEEE open & big data conference.

El Archi, Y., Benbba, B., Dávid, L. D., & Cardoso, L. (Eds.). (2024). *Promoting Responsible Tourism With Digital Platforms*. IGI Global., DOI: 10.4018/979-8-3693-3286-3

Elhaj, M. (2012). Preferences for Online vs. Traditional Travel Reservation. *Asean Journal of Hospitality and Tourist.*, 10(2), 100–109. DOI: 10.5614/ajht.2011.10.2.03

Elluri, L., Mandalapu, V., Vyas, P., & Roy, N. (2023). Recent Advancements in Machine Learning for Cybercrime Prediction. *Journal of Computer Information Systems*, •••, 1–15. DOI: 10.1080/08874417.2023.2270457

Eloranta, S., & Boman, M. (2022). Predictive models for clinical decision making. Deep dives in practical machine learning. *Journal of Internal Medicine, 292*(2), 278–295. https.//DOI: 10.1111/joim.13483

Emmanuel, I. E., & Damachi, G. U. (2015). *Employees' Participation in Decision Making and the Hospitality Industry in Nigeria. An Investigative Study of Selected Hotels in the Federal Capital Territory*. Academic Journal of Economic Studies.

Erol, I., & Neuhofer, I. O., Dogru (Dr. True), T., Oztel, A., Searcy, C., & Yorulmaz, A. C. (. (2022). Improving sustainability in the tourism industry through blockchain technology: Challenges and opportunities. *Tourism Management*, 93. Advance online publication. DOI: 10.1016/j.tourman.2022.104628

Escorcia-Gutierrez, J., Gamarra, M., Leal, E., Madera, N., Soto, C., Mansour, R. F., Alharbi, M., Alkhayyat, A., & Gupta, D. (2023). Sea turtle foraging algorithm with hybrid deep learning-based intrusion detection for the internet of drones environment. *Computers & Electrical Engineering*, 108, 108704. DOI: 10.1016/j.compeleceng.2023.108704

Escudeiro, N., Escudeiro, P., Cunha, B., & Gouveia, M. C. (2023). Inclusive Cultural Heritage Tourism. In Abreu, A., Carvalho, J. V., Liberato, D., & Galdames, I. S. (Eds.), *Advances in Tourism, Technology and Systems* (Vol. 340, pp. 207–217). Springer Nature Singapore., DOI: 10.1007/978-981-19-9960-4_19

European Commission. (2016). General Data Protection Regulation (GDPR). Retrieved from https://eur-lex.europa.eu/legal-content/EN/TXT/PDF/?uri=CELEX:32016R0679

Fahad Binhowemel, S., Alfakhri, M. O., Alreshaid, K. M., & Alyani, A. M. (2023). The Role of Artificial Intelligence in Diabetes Research, Diagnosis and Prognosis. A Narrative Review. [http.//www.jhidc.org/]. *Journal of Health Informatics in Developing Countries*, 17(2), 2023.

Falwadiya, H., & Dhingra, S. (2022). Blockchain technology adoption in government organizations: A systematic literature review. *J. Global Oper. Strat. Sourcing*, 15(3), 473–501. DOI: 10.1108/JGOSS-09-2021-0079

Fan, Y., Long, E., Cai, L., Cao, Q., Wu, X., & Tong, R. (2021). Machine Learning Approaches to Predict Risks of Diabetic Complications and Poor Glycemic Control in Nonadherent Type 2 Diabetes. *Frontiers in Pharmacology*. https.//DOI: 10.3389/fphar.2021.665951

Fanning, K., & Centers, D. P. (2016). Blockchain and its coming impact on financial services. *Journal of Corporate Accounting & Finance*, 27(5), 53–57. DOI: 10.1002/jcaf.22179

Faria, J. R., & Vilela, A. S. (2020). Corporate social responsibility and the telecommunication sector: A systematic review. *Telematics and Informatics*, 49, 101366. DOI: 10.1016/j.tele.2020.101366

Fauziah, Z., Latifah, H., Omar, X., Khoirunisa, A., & Millah, S. (2020). Application of blockchain technology in smart contracts: A systematic literature review. [ATT]. *Aptisi Transactions on Technopreneurship*, 2(2), 160–166. DOI: 10.34306/att.v2i2.97

Fernández, A. S. (2022). *BACHELOR ' S THESIS Blockchain in the hospitality industry : Identifying main applications Blockchain in the hospitality industry : Identifying main applications Antonio Salamanca Fernández Bachelor ' s Thesis Faculty of Tourism University of the Balearic Islands*.

Field, A. (2009). *Discovering statistics using spss*. sage.

Filimonau, V., & Naumova, E. (2020). The blockchain technology and the scope of its application in hospitality operations. *International Journal of Hospitality Management*, 87, 102383. DOI: 10.1016/j.ijhm.2019.102383

Firdous, S., Imran, M., Ullah, Z., & Zia, M. Q. (2020). Performance Analysis of Blockchain-Based Cloud Storage Systems using MG1 Queue. *IEEE Access : Practical Innovations, Open Solutions*, 8, 18081–18091.

Firoj, K., & Mohammad, B. T. (2024). Measuring sustainability in the broadcasting media industry in Bangladesh. *I-Manager's. Journal of Management*, 18(3), 51. DOI: 10.26634/jmgt.18.3.20234

Fjermestad, J., & Romano, N. C.Jr. (2003). Electronic customer relationship management: Revisiting the general principles of usability and resistance – an integrative implementation framework. *Business Process Management Journal*, 9(5), 572–591. DOI: 10.1108/14637150310496695

Fornell, C., & Larcker, D. F. (1981). Evaluating structural equation models with unobservable variables and measurement error. *JMR, Journal of Marketing Research*, XVIII(February), 39–50. DOI: 10.1177/002224378101800104

Forsström, S. (2018). Blockchain. *Research Reports (Montgomery)*, (December), 1–12.

Fragniere, E., & Yagci, K. (2021). Key Terms: a Glimpse Into the World of Cyber-Attacks. In E. Fragniere, & K. Yagci, *Network & cyber security in Hospitality and Tourism* (p. 23). South Florida: USF M3 Publishing. doi:https://www.doi.org/10.5038/9781732127593

Gabriel Raicu, A. R. (2022, DECEMBER 20). CYBERSECURITY STRATEGIES IN INDUSTRY 4.0. *International Journal of Modern Manufacturing Technologies*. DOI: 10.54684/ijmmt.2022.14.3.233

Gangula, R., Vutukuru, M. M., & Kumar, R. (2024). Hybridization of Bottlenose Dolphin Optimization and Artificial Fish Swarm Algorithm with Efficient Classifier for Detecting the Network Intrusion in Internet of Things (IoT). *International Journal of Intelligent Systems and Applications in Engineering*, 12(6s), 220–232.

Ganji, K., & Afshan, N. (2024). A bibliometric review of Internet of Things (IoT) on cybersecurity issues. *Journal of Science and Technology Policy Management*.

Gans, J. S., & Halaburda, H. (2018). Some economics of private digital currency. *The Journal of Economic Perspectives*, 31(4), 3–22. DOI: 10.1257/jep.31.4.3

García, G., Dos Anjos, S., & Doğan, S.GARCİA. (2021). Online Travel Agencies and Their Role in the Tourism Industry. [AHTR]. *Advances in Hospitality and Tourism Research*, 10(3), 361–386. Advance online publication. DOI: 10.30519/ahtr.865546

Garcia, L., Martinez, E., & Perez, R. (2022). Scalability Solutions for Blockchain: A Comprehensive Review. *International Journal of Blockchain Applications*, 6(1), 45–61.

Garg, G., Sharma, S., Choudhury, T., & Kumar, P. (2017, August). Crop productivity based on IoT. In *2017 International Conference On Smart Technologies For Smart Nation (SmartTechCon)* (pp. 223-226). IEEE.

Gervais, A., Karame, G. O., Wüst, K., & Capkun, S. (2016). On the security and performance of proof of work blockchains. In *Proceedings of the 2016 ACM SIGSAC Conference on Computer and Communications Security* (pp. 3-16). DOI: 10.1145/2976749.2978341

Ghazaleh, M. A., & Zabadi, A. M. (2021). BlockChain (BC) Upending Customer Experience: Promoting a New Customer Relationship Management (CRM) Structure Using Blockchain Technology (BCT). *Journal of Management and Sustainability*, 11(1), 203. DOI: 10.5539/jms.v11n1p203

Gipp, B., Meuschke, N., & Gernandt, A. (2018). Decentralized trusted timestamping using the crypto currency bitcoin. In *Proceedings of the 11th International Conference on Availability, Reliability and Security (ARES)* (pp. 1-10).

Gislainy, Laise, da, Silva., Luiz, Mendes, Filho. (2024). 5. Proposição de Fatores que influenciam o uso de Criptomoedas para Pagamento de Serviços Turísticos: Uma Revisão Sistemática da Literatura e Bibliometria. DOI: 10.18226/21789061.v16i1p140

Giudici, G., & Adhami, S. (2020). Decentralized finance (DeFi) and the future of banking. *Journal of Corporate Finance*, 67, 101876. DOI: 10.1016/j.jcorpfin.2020.101876

Glaser, F. (2017). Pervasive decentralisation of digital infrastructures: A framework for blockchain enabled system and use case analysis. Journal of Peer Production, 9.

Goodell, G., & Aste, T. (2019). A decentralized digital identity architecture. *Frontiers in Blockchain*, 2, 491305. DOI: 10.3389/fbloc.2019.00017

Gray, J., & Rumpe, B. (2015). Models for Digitalization. *Software & Systems Modeling*, 4(4), 1319–1320. DOI: 10.1007/s10270-015-0494-9

Greenberg, P. (2010). The impact of CRM 2.0 on customer insight. *Journal of Business and Industrial Marketing*, 25(6), 410–419. DOI: 10.1108/08858621011066008

Gretzel, U., & Yoo, K.-H. (2008). Use and Impact of Online Travel Reviews. *Information and Communication Technologies in Tourism*, 2008, 35–46. DOI: 10.1007/978-3-211-77280-5_4

Grigg, I. (2005). Triple entry accounting. Ian Grigg. https://iang.org/papers/triple_entry.html

Grimm, P. W., Grossman, M. R., & Cormack, G. V. (2021). Artificial intelligence as evidence. *Nw. J. Tech. & Intell. Prop.*, 19, 9.

Grobelna, A. (2015). Intercultural Challenges Facing the Hospitality Industry. Implications for Education and Hospitality Management. *Journal of Intercultural Management*. https.//DOI: 10.1515/joim-2015-0023

Guan, Z., Li, H., Liu, R., Cai, C., Liu, Y., Li, J., Wang, X., Huang, S., Wu, L., Liu, D., Yu, S., Wang, Z., Shu, J., Hou, X., Yang, X., Jia, W., & Sheng, B. (2023). Artificial intelligence in diabetes management. Advancements, opportunities, and challenges. In *Cell Reports Medicine*. https.//DOI: 10.1016/j.xcrm.2023.101213

Guizzardi, A., Pons, F., Angelini, G., & Ranieri, E. (2020). Big data from dynamic pricing: A smart approach to tourism demand forecasting. *International Journal of Forecasting*, 37(3), 1049–1060. Advance online publication. DOI: 10.1016/j.ijforecast.2020.11.006

Guleria, A., Krishan, K., Sharma, V., & Kanchan, T. (2024). *Global adoption of facial recognition technology with special reference to India—Present status and future recommendations*. Medicine, Science and the Law/Medicine, Science and the Law., DOI: 10.1177/00258024241227717

Gunavathi, R., & Bharathi, K. M. (2024). 2 Cybercrimes in the. *Artificial Intelligence for Cyber Defense and Smart Policing*, 21.

Gupta, A., Kondeti, S., & Deka, G. C. (2021). Blockchain technology and applications: A bibliometric study. *Journal of Industrial Integration and Management*, 6(4), 481–503. DOI: 10.5267/j.jiim.2020.11.006

Gupta, C. P., & Kumar, V. R. (2022, June). Artificial Intelligence and Internet of Things: Revolutionizing the implementation of Customer Relationship Management. In *2022 ASU International Conference in Emerging Technologies for Sustainability and Intelligent Systems (ICETSIS)* (pp. 60-66). IEEE. DOI: 10.1109/ICETSIS55481.2022.9888821

Gupta, M. (2018). Blockchain for Hospitality. *John Wiley & Sons. Inc*, 2, 44.

Gupta, R., & Misra, S. C. (2018). Blockchain in hospitality and tourism industry: A review, taxonomy and synthesis. *International Journal of Information Management*, 42, 159–181.

Gururaj, H. L., Janhavi, V., Holla, A. M., Kumar, A. A., Bhumika, R., & Goundar, S. (2021). Decentralised application for crowdfunding using blockchain technology. *International Journal of Blockchains and Cryptocurrencies*, 2(1), 68–82. DOI: 10.1504/IJBC.2021.117809

Hagendorff, T. (2019). From privacy to anti-discrimination in times of machine learning. *Ethics and Information Technology*, 21(4), 331–343. DOI: 10.1007/s10676-019-09510-5

Hair, F. J., Black, C. W., Babin, J. B., & Amderson, E. R. (2010). Multivariate Data Analysis (7th ed.). pearson prentice Hall.

Hajric, V. (2022). Crypto Crash Erases More Than $1 Trillion in Market Value". *Bloomberg*, 22 January 2022. Available at: https://www.bloomberg.com/news/articles/2022-01-21/crypto-meltdown-erases-more-than-1-trillion-in-market-value (accessed 10 December 2022).

Hall, C. M., Prayag, G., Safonov, A., Coles, T., Gössling, S., & Naderi Koupaei, S. (2022). Airbnb and the sharing economy. *Current Issues in Tourism*, 25(19), 3057–3067. DOI: 10.1080/13683500.2022.2122418

Hamad, S. I. (2023). A review of deep learning applied to cyber security. *Texas Journal of Engineering and Technology*, 22, 49–57.

Hamaguchi, Y. (2024). A survey of sustainable development in economic growth theory: Achievements and future directions. In Arouri, M., & Gomes, M. (Eds.), *Handbook on Energy and Economic Growth* (pp. 128–153). Edward Elgar Publishing., DOI: 10.4337/9781802204803.00013

Han, D.-I. D., Bergs, Y., & Moorhouse, N. (2022). Virtual reality consumer experience escapes: Preparing for the metaverse. *Virtual Reality (Waltham Cross)*, 26(4), 1443–1458. Advance online publication. DOI: 10.1007/s10055-022-00641-7

Hardjono, T., & Smith, A. (2018). *Introduction to decentralized identity*. O'Reilly Media, Inc.

Harjanti, D. (2019). Burnout and Employee Performance in Hospitality Industry. The Role of Social Capital. *Jurnal Teknik Industri*. https.//DOI: 10.9744/jti.21.1.15-24

Hemamalini, V., Mishra, A. K., Tyagi, A. K., & Kakulapati, V. (2024). Artificial Intelligence–Blockchain-Enabled–Internet of Things-Based Cloud Applications for Next-Generation Society. *Automated Secure Computing for Next-Generation Systems*, 65-82.

Hight, S. K., Gajjar, T., & Okumus, F. (2019). Managers from "Hell" in the hospitality industry. How do hospitality employees profile bad managers? *International Journal of Hospitality Management*. https.//DOI: 10.1016/j.ijhm.2018.06.018

Hileman, G., & Rauchs, M. (2017). Global cryptocurrency benchmarking study. Cambridge Centre for Alternative Finance. https://www.jbs.cam.ac.uk/faculty-research/centres/alternative-finance/publications/global-cryptocurrency/

Hochschwarzer, D. (2019). *Impact factors on the adoption of Blockchain Technology in the Hotel In-dustry*. 206. https://www.modul.ac.at/uploads/files/Theses/Master/Grad_2019/David_Hochschwarzer_-_no_sig.pdf

Hoffmann, K., Ivanova, M., & Kubicek, B. (2020). The potentials of blockchain technology for governance. *Policy and Internet*, 12(3), 310–327. DOI: 10.1002/poi3.231

Hoijtink, M., & Planqué-van Hardeveld, A. (2022). Machine learning and the platformization of the military: A study of google's machine learning platform TensorFlow. *International Political Sociology*, 16(2), olab036. DOI: 10.1093/ips/olab036

Holub, M., & Johnson, J. (2018). Bitcoin research across disciplines. *The Information Society, 34*(2), 114-126. https.//DOI: <ALIGNMENT.qj></ALIGNMENT>10.1080/01972243.2018.1413556

Hong, J. (2018). Rise of the Sharing Economy and the Future of Travel and Tourism Industry. *Journal of Business and Hotel Management.*, 07(2). Advance online publication. DOI: 10.4172/2169-0286.1000180

Horst, T. Daniel, T., Leung., Andrei, O., J., Kwok., Aaron, Tham. (2021). 3. Crypto-currency adoption in travel and tourism – an exploratory study of Asia Pacific travellers. *Current Issues in Tourism*. Advance online publication. DOI: 10.1080/13683500.2020.1863928

Hosny, A., Parmar, C., Quackenbush, J., Schwartz, L. H., & Aerts, H. J. W. L. (2018). Artificial intelligence in radiology. *Nature Reviews Cancer, 18*(8), 500–510. https.//DOI: 10.1038/s41568-018-0016-5

House, R. J. (1971). A Path Goal Theory of Leader Effectiveness. *Administrative Science Quarterly*. https.//DOI: 10.2307/2391905

Howarth, J. (2023). *Average Customer Retention By Industry*. https.//explodingtopics.com/blog/customer-retention-rates

https.//docs.essif.sk/en/about-essif-framework/ [Accessed on June 30, 2024]

https.//ktdi.org/ [Accessed on June 30, 2024]

https.//myidalliance.org/ [Accessed on July 1, 2024]

https.//www3.weforum.org/docs/WEF_KTDI_Specifications_Guidance_2020.pdf [Accessed on June 30, 2024]

https://wttc.org/research/economic-impact

https://www.unwto.org/news/tourism-s-importance-for-growth-highlighted-in-world-economic-outlook-report

Huang, S., Yang, J., Fong, S., & Zhao, Q. (2020). Artificial intelligence in cancer diagnosis and prognosis. Opportunities and challenges. In *Cancer Letters*. https.// DOI: 10.1016/j.canlet.2019.12.007

Huang, D. H., & Chueh, H. E. (2022). Behavioral intention to continuously use learning apps: A comparative study from Taiwan universities. *Technological Forecasting and Social Change*, 177(1), 121531. DOI: 10.1016/j.techfore.2022.121531

Huh, S., & Lee, S. (2017). Implementing blockchain-based national academic credentialing system. In 2017 19th International Conference on Advanced Communication Technology (ICACT) (pp. 514-518). IEEE.

Huh, S., Cho, S., & Kim, S. (2017). Managing Risk of Supply Chain Disruption Using Blockchain Technology. In *Proceedings of the 2017 International Conference on Information Networking (ICOIN)* (pp. 310-315).

Huh, S., Cho, S., Kim, S., & Kim, H. (2017). A Blockchain-Based Development of the Internet of Things (IoT) for Food Supply Chain Integrity. In *International Conference on Open Source Systems and Technologies* (pp. 277–289).

Iansiti, M., & Lakhani, K. R. (2017). The truth about blockchain. *Harvard Business Review*, 95(1), 118–127.

IBM. (2016). Hyperledger fabric v0. 6 architecture. Retrieved from https://github.com/hyperledger/fabric/blob/v0.6/docs/architecture/README.md

Idian, M. J. I., Hassan, M. K., & Terzungwe, A. S. (2023). Artificial Intelligence, Blockchain, Machine Learning, and Customer Relationship Management. Bincang Sains dan Teknologi, 2(01), 16-20.

Irannezhad, E., & Mahadevan, R. (2021). Is blockchain tourism's new hope? In *Journal of Hospitality and Tourism Technology* (Vol. 12, Issue 1, pp. 85–96). Emerald Group Holdings Ltd. DOI: 10.1108/JHTT-02-2019-0039

Irene, Domenicale., Cristina, Viano., Claudio, Schifanella. (2024). 1. Blockchain for local communities: an exploratory review of token economy aspects. Frontiers in blockchain, DOI: 10.3389/fbloc.2024.1426802

Irfan, M., Elmogy, M., & El-Sappagh, S. (Eds.). (2023). *The impact of AI innovation on financial sectors in the era of industry 5.0*. IGI Global.

Isaacson, W. (2012). *Real Leadership Lessons*. https.//hbr.org/2012/04/the-real-leadership-lessons-of-steve-jobs

Itani, M., Basheer, H., & Eddine, F. (2023, July). Attack Detection in IoT-Based Healthcare Networks Using Hybrid Federated Learning. In *2023 International Conference on Smart Applications, Communications and Networking (SmartNets)* (pp. 1-7). IEEE. DOI: 10.1109/SmartNets58706.2023.10216144

Jack Holdsworth, E. A. (2017). An Effective Immersive Cyber Security Awareness Learning Platform for Businesses in the Hospitality Sector. DOI: 10.1109/REW.2017.47

Jain, G., Kamble, S. S., Ndubisi, N. O., Shrivastava, A., Belhadi, A., & Venkatesh, M. (2022). Antecedents of Blockchain-Enabled E-commerce Platforms (BEEP) adoption by customers – A study of second-hand small and medium apparel retailers. *Journal of Business Research*, 149(1), 576–588. DOI: 10.1016/j.jbusres.2022.05.041

Jain, P., Singh, R. K., Mishra, R., & Rana, N. (2023). Emerging dimensions of blockchain application in tourism and hospitality sector: A systematic literature review. *Journal of Hospitality Marketing & Management*, 32(3), 1–23. DOI: 10.1080/19368623.2023.2184440

Jenik, I., Helfenstein, S., Wieder, P., & Murer, M. (2019). Blockchain in hospitality: A systematic literature review and research agenda. *Journal of Hospitality and Tourism Technology*.

Jha, M. (2024). The role of digital transformation in business and its impact on sustainable development goals (sdgs) in the tourism sector. *SDGs Studies Review*, 5, e010. DOI: 10.37497/sdgs.v5igoals.10

Jian, Y., Pasquier, M., Sagahyroon, A., & Aloul, F. (2021). A Machine Learning Approach to Predicting Diabetes Complications. *Healthcare, 9*(12), 1712. https.// DOI: 10.3390/healthcare9121712

Jiang, L., Li, J., & Tian, L. (2018). Blockchain-based secure identity and data sharing for the Internet of Things. *Future Generation Computer Systems*, 82, 668–675.

Jiang, Y., Wu, J., Yu, X., Wang, X., & Liu, J. (2020). Performance Analysis of Permissioned Blockchain Systems with MG1 Queues. *Future Generation Computer Systems*, 114, 537–548.

Johannes Sedlmeir, Reilly Smethurst, Alexander Rieger, and Gilbert Fridgen. Digital identities and verifiable credentials. Business &amp Information Systems Engineering, 63(5).603–613, October 2021.

John, Matthew, Wnuk. (2017). 2. Flexible payment services for travel and credit cards

Johnson, A. L., & Smith, B. R. (2022). Performance Analysis of MG1 Queue in Blockchain for Business Transactions. *International Journal of Blockchain Research*, 3(1), 28–45.

Johnson, T., & Smith, J. (2020). Regulatory Considerations for Blockchain Adoption in the Hospitality Industry. *Journal of Hospitality Regulation and Compliance*, 12(2), 78–94.

Kabir, F., Khan, M. R., Mia, M. N., & Talukder, M. B. (2024). Implications of Artificial Intelligence (AI) in the Hotel Industry. In Talukder, M., Kumar, S., & Tyagi, P. (Eds.), *Hotel and Travel Management in the AI Era* (pp. 357–378). IGI Global., DOI: 10.4018/979-8-3693-7898-4.ch017

Kagiyama, N., Shrestha, S., Farjo, P. D., & Sengupta, P. P. (2019). Artificial Intelligence. Practical Primer for Clinical Research in Cardiovascular Disease. *Journal of the American Heart Association, 8*(17). https.//DOI: 10.1161/JAHA.119.012788

Kaptein, M. (2024). *Reconciling Shareholder Theory and Stakeholder Theory: The social responsibility of business is to serve its shareholders by serving its stakeholders*. DOI: 10.13140/RG.2.2.28364.39047

Karame, G. O., & Androulaki, E. (2016). Two Bitcoins at the price of one? Double-spending attacks on fast payments in Bitcoin. In *Proceedings of the 2012 ACM conference on Computer and communications security* (pp. 906-917). ACM. DOI: 10.1145/2976749.2978392

Katschnig, M. (2022). *The impact of blockchain technology on hotel booking systems. May.*

Katyal, S. K. (2019). Private accountability in the age of artificial intelligence. *UCLA Law Review. University of California, Los Angeles. School of Law*, 66, 54.

Kaushik, K. (2024). Leveraging Deep Learning Techniques for Securing the Internet of Things in the Age of Big Data. *Applying Artificial Intelligence in Cybersecurity Analytics and Cyber Threat Detection*, 309.

Khalilzadeh, J., Ozturk, A. B., & Bilgihan, A. (2017). Security-related factors in extended UTAUT model for NFC based mobile payment in the restaurant industry. *Computers in Human Behavior*, 70, 460–474. DOI: 10.1016/j.chb.2017.01.001

Khan, M., Alam, M. M., & Islam, S. (2021). Exploring the Potential Application of Blockchain Technology in Hospitality Management: Challenges and Opportunities. In Handbook of Research on Blockchain Technology (pp. 245-267). IGI Global.

Khan, Ms & Irfan, Zainab & Muley, Kirti. (2023). CHATBOT ADOPTION IN TRAVEL AND TOURISM SERVICES. 2.

Khan, N., & Efthymiou, M. (2021). The use of biometric technology at airports: The case of customs and border protection (CBP). *International Journal of Information Management Data Insights,* 1 (2) 2021.100049, ISSN 2667-0968

Khan, M. S., Woo, M., Nam, K., & Chathoth, P. K. (2017). Smart city and smart tourism: A case of Dubai. *Sustainability (Basel)*, 9(12), 2279. Advance online publication. DOI: 10.3390/su9122279

Khanna, A., Sah, A., Choudhury, T., & Maheshwari, P. (2020). Blockchain Technology for Hospitality Industry. *Lecture Notes in Business Information Processing*, 402(November), 99–112. DOI: 10.1007/978-3-030-63396-7_7

Khanna, V., & Sultania, A. (2021). Blockchain technology in travel and tourism: A systematic review. *Tourism Management Perspectives*, 37, 100796. DOI: 10.1016/j.tmp.2020.100796

Kim, J., Song, H. J., & Lee, C. K. (2016). Effects of corporate social responsibility and internal marketing on organizational commitment and turnover intentions. *International Journal of Hospitality Management*. https.//DOI: 10.1016/j.ijhm.2016.02.007

Kim, H., Kim, H. S., & Lee, S. G. (2018). Beyond the hype: What is blockchain? *IT Professional*, 20(6), 15–20.

Kim, J. J., Radic, A., Chua, B. L., Koo, B., & Han, H. (2022). Digital currency and payment innovation in the hospitality and tourism industry. *International Journal of Hospitality Management*, 107, 103314. DOI: 10.1016/j.ijhm.2022.103314

Kizildag, M., Dogru, T., Zhang, T., Mody, M. A., Altin, M., Ozturk, A. B., & Ozdemir, O. (2020). Blockchain: A paradigm shift in business practices. *International Journal of Contemporary Hospitality Management*, 32(3), 953–975. DOI: 10.1108/IJCHM-12-2018-0958

Kochhar, S. K., Bhatia, A., & Tomer, N. (2023). Using Deep Learning and Big Data Analytics for Managing Cyber-Attacks. In *New Approaches to Data Analytics and Internet of Things Through Digital Twin* (pp. 146–178). IGI Global.

Kollmann, T., Hensellek, S., de Cruppe, K., & Sirges, A. (2020). Toward a renaissance of cooperatives fostered by Blockchain on electronic marketplaces: A theory-driven case study approach. *Electronic Markets*, 30(2), 273–284. DOI: 10.1007/s12525-019-00369-4

Kongsorot, Y., Musikawan, P., Aimtongkham, P., You, I., Benslimane, A., & So-In, C. (2023). An Intrusion Detection and Identification System for Internet of Things Networks Using a Hybrid Ensemble Deep Learning Framework. *IEEE Transactions on Sustainable Computing*, 8(4), 596–613. DOI: 10.1109/TSUSC.2023.3303422

Kopanaki, E., Stroumpoulis, A., & Oikonomou, M. (2021). The Impact of Blockchain Technology on Food Waste Management in the Hospitality Industry. *ENTRENOVA - ENTerprise REsearch InNOVAtion, 7*(1), 428–437. DOI: 10.54820/CQRJ6465

Kordzadeh, N., & Ghasemaghaei, M. (2022). Algorithmic bias: Review, synthesis, and future research directions. *European Journal of Information Systems*, 31(3), 388–409. DOI: 10.1080/0960085X.2021.1927212

Krietemeyer, M. (2019). *Blockchain Technologies' Influence on Hotel Bookings.*

Kshetri, N. (2017). Will blockchain emerge as a tool to break the poverty chain in the Global South? *Third World Quarterly, 38*(8), 1710-1732. https.//DOI: <ALIGNMENT.qj></ALIGNMENT>10.1080/01436597.2017.1282992

Kshetri, N. (2017). Can blockchain strengthen the internet of things? *IT Professional*, 19(4), 68–72. DOI: 10.1109/MITP.2017.3051335

Kud, A. (2023). Global problem of growing economic inequality and tokenization of assets as a prospect of its solution. *Economic Analysis*, 33(2), 7–24. DOI: 10.35774/econa2023.02.007

Kumar, A. (2024). Cybersecurity Threat Detection using Machine Learning and Network Analysis. *Journal of Artificial Intelligence General science (JAIGS) ISSN: 3006-4023, 1*(1), 38-46.

Kumar, P., Gowda, D. Y., & Prakash, A. M. (2024). Machine Learning in Cybersecurity: A Comprehensive Survey of Data Breach Detection, Cyber-Attack Prevention, and Fraud Detection. *Pioneering Smart Healthcare 5.0 with IoT, Federated Learning, and Cloud Security*, 175-197.

Kumar, A. K., Vadivukkarasi, K., & Dayana, R. (2023, February). A Novel Hybrid Deep Learning Model for Botnet Attacks Detection in a Secure IoMT Environment. In *2023 International Conference on Intelligent Systems for Communication, IoT and Security (ICISCoIS)* (pp. 44-49). IEEE. DOI: 10.1109/ICISCoIS56541.2023.10100396

Kumar, S., Talukder, M. B., Kabir, F., & Kaiser, F. (2023). Challenges and Sustainability of Green Finance in the Tourism Industry: Evidence From Bangladesh. In Taneja, S., Kumar, P., Grima, S., Ozen, E., & Sood, K. (Eds.), (pp. 97–111). Advances in Finance, Accounting, and Economics. IGI Global., DOI: 10.4018/979-8-3693-1388-6.ch006

Kumar, S., Talukder, M. B., & Tyagi, P. K. (2024). The Impact of Artificial Intelligence on Improving Efficiency in Service and Implementing Best Practices in Service Marketing. In Nadda, V., Tyagi, P., Singh, A., & Singh, V. (Eds.), *AI Innovations in Service and Tourism Marketing* (pp. 57–79). IGI Global., DOI: 10.4018/979-8-3693-7909-7.ch004

Kumar, V., & Reinartz, W. (2018). *Customer Relationship Management: Concept, Strategy, and Tools*. Springer. DOI: 10.1007/978-3-662-55381-7

Kuperberg, M. (2019). Blockchain-based identity management. A survey from the enterprise and ecosystem perspective. *IEEE Transactions on Engineering Management*, 67(4), 1008–1027. DOI: 10.1109/TEM.2019.2926471

Lacity, M. C. (2020). *Blockchain Foundations: For the Internet of Value*. University of Arkansas Press.

La, J., & Heiets, I. (2021). The Impact Of Digitalization And Intelligentization On Air Transportation System. *Aviation*, 25(3), 159–170. DOI: 10.3846/aviation.2021.15336

Lampropoulos, K., & Denazis, S. (2011). Identity management directions in future internet. *IEEE Communications Magazine*, 49(12), 74–83. DOI: 10.1109/MCOM.2011.6094009

Lasi, H., Fettke, P., Kemper, H. G., Feld, T., & Hoffmann, M. (2014). Industry 4.0. *Business and Information Systems Engineering, 6*(4), 239–242. https.//DOI: 10.1007/s12599-014-0334-4

Latif, S., Boulila, W., Koubaa, A., Zou, Z., & Ahmad, J. (2024). DTL-IDS: An optimized Intrusion Detection Framework using Deep Transfer Learning and Genetic Algorithm. *Journal of Network and Computer Applications*, 221, 103784. DOI: 10.1016/j.jnca.2023.103784

Lee, H., & Kelley, D. (2008). Building dynamic capabilities for innovation. An exploratory study of key management practices. *R and D Management*. https.//DOI: 10.1111/j.1467-9310.2008.00506.x

Lee, H., & Guillet, D. (2013). An Examination of the Relationship between Online Travel Agents and Hotels: A Case Study of Choice Hotels International and Expedia.com. *Cornell Hospitality Quarterly*, 54(1), 95–107. DOI: 10.1177/1938965512454218

Lee, I., & Shin, Y. J. (2020). Machine learning for enterprises: Applications, algorithm selection, and challenges. *Business Horizons*, 63(2), 157–170. DOI: 10.1016/j.bushor.2019.10.005

Lee, M., Ahn, J., Shin, M., Kwon, W., & Back, K.-J. (2021). Integrating technology to service innovation: Key issues and future research directions in hospitality and tourism. *Journal of Hospitality and Tourism Technology*, 12(1), 19–38. DOI: 10.1108/JHTT-01-2019-0013

Lenka, S., Parida, V., & Wincent, J. (2016). Digitalization capabilities as enablers of Value Co-Creation in servitizing firms. *Psychology and Marketing*, 34(1), 92–100. DOI: 10.1002/mar.20975

Li, J., He, Q., Liang, R., & Jiang, B. 2021. Smart tourism identity authentication service based on blockchain and decentralized identifier. In *Blockchain and Trustworthy Systems. Third International Conference, BlockSys 2021,Guangzhou, China,August 5–6, 2021, Revised Selected Papers 3* (pp. 545-558). Springer Singapore. DOI: 10.1007/978-981-16-7993-3_42

Liao, Rouya. (2020). The value of traditional travel agency in the digital age.

Li, C., Zhang, Y., & Wang, Q. (2021). Modeling and Analysis of MG1 Queue in Blockchain-Based Travel business process Management. *Journal of Applied Blockchain*, 2(2), 85–102.

Lightbody, D., Ngo, D. M., Temko, A., Murphy, C. C., & Popovici, E. (2024). Dragon_Pi: IoT Side-Channel Power Data Intrusion Detection Dataset and Unsupervised Convolutional Autoencoder for Intrusion Detection. *Future Internet*, 16(3), 88. DOI: 10.3390/fi16030088

Li, H., & Dong, S. (2024). Image steganalysis algorithm based on deep learning and attention mechanism for computer communication. *Journal of Electronic Imaging*, 33(1), 013015–013015. DOI: 10.1117/1.JEI.33.1.013015

Li, L., Zhao, T., Xie, Y., & Feng, Y. (2020). Interpretable machine learning based on integration of nlp and psychology in peer-to-peer lending risk evaluation. In *Natural Language Processing and Chinese Computing: 9th CCF International Conference, NLPCC 2020, Zhengzhou, China, October 14–18, 2020* [Springer International Publishing.]. *Proceedings*, 9(Part II), 429–441.

Limna, P. (2023). Artificial Intelligence (AI) in the Hospitality Industry. A Review Article. *International Journal of Computing Sciences Research*. https.//DOI: 10.25147/ijcsr.2017.001.1.103

Lipsa, S., & Dash, R. K. (2023). A novel intrusion detection system based on deep learning and random forest for digital twin on IOT platform. *Int. J. Sch. Res. Eng. Technol*, 2, 51–64.

Li, T., Wang, H., & Lin, Y. (2024). Selection of renewable energy development path for sustainable development using a fuzzy MCDM based on cumulative prospect theory: The case of Malaysia. *Scientific Reports*, 14(1), 15082. DOI: 10.1038/s41598-024-65982-6 PMID: 38956184

Liu, C., Chen, B., Shao, W., Zhang, C., Wong, K., & Zhang, Y. (2024). Unraveling Attacks in Machine Learning-based IoT Ecosystems: A Survey and the Open Libraries Behind Them. arXiv preprint arXiv:2401.11723.

Liu, M. T., Wang, S., McCartney, G., & Wong, I. A. (2021). Taking a break is for accomplishing a longer journey: Hospitality industry in Macao under the COVID-19 pandemic. *International Journal of Contemporary Hospitality Management*, 33(4), 1249–1275. DOI: 10.1108/IJCHM-07-2020-0678

Liu, Y., Peng, S., Zhang, M., Shi, S., & Fu, J. (2024). Towards secure and efficient integration of blockchain and 6G networks. *PLoS One*, 19(4), e0302052. DOI: 10.1371/journal.pone.0302052 PMID: 38603725

Liu, Y., Wang, Q., Xie, L., & Xu, Z. (2020). Performance Analysis of MG1 Queue Based on Blockchain in Travel business process Reengineering. In *Proceedings of the 2020 International Conference on Advanced Information Technologies and Applications (ICAITA)* (pp. 193-196).

Liu, Y., Xiang, Y., & Lu, R. (2020). A Performance Analysis Model for Consortium Blockchain Systems based on MG1 Queue. *IEEE Access : Practical Innovations, Open Solutions*, 8, 92507–92519.

Liu, Y., Zhang, H., & Wang, X. (2022). Modeling and analysis of MG1 queue in blockchain for secure data sharing in business applications. *Journal of Blockchain Applications*, 2(1), 38–52.

Liu, Y., Zhang, H., & Wang, X. (2022). Modeling and Analysis of MG1 Queue in Blockchain for Secure Data Sharing in Business Applications. *Journal of Blockchain Research*, 3(2), 79–96.

Li, X., Chen, J., & Wang, Y. (2021). Modeling and analysis of MG1 queue in blockchain for travel business process integration. *International Journal of Blockchain and Cryptocurrency*, 2(2), 109–124.

Li, X., Chen, Y., & Liu, Z. (2021). Modeling and simulation of MG1 queue in blockchain-based supply chain management. *Journal of Applied Blockchain Research*, 1(2), 57–72.

Li, Y., Xiong, Y., Li, X., & Zhang, W. (2020). Performance Analysis of MG1 Queue Based on Blockchain in Travel business process Management Systems. In *Proceedings of the 2020 International Conference on Artificial Intelligence and Industrial Automation (AIIA)* (pp. 147-151).

Li, Z., Li, X., & Luo, M. (2021). Performance Modeling and Analysis of Blockchain-based Systems with MG1 Queues. *Journal of Computer Research and Development*, 58(7), 1571–1583.

Lone, A. N., Mustajab, S., & Alam, M. (2023). A comprehensive study on cybersecurity challenges and opportunities in the IoT world. *Security and Privacy*, 6(6), e318. DOI: 10.1002/spy2.318

LUDYNIA. A. (2024). *Cybersecurity in the Hospitality Industry.* Shiji Group. Retrieved from https://www.hospitalitynet.org/news/4120586.html

Luecking, M., Fries, C., Lamberti, R., & Stork, W. 2020, May. Decentralized identity and trust management framework for Internet of Things. In *2020 IEEE International Conference on Blockchain and Cryptocurrency (ICBC)* (pp. 1-9). IEEE. DOI: 10.1109/ICBC48266.2020.9169411

Lui, A., & Lamb, G. W. (2018). Artificial intelligence and augmented intelligence collaboration: Regaining trust and confidence in the financial sector. *Information & Communications Technology Law*, 27(3), 267–283. DOI: 10.1080/13600834.2018.1488659

M. K. N., S., V., P., V., & S., B. (2024). Blockchain and Its Role in Leadership: In A. Agnihotri, R. Agarwal, A. Maurya, M. Sinha, & B. Balusamy (Eds.), *Advances in Business Strategy and Competitive Advantage* (pp. 179–205). IGI Global. DOI: 10.4018/979-8-3693-1946-8.ch010

MacCallum, R. C., Browne, M. W., & Sugawara, H. M. (1996). Power analysis and determination of sample size for covariance structure modeling. *Psychological Methods*, 1(2), 130–149. DOI: 10.1037/1082-989X.1.2.130

Mahamuni, N., Nikam, H., Pattewar, G., Loka, O., & Patil, R. 2022, September. Management of IoT devices data security using blockchain and proxy re-encryption algorithm. In *International Conference on Emerging Technologies and Intelligent Systems* (pp. 551-558). Cham. Springer International Publishing.

Mahamuni, N., Pattewar, G., Nikam, H., Loka, O., & Patil, R. 2022, September. A blockchain and proxy re-encryption based approach for IoT data security. a review. In *International Conference on Emerging Technologies and Intelligent Systems* (pp. 587-595). Cham. Springer International Publishing.

Mahmoudi, N., & Duman, E. (2015). Detecting credit card fraud by modified Fisher discriminant analysis. *Expert Systems with Applications*, 42(5), 2510–2516. DOI: 10.1016/j.eswa.2014.10.037

Mahtani, A. (2024). Practical Implications. In A. Mahtani, *The Objects of Credence* (1st ed., pp. 105–137). Oxford University PressOxford. DOI: 10.1093/oso/9780198847892.003.0006

Makhdoomi, A., & Khaki, A. A. (2023). Journey to Resilience: Sustainable Tourism and Community Participation in Jammu and Kashmir. *International Journal of Management and Development Studies*, 12(12), 41–48. DOI: 10.53983/ijmds.v12n12.005

Makoto, N. (2020). *5. The present and future of digital-community currencies: RAMICS 2019 in Hida–Takayama keynote speech.* Evolutionary and Institutional Economics Review., DOI: 10.1007/s40844-020-00177-y

Manimaran, M., Dhar, M., Norabuena-Figueroa, R., Mahaveerakannan, R., Saraswathi, S., & Selvakumarasamy, K. (2023). Implementing Machine Learning-based Autonomic Cyber Defense for IoT-enabled Healthcare Devices. *Journal of Artificial Intelligence and Technology*, 3(4), 162–172. DOI: 10.37965/jait.2023.0209

Mansour, S., & Tremblay, D.-G. (2018). Work–family conflict/family–work conflict, job stress, burnout and intention to leave in the hotel industry in Quebec (Canada). moderating role of need for family friendly practices as "resource passageways." *The International Journal of Human Resource Management, 29*(16), 2399–2430. https.//DOI: 10.1080/09585192.2016.1239216

Mantas, P., Ioannou, Z.-M., Viennas, E., Pavlidis, G., & Sakkopoulos, E. (2022). Digital gifts and tourism mementos: A sustainable approach. *Sustainability (Basel)*, 14(1), 98. DOI: 10.3390/su14010098

Ma, Q., Rosnon, M. R., Razak, M. A. A., Amin, S. M., & Burhan, N. A. S. (2024). Exploring the driving forces of community sustainable development based on ABCD theory—A case study of Yucun village China. *Journal of Infrastructure. Policy and Development*, 8(8), 5815. DOI: 10.24294/jipd.v8i8.5815

Marshall, C., & Rossman, G. B. (2014). *Designing Qualitative Research.* Sage publications.

Martin-Fuentes, E., & Mellinas, J. (2018). Hotels that most rely on Booking.com – online travel agencies (OTAs) and hotel distribution channels. *Tourism Review*, 73(4), 465–479. DOI: 10.1108/TR-12-2017-0201

Maythu, Y., Kwok, A. O. J., & Teh, P. L. (2024). Blockchain technology diffusion in tourism: Evidence from early enterprise adopters and innovators. *Heliyon*, 10(2), e24675. DOI: 10.1016/j.heliyon.2024.e24675 PMID: 38304774

McKendrick, K. (2019). Artificial intelligence prediction and counterterrorism. *London: The Royal Institute of International Affairs-Chatham House, 9*.

Mendling, J., Weber, I., van der Aalst, W. M., Brocke, J. V., Cabanillas, C., Daniel, F., & Weidlich, M. (2018). Blockchains for business process management–challenges and opportunities. [TMIS]. *ACM Transactions on Management Information Systems*, 9(1), 1–16. DOI: 10.1145/3183367

Meng, Weiyi. (2009). Metasearch Engines. .DOI: 10.1007/978-0-387-39940-9_217

Messai, M. L., & Seba, H. (2023, June). POSTER: Activity Graph Learning for Attack Detection in IoT Networks. In *2023 IEEE 24th International Symposium on a World of Wireless, Mobile and Multimedia Networks (WoWMoM)* (pp. 320-322). IEEE.

Messai, M. L., & Seba, H. (2023, August). IoT Network Attack Detection: Leveraging Graph Learning for Enhanced Security. In *Proceedings of the 18th International Conference on Availability, Reliability and Security* (pp. 1-7). DOI: 10.1145/3600160.3605053

Mhlanga, D. (2021). Financial inclusion in emerging economies: The application of machine learning and artificial intelligence in credit risk assessment. *International journal of financial studies, 9*(3), 39.

Mijwil, M., & Aljanabi, M. (2023). Towards artificial intelligence-based cybersecurity: The practices and ChatGPT generated ways to combat cybercrime. *Iraqi Journal For Computer Science and Mathematics*, 4(1), 65–70.

Mijwil, M., Salem, I. E., & Ismaeel, M. M. (2023). The significance of machine learning and deep learning techniques in cybersecurity: A comprehensive review. *Iraqi Journal For Computer Science and Mathematics*, 4(1), 87–101.

Mishra, A. K., Hemamalini, V., & Tyagi, A. K. (2024). Digital Forensics with Emerging Technologies: Vision and Research Potential for Future. *Conversational Artificial Intelligence*, 675-697.

Mittal, H. (2024). Software security: Threats, solutions and challenges. *Computer Software and Media Applications*, 6(1), 3769. DOI: 10.24294/csma.v6i1.3769

Mofokeng, N., & Fatima, T. (2018). Future tourism trends: Utilizing non-fungible tokens to aid wildlife conservation. *African Journal of Hospitality, Tourism and Leisure*, 7(4), 1–20.

Mohamed, L. M. (2016). Assessing the effects of transformational leadership. A study on Egyptian hotel employees. *Journal of Hospitality and Tourism Management*. https.//DOI: 10.1016/j.jhtm.2016.04.001

Mohammad Badruddoza Talukder. Sanjeev Kumar, I. R. Das. (2024). Implications of Blockchain Technology- Based Cryptocurrency in the Cloud for the Hospitality Industry. In *Emerging Trends in Cloud Computing Analytics, Scalability, and Service Models* (p. 19). https://doi.org/DOI: 10.4018/979-8-3693-0900-1.ch018

Mohammad Badruddoza Talukder. Sanjeev Kumar, I. R. Das. (2024). Perspectives of Digital Marketing for the Restaurant Industry. In *Advancements in Socialized and Digital Media Communications* (p. 17). https://doi.org/DOI: 10.4018/979-8-3693-0855-4.ch009

Mohammad, B. T., & Fahmida, K. (2023). Economic impact of river tourism: Evidence of Bangladesh. *I-Manager's. Journal of Management*, 18(2), 47. DOI: 10.26634/jmgt.18.2.20235

Mohammad, B. T., Mushfika, H., & Iva, R. D. (2024). Opportunities of tourism and hospitality education in bangladesh: Career perspectives. *I-Manager's. Journal of Management*, 18(3), 21. DOI: 10.26634/jmgt.18.3.20385

MOHANTY, R. K., & JYOTHI, N. (2015). A Secured Framework for Protecting Sensitive Information from Unauthorized Users.

Mohanty, R. K., Kumar, A. P., Padmaja, R., & Prashanthi, V. (2024). Deep Learning for Analyzing User and Entity Behaviors: Techniques and Applications. In *Consumer and Organizational Behavior in the Age of AI* (pp. 219-250). IGI Global.

Mohanty, R. K., Sahoo, S. P., & Kabat, M. R. (2022, October). A Survey on Emerging Technologies in Wireless Body Area Network. In *2022 13th International Conference on Computing Communication and Networking Technologies (ICCCNT)* (pp. 1-5). IEEE.

Mohanty, R. K., Sahoo, S. P., & Kabat, M. R. (2023, June). A Network Reliability based Secure Routing Protocol (NRSRP) for Secure Transmission in Wireless Body Area Network. In *2023 8th International Conference on Communication and Electronics Systems (ICCES)* (pp. 663-668). IEEE.

Mohanty, R. K., Sahoo, S. P., & Kabat, M. R. (2024). Thermal-energy-efficient-secured-link reliable and delay-aware routing protocol (TESLDAR) for wireless body area networks. *International Journal of Computers and Applications*, 1-13. IEEE. (2021, June 25). Hyperledger, Ethereum, and blockchain technology: A short overview.

Mohanty, R. K., Motupalli, R. K., Manju, D., Gangappa, M., Gouthami, B., & Mounika, G. (2023, December). Energy-Efficient Cluster Based Routing Protocol to Enhance the Lifetime of Wearable Wireless Body Area Networks (WBAN). In *2023 OITS International Conference on Information Technology (OCIT)* (pp. 71-76). IEEE. DOI: 10.1109/OCIT59427.2023.10431071

Mohanty, R. K., Sahoo, S. P., & Kabat, M. R. (2023). Sustainable remote patient monitoring in wireless body area network with Multi-hop routing and scheduling: A four-fold objective based optimization approach. *Wireless Networks*, 29(5), 2337–2351. DOI: 10.1007/s11276-023-03276-x

Montasari, R. (2024). Machine Learning and Deep Learning Techniques in Countering Cyberterrorism. In *Cyberspace, Cyberterrorism and the International Security in the Fourth Industrial Revolution: Threats, Assessment and Responses* (pp. 135–158). Springer International Publishing. DOI: 10.1007/978-3-031-50454-9_8

Moreno, A., Gómez, M., & Ponce, P. (2019). A Blockchain-based identity management system for the hospitality industry. In 2019 3rd International Conference on Advances in Science, Engineering and Robotics Technology (ICASERT) (pp. 1-5). IEEE.

Mottaghi, S. F., Steininger, B. I., & Yanagawa, N. (2024). Real Estate Insights: The current state and the new future of tokenization in real estate. *Journal of Property Investment & Finance*, 42(6), 614–620. Advance online publication. DOI: 10.1108/JPIF-07-2024-0087

Moustafa, N., Koroniotis, N., Keshk, M., Zomaya, A. Y., & Tari, Z. (2023). Explainable intrusion detection for cyber defences in the internet of things: Opportunities and solutions. *IEEE Communications Surveys and Tutorials*, 25(3), 1775–1807. DOI: 10.1109/COMST.2023.3280465

Mühlhoff, R. (2021). Predictive privacy: Towards an applied ethics of data analytics. *Ethics and Information Technology*, 23(4), 675–690. DOI: 10.1007/s10676-021-09606-x

Mukta, S. N. (2023). *Blockchain Technology : An Overview Blockchain Technology : An Overview Shamima Nasrin Mukta Assistant Professor Department of Humanities. March.*

Mulaik, S. A. (1987). A Brief History of the Philosophical Foundations of Exploratory Factor Analysis. *Multivariate Behavioral Research*, 22(3), 267–305. DOI: 10.1207/s15327906mbr2203_3 PMID: 26776378

Mulyan, A., & Martoni, A. (2024). Community Participation in Village Tourism Development. *International Journal of Multicultural and Multireligious Understanding*, 11(3), 120. DOI: 10.18415/ijmmu.v11i3.5559

Muñoz, Andrés & del Vas, Ginesa & Yi, Yee. (2019). An integral mobile application for pre-travel, on-site and post-travel stages. 4. 7-17.

Murtagh, N., Gatersleben, B., & Uzzell, D. (2012). Multiple identities and travel mode choice for regular journeys. *Transportation Research Part F: Traffic Psychology and Behaviour*, 15(5), 514–524. DOI: 10.1016/j.trf.2012.05.002

Naik, N., & Jenkins, P. 2017, May. Securing digital identities in the cloud by selecting an apposite Federated Identity Management from SAML, OAuth and OpenID Connect. In *2017 11th International Conference on Research Challenges in Information Science (RCIS)* (pp. 163-174). IEEE.

Nakamoto, S. (2008). Bitcoin. A Peer-to-Peer Electronic Cash System.

Nakamoto, S. (2008). Bitcoin: A peer-to-peer electronic cash system. Bitcoin.org. https://bitcoin.org/bitcoin.pdf

Nakamoto, S. (2008). Bitcoin: A peer-to-peer electronic cash system. Retrieved from https://bitcoin.org/bitcoin.pdf

Nakamoto, S. (2019). *Bitcoin: A Peer-to-peer Electronic Cash System. Technical report*. Manubot.

Namasudra, Suyel & Akkaya, Kemal. (2023). Introduction to Blockchain Technology. .DOI: 10.1007/978-981-19-8730-4_1

Nandan, M., & Dey, S. (2023). Cybersecurity: Techniques and Applications to Combat Vicious Threats in Modern-Era Indices. In *AI-Aided IoT Technologies and Applications for Smart Business and Production* (pp. 248-270). CRC Press.

Narayanan, A., Bonneau, J., Felten, E., Miller, A., & Goldfeder, S. (2016). *Bitcoin and Cryptocurrency Technologies*. Princeton University Press.

Narayanan, A., Bonneau, J., Felten, E., Miller, A., & Goldfeder, S. (2016). *Bitcoin and Cryptocurrency Technologies: A Comprehensive Introduction*. Princeton University Press.

Narayana, Y. V., & Sreedevi, M. (2023, October). DDCATF: Deep Learning Approach for Detection of Cybercrime Activities Based on Temporal Features. In *2023 International Conference on Self Sustainable Artificial Intelligence Systems (ICSSAS)* (pp. 462-469). IEEE. DOI: 10.1109/ICSSAS57918.2023.10331644

Nassar, A., & Kamal, M. (2021). Ethical Dilemmas in AI-Powered Decision-Making: A Deep Dive into Big Data-Driven Ethical Considerations. *International Journal of Responsible Artificial Intelligence*, 11(8), 1–11.

Naumov, E. A. (2024). Sustainable Economic Development: Theory of Institutional Constructivism. *Economics: The Strategy and Practice*, 19(1), 46–56. DOI: 10.51176/1997-9967-2024-1-46-56

Naz, Muqaddas, et al. "A secure data sharing platform using blockchain and interplanetary file system." Sustainability 11.24 (2019). 7054.

Nehinbe, J. O., Benson, J. A., & Chibuzor, L. (2023). The classification of the investigations and punishment for crime syndicates that relate to intrusions against IoT-based healthcare systems. In *Blockchain Technology Solutions for the Security of IoT-Based Healthcare Systems* (pp. 113–131). Academic Press. DOI: 10.1016/B978-0-323-99199-5.00010-0

Neisse, A. R., Dondio, B., & Dumas, M. B. (2017). Towards Blockchain-based Travel business process Execution. In *Proceedings of the 2017 IEEE 21st International Enterprise Distributed Object Computing Conference (EDOC)*.

Nguyen, H., Nawara, D., & Kashef, R. (2024). Connecting the Indispensable Roles of IoT and Artificial Intelligence in Smart Cities: A Survey. *Journal of Information and Intelligence*.

Nguyen, T. T., Truong, T. T., & Da Nguyen, L. T. (2023). Blockchain in Hospitality and Tourism: A Game-Changer for Asian Markets. *International Journal of Research Publication and Reviews*, 4(6), 3209–3213. DOI: 10.55248/gengpi.4.623.46183

Nisha, S. R., & Muthurajkumar, S. (2023). Semantic Graph Based Convolutional Neural Network for Spam e-mail Classification in Cybercrime Applications. *International Journal of Computers, Communications & Control*, 18(1).

Niu, T., Li, W., & Liu, Y. (2024). DarkGuardNet: A deep learning framework for imbalanced dark web traffic identification and application classification.

Nkoro, E. C., Njoku, J. N., Nwakanma, C. I., Lee, J. M., & Kim, D. S. (2024). Zero-Trust Marine Cyberdefense for IoT-Based Communications: An Explainable Approach. *Electronics (Basel)*, 13(2), 276. DOI: 10.3390/electronics13020276

Norman, Shaw. (2018). 2. Helping the Local Community with Crypto-Currency: A Case Study.. DOI: 10.1007/978-3-319-91716-0_52

Nov, O., & Ye, C. (2008). Personality and technology acceptance. Personal innovativeness in IT, openness and resistance to change. *Proceedings of the Annual Hawaii International Conference on System Sciences*. https.//DOI: 10.1109/HICSS.2008.348

Nugraha, R. N., & Ramdani, A. (2024). Community-Based Tourism in the Development of Curug Leuwi Hejo, Bogor. *West Science Interdisciplinary Studies*, 2(05), 1099–1108. DOI: 10.58812/wsis.v2i05.919

Nur Muharam, I., Tussyadiah, I. P., & Kimbu, A. N. (2024). A theoretical model of user acceptance of blockchain-based peer-to-peer accommodation. *Current Issues in Tourism*, 27(7), 1008–1025. DOI: 10.1080/13683500.2022.2164485

Nyaletey, E., "BlockIPFS-blockchain-enabled interplanetary file system for forensic and trusted data traceability." *2019 IEEE International Conference on Blockchain (Blockchain)*. IEEE, 2019. DOI: 10.1109/Blockchain.2019.00012

Nyarko, B. N. E., Bin, W., Zhou, J., Odoom, J., Danso, S. A., & Addai, G. E. S. (2024). Forensic detection of heterogeneous activity in data using deep learning methods. *Intelligent Systems with Applications*, 21, 200303. DOI: 10.1016/j.iswa.2023.200303

Nyoman Surpa Adisastra, I.I Nyoman Surpa AdisastraBagus Ade Tegar Prabawa. (2024). Strengthening the role of customary villages in spiritual tourism management in Bali. *Ride: Journal of Cultural Tourism and Religious Studies*, 2(1), 54–63. DOI: 10.25078/ride.v2i1.3623

O'Connor, P., & Murphy, J. (2004). Research on information technology in the hospitality industry. *International Journal of Hospitality Management*, 23(5), 473–484. Advance online publication. DOI: 10.1016/j.ijhm.2004.10.002

O'Dwyer, K. J., & Malone, D. (2014). Bitcoin mining and its energy footprint. In Proceedings of the 25th IET Irish Signals & Systems Conference (ISSC 2014) (pp. 280-285). DOI: 10.1049/cp.2014.0699

Odeh, A., & Abu Taleb, A. (2023). Ensemble-Based Deep Learning Models for Enhancing IoT Intrusion Detection. *Applied Sciences (Basel, Switzerland)*, 13(21), 11985. DOI: 10.3390/app132111985

Omar, I. A., Hasan, H., Jayaraman, R., Salah, K., Omar, M., Dhabi, A., Emirates, U. A., Science, C., Dhabi, A., & Emirates, U. A. (2019). *Using blockchain technology to achiece sustainabilty in the hospitality industry by recuing food waste.*

Önder, I., & Gunter, U. (2022). Blockchain: Is it the future for the tourism and hospitality industry? *Tourism Economics*, 28(2), 291–299. DOI: 10.1177/1354816620961707

Ortiz-Ruiz, E., Bermejo, J. R., Sicilia, J. A., & Bermejo, J. (2024). Machine Learning Techniques for Cyberattack Prevention in IoT Systems: A Comparative Perspective of Cybersecurity and Cyberdefense in Colombia. *Electronics (Basel)*, 13(5), 824. DOI: 10.3390/electronics13050824

Övgü, Açiksözlü., Ilbey, Varol., Nur, Neşe, Şahin. (2022). 1. Touristic coins: evaluation of the use of crypto coins in tourism businesses by tourism students. Social science development journal, DOI: 10.31567/ssd.759

Paatlan, S., & Ranga, J. (2023). Responsible Practices by Tour Guides Promoting Sustainable Tourism. In Nadda, V., Tyagi, P. K., Moniz Vieira, R., & Tyagi, P. (Eds.), (pp. 81–90). Advances in Logistics, Operations, and Management Science. IGI Global., DOI: 10.4018/979-8-3693-2065-5.ch006

Paddalwar, S., Ragha, L., & Mane, V. (2023). Cyber threat mitigation using machine learning, deep learning, artificial intelligence, and blockchain. In *Intelligent Approaches to Cyber Security* (pp. 163–179). Chapman and Hall/CRC. DOI: 10.1201/9781003408307-14

Panai, E. (n.d.). A Cyber Security Framework for Independent Hotels. Retrieved from https://www.researchgate.net/profile/Enrico-Panai/publication/325780143_A_Cyber_Security_Framework_for_Independent_Hotels/links/5b235fe2aca272277fb0f8ee/A-Cyber-Security-Framework-for-Independent-Hotels.pdf

Payne, A., & Frow, P. (2005). A strategic framework for customer relationship management. *Journal of Marketing*, 69(4), 167–176. DOI: 10.1509/jmkg.2005.69.4.167

Peng, K., Tao, X., Jiang, J., & Zhai, J. (2023). The Experience Design of Cultural Heritage Tourism in the Perspective of Gamification. In Marcus, A., Rosenzweig, E., & Soares, M. M. (Eds.), *Design, User Experience, and Usability* (Vol. 14034, pp. 127–146). Springer Nature Switzerland., DOI: 10.1007/978-3-031-35705-3_10

Pereira, B. A., Lohmann, G., & Houghton, L. (2021). Innovation and value creation in the context of aviation: A Systematic Literature Review. *Journal of Air Transport Management*, 94, 102076. DOI: 10.1016/j.jairtraman.2021.102076

Pesonen, Juho & Tussyadiah, Iis. (2017). Peer-to-peer accommodation: drivers and user profiles. .DOI: 10.1007/978-3-319-51799-5

Petrov, S. V. (2024). Methods for assessing risks of sustainable development of an enterprise: Theory and empirical analysis. *Economic Analysis: Theory and Practice*, 23(4), 713–734. DOI: 10.24891/ea.23.4.713

Pham, C. T., & Thi Nguyet, T. T. (2023). Determinants of blockchain adoption in news media platforms: A perspective from the Vietnamese press industry. *Heliyon*, 9(1), e12747. Advance online publication. DOI: 10.1016/j.heliyon.2022.e12747 PMID: 36685429

Pilkington, M. (2016). Blockchain Technology: Principles and Applications. In Research Handbook on Digital Transformations (pp. 225–253).

Pilkington, M. (2015). *Blockchain technology: Principles and applications. Research Handbook on Digital Transformations*. Edward Elgar Publishing.

Plageras, A., Stergiou, C. L., & Psannis, K. (2024). Secure Edge Communications Over the IoT.

Pocher, N., Zichichi, M., Merizzi, F., Shafiq, M. Z., & Ferretti, S. (2023). Detecting anomalous cryptocurrency transactions: An AML/CFT application of machine learning-based forensics. *Electronic Markets*, 33(1), 37. DOI: 10.1007/s12525-023-00654-3

Pradhan, B., Roy, M., & Bhatia, S. (2023). Enhancing Tourists' Satisfaction Through Blockchain Technology. *PUSA Journal of Hospitality and Applied Sciences*, 9(2), 37–47. DOI: 10.48165/pjhas.2023.9.2.5

Prados-Castillo, J. F., Torrecilla-García, J. A., Andraz, G., & Guaita Martínez, J. M. (2023). Blockchain in Peer-to-Peer Platforms: Enhancing Sustainability and Customer Experience in Tourism. *Sustainability (Basel)*, 15(22), 15968. DOI: 10.3390/su152215968

Preukschat, A., & Reed, D. (2021). *Self-sovereign identity*. Manning Publications.

Pritee, Z. T., Anik, M. H., Alam, S. B., Jim, J. R., Kabir, M. M., & Mridha, M. F. (2024). Machine learning and deep learning for user authentication and authorization in cybersecurity: A state-of-the-art review. *Computers & Security*, 140, 103747. DOI: 10.1016/j.cose.2024.103747

Priyadarshini, I., Mohanty, P., Alkhayyat, A., Sharma, R., & Kumar, S. (2023). SDN and application layer DDoS attacks detection in IoT devices by attention-based Bi-LSTM-CNN. *Transactions on Emerging Telecommunications Technologies*, 34(11), e4758. DOI: 10.1002/ett.4758

Psefti, Dimitra & Poulaki, Ioulia & Alkistis, Papaioannou & Katsoni, Vicky. (2021). The Evolution of Online Travel Agencies in the Last Decade: E-Travel SA as an Exceptional Paradigm. .DOI: 10.1007/978-3-030-72469-6_40

Querido, P. C. Blockchain Based Identity Management and Ticketing for MaaS. MS thesis. Universidade de Lisboa (Portugal), 2020.

Radic, A., Law, R., Lück, M., Kang, H., Ariza-Montes, A., Arjona-Fuentes, J. M., & Han, H. (2020). Apocalypse now or overreaction to coronavirus: The global cruise tourism industry crisis. *Sustainability (Basel)*, 12(17), 6968. DOI: 10.3390/su12176968

Radic, A., Quan, W., Antonio, A. M., Lee, J. S., & Han, H. (2022). You can't hold the tide with a broom: Cryptocurrency payments and tourism in South Korea and China. *Tourism Management Perspectives*, 43(1), 101000. DOI: 10.1016/j.tmp.2022.101000

Radic, A., Quan, W., Koo, B., Chua, B. L., Kim, J. J., & Han, H. (2022a). Central bank digital currency as a payment method for tourists: Application of the theory of planned behavior to digital Yuan/Won/Dollar choice. *Journal of Travel & Tourism Marketing*, 39(2), 152–172. DOI: 10.1080/10548408.2022.2061677

Ragnedda, M., & Destefanis, G. (2020). Blockchain: A disruptive technology. Ragnedda, M. & Destefanis, G. (Eds.). *Blockchain and Web 3.0: Social, Economic, and Technological Challenges*. Routledge, New York, NY.

Rai, R., & Sahu, C. K. (2020). Driven by data or derived through physics? a review of hybrid physics guided machine learning techniques with cyber-physical system (cps) focus. *IEEE Access : Practical Innovations, Open Solutions*, 8, 71050–71073. DOI: 10.1109/ACCESS.2020.2987324

Rajkumar, S., Sheeba, S. L., Sivakami, R., Prabu, S., & Selvarani, A. (2023). An IoT-Based Deep Learning Approach for Online Fault Detection Against Cyber-Attacks. *SN Computer Science*, 4(4), 393. DOI: 10.1007/s42979-023-01808-y

Rakha, M. A., Khan, I. U., Ouaissa, M., Ouaissa, M., & Ayub, M. Y. (2024). Hybrid Model for IoT-Enabled Intelligent Towns Using the MQTT-IoT-IDS2020 Dataset. In *Cyber Security for Next-Generation Computing Technologies* (pp. 159-176). CRC Press.

Rana, R. L., Adamashvili, N., & Tricase, C. (2022). The Impact of Blockchain Technology Adoption on Tourism Industry: A Systematic Literature Review. *Sustainability (Basel)*, 14(12), 7383. Advance online publication. DOI: 10.3390/su14127383

Ransbotham, S., & Mitra, S. (2018). Blockchain: What does it mean for consumers? *MIT Sloan Management Review*, 59(4), 1–6.

Rashideh, W. (2020). Blockchain technology framework: Current and future perspectives for the tourism industry. *Tourism Management*, 80, 104125. DOI: 10.1016/j.tourman.2020.104125

Rathee, G., Iqbal, R., Kerrache, C. A., & Song, H. (2024). TrustNextGen: Security Aspects of Trustworthy Next Generation Industrial Internet of Things (IIoT). *IEEE Internet of Things Journal*, 11(15), 25568–25576. DOI: 10.1109/JIOT.2024.3361801

Reddy, B. B., Pasha, S. G., Kameswari, M., Chinkera, R., Fatima, S., Bhargava, R., & Shrivastava, A. (2024). Classification Approach for Face Spoof Detection in Artificial Neural Network Based on IoT Concepts. *International Journal of Intelligent Systems and Applications in Engineering*, 12(13s), 79–91.

Rigby, D. K., Reichheld, F. F., & Schefter, P. (2002). Avoid the four perils of CRM. *Harvard Business Review*. PMID: 11894676

Rim, B., Sung, N. J., Min, S., & Hong, M. (2020). Deep learning in physiological signal data. A survey. In *Sensors (Switzerland)*. https.//DOI: 10.3390/s20040969

Rosenfeld, M. (2011). Overview of blockchain technology: Architecture and consensus algorithms. In *Financial Cryptography and Data Security* (pp. 507–527). Springer., DOI: 10.1007/978-3-642-19348-4_33

Roshanaei, M. (2024). Enhancing Mobile Security through Comprehensive Penetration Testing. *Journal of Information Security*, 15(2), 63–86. DOI: 10.4236/jis.2024.152006

Ruangkanjanases, A., Qhal, E. M. A., Alfawaz, K. M., & Hariguna, T. (2023). Examining the Antecedents of Blockchain Usage Intention: An Integrated Research Framework. *Sustainability (Basel)*, 15(4), 3500. Advance online publication. DOI: 10.3390/su15043500

Rudzeyt, O., Nedyak, A., & Zainetdinov, A. (2020). Tokenization of assets and products. *Russian Journal of Resources. Conservation & Recycling*, 7(2). Advance online publication. DOI: 10.15862/10INOR220

Rusch, J. (2003). Computer and Internet Fraud: A Risk Identification Overview. *Computer Fraud & Security*, 2003(6), 6–9. DOI: 10.1016/S1361-3723(03)06008-1

Saha, S. (2024). SECURITY IN IOT USING ARTIFICIAL INTELLIGENCE. *The Fusion of Artificial Intelligence and Soft Computing Techniques for Cybersecurity*.

Sahingoz, O. K., Buber, E., & Kugu, E. (2024). DEPHIDES: Deep Learning Based Phishing Detection System. *IEEE Access : Practical Innovations, Open Solutions*, 12, 8052–8070. DOI: 10.1109/ACCESS.2024.3352629

Said, S. (2023). The Role of Artificial Intelligence (AI) and Data Analytics in Enhancing Guest Personalization in Hospitality. *Journal of Modern Hospitality*, 2(1), 1–13. DOI: 10.47941/jmh.1556

Saiyed, M. F., & Al-Anbagi, I. (2024). A Genetic Algorithm-and t-Test-Based System for DDoS Attack Detection in IoT Networks. *IEEE Access : Practical Innovations, Open Solutions*, 12, 25623–25641. DOI: 10.1109/ACCESS.2024.3367357

Sakthibalan, P., Saravanan, M., Ansal, V., Rajakannu, A., Vijayalakshmi, K., & Vani, K. D. (2024). A Federated Learning Approach for ResourceConstrained IoT Security Monitoring. In *Handbook on Federated Learning* (pp. 131–154). CRC Press.

Saltz, J., Skirpan, M., Fiesler, C., Gorelick, M., Yeh, T., Heckman, R., & Beard, N. (2019). Integrating ethics within machine learning courses. [TOCE]. *ACM Transactions on Computing Education*, 19(4), 1–26. DOI: 10.1145/3341164

Sambasivan, N., Arnesen, E., Hutchinson, B., Doshi, T., & Prabhakaran, V. (2021, March). Re-imagining algorithmic fairness in india and beyond. In *Proceedings of the 2021 ACM conference on fairness, accountability, and transparency* (pp. 315-328). DOI: 10.1145/3442188.3445896

Samsudeen, S., & Thomas, L. (2024). Cybersecurity Warning System Using Diluted Convolutional Neural Network Framework for IOT Attack Prevention. *International Journal of Intelligent Engineering & Systems*, 17(1).

Santhanam, N., Kamalanabhan, T. J., Dyaram, L., & Ziegler, H. (2017). Impact of human resource management practices on employee turnover intentions. Moderating role of psychological contract breach. *Journal of Indian Business Research*. https.// DOI: 10.1108/JIBR-10-2016-0116

Sarma, R. (2019)... *Study Paper on Security Aspects of Blockchain.*, 6(3), 104–107.

Sarnacchiaro, P., Luongo, S., Sepe, F., & Della Corte, V. (2024). The role of blockchain technology in the tourism industry: Analyzing the factors affecting its adoption. *Quality & Quantity*, 0123456789. Advance online publication. DOI: 10.1007/s11135-024-01836-7

Sarvamangala, D. R., & Kulkarni, R. V. (2022). Convolutional neural networks in medical image understanding. a survey. In *Evolutionary Intelligence*. https.//DOI: 10.1007/s12065-020-00540-3

Savin-Baden, M., & Major, C. H. (2013). *Qualitative Research: The Essential Guide to Theory and Practice*. Routledge.

Schatsky, D., Muraskin, R., & Shetty, M. (2019). How blockchain could improve privacy for travelers. *Harvard Business Review*.

Schmitt, M. (2020). Artificial intelligence in business analytics, capturing value with machine learning applications in financial services.

Scott, J. (2024). On the Practical Implications of Universalism and its Relation to Suffering. *The Expository Times*, 135(9), 366–376. DOI: 10.1177/00145246241251575

Segovia-Vargas, M. J. (2024). Money Laundering in the Age of Cybercrime and Emerging Technologies.

Selbst, A. D., & Barocas, S. (2018). The intuitive appeal of explainable machines. *Fordham Law Review*, 87, 1085.

Shabani, N., & Munir, A. (2020). *A Review of Cyber Security Issues in.* doi:DOI: DOI: 10.1007/978-3-030-52243-8_35

Shah, A., & Krishnan, R. (2019). Decentralized travel booking platforms using blockchain technology. An empirical study. *Journal of Travel Research, 58*(7), 1234-1245. https.//DOI: <ALIGNMENT.qj></ALIGNMENT>10.1177/0047287518807639

Shah, T., & Mulla, Z. R. (2013). Leader Motives, Impression Management, and Charisma. A Comparison of Steve Jobs and Bill Gates. *Management and Labour Studies*. https.//DOI: 10.1177/0258042X13509736

Shaikh, J., Butt, Y. A., & Naqvi, H. F. (2024). Effective Intrusion Detection System Using Deep Learning for DDoS Attacks. *The Asian Bulletin of Big Data Management*, 4(1). Advance online publication. DOI: 10.62019/abbdm.v4i1.113

Shamim, S., Cang, S., Yu, H., & Li, Y. (2016). Management approaches for Industry 4.0. A human resource management perspective. *2016 IEEE Congress on Evolutionary Computation, CEC 2016*. https.//DOI: 10.1109/CEC.2016.7748365

Shamim, S., Cang, S., Yu, H., & Li, Y. (2017). Examining the feasibilities of Industry 4.0 for the hospitality sector with the lens of management practice. *Energies*. https.//DOI: 10.3390/en10040499

Sharma, A., Mansotra, V., & Singh, K. (2023). Detection of Mirai Botnet Attacks on IoT devices Using Deep Learning. *Journal of Scientific Research and Technology*, 174-187.

Sharma, N., & Annaboina, K. (2024). Analytical Study On Prevention And Detection Of Financial Cybercrime And Frauds Using Transaction Pattern Generation Tool. *Journal of Scientific Research and Technology*, 9-31.

Sharma, R., Dhamija, P., & Jain, P. (2020). Blockchain Technology in Hospitality and Tourism Industry: A Comprehensive Review. In Sustainable Development Goals and Sustainable Supply Chains in the Post-Covid Era (pp. 267–279).

Sharma, M., Sehrawat, R., Daim, T., & Shaygan, A. (2021). Technology assessment: Enabling Blockchain in hospitality and tourism sectors. *Technological Forecasting and Social Change*, 169, 120810. DOI: 10.1016/j.techfore.2021.120810

Sharma, R., & Maheshwari, P. (2021). Blockchain technology in supply chain management and business. *Operations and Supply Chain Management: An International Journal*, 14(1), 21–37. DOI: 10.31387/oscm058

Sharma, T., Chen, J., & Liu, W. Y. (2020). Eco-innovation in hospitality research (1998-2018): A systematic review. *International Journal of Contemporary Hospitality Management*, 32(2), 913–933. DOI: 10.1108/IJCHM-01-2019-0002

Shubhneet. (2024). *Automation in the Hospitality Sector*. https.//indiaai.gov.in/article/ai-and-automation-in-the-hospitality-sector

Shukla, R. K., & Tiwari, A. K. (2024). Security Analysis of the Cyber Crime. In *The Ethical Frontier of AI and Data Analysis* (pp. 257–271). IGI Global. DOI: 10.4018/979-8-3693-2964-1.ch016

Singh, A., & Bathla, G. (2023). Fostering Creativity and Innovation: Tourism and Hospitality Perspective. In Embracing Business Sustainability Through Innovation and Creativity in the Service Sector (pp. 70-83). IGI Global.

Singh, B. (2023). Blockchain Technology in Renovating Healthcare: Legal and Future Perspectives. In *Revolutionizing Healthcare Through Artificial Intelligence and Internet of Things Applications* (pp. 177-186). IGI Global.

Singh, B., & Kaunert, C. (2024). Future of Digital Marketing: Hyper-Personalized Customer Dynamic Experience with AI-Based Predictive Models. *Revolutionizing the AI-Digital Landscape: A Guide to Sustainable Emerging Technologies for Marketing Professionals*, 189.

Singh, B., & Kaunert, C. (2024). Harnessing Sustainable Agriculture Through Climate-Smart Technologies: Artificial Intelligence for Climate Preservation and Futuristic Trends. In *Exploring Ethical Dimensions of Environmental Sustainability and Use of AI* (pp. 214-239). IGI Global.

Singh, C., Singh, R., Tiwari, M., & Hazela, B. (2024). Analyse and Predict the Detection of the Cyber-Attack Process by Using a Machine-Learning Approach. *EAI Endorsed Transactions on Internet of Things, 10*.

Singh, B. (2023). Federated Learning for Envision Future Trajectory Smart Transport System for Climate Preservation and Smart Green Planet: Insights into Global Governance and SDG-9 (Industry, Innovation and Infrastructure). *National Journal of Environmental Law*, 6(2), 6–17.

Singh, B. (2023). Tele-Health Monitoring Lensing Deep Neural Learning Structure: Ambient Patient Wellness via Wearable Devices for Real-Time Alerts and Interventions. *Indian Journal of Health and Medical Law*, 6(2), 12–16.

Singh, B. (2023). Unleashing Alternative Dispute Resolution (ADR) in Resolving Complex Legal-Technical Issues Arising in Cyberspace Lensing E-Commerce and Intellectual Property: Proliferation of E-Commerce Digital Economy. *Revista Brasileira de Alternative Dispute Resolution-Brazilian Journal of Alternative Dispute Resolution-RBADR*, 5(10), 81–105. DOI: 10.52028/rbadr.v5i10.ART04.Ind

Singh, B. (2024). Lensing Legal Dynamics for Examining Responsibility and Deliberation of Generative AI-Tethered Technological Privacy Concerns: Infringements and Use of Personal Data by Nefarious Actors. In Ara, A., & Ara, A. (Eds.), *Exploring the Ethical Implications of Generative AI* (pp. 146–167). IGI Global., DOI: 10.4018/979-8-3693-1565-1.ch009

Singh, B. (2024). Social Cognition of Incarcerated Women and Children: Addressing Exposure to Infectious Diseases and Legal Outcomes. In Reddy, K. (Ed.), *Principles and Clinical Interventions in Social Cognition* (pp. 236–251). IGI Global., DOI: 10.4018/979-8-3693-1265-0.ch014

Singh, B., & Kaunert, C. (2024). Integration of Cutting-Edge Technologies such as Internet of Things (IoT) and 5G in Health Monitoring Systems: A Comprehensive Legal Analysis and Futuristic Outcomes. *GLS Law Journal*, 6(1), 13–20. DOI: 10.69974/glslawjournal.v6i1.123

Singh, B., Kaunert, C., & Vig, K. (2024). Reinventing Influence of Artificial Intelligence (AI) on Digital Consumer Lensing Transforming Consumer Recommendation Model: Exploring Stimulus Artificial Intelligence on Consumer Shopping Decisions. In Musiolik, T., Rodriguez, R., & Kannan, H. (Eds.), *AI Impacts in Digital Consumer Behavior* (pp. 141–169). IGI Global., DOI: 10.4018/979-8-3693-1918-5.ch006

Singh, N. J., Hoque, N., Singh, K. R., & Bhattacharyya, D. K. (2023). Botnet-based IoT network traffic analysis using deep learning. *Security and Privacy*, •••, 355.

Siwakoti, Y. R., Bhurtel, M., Rawat, D. B., Oest, A., & Johnson, R. C. (2023). Advances in IOT security: Vulnerabilities, enabled Criminal Services, attacks and countermeasures. *IEEE Internet of Things Journal*, 10(13), 11224–11239. DOI: 10.1109/JIOT.2023.3252594

Smith, A., & Yurkovich, A. (2019). The Impact of Blockchain Technology on the Hospitality Industry: A Systematic Review. *International Journal of Hospitality Management*, 81, 228–241.

Smith, K., Jones, M., & Brown, D. (2019). Enhancing Data Security in the Hospitality Industry through Blockchain Technology. [Springer.]. *International Journal of Hospitality Management*, 38(4), 257–272.

Soliman, S., Oudah, W., & Aljuhani, A. (2023). Deep learning-based intrusion detection approach for securing industrial Internet of Things. *Alexandria Engineering Journal*, 81, 371–383. DOI: 10.1016/j.aej.2023.09.023

Son-Turan, S. (2023). Tokenization and NFTs: A Tokenized Income Sharing Model for Higher Education as a Potential Solution for Student Debt in the USA. In Lenart-Gansiniec, R., Wenzlaff, K., & Späth, S. (Eds.), *Crowdfunding in Higher Education Institutions* (pp. 145–158). Springer International Publishing., DOI: 10.1007/978-3-031-30069-1_9

Sorenson, A. (2018). A Paradigm Shift in How We Travel. Retrieved from https://www.linkedin.com/pulse/paradigm-shift-how-we-travel-arne-sorenson1/?trackingId=a4BJrFrz9F1wMNEGQ6Yyxg%3D%3D&lipi=urn%3Ali%3Apage%3 Ad_flagship3_search_srp_content%3BnWePi4GxTuq7E3Fm%2FwAfdQ%3D%3D&licu=urn%3Ali%3Acontrol%3Ad_flagship3_search_srp_co

Sota, S., Chaudhry, H., & Srivastava, M. K. (2020). Customer relationship management research in hospitality industry: A review and classification. *Journal of Hospitality Marketing & Management*, 29(1), 39–64. DOI: 10.1080/19368623.2019.1595255

Souto, T., Baptista, A., Tavares, D., Queirós, C., & António, M. (2013). Facial emotional recognition in schizophrenia: Preliminary results of the virtual reality program for facial emotional recognition. *Archives of Clinical Psychiatry*, 40(4), 129–134. DOI: 10.1590/S0101-60832013000400001

Sowmya, B. J., Hanumantharaju, R., Kumar, D. P., & Srinivasa, K. G. (2023). Identification of authorship and prevention of fraudulent transactions/cybercrime using efficient high performance machine learning techniques. *International Journal of Business Intelligence and Data Mining*, 22(1-2), 144–169. DOI: 10.1504/IJBIDM.2023.127312

Sri, P. S. G. A., & Bhaskari, D. L. (2018). A study on blockchain technology. *International Journal of Engineering and Technology(UAE)*, 7, 418–421. DOI: 10.14419/ijet.v7i2.7.10757

Stockburger, L., Kokosioulis, G., Mukkamala, A., Mukkamala, R. R., & Avital, M. (2021). Blockchain-enabled decentralized identity management. The case of self-sovereign identity in public transportation. *Blockchain.Research and Applications*, 2(2), 100014. DOI: 10.1016/j.bcra.2021.100014

Storbacka, K., Strandvik, T., & Grönroos, C. (1994). Managing customer relationships for profit: The dynamics of relationship quality. *International Journal of Service Industry Management*, 5(5), 21–38. DOI: 10.1108/09564239410074358

Su, K.-W., Chiu, P.-C., & Lin, T.-H. (2022). Establishing a blockchain online travel agency with a human–computer interaction perspective. *Journal of Hospitality and Tourism Technology*, ahead-of-print .DOI: 10.1108/JHTT-01-2021-0038

Sudhakar, & Kumar, S. (2023, April). ABBDIoT: Anomaly-based botnet detection using machine learning model in the Internet of Things network. In *International Conference on IoT, Intelligent Computing and Security: Select Proceedings of IICS 2021* (pp. 235-245). Singapore: Springer Nature Singapore.

Sultan, K., Ruhi, U., & Lakhani, R. (2018). Conceptualizing blockchains: Characteristics & applications. *arXiv preprint arXiv:1806.03693*.

Sumariadhi, N. W.Ni Wayan Sumariadhi. (2023). Green Tourism: Promoting Sustainable Practices for a Responsible Future. [International Journal of Social Studies]. *Samā Jiva Jnānam*, 1(1), 19–25. DOI: 10.25078/ijoss.v1i1.2976

Sun, C., Zhang, X., & Liu, Y. (2019). Blockchain for Travel business process Management: A Review. *Enterprise Information Systems*, 13(7), 828–854.

Supanti, D., Butcher, K., & Fredline, L. (2015). Enhancing the employer-employee relationship through corporate social responsibility (CSR) engagement. *International Journal of Contemporary Hospitality Management*. https.//DOI: 10.1108/IJCHM-07-2014-0319

Sutarjo, M., & Yuniarsih, A. (2024). Community participation in developing situ janggala tourism in panawuan village, cigandamekar district, kuningan district. *Journal of Economic Development and Village Building*, 2(1), 28–33. DOI: 10.59261/jedvb.v2i1.14

Swan, M. (2015). *Blockchain: blueprint for a new economy. " O'Reilly Media, Inc.". Tapscott, D., & Tapscott, A. (2016). Blockchain revolution: How the technology behind bitcoin is changing money, business, and the world*. Penguin.

Swan, M. (2015). *Blockchain: Blueprint for a new economy*. O'Reilly Media, Inc.

Swiątkowska, J. (2020). Tackling cybercrime to unleash developing countries' digital potential. *Pathways for Prosperity Commission Background Paper Series*, 33, 2020–01.

Swift, R. S. (2001). *Accelerating Customer Relationships: Using CRM and Relationship Technologies*. Prentice Hall.

Szabo, N. (1996). Smart contracts: Building blocks for digital markets. Retrieved from https://www.fon.hum.uva.nl/rob/Courses/InformationInSpeech/CDROM/Literature/LOTwinterschool2006/szabo.best.vwh.net/smart_contracts_2.html

Szabo, N. (1997). Formalizing and securing relationships on public networks. *First Monday*, 2(9). Advance online publication. DOI: 10.5210/fm.v2i9.548

Szajna, B. (1996). Empirical Evaluation of the Revised Technology Acceptance Model. *Management Science*, 42(1), 85–92. DOI: 10.1287/mnsc.42.1.85

Takabi, H., Joshi, J. B., & Ahn, G.-J. (2019). Security and privacy challenges in blockchain-based ecosystems. *IEEE Security and Privacy*, 17(6), 4–5.

Takale, Dattatray & Damke, Sahil & Mehra, Sujal & Burkule, Sanskruti & Tadge, Nidhi. (2024). Applications of Blockchain in Tourism Industry.

Takeda, A., & Ito, Y. (2021). A review of FinTech research. *International Journal of Technology Management*, 86(1), 67–88. DOI: 10.1504/IJTM.2021.115761

Talukder, M. B. (2020). An Appraisal of the Economic Outlook for the Tourism Industry, Specially Cox's Bazar in Bangladesh. *i-manager's Journal on Economics & Commerce,* 2(1), 23-35. DOI: 10.26634/jecom.2.1.17285

Talukder, M. B., & Kumar, S. (2024), “The Development of Human Capital in The Hospitality Business”, Taneja, S., Kumar, P., Reepu, Balusamy, B., Sood, K. and Grima, S. (Ed.) *Sustainability Development through Green Economics* (*Contemporary Studies in Economic and Financial Analysis, Vol. 114*), Emerald Publishing Limited, Leeds, pp. 21-38. DOI: 10.1108/S1569-375920240000114002

Talukder, M. B., . . . (Eds.). (2024). Impact of AI and Tech-Driven Solutions in Hospitality and Tourism. IGI Global, 2024. DOI: 10.4018/979-8-3693-6755-1

Talukder, M. B., Kabir, F., Kaiser, F., & Lina, F. Y. (2024). Digital Detox Movement in the Tourism Industry: Traveler Perspective. In *Business Drivers in Promoting Digital Detoxification* (pp. 91-110). IGI Global. DOI: 10.4018/979-8-3693-1107-3.ch007

Talukder, M. B., Kumar, S., Kaiser, F., & Mia, Md. N. (2024). Pilgrimage Creative Tourism: A Gateway to Sustainable Development Goals in Bangladesh. In M. Hamdan, M. Anshari, N. Ahmad, & E. Ali (Eds.), *Advances in Public Policy and Administration* (pp. 285–300). IGI Global. DOI: 10.4018/979-8-3693-1742-6.ch016

Talukder, M. B. (2020). The Future of Culinary Tourism: An Emerging Dimension for the Tourism Industry of Bangladesh. I-Manager's. *Journal of Management*, 15(1), 27. DOI: 10.26634/jmgt.15.1.17181

Talukder, M. B. (2024). Implementing Artificial Intelligence and Virtual Experiences in Hospitality. In *Innovative Technologies for Increasing Service Productivity* (pp. 145–160). IGI Global., DOI: 10.4018/979-8-3693-2019-8.ch009

Talukder, M. B., Lina, F. Y., Kumar, S., & Khan, M. R. (2024). Data-Driven Personalization in the Sharing Economy. In Ordóñez de Pablos, P. (Ed.), *Building Climate Neutral Economies Through Digital Business and Green Skills* (pp. 277–300). IGI Global., DOI: 10.4018/979-8-3693-5673-9.ch012

Tama, P., Tudoran, R., & Dimon, C. V. (2017). Blockchain-Based Smart Contracts for Decentralized Travel business processes. In *Proceedings of the 2017 International Conference on Development and Application Systems.*

Tamilmani, K., Rana, N. P., Wamba, S. F., & Dwivedi, R. (2021). The extended Unified Theory of Acceptance and Use of Technology (UTAUT2): A systematic literature review and theory evaluation. *International Journal of Information Management*, 57(1), 102269. DOI: 10.1016/j.ijinfomgt.2020.102269

Tamrakar, S., Ekberg, J. E., & Asokan, N. 2011, October. Identity verification schemes for public transport ticketing with NFC phones. In *Proceedings of the sixth ACM workshop on Scalable trusted computing* (pp. 37-48). DOI: 10.1145/2046582.2046591

Tandafatu, N., Ermilinda, L., Darkel, M., & Brekmans, Y. (2024). Digital Transformation in Tourism: Exploring the Impact of Technology on Travel Experiences. *International Journal of Multidisciplinary Approach Sciences and Technologies.*, 1(1), 55–64. DOI: 10.62207/w3vsg352

Tapscott, D., & Tapscott, A. (2016). *Blockchain Revolution. How the Technology Behind Bitcoin Is Changing Money, Business, and the World*. Penguin.

Tapscott, D., & Tapscott, A. (2016). *Blockchain revolution: How the technology behind Bitcoin and other cryptocurrencies is changing the world*. Penguin Random House.

Tapscott, D., & Tapscott, A. (2016). *Blockchain revolution: How the technology behind Bitcoin is changing money, business, and the world*. Penguin.

Tapscott, D., & Tapscott, A. (2017). How blockchain will change organizations. *MIT Sloan Management Review*, 58(2), 10–13.

Tasca, P., Tessone, C. J., & Schweitzer, F. (2018). The evolution of the Bitcoin economy: Extracting and analyzing the network of payment relationships. *The Journal of Risk Finance*, 19(2), 94–126. DOI: 10.1108/JRF-03-2017-0059

TEJASVI, K., BEGUM, R., & JABBAR, M. (2024). SECURITY IN IOT: SYSTEMATIC REVIEW. *The Fusion of Artificial Intelligence and Soft Computing Techniques for Cybersecurity*, 217.

Tepe, Y. (2020). *Decentralisation of hotel and tourism industry : Effects of blockchain technology in hotel booking systems*. 1–109.

Thapaliya, S., & Sharma, P. K. (2023). Cyber Forensic Investigation in IoT Using Deep Learning Based Feature Fusion in Big Data. *International Journal of Wireless Information Networks*, 30(1), 16–29.

Thapaliya, S., & Sharma, P. K. (2023). Optimized deep neuro fuzzy network for cyber forensic investigation in big data-based IoT infrastructures. [IJISP]. *International Journal of Information Security and Privacy*, 17(1), 1–22. DOI: 10.4018/IJISP.315819

Thees, H., Erschbamer, G., & Pechlaner, H. (2020). The Application of Blockchain in Tourism: Use Cases in the Tourism Value System. *European Journal of Tourism Research*, 26, 2602. Advance online publication. DOI: 10.54055/ejtr.v26i.1933

Thies, F., Wallbach, S., Wessel, M., Besler, M., & Benlian, A. (2022). Initial coin offerings and the cryptocurrency hype - the moderating role of exogenous and endogenous signals. *Electronic Markets*, 32(3), 1691–1705. DOI: 10.1007/s12525-021-00460-9

Tian, X., Xie, L., & Ai, H. (2024). Exploring the Path of Sustainable Cultural Tourism under the Context of Rural Revitalization: Taking Yantianzi, Hong Kong as an Example. *Journal of Humanities and Social Sciences Studies*, 6(2), 25–29. DOI: 10.32996/jhsss.2024.6.2.4

Tippins, N. T., Oswald, F. L., & McPhail, S. M. (2021). Scientific, legal, and ethical concerns about AI-based personnel selection tools: A call to action. *Personnel Assessment and Decisions*, 7(2), 1. DOI: 10.25035/pad.2021.02.001

Tok, Y. C., & Chattopadhyay, S. (2023). Identifying threats, cybercrime and digital forensic opportunities in Smart City Infrastructure via threat modeling. *Forensic Science International Digital Investigation*, 45, 301540. DOI: 10.1016/j.fsidi.2023.301540

Tong, J., Li, Y., & Yang, Y. (2024). System Construction, Tourism Empowerment, and Community Participation: The Sustainable Way of Rural Tourism Development. *Sustainability (Basel)*, 16(1), 422. DOI: 10.3390/su16010422

Treiblmaier, H. (2022a). Defining the Internet of Value. Vadgama, N., Xu, J. & Tasca, P. (Eds.). *Enabling the Internet of Value: How Blockchain Connects Global Business*. Springer Nature, Switzerland, 3-13. DOI: 10.1007/978-3-030-78184-2_1

Treiblmaier, H. (2021). *Need some inspiration for blockchain research? Try tokenization!* Academia Letters., DOI: 10.20935/AL2937

Treiblmaier, H. (2021). The token economy as a key driver for tourism: Entering the next phase of blockchain research. *Annals of Tourism Research*, 91, 103177. DOI: 10.1016/j.annals.2021.103177

Treiblmaier, H. (2022). *Blockchain Transformation in the Tourism and Hospitality Sector*. DOI: 10.13140/RG.2.2.10663.01441

Treiblmaier, H. (2022b). Do cryptocurrencies really have (no) intrinsic value? *Electronic Markets*, 32(3), 1749–1758. DOI: 10.1007/s12525-021-00491-2

Treiblmaier, H., Chua, C. E. H., & Kreuzer, E. (2020). The Future of Blockchain in the Hospitality Industry: A Delphi Study. *Journal of Hospitality and Tourism Technology*.

Tschorsch, F., & Scheuermann, B. (2016). Bitcoin and beyond: A technical survey on decentralized digital currencies. *IEEE Communications Surveys and Tutorials*, 18(3), 2084–2123. DOI: 10.1109/COMST.2016.2535718

Tufani, J. A. (2024). Stakeholder perspectives on mosque management and accountability: A stakeholder theory approach. *Indonesian Journal of Multidisciplinary Science*, 3(4), 385–390. DOI: 10.55324/ijoms.v3i4.824

Turchini, G. (2019). *Handbook of Research on Blockchain Technology*. IGI Global.

Turetzky, A., & Adi, Y. (2024). *LAST: Language Model Aware Speech Tokenization* (Version 1). arXiv. DOI: 10.48550/ARXIV.2409.03701

Tyagi, A. K., Aswathy, S. U., & Abraham, A. (2020). Integrating blockchain technology and artificial intelligence: Synergies perspectives challenges and research directions. *Journal of Information Assurance and Security*, 15(5), 1554.

Tyan, I., Yagüe, M. I., & Guevara-Plaza, A. (2020). Blockchain technology for smart tourism destinations. *Sustainability (Basel)*, 12(22), 1–11. DOI: 10.3390/su12229715

Tyan, I., Yagüe, M., & Guevara-Plaza, A. (2021). Blockchain adoption in tourism:Grounded theory-based conceptual model. *Ara: Revista de Investigación En Turismo*, 10(1), 68–89. DOI: 10.1344/ara.v10i1.32819

Utami, S. H., Purnama, A. A., Hidayanto, A. N., Utami, S. H., Purnama, A. A., & Hidayanto, A. N. (2022). Fintech Lending in Indonesia: A Sentiment Analysis, Topic Modelling, and Social Network Analysis using Twitter Data. *International Journal of Applied Engineering & Technology*, 4(1), 50–56.

Valentinov, V., Imami, D., & Xhoxhi, O. (2024). Contract farming in transitional economies: A stakeholder theory perspective. *The International Food and Agribusiness Management Review*, 27(4), 1–17. DOI: 10.22434/ifamr1099

Valeri, M., & Baggio, R. (2021). A critical reflection on the adoption of blockchain in tourism. *Information Technology & Tourism*, 23(2), 121–132. DOI: 10.1007/s40558-020-00183-1

Van Der Sluis, L. E. c. (2004). Designing the workplace for learning and innovation . Organizational factors affecting learning and innovation. *Development and Learning in Organizations. An International Journal*. https.//DOI: 10.1108/14777280410554942

Varma, P., Nijjer, S., Sood, K., Grima, S., & Rupeika-Apoga, R. (2022). Thematic Analysis of Financial Technology (Fintech) Influence on the Banking Industry. *Risks*, 10(10), 186. DOI: 10.3390/risks10100186

Vasan, D., Hammoudeh, M., & Alazab, M. (2024). Broad Learning: A GPU-Free Image-based Malware Classification. *Applied Soft Computing*, 154, 111401. DOI: 10.1016/j.asoc.2024.111401

Vatambeti, R., & Mamidisetti, G. (2023). Routing attack detection using ensemble deep learning model for IIoT. *Inf. Dyn. Appl*, 2(1), 31–41. DOI: 10.56578/ida020104

Venkatasubramanian, M., Lashkari, A. H., & Hakak, S. (2023). Iot malware analysis using federated learning: A comprehensive survey. *IEEE Access : Practical Innovations, Open Solutions*, 11, 5004–5018. DOI: 10.1109/ACCESS.2023.3235389

Venkatesh, V. (2022). Adoption and use of AI tools: A research agenda grounded in UTAUT. *Annals of Operations Research*, 308(1–2), 641–652. DOI: 10.1007/s10479-020-03918-9

Venkatesh, V., & Davis, F. D. (2000). Theoretical extension of the Technology Acceptance Model: Four longitudinal field studies. *Management Science*, 46(2), 186–204. DOI: 10.1287/mnsc.46.2.186.11926

Venkatesh, V., Smith, R. H., Morris, M. G., Davis, G. B., Davis, F. D., & Walton, S. M. (2003). User acceptance of information technology: Toward a unified view. *Management Information Systems Quarterly*, 27(3), 425–478. DOI: 10.2307/30036540

Vieira, S., Pinaya, W. H. L., & Mechelli, A. (2017). Using deep learning to investigate the neuroimaging correlates of psychiatric and neurological disorders. Methods and applications. In *Neuroscience and Biobehavioral Reviews*. https.//DOI: 10.1016/j. neubiorev.2017.01.002

Vijendran, Vijaikanth., A, Boyle. (2023). 4. The Use of Crypto-currencies as a Tool for the Development of Marketing in Tourism. Smart Innovation, Systems and Technologies, DOI: 10.1007/978-981-19-9099-1_1

Virmani, D., Ravishankar, T. N., & Tesfayohanis, M. (2023). 6 IoT attack detection using quantum deep learning in large-scale networks. *Quantum-Safe Cryptography Algorithms and Approaches: Impacts of Quantum Computing on Cybersecurity*, 67.

Voshmgir, S. (2020). *Token Economy: How the Web3 reinvents the Internet* (2nd ed.). BlockchainHub Berlin.

Wang, D., Zheng, X., Zheng, X., & Zhang, S. (2020). An Analytical Model for Blockchain Systems based on MG1 Queue. *International Journal of Distributed Sensor Networks*, 16(4), 1550147720917117.

Wang, H., Li, M., & Li, C. (2020). Performance evaluation of MG1 queue in blockchain-based financial transactions. *International Journal of Blockchain and Cryptocurrency Research*, 1(1), 78–93.

Wang, H., Liu, M., & Li, J. (2021). MG1 Queue Analysis in Blockchain-Based Supply Chain Management for Business Applications. *Journal of Blockchain Applications*, 3(2), 115–132.

Wang, Q., Lin, L., Hu, X., Liu, L., & Shen, Z. (2021). Performance Analysis of MG1 Queue Based on Blockchain for Travel business process. In *Proceedings of the 2021 IEEE International Conference on Information Science, Electronics and Electrical Engineering (ISEEE)* (pp. 417-420).

Wang, Z., Li, J., Guo, C., & Huang, Y. (2021). Performance Analysis of MG1 Queue Based on Blockchain in Travel business process Integration. In *Proceedings of the 2021 International Conference on Cloud Computing and Intelligence Systems (CCIS)* (pp. 93-97).

Wang, Z., Xu, Q., Li, Z., & Xu, K. (2020). Modeling and Performance Analysis of Blockchain-based Supply Chain Systems using MG1 Queues. *Journal of Ambient Intelligence and Humanized Computing*, 11(7), 3055–3066.

Wang, Z., Zhang, H., & Liu, Q. (2023). Performance Analysis of MG1 Queue in Blockchain for Travel business process Reengineering. *Journal of Blockchain Technology and Applications*, 5(1), 34–51.

Waring, J., Lindvall, C., & Umeton, R. (2020). Automated machine learning. Review of the state-of-the-art and opportunities for healthcare. In *Artificial Intelligence in Medicine*. https.//DOI: 10.1016/j.artmed.2020.101822

Waris, A., Malang, P. N., Rachmawati, I. K., Bukhori, M., Majidah, Y., & Hidayatullah, S. (2020). Analysis Of Use Of Mobile Banking With Acceptance And Use Of Technology (UTAUT) Article in. *International Journal of Scientific & Technology Research*. www.ijstr.org

Werbach, K. (2018). *The Blockchain and the New Architecture of Trust*. MIT Press. DOI: 10.7551/mitpress/11449.001.0001

Willie, P. (2019). Can all sectors of the hospitality and tourism industry be influenced by the innovation of Blockchain technology? *Worldwide Hospitality and Tourism Themes*, 11(2), 112–120. DOI: 10.1108/WHATT-11-2018-0077

Wilson, R., & White, S. (2023). Cost Analysis of Blockchain Deployment Models for Hospitality Businesses. *Journal of Hospitality Technology*, 17(1), 32–47.

Wong, L. W., Tan, G. W. H., Lee, V. H., Ooi, K. B., & Sohal, A. (2020). Unearthing the determinants of Blockchain adoption in supply chain management. *International Journal of Production Research*, 58(7), 2100–2123. DOI: 10.1080/00207543.2020.1730463

Wu, H.-C., Cheng, C.-C., Chen, Y.-C., & Hong, W. (2018). Towards green experiential loyalty: Driving from experiential quality, green relationship quality, environmental friendliness, green support and green desire. *International Journal of Contemporary Hospitality Management*, 30(3), 1374–1397. DOI: 10.1108/IJCHM-10-2016-0596

Wu, L., Peng, Q., & Lembke, M. (2023). Research trends in cybercrime and cybersecurity: A review based on web of science core collection database. *International Journal of Cybersecurity Intelligence & Cybercrime*, 6(1), 5–28. DOI: 10.52306/2578-3289.1154

Wut, T. M., & Xu, J. (Bill), & Wong, S. mun. (2021). Crisis management research (1985–2020) in the hospitality and tourism industry: A review and research agenda. In *Tourism Management* (Vol. 85). Elsevier Ltd. DOI: 10.1016/j.tourman.2021.104307

Wynn, M., & Lam, C. (2023). Digitalisation and IT Strategy in the Hospitality Industry. *Systems*, 11(10), 501. Advance online publication. DOI: 10.3390/systems11100501

Xiang, Z., & Gretzel, U. (2010). Role of Social Media in Online Travel Information Search. *Tourism Management*, 31(2), 179–188. DOI: 10.1016/j.tourman.2009.02.016

Xiao, X., Zhang, Y., Dong, X., Wang, L., Xiang, Y., & Cao, X. (2022). Fair Outsourcing Paid in Fiat Money Using Blockchain. *IEEE Transactions on Services Computing*, •••, 1–14. DOI: 10.1109/TSC.2022.3214615

Xiong, Y., Xia, S., & Wang, X. (2020). Artificial intelligence and business applications, an introduction. *International Journal of Technology Management*, 84(1/2), 1–7. DOI: 10.1504/IJTM.2020.112615

Xu, J., Wang, Y., & Zhou, L. (2021). Performance Evaluation of MG1 Queue in Blockchain-Based Logistics Management Systems. In *Proceedings of the International Conference on Blockchain* (pp. 301-316).

Xu, J., Wang, Y., & Zhou, L. (2021). Performance evaluation of MG1 queue in blockchain-based logistics management systems. *International Journal of Blockchain Studies*, 4(2), 89–105.

Xu, J., Wu, Z., & Li, L. (2020). Blockchain-based Decentralized Workflow Management System for Travel business process Execution. *Journal of Ambient Intelligence and Humanized Computing*, 11(6), 2345–2358.

Xu, X., Weber, I., Staples, M., Zhu, L., Bosch, J., Bass, L., & Rimba, P. (2019). A Taxonomy of Blockchain-Based Systems for Architecture Design. *IEEE Software*, 36(6), 38–44.

Xu, X., Weber, I., Staples, M., Zhu, L., Bosch, J., Bass, L., & Rimba, P. (2020). A taxonomy of blockchain-based systems for architecture design. In *Proceedings of the 40th International Conference on Software Engineering (ICSE '18)*, May 27-June 3, 2018, Gothenburg, Sweden. IEEE Press.

Yang, X., Chen, A., PourNejatian, N., Shin, H. C., Smith, K. E., Parisien, C., Compas, C., Martin, C., Costa, A. B., Flores, M. G., Zhang, Y., Magoc, T., Harle, C. A., Lipori, G., Mitchell, D. A., Hogan, W. R., Shenkman, E. A., Bian, J., & Wu, Y. (2022). A large language model for electronic health records. *Npj Digital Medicine*. https.//DOI: 10.1038/s41746-022-00742-2

Yang, Y., Zhang, L., Du, M., Bo, J., Liu, H., Ren, L., Li, X., & Deen, M. J. (2021). A comparative analysis of eleven neural networks architectures for small datasets of lung images of COVID-19 patients toward improved clinical decisions. *Computers in Biology and Medicine*. https.//DOI: 10.1016/j.compbiomed.2021.104887

Yele, S., & Litoriya, R. (2024). Blockchain-based secure dining: Enhancing safety, transparency, and traceability in food consumption environment. *Blockchain: Research and Applications*, 100187(2), 100187. Advance online publication. DOI: 10.1016/j.bcra.2023.100187

Yermack, D. (2015). Is Bitcoin a real currency? An economic appraisal. In *Handbook of digital currency: Bitcoin, innovation, financial instruments, and big data* (pp. 31–43). Academic Press. DOI: 10.1016/B978-0-12-802117-0.00002-3

Yi, M. Y., & Hwang, Y. (2003). Predicting the use of web-based information systems. Self-efficacy, enjoyment, learning goal orientation, and the technology acceptance model. *International Journal of Human Computer Studies*. https.//DOI: 10.1016/S1071-5819(03)00114-9

Yli-Huumo, J., Ko, D., Choi, S., Park, S., & Smolander, K. (2016). Where is current research on blockchain technology?—A systematic review. *PLoS One*, 11(10), e0163477. DOI: 10.1371/journal.pone.0163477 PMID: 27695049

Yuan, X., Chen, J., Zhang, K., Wu, Y., & Yang, T. (2022). A Stable AI-Based Binary and Multiple Class Heart Disease Prediction Model for IoMT. *IEEE Transactions on Industrial Informatics*. https.//DOI: 10.1109/TII.2021.3098306

Yu, H., Yang, Y., & Zhang, Y. (2019). A Blockchain-Based Supply Chain Finance System for Travel business processes Optimization. In *Proceedings of the 2019 IEEE International Conference on Industrial Cyber Physical Systems (ICPS).*

Zailani, S. H. M., Iranmanesh, M., & Nikbin, D. (2019). Determinants of blockchain technology adoption in hospitality supply chain: A decision-making framework. *International Journal of Hospitality Management*, 76, 251–262.

Zavolokina, L., Zani, N., & Schwabe, G. (2023). Designing for Trust in Blockchain Platforms. *IEEE Transactions on Engineering Management*, 70(3), 849–863. DOI: 10.1109/TEM.2020.3015359

Zeng, D., Alqahtani, S., & Tian, D. (2020). An Efficient Blockchain-based Approach for Secure Data Sharing in Business Applications. *Future Generation Computer Systems*, 107, 1041–1052.

Zervas, G., Proserpio, D., & Byers, J. W. (2017). The Rise of the Sharing Economy: Estimating the Impact of Airbnb on the Hotel Industry. *JMR, Journal of Marketing Research*, 54(5), 687–705. DOI: 10.1509/jmr.15.0204

Zhang, A., Lipton, Z. C., Li, M., & Smola, A. J. (2023). *Dive into deep learning*. Cambridge University Press.

Zhang, H., Zhou, J., Zhang, J., & Zhang, W. (2019). Performance Analysis of MG1 Queue Based on Blockchain in Travel business process Optimization. In *Proceedings of the 2019 IEEE International Conference on Industrial Cyber Physical Systems (ICPS)* (pp. 89-93).

Zhang, L., Wang, Q., & Li, J. (2022). Performance analysis of MG1 queue in blockchain for travel business process management. *International Journal of Blockchain Research*, 2(1), 45–62.

Zhang, L., Xiong, F., Tang, Y., & Zeng, M. (2021). Performance Analysis of MG1 Queue-Based Blockchain Consensus Protocol for Business Applications. *Journal of Systems Engineering and Electronics*, 32(4), 831–842.

Zhang, Q., Liu, H., & Yang, W. (2020). Performance Modeling and Simulation of MG1 Queue in Blockchain for Travel business process Optimization. In *Proceedings of the International Conference on Blockchain* (pp. 401-416).

Zhang, Q., Liu, H., & Yang, W. (2020). Performance modeling and simulation of MG1 queue in blockchain for travel business process optimization. *International Journal of Blockchain and Distributed Systems*, 1(2), 117–132.

Zhang, R., Yu, W., Mao, Y., & Zhang, X. (2020). An MG1-based Performance Analysis Model for Blockchain Networks. *Journal of Computational Science*, 43, 101149.

Zhang, W., Chen, Q., & Liu, X. (2023). Analysis of MG1 queue in blockchain-based smart contracts for travel business processes. *International Journal of Business Blockchain*, 3(2), 145–162.

Zhang, W., Chen, Q., & Liu, X. (2023). Performance Analysis of MG1 Queue in Blockchain-Based Smart Contracts for Travel business processes. In *Proceedings of the International Conference on Blockchain* (pp. 201-216).

Zhang, X., Liu, L., Lan, M., Song, G., Xiao, L., & Chen, J. (2022). Interpretable machine learning models for crime prediction. *Computers, Environment and Urban Systems*, 94, 101789. DOI: 10.1016/j.compenvurbsys.2022.101789

Zhang, Y., Suleiman, B., Alibasa, M. J., & Farid, F. (2024). Privacy-Aware Anomaly Detection in IoT Environments using FedGroup: A Group-Based Federated Learning Approach. *Journal of Network and Systems Management*, 32(1), 20. DOI: 10.1007/s10922-023-09782-9

Zhang, Y., Xiong, F., Xie, Y., Fan, X., & Gu, H. (2020). The impact of artificial intelligence and blockchain on the accounting profession. *IEEE Access : Practical Innovations, Open Solutions*, 8, 110461–110477. DOI: 10.1109/ACCESS.2020.3000505

Zhang, Z., Al Hamadi, H., Damiani, E., Yeun, C. Y., & Taher, F. (2022). Explainable artificial intelligence applications in cyber security: State-of-the-art in research. *IEEE Access : Practical Innovations, Open Solutions*, 10, 93104–93139. DOI: 10.1109/ACCESS.2022.3204051

Zhao, S., Zhang, Y., & Li, Y. (2020). Performance Analysis of MG1 Queue in Blockchain for Travel business process Execution. In *Proceedings of the 2020 International Conference on Artificial Intelligence and Big Data (ICAIBD)* (pp. 335-338).

Zheng, Z., Xie, S., Dai, H., Chen, X., & Wang, H. (2017a). An Overview of Blockchain Technology: Architecture, Consensus, and Future Trends. *Proceedings - 2017 IEEE 6th International Congress on Big Data, BigData Congress 2017, October*, 557–564. DOI: 10.1109/BigDataCongress.2017.85

Zheng, Z., Xie, S., Dai, H. N., Chen, X., & Wang, H. (2018). Blockchain challenges and opportunities: A survey. *International Journal of Web and Grid Services*, 14(4), 352–375. DOI: 10.1504/IJWGS.2018.095647

Zhou, B., Yang, G., Shi, Z., & Ma, S. (2024). Natural Language Processing for Smart Healthcare. *IEEE Reviews in Biomedical Engineering, 17*, 4–18. https.//DOI: 10.1109/RBME.2022.3210270

Zhou, M. X., & Xu, W. J. (2018). Research on Blockchain Technology Application in Travel business process Reengineering. In Proceedings of the 2018 IEEE International Conference on Big Data and Smart Computing (BigComp). Qureshi, N., Hijazi, I., & Nasser, Y. (2018). A Review of Blockchain Technology in Travel business process Management Systems. In Proceedings of the 2018 7th International Conference on Industrial Technology and Management (ICITM).

Zhou, Y., Li, H., Chen, J., & He, T. (2020). Modeling and Analysis of Blockchain Consensus Algorithms using MG1 Queue. *Peer-to-Peer Networking and Applications*, 13(2), 534–546.

Zhu, H., & Zhou, Z. Z. (2016). Analysis and outlook of applications of blockchain technology to equity crowdfunding in China. *Financial Innovation*, 2(1), 1–11. DOI: 10.1186/s40854-016-0044-7

Zhu, N., Sheng, Q. Z., Ngu, A. H. H., & Li, X. (2018). How blockchain reshapes the sharing economy: A research agenda. *World Wide Web (Bussum)*, 21(4), 1081–1108.

Zhu, X., & Badr, Y. 2018, July. A survey on blockchain-based identity management systems for the Internet of Things. In *2018 IEEE International Conference on Internet of Things (iThings) and IEEE Green Computing and Communications (GreenCom) and IEEE Cyber, Physical and Social Computing (CPSCom) and IEEE Smart Data (SmartData)* (pp. 1568-1573). IEEE. DOI: 10.1109/Cybermatics_2018.2018.00263

Zielińska, A. (2020). Application possibilities of blockchain technology in the energy sector. *E3S Web of Conferences, 154*. DOI: 10.1051/e3sconf/202015407003

Ziwei, H., Dongni, Z., Man, Z., Yixin, D., Shuanghui, Z., Chao, Y., & Chunfeng, C. (2024). The applications of internet of things in smart healthcare sectors: A bibliometric and deep study. *Heliyon*, 10(3), e25392. DOI: 10.1016/j.heliyon.2024.e25392 PMID: 38356528

Zohar, A. (2015). Bitcoin. under the hood. *Communications of the ACM, 58*(9), 104-113. https.//DOI: 10.1145/2699415

Zohar, A. (2015). Bitcoin: Under the hood. *Communications of the ACM*, 58(9), 104–113. DOI: 10.1145/2701411

About the Contributors

Riktesh Srivastava has a PhD in Electronics Engineering and has Qualifications in Management from the Indian Institute of Management, Ahmedabad (IIMA). He obtained certifications on Marketing at Wharton School, University of Pennsylvania, USA, Electronic Commerce at NTU, Singapore, and Innovation and Information Technology Management at IIMB, India. Currently, he is Associate Professor, MBA at City University College of Ajman, UAE.

Varinder Singh Rana is presently working as Department Chair of Hospitality and Tourism Management at City University Ajman, Ajman, UAE. He received his Doctorate (Ph.D.) in Hospitality from Amity University, Noida, and completed his post-graduation in Hotel Management and Catering Technology from St Peters University, Chennai. He obtained his Bachelor's in Hotel Management from Bangalore University in 2001. He has over 21 years of experience in Academia and Industry. He has provided his services to CT University, GNA University, Lovely Professional University, Punjab Tourism Development Corporation, and various reputed hotels. He has 12 National records in the Limca Book of Records. He is a member of the Board of Management and the Board of Studies of various Universities. He has authored 12 books and 32 research papers in International Journals. He has a vast experience in research and he has organized more than 20 International conferences. He has been invited as a keynote speaker, session chair, and panelist in more than 50 research conferences and seminars. He is a member of the editorial board of five International and three National Journals. He is a certified hospitality educator from American Hotel and Lodging Education Institute. He is the General Secretary of the Chefs Association of Five Rivers which is the nodal body of the Indian Federation of Culinary Associations (IFCA). He served as head chef to the honorable President of India and the President of the Republic of Afghanistan during their visit to Punjab. He is a certified Master Trainer of the Food Safety and Standards Authority of India. He has been awarded by Phagwara Administration for outstanding professional work in 2017. He has been awarded the Best Culinary Educator award by the Indian Federation of Culinary Association (A Nodal Body of the Ministry of Tourism, Government of India). He grabbed Two Silver Medals and one Bronze medal for the Republic of India at the International Culinary Challenge, Uzbekistan where 22 countries participated. He has been associated with many projects of the Punjab Heritage and Tourism Promotion Board (PHTPB).

***

Shailja Bakshi is a Commerce graduate with Post Graduation in Commerce and Management with UGC NET and CG SET Qualified, a seasoned professional, a keen researcher of Pt. Ravishankar Shukla University, Raipur, an enthusiast, and a motivated academician. Ms. Shailja Bakshi has spent more than 7 years of career span into teaching in ITM University, Raipur and MATS University, Raipur with a dominant blend of administrative responsibilities and research activities. A key area of her interest is Mercantile Law, Finance and Economics. She has been actively involved in academic audits, training teachers, and understanding the aspects of effective class delivery like class control, the quantum of content and quality of content with innovativeness and initiatives in the teaching-learning process. She has been associated with reputed universities and her research work has been published in many journals of national and international repute. She is currently serving as Assistant Professor at MATS University, Raipur.

Gaurav Bathla is having over fourteen years of experience in Academia & Industry and presently working as Professor in School of Hotel Management, Airlines and Tourism at CT University Punjab. He has received his Doctorate (PhD) in Hotel Management and Tourism from GNA University, Punjab. Dr. Bathla has authored more than 30 research papers in Scopus Indexed, UGC Approved and Peer Review Journals. He has been associated with many universities and hotel management institutions for their curriculum development and examination system. Dr. Bathla is editorial / reviewer board member of more than 8 National & International Journals. He has also organized various conferences and Faculty Development Programs in the field of Hospitality and Tourism.

G. Sowmya is an Assistant Professor in the Department of Computer Science and Engineering at MLRIT, Hyderabad, with over a decade of teaching experience. Currently pursuing a Ph.D. in CSE from JNTUH, her research focuses on the formal verification of smart contracts. Sowmya holds an M.Tech and B.Tech in CSE and has received the prestigious Prathibha Award for academic excellence. She has contributed to numerous international journals and conferences, authored several patents, and actively engages in various FDPs and certifications, particularly in Blockchain, AI, and IoT. She has also conducted workshops and webinars on cutting-edge technologies such as blockchain and machine learning **Work Experience:** - **Assistant Professor in CSE**, MLR Institute of Technology, Hyderabad (December 2012 - Present) **Education:** - **Pursuing Ph.D.** in Computer Science and Engineering, JNTUH Hyderabad, TG - **Research Topic:** An Efficient Tool for Formal Verification of Smart Contracts - **Guide:** Dr. R. Sridevi - **M.Tech** in Computer Science and Engineering, Jaya Prakash Narayan College of Engineering, Mahabubnagar, TG (2012) - **B.Tech** in Computer Science and Engineering, Jaya Prakash Narayan College of Engineering, Mahabubnagar, TG (2009) - **Intermediate (MPC)**, Scholors Junior College, Wanaparthy, TG (2005) - **SSC**, Sri Vivekananda School, Wanaparthy, TG (2003) **Awards:** - **Prathibha Award** for Securing 972 marks in Intermediate by Govt of AP (2005) **Patents:** 1. Digital Recipe sharing and copyright protection using blockchain (2023) 2. System/Method to recognize Emotion from text and feedback Analysis **Publications:** - Authored multiple international journal papers and conference papers on topics like machine learning, IoT, blockchain, and big data. - Contributed book chapters on finance transformation and integrating AI, ML, blockchain, and IoT for supply chain optimization. **Subjects Taught:** - Digital Logic Design - Computer Organization - Java, C, C++ - FLAT-Formal Languages and Automata Theory - Mobile Application Development using Android - Web Technologies and Programming - Cognitive computing - Artificial Intelligence **Certifications:** - Multiple NPTEL online certifications on topics such as blockchain, theory of computation, programming in Java, C++, Python, and more. - IUCEE Certification (2020) **FDPs Attended:** - Attended numerous Faculty Development Programs on diverse topics including DBMS, Python, blockchain, IoT, AI, data science, cybersecurity, and more. **Other Information:** - Qualified in TS-SET (2018) - Conducted a webinar on Blockchain Technology in Cyber Crime Investigation for the Police Academy organized by the Central Detective Training Institute Hyderabad (2023)

A. K. Haghi, Ph.D., is a retired professor and has written, co-written, edited or co-edited more than 1000 publications, including books, book chapters, and papers in refereed journals with over 4000 citations and h-index of 33, according to Google Scholar database. He was appointed as Honorary Research Associate (HRA) of Bioprocesses and Bioproducts Group, Facultad de Ciencias Químicas, Universidad Autónoma de Coahuila, Saltillo, Coahuila, México. He has also been appointed as Honorary Research Associate (HRA) at Chemistry Centre, University of Coimbra, Portugal and held a Senior Research Fellowship (SRF) at the Tbilisi State University. He has supervised several PhD and MSc theses at the University of Guilan and co-supervised international doctoral projects. Professor Haghi holds a BSc in urban and environmental engineering from the University of North Carolina (USA) and holds two MSc, one in mechanical engineering from North Carolina State University (USA) and another one in applied mechanics, acoustics, and materials from the Université de Technologie de Compiègne (France). He was awarded a PhD in engineering sciences at Université de Franche-Comté (France).

Christian Kaunert is Professor of International Security at Dublin City University, Ireland. He is also Professor of Policing and Security, as well as Director of the International Centre for Policing and Security at the University of South Wales. In addition, he is Jean Monnet Chair, Director of the Jean Monnet Centre of Excellence and Director of the Jean Monnet Network on EU Counter-Terrorism (www.eucter.net).

Musfiqur Rahoman Khan is an accomplished author and Teaching Assistant at the Department of Tourism and Hospitality Management at Daffodil Institute of IT (DIIT), Dhaka, Bangladesh. He holds a Bachelor's degree in Business Administration (BBA), majoring in Tourism and Hospitality Management, from the same institute. With a strongo academic background and a passion for exploring the intersection of travel and culture, Musfiq's diverse areas of interest include Adventure tourism, Cultural tourism, and Wildlife tourism. Through his teaching and writing, he strives to inspire others to discover the richness and diversity of the world through travel.

Rupam Konar is the Programme Director for PhD (Hospitality and Tourism) & MSc. (Tourism) programmes and also a Senior Lecturer in the School of Hospitality, Tourism & Events at Taylor's University, Malaysia. He also serves as a managing editor for the SCOPUS-indexed Asia Pacific Journal of Innovation in Hospitality and Tourism and also as an Associate Director at the Centre for Research and Innovation in Tourism (CRiT). Dr. Rupam is a Certified Microsoft Innovative Educator. His specialization area includes service innovation, service management, and service design within the hospitality industry. Within his research interest, he has published over 25 articles and book chapters in international refereed journals and has successfully complemented many national and privately funded research projects. With his gained years of experience in the hospitality sector and academia, he is now really intrigued by the possibilities and innovative changes he can contribute to these industries.

Pankaj Kumar is currently working as an Assistant Professor in Faculty of Commerce and Management, United University, Prayagraj, Uttar Pradesh. He has completed his Ph.D. in Finance from Faculty of Commerce, Banaras Hindu

University and published number of research papers in ABDC and Care listed journals.

Kumari Neelam is currently pursuing her Ph.D. in Finance from the Department of Commerce, Mahatma Gandhi Kashi Vidyapith, Varanasi, Uttar Pradesh. She has published a number of research papers in ABDC and peer-reviewed journals. Her research interests include corporate finance, financial markets, and investment strategies. Additionally, she has presented her work at various national and international conferences, receiving commendations for her contributions to the field.

Varinder Singh Rana is presently working as Department Chair of Hospitality and Tourism Management at City University Ajman, Ajman, UAE. He received his Doctorate (Ph.D.) in Hospitality from Amity University, Noida, and completed his post-graduation in Hotel Management and Catering Technology from St Peters University, Chennai. He obtained his Bachelor's in Hotel Management from Bangalore University in 2001. He has over 21 years of experience in Academia and Industry. He has provided his services to CT University, GNA University, Lovely Professional University, Punjab Tourism Development Corporation, and various reputed hotels. He has 12 National records in the Limca Book of Records. He is a member of the Board of Management and the Board of Studies of various Universities. He has authored 12 books and 32 research papers in International Journals. He has a vast experience in research and he has organized more than 20 International conferences. He has been invited as a keynote speaker, session chair, and panelist in more than 50 research conferences and seminars. He is a member of the editorial board of five International and three National Journals. He is a certified hospitality educator from American Hotel and Lodging Education Institute. He is the General Secretary of the Chefs Association of Five Rivers which is the nodal body of the Indian Federation of Culinary Associations (IFCA). He served as head chef to the honorable President of India and the President of the Republic of Afghanistan during their visit to Punjab. He is a certified Master Trainer of the Food Safety and Standards Authority of India. He has been awarded by Phagwara Administration for outstanding professional work in 2017. He has been awarded the Best Culinary Educator award by the Indian Federation of Culinary Association (A Nodal Body of the Ministry of Tourism, Government of India). He grabbed Two Silver Medals and one Bronze medal for the Republic of India at the International Culinary Challenge, Uzbekistan where 22 countries participated. He has been associated with many projects of the Punjab Heritage and Tourism Promotion Board (PHTPB).

Premendra Sahu is an Associate Professor of Marketing at MATS University Raipur Chhattisgarh. He has a research and teaching experience of more than 15 years. His current research interest targets the analysis of the consumer behaviour of millennials in marketing. His has an expertise in the application of analytics in business, with specific emphasis to marketing, sustainability, retailing and e-commerce. He has used many statistical tools in his research including SPSS, SmartPLS, Excel and R. He is also assisting numerous startups in their digital and analytical needs.

Partho Pratim Seal has more than two decades of experience in academics and hospitality. An avid wordsmith who believes that writing is the most influential and resourceful medium to disseminate information has authored four books Computers in Hotels: Concepts and Application, Food & Beverage Management, and How to Succeed in Hotel Management Job Interviews and Food Anthropology in India. His interest is in Marketing, Education, and Culinary. He has published research papers in indexed international journals and is also a reviewer of international journals.

Vikas Sharma is an alumnus of IHM Gwalior. He has 7 years of experience, including teaching and industry experience in luxury brands like ITC grand Bharat Gurugram, The Leela Ambience Hotel and Residences Gurugram and Le Meridian Gurugram. Currently he is associated with Swami Vivekanand Subharti University, Bhikaji Cama Subharti college of Hotel Management as Assistant Professor. Also He is currently pursuing PhD in Hotel Management from Swami Vivekanand Subharti University and has completed Masters in Travel and Tourism Management. He has 7 patents published and also published 8 research papers in various national and international journals. He has attended 15 FDPs and workshops. He has also presented research papers in many national and international conferences

Amrik Singh is working as Professor in the School of Hotel Management and Tourism at Lovely Professional University, Punjab, India. He obtained his Ph.D. degree in Hotel Management from Kurukshetra University, Kurukshetra. He started his academic career at Lovely Professional University, Punjab, India in the year 2007. He has published more than 40 research papers in UGC and peer-reviewed and Scopus/Web of Science) journals. He has published 12 patents and 01 patent has been granted in the inter-disciplinary domain. Dr. Amrik Singh participated and acted as a resource person in various national and international conferences, seminars, research workshops, and industry talks. His area of research interest is accommodation management, ergonomics, green practices, human resource management in hospitality, waste management, AR VR in hospitality, etc. He is currently guiding 8Ph.D. scholars and 2 Ph.D. scholars have been awarded Ph.D.

Bhupinder Singh working as Professor at Sharda University, India. Also, Honorary Professor in University of South Wales UK and Santo Tomas University

Tunja, Colombia. His areas of publications as Smart Healthcare, Medicines, fuzzy logics, artificial intelligence, robotics, machine learning, deep learning, federated learning, IoT, PV Glasses, metaverse and many more. He has 3 books, 139 paper publications, 163 paper presentations in international/national conferences and seminars, participated in more than 40 workshops/FDP's/QIP's, 25 courses from international universities of repute, organized more than 59 events with international and national academicians and industry people's, editor-in-chief and co-editor in journals, developed new courses. He has given talks at international universities, resource person in international conferences such as in Nanyang Technological University Singapore, Tashkent State University of Law Uzbekistan; KIMEP University Kazakhstan, All'ah meh Tabatabi University Iran, the Iranian Association of International Criminal law, Iran and Hague Center for International Law and Investment, The Netherlands, Northumbria University Newcastle UK,

Sujay Vikram Singh is a Senior Research Fellow currently pursuing a doctorate at Banaras Hindu University. He graduated and post-graduated from IHM Lucknow. His research interests include Hospitality, CRM, Service Marketing, Service Quality, and Systematic Literature Reviews. He has published papers in various handbooks and journals. His recent journal publications include the *International Journal of Market Research* (Sage Publishing) [ABDC-A, Scopus] and the *Journal of Global Information Management* (IGI Publishing) [Scopus, ABDC-A]. Sujay has also been a reviewer for tourism and management journals and has presented and published papers at various national and international conferences and seminars. He has received best paper awards at several conferences, including those held at IHM Bhopal, Subharati University, and Delhi University.

Pravin Chandra Singh is currently working as an Assistant Professor at MSMSR, Mats University, Chhattisgarh. Prior to Mats University he was associated with Raffles University, Rajasthan. He has done his Doctorate from IM-BHU in Marketing and published several research papers in the journal and publisher of repute Like IIM-S, Elsevier, Emerald, IGI- Global, PBRI. His research interests includes Advertising, Corporate Social Responsibility, Marketing and his credential may be verified on various research platforms like Google Scholar, SSRN, LinkedIn, Academia, and Research Gate.

Ankit Srivastava is currently working as Assistant Professor in Bhikaji Cama Subharti College of Hotel Management, Swami Vivekanand Subharti University, Meerut.

Mohammad Badruddoza Talukder is an Associate Professor, College of Tourism and Hospitality Management, IUBAT - International University of Business

Agriculture and Technology, Dhaka-1230, Bangladesh. He holds PhD in Hotel Management from Lovely Professional University, India. He has been teaching various courses in the Department of Tourism and Hospitality at various universities in Bangladesh since 2008. His research areas include tourism management, hotel management, hospitality management, food & beverage management, and accommodation management, where he has published research papers in well-known journals in Bangladesh and abroad. Mr. Talukder is one of the executive members of the Tourism Educators Association of Bangladesh. He has led training and consulting for a wide range of hospitality organizations in Bangladesh. He just became an honorary facilitator at the Bangladesh Tourism Board's Bangabandhu international tourism and hospitality training institution.

Shiv Mohan is currently working as Head of Institution in Bhikaji Cama Subharti College of Hotel Management, Swami Vivekanand Subharti University, Meerut.

Index

A

B

C

D

E

F

G

H

I

L

M

N

O

P

R

S

T

V

www.ingramcontent.com/pod-product-compliance
Lightning Source LLC
LaVergne TN
LVHW080346011026
849161LV00009B/2203
9798369365625